STUDENT DISSENT IN THE SCHOOLS

STUDENT DISSENT

IN THE SCHOOLS

Edited by
Irving G. Hendrick
Reginald L. Jones

University of California, Riverside

HOUGHTON MIFFLIN COMPANY • BOSTON

NEW YORK • ATLANTA • GENEVA, ILLINOIS • DALLAS • PALO ALTO

Printed in the U.S.A.

Library of Congress Catalog Card Number: 78-168854

ISBN: 0-395-12624-X

Photo Credits:

facing p. 1 © 1970 Stephen Shames/Photon West
p. 64 Anna Kaufman Moon/Stock Boston
p. 282 Mike Mazzaschi/Stock Boston

CONTENTS

PREFACE

Over the past several years it has become painfully clear that tensions between activist students and school authorities are being strained to the limits of their mutual endurance. In reflecting upon the social dynamics of student dissent and activism in public schools, the editors are convinced that much work is needed if students and practitioners of education are going to develop a sense of what is happening and be able to deal with it. The focus in the present volume is limited to the public schools, especially public secondary schools. Readers seeking literature on college student activism will find it in abundance in numerous other sources.

Our goal was to strive for a balanced perspective on the topics identified. Obviously, the coverage is not exhaustive, but a number of important issues are explored. We attempted to find out what students are distressed about, how many are involved in protest activity, how their displeasure and discomfort is being expressed, and what can be done to resolve the conflict. The book's organization and the selections included in it reflect these concerns.

An effort has been made to draw opinion and insights from as broad a cross section of observers and participants as necessary to gain the perspective we seek. Consequently, the works of sociologists, students, professional writers, and psychiatrists have been brought together. It was felt that the problems facing students, the schools, and society at large are much too serious to permit us the luxury of academic arrogance. Insights into what is wrong, what is at stake, and what can be done to help solve the problems of distressed and disillusioned youth are not limited to any particular group. We have felt no trepidations about including the works of Edgar Friedenberg, J. Edgar Hoover, and activist teenagers in the same volume.

Part I, "Society's Problem," emphasizes the nature and extent of student activism and includes some informed speculation on why students are disenchanted with their schools and society at large. Part II, "Dimensions of Alienation and Activism," includes a sample of activist demands as presented by activists themselves, a look at the drug problem, racial conflict in the schools, and several facets of the student rights issue. All relate to dimensions of student alienation and/or activism, albeit they represent vastly different types of problems, e.g., the freedom of press issue is actually a subcategory of the larger student rights issue while the drug issue is scarcely related to student rights at all. A final section, "Direction for the Future," is intended to stimulate the reader's imagination with regard to finding a way out of a tense and largely unproductive conflict situation. Whether or not educators possess the collective wisdom, will, and capacity to offer viable solutions to the problems discussed are themselves formidable questions.

In the course of organizing the format, making the selections, and writing the chapter introductions, the editors were assisted in several important ways. Readers and critics of the original outline included Fred M. Newmann of the University of Wisconsin, Jack R. Frymier of the Ohio State University, Gary D. Fenstermacher of U.C.L.A., Frederick R. Smith of Indiana University, and our colleague in the Department of Education at U.C.R., Robin J. McKeown. Sam Feldman, San Fernando Valley State College, and F. K. Heussenstamm, California State College, Los Angeles, generously permitted us to read and use their collections of underground newspapers. Valerie Bennett, Eddie Knopf, Ruby Tapia and Faith Lewis helped in numerous ways, including data gathering, record keeping, proofreading, and typing. The efforts of all who helped are sincerely appreciated; as always, the editors assume all responsibilities.

I.G.H. and R.L.J.

University of California, Riverside

PART ONE

SOCIETY'S PROBLEM

FOR WHAT IT'S WORTH

There's something happenin' here.
What it is ain't exactly clear.
There's a man with a gun over there,
Tellin' me I've got to beware.
It's time we stop, children,
What's that sound?
Everybody look what's goin' down.

There's battle lines bein' drawn,
Nobody's right if everybody's wrong.
Young people speakin' their minds,
Gettin' so much resistance from behind.
It's time we stop, children,
What's that sound?
Everybody look what's goin' down.

What a field day for the heat.
A thousand people in the street,
Singin' songs and carryin' signs.
Mostly saying, "Hooray for our side."
It's time we stop, children,
What's that sound?
Everybody look what's goin' down.

Paranoia strikes deep,
Into your life it will creep.
It starts when you're always afraid,
Step out of line, the Man come
And take you away.
You better stop, hey,
What's that sound?
Everybody look what's goin' down.

Stephen Stills (for The Buffalo Springfield)

ALIENATION, ACTIVISM AND DISRUPTION:
AN INTRODUCTION

A frequent observation made by journalists and scholars alike over the past several years has been that a marked social upheaval has occurred in America's secondary schools. A visit to almost any urban high school, and many rural ones as well, will reveal substantial change from what was considered normal even a decade earlier. Many changes relate directly or indirectly to the issue of student rights, be the issue of the moment student dress, political advocacy, a free press, or some current moral cause. Clearly students have been active in stimulating changes. Clearly also, thanks to the effectiveness of their own peer group communication network and the adult world's media, they have been sharing experiences concerning "in" happenings with others outside of their neighborhoods.

The parameters of student alienation, activism, dissent, and disruption are somewhat hard to define. That may explain the attractiveness of using the rather imprecise term "student unrest" when describing the many types of activist behavior. In the first place, it should be acknowledged that in spite of much purple prose to the contrary, many students, perhaps a majority, are still "politically apathetic." They have identified with and accepted the values of their parents; consequently they are little heard from. More importantly, there is considerable reason to believe that the majority does not make a significant difference when it comes to establishing trends.

Adolescents who reject the traditional values of society, rebel against institutional authority, but are uninvolved politically, are often identified as "alienated youth." Although there are substantial numbers of students who fit this definition, the principal population focused on in this volume are those who turn their disenchantment into action. Thus, since they believe that some of the major values of contemporary society are reprehensible, they dedicate themselves to fighting, demonstrating, and protesting those policies. In a word, they are "activists."

Some literature characterizes activist students as not only vigorously opposing existing social and political policies but also as willing to use a variety of means, including some of marginal legality, to effect change. When used in this way, the term implies that "activists" work on the periphery of the established society. Because their behavior is guided by a moral-ethical justification, only rarely are they categorized as "anti-social youth" or as delinquents. However, one American historian did go so far as to suggest that the most vocal and violent disruptors of American society were not merely radicals, but a "new species of barbarian."[1]

Given the broad range of motivations operating in the lives of students, it is par-

[1] Daniel J. Boorstin, *The Decline of Radicalism: Reflections on America Today* (New York: Random House, 1969).

ticularly difficult to generalize about the causes of activist behavior. The almost inevitable failure of society to measure up to the idealized model envisioned by the student is one reasonable explanation for student activism. As young people become capable of hypothetical thinking and begin to anticipate what the good life should entail, they are likely to find existing society wanting.[2] Inhelder and Piaget refer to this developmental juncture as the "idealistic crisis" and suggest that the key consideration is how adolescents react to the crisis.[3] Presumably most are able to resolve it by focusing on professional or vocational objectives in the adult world, thereby leading themselves away from the dangers of purely formal-istic, hypothetical thought. Historically, secondary school youth have not been critics of society. Rarely has their idealism led to revolutionary or even activist behavior.

The extent of student activism has been defined by several notable national opinion samples and status surveys made since 1968. Stephen K. Bailey, reporting evidence from a cross section of 27 secondary schools in his Syracuse study, found that 85 percent of the schools responding in June, 1970, had experienced some type of disruption over the past three years.[4] Not all of his findings are particularly surprising, e.g., larger schools have more problems than smaller ones; others are controversial, e.g., disruption is positively related to integration. While it can be documented statistically that large, racially mixed schools have more problems than other schools, it is less than clear just what has been proved. For example, it may only serve to prove that "integration" has not yet occurred. Few students of integration have seen desegregation, i.e., bringing the races together in the same building, as anything but a first step toward integration.

The largest—although perhaps the least publicized—of the major surveys was conducted for the years 1968-69 by the House Subcommittee on General Education. All 29,000 public and private secondary schools were included. According to an *Education U.S.A.* report of the results, 18 percent of the respondents had experienced "serious protests,"[5] including protests con-cerning disciplinary rules, dress codes, school services and facilities, and curricu-lum policy. Sit-ins were the most popular form of expression in smaller schools, while the distribution of underground newspapers led the list of activist expres-sion in larger schools. Among the 20 percent of schools reporting a significant in-

[2] A detailed discussion of student activism together with an extensive series of definitions concerning "politically apathetic youth," "alienated youth," "individualist youth," "activist youth," "constructivist youth," and "anti-social youth" is included in Jeanne H. Block, Norma Haan, and M. Brewster Smith, "Activism and Apathy in Contemporary Adolescents," in James F. Adams, ed., *Understanding Adolescence* (Boston: Allyn and Bacon, 1968), pp. 198-231.
[3] Barbel Inhelder and Jean Piaget, *The Growth of Logical Thinking from Childhood to Adolescence* (New York: Basic Books, 1958).
[4] Stephen K. Bailey, *Disruption in Urban Public Secondary Schools* (Washington, D.C.: National Association of Secondary School Principals, 1970).
[5] "Serious Protest Found in 18% of High Schools," *Education U.S.A.*, March 2, 1970.

crease in minority group enrollment over the past five years, 22 percent experienced student protests, compared to 16 percent in schools without a significant increase in such enrollment. With school size, location, and conditions not reported, it is difficult to infer what the finer implications of this data might be.

Of all the activism surveys, the one most widely publicized among schoolmen was the one conducted by J. Lloyd Trump and Jane Hunt for the National Association of Secondary School Principals in 1969. Their central finding was that 59 percent of the high schools and 56 percent of the junior highs reported experiencing some form of student protest. Suburban senior highs led the list with 69 percent, followed by urban senior highs (63 percent) and suburban junior highs (61 percent). In no case was the percentage low. Even among rural junior highs 48 percent reported protest activity. As with the other studies, the grievance list was headed by dress and hair-length requirements, followed by alleged overly restrictive smoking regulations, poor cafeteria service, poor assemblies, and censorship of campus speakers or publications.[6]

Only a fourth of the schools surveyed by Trump experienced activism in the area of national issues such as race relations, the peace movement, or the draft. Indeed, one of the prominent themes from the high school reports is that local issues, rather than national issues, head the list of grievances. This is not to suggest that an active minority of students has not been prepared to press a mimeograph machine into service to protest ROTC on campus, the war in Vietnam, or the failure of the school cafeteria to boycott non-union grapes and lettuce. It may suggest that most activist students are comparatively more interested in a redress of local grievances than they are in supporting an international revolution or a basic restructuring of their own society.

The formation of student movements in general, including those on college campuses, may be a reflection of technological, cultural, and economic changes that require newer forms and mechanisms for the distribution of political power. Although the present high school student movement is unprecedented, its parent college movement is not. Advances in communication through the media, a progressively closer affinity between college and high school students, plus a generally more sophisticated examination of ideas by the brighter high school students in their own classes, help to account for the rise of activism in the schools. The rise of activism in the society at large is doubtlessly a factor also. It is little wonder, for example, that Black and Spanish-speaking youth have become increasingly more assertive as adults in their communities and have become increasingly aware of the discrimination, oppression, and unequal opportunities which have been theirs to experience. Paralleling the student protest movement in the United States, at least in time, has been a larger international movement centered

[6] J. Lloyd Trump and Jane Hunt, *Report on a National Survey of Secondary School Principals on the Nature and Extent of Student Activism* (Washington: National Association of Secondary School Principals, [1969]), 7 pp. (mimeo).

in Europe and Japan. It is likely that this wider movement has had an impact on American college students, who in turn have influenced the younger high school protestors.

Within the American experience itself there has been ample precedent for activist behavior by students, at least on the college level. Protests, violent at times, have been waged since the nineteenth century against dormitory life and various rules of student governance. Although serious protest was not the hallmark of American collegiate life during the 1920's, the depression of the 1930's and the pre-World War II period were marked by protest of a political character. Among the surprising developments surrounding campus protest activity during the 1960's was that it was engaged in by so many, followed a decade of comparative quiet on campuses, and happened during a time of general prosperity. The student movement of the thirties, as contrasted to the more recent upheaval, had been tied rather closely to the mainstream of liberal and radical thought and was more intellectual in its appeal.

More recently, it appears that students have been leading more and following less, albeit the intellectual antecedents of their movement are attributable to adults. C. Wright Mills was well over thirty when he wrote a "Letter to the New Left," thereby doing much to establish himself as the most influential theorist behind the new left movement at large and the early Students for a Democratic Society (SDS) organization in particular. So was Howard Zinn, the only white person elected to the early Student Nonviolent Coordinating Committee (SNCC) and one who roundly condemned much intellectual activity as the aimless dredging up of what is and what was, rather than a creative recollection of experience pointed at the betterment of human life. An insistence on action—direct and immediate action—is perhaps the key point which decisively distinguishes between new left radicalism and all varieties of liberalism.[7]

If it can be assumed that many secondary school pupils are rather psychologically and physically akin to most college students, it is not surprising that the rebellion of the latter would affect the high schools. It is clear that radical thought is now present in some of the nation's high schools, especially the larger urban and suburban ones, and that working for the revolution is a serious pastime for a small number of activists. This does not suggest that even a substantial minority of high school activists have any use for the SDS; indeed, some see it as a college student dominated group with goals irrelevant to high school students. Thus, while it is relatively easy to document SDS activity and attempted activity in the schools, it is more difficult to document its success.

While it would be naive to discuss student activism without giving due attention to the SDS, it would be a mistake for the reader to infer that the SDS is having a tremendous influence on high school students. There is no evidence that even a substantial minority of students support promoting social and political revolution

[7] See Staughton Lynd, "The New Left," *The Annals of the American Academy of Political and Social Science*, no. 382, March, 1969, and the Staff Report of the National Commission on the Causes and Prevention of Violence, *The Politics of Protest*.

through the school. At the same time, there is ample evidence that activists, including both those of a revolutionary ilk and those of a more moderate persuasion, have given school officials in particular and society in general good cause for reexamining social and educational values and policies. The chapters which follow contain evidence in support of this contention.

ONE

VALUES IN TRANSITION

There was a time once, as late as the 1950's, when the basic values of our society were seldom questioned by youth, at least not in large and significant numbers. Youth seemed to accept its role and station—to be socialized, to be bent and molded in preparation for maintaining the culture and extending it. Society's goals were shared—or certainly not questioned; one simply bided his time while being prepared by family and school. Indeed, one key purpose of education has always been to provide cultural continuity until adulthood, when one would move into the mainstream and either take his rightful place or create one. These were the aspirations of the middle class, the affluent, and even the poor and the Black who believed in these goals—and who worked toward them, or at worst, showed no distaste for them. Much has changed. These are days of conflict, of alienation, of dissent; these are the days of the generation gap. Many goals of society are not accepted, and, indeed, they are being actively challenged.

How real is the gap and what factors contribute to it? Are these marked differences in values between youth and their elders more real than was true one or two decades ago? These are the concerns of the present Chapter.

No easy answers to problems of intergenerational conflict can be promised, for as Robert Grinder notes:

> The nature of the youth culture thrust has been discussed profusely, but unanimity among commentators is wholly lacking. To sift among the viewpoints for cogency and relevance means to grapple with two problems: (a) the commentary is often more an intuitive expression of personal feeling than a result of scientific inquiry, and (b) discussions are often based upon conceptions of human nature that vary according to the proclivities of the commentator."[1]

Several main themes highlight intergenerational conflict; several perspectives bear on the problems, and certain of these are represented in the present chapter.

In the first article, "The Generation Gap," Edgar Friedenberg asks if the generation gap represents a real phenomenon or indeed if the activity of contemporary adolescents is no different from those of his elders? Friedenberg's answer is an emphatic yes—the generation gap represents "a genuine class conflict between the

[1] Robert E. Grinder, "Distinctiveness and Thrust in the American Youth Culture," *Journal of Social Issues*, 25 (Spring, 1969): 10.

dominant and exploitative older generation and youth who are slowly becoming aware of what is happening to them as demands on them are, in the language of the time, escalated." The current conflict does not result from the fact that the young wish to replace the old, but rather, as Friedenberg notes, from their declaration that "they will not even accept, when their turn comes, the kinds of roles—in the kind of society—which their parents have held." Friedenberg speculates broadly about sources and causes of the conflict—compulsory school attendance, the Selective Service system, the Vietnam War, the social insensitivity of responsible government officials, and the repressive nature of public schools.

Herzog and Sudia, in "The Generation Gap in the Eyes of Youth," analyze the youth view as represented by 407 college preparatory students in metropolitan areas who responded to a mail questionnaire. Although the sample is biased in that students from non-metropolitan areas were not represented, the article does point up the main concerns of a significant group of adolescents and confirms the presence of a generation gap. According to the authors, almost 50 percent of the respondents report that the generation gap is viewed as a real problem, and a few add that it is worse than in former years. The other half is about equally divided: one group suggests that the gap is not viewed as a problem at all, while the other says the generational conflict is seen as a problem by some young people but not by others. Importantly, the article touches upon the main grievances as reported by the teenagers themselves.

A psychodynamic (psychiatrically oriented) explanation of dissent and activism among youth is presented by Philips and Szurek. Such a view is offered in contrast to sociological writings (e.g., Friedenberg, and others), which in the authors' opinion "do not always seem sufficient to account for the behavior of many participant young individuals . . . ."

Unlike sociological explanations, which look largely to societal and external forces as the root causes of activism and dissent. Philips's and Szurek's focus is upon "psychodynamic factors involved in the individual's experiences with his family that impel him to what often seems self-destructive activity." Two case studies are presented as illustrative of processes alluded to above. The subjects, while college students, both manifested clear problems while in high school. Indeed, problems of dissent in high school actually led to psychiatric referral in the case of one student. The case studies are intended only to be illustrative and supportive of the authors' thesis, which centers on psychodynamic factors as causative agents in student revolt. Such psychiatrically oriented data and the inferences drawn from them must, understandably, be regarded as tentative until more widespread supporting data become available.

The Philips-Szurek thesis is a psychiatric pathology-oriented one—i.e., we must look at the intrafamily dynamic for elements of unhealthiness. While many do not concur in this view, it does define one of the two poles of explanation commonly used to account for student activism and dissent, i.e., the sick society versus the sick adolescent. The Philips and Szurek article clearly focuses upon sick psychodynamic family relationships and by inference upon the sick individual. On the other hand, it is noteworthy that the authors also acknowledge that there are activists whose behavior is nonpathological.

Articles selected for this chapter range from the largely factual and descriptive piece by Herzog and Sudia, through the quasi-factual and interpretive article by Philips and Szurek, to Friedenberg's sociologically oriented treatise. They represent several perspectives on forces which lead to activism and dissent among certain adolescents, including sociologial factors and interpersonal family dynamics. A third view, included in Chapter 2, is represented by the responses of students themselves.

Analyses which focus upon either pathological family relationships or upon societal problems as causes of activism and dissent do not gain universal acceptance. Some, for example, assert that the structure of the schools is a contributing cause. (see Chapter 9). A more conservative view attributes many problems to parental permissiveness and a lack of parent discipline. Witness Harriet Van Horne's "Generation of Tyrants," which follows this theme, i.e., if parents would exercise stricter controls in dealing with their children few problems would ensue.

The final article of the present chapter, Robert Rosenstone's "The Times They Are A-Changin: The Music of Protest," looks at activism and dissent in the context of folk-rock music. Here, in an incisive and insightful article, Rosenstone traces the history and main threads of current rock music with some attention to the purposes served by rock. Many of youth's concerns and values are skillfully analyzed and interpreted.

THE GENERATION GAP

EDGAR Z. FRIEDENBERG

Abstract: The "generation gap" between youth and adults in contemporary American society reflects a real and serious conflict of interest rather than mutual misunderstanding. In an open, bureaucratic society, sanctions against nepotism and the attrition of property through inheritance taxes lessen the utility of each generation to the other: the young cannot succeed. Youth, moreover, is a discriminated-against minority in America—more seriously so than any ethnic minority. It is excluded from economic opportunity, and is seriously exploited by being forced to supply, as members of the Armed Forces, its services at a fraction of their market value. School attendance is less obviously exploitive, but is as much a forced sub-

From *The Annals of the American Academy of Political and Social Science,* No. 382 (March, 1969), 32-42. Reprinted with the permission of the author and the publisher.

Edgar Z. Friedenberg is Professor of Education at Dalhousie University, Halifax, Nova Scotia.

sidy of the social and economic system by the young as "an opportunity to invest in the future." Compulsory school attendance, the juvenile court system, and the Selective Service System all operate as serious, age-graded constraints from which adults are exempt—these constraints, indeed, define youth as a social role. Informal and often abusive constraint by schools and law-enforcement officials exacerbate the conflict. The humiliation of, particularly, youth from the upper-middle and upper classes, especially those prone to dissent, is functional in preventing the disruption of a democratic society by the hostilities of the "lumpen-bourgeoisie."

The idea that what separates us from the young is something so passive that it may justly be called a "generation gap" is, I believe, itself a misleading article of middle-aged liberal ideology, serving to allay anxiety rather than to clarify the bases of intergenerational conflict. It is true, to be sure, that the phrase is strong enough to describe the barrier that separates many young people from their elders, for a majority still accept our society as providing a viable pattern of life and expectations for the future. Liberalism dies hard, and most young people, like some Negroes even today, are still willing to attribute their difficulties with their elders and society to mutual misunderstanding.

I believe, however, that this is a false position. Though most adults maintain a benevolent posture in expressing their public attitudes toward youth and—though, I think, steadily fewer—young people still accept this as what their elders intend in principle, both young and old seem trapped in a false view of what is actually a profound conflict of interest in our society. What appears to be a consequence of mere cultural lag in responding to a new social and political maturity in the young, with distressing but unintended repressive consequences, is rather the expression of what has become genuine class-conflict between a dominant and exploitive older generation and youth who are slowly becoming more aware of what is happening to them as demands on them are, in the language of the time, escalated.[1]

DISCONTINUITY IN AN OPEN SOCIETY

In all societies, so far as I know, young people enter the social system in subordinate roles while older people run things. This is true even in technically primitive cultures where the crude physical strength of youth is still of real productive advantage. Is there always a generational conflict? And, if so, does it always reflect

---

[1] I am indebted to John and Margaret Rowntree, of York University and the University of Toronto, respectively, for demonstrating, in their paper "The Political Economy of Youth in the United States," the class-dynamics of generational conflict. This document, prepared for presentation at the First Annual Meeting of the Committee on Socialist Studies in Calgary, Alberta, in June 1968, was published in the Montreal quarterly journal *Our Generation*, Vol. 6, No. 1, 1968. Their radical analysis simplifies many apparent paradoxes in the relationship between the generations.

as profound a division, and as severe a conflict of interest, as generational conflict in America today?

There is, I believe, indeed an inherent basis for such a conflict in the fact that the old dominate the young and the young wish to replace them, but it is not as severe in most societies as in ours. Here, it has become different in kind, as the brightest and most articulate of the young declare that they will not even accept, when their turn comes, the kinds of roles—in the kind of society—which their parents have held. As Bruno Bettelheim[2] pointed out in a classic paper some years ago, factors that have traditionally mitigated generational conflict have become feeble or inoperative even in this country. The family, for example, which is the context within which the strongest—albeit ambivalent—affectual ties between the generations are formed, plays a decreasing role in the lives of its members and, certainly, in the socialization of the young. It has less effect on their life-chances than it once had. If the Victorian father or the head of a traditional rural household was often a tyrant, and more or less accepted as such by his neighbors and his children, he was also a man who felt that he could transmit his wealth, his trade, and his position in the community, by inheritance. His relationship to his sons was not purely competitive but complementary as well; it was they who would have to carry on his work as his own powers failed, and on whom he was therefore ultimately dependent if his accomplishment in life was to lead to anything permanent. The proper attitude of father to son—both the authority and the underlying tenderness—took account of this mutual though unequal dependency. And while excessive and inconsiderate longevity in a father might make his son's position grotesque, as that of mad old George III did to the Prince Regent's position, the problems of succession were usually made less abrasive by the recognition of mutual need.

Moreover, so long as society changed slowly, elders really knew more that was useful than the young did; they were wiser; their authority was based on real superiority in the subtle techniques of living. This was never a very strong bond between the generations in America, where the sons of immigrants have always been as likely to find their greenhorn parents a source of embarrassment as of enlightenment; and generational conflict has probably always been more severe here than in more subtle cultures—or would have been had there not also been a continent to escape into and develop.

But, today, the older generation has become not merely an embarrassment, but often an obstructive irrelevance to the young. We cannot even defend our former functions with respect to youth; for the ethos of modern liberalism condemns as inequitable, and a violation of equal opportunity, the arrangements on which continuity between the generations has been based. Bourgeois emphasis on private property and the rights of inheritance gave to the family the function of providing this continuity, which, under feudal conditions, would have been shared among

[2] Bruno Bettelheim, "The Problem of Generations," *Daedalus*, Vol. 91, No. 1 (Winter 1962), pp. 68-96.

several institutions—apprenticeship, for example. But the development of an open, bureaucratic society has weakened the influence of the family, and has transferred the task of distributing status among claimants primarily to the schools, which profess to judge them, so far as possible, without regard to their antecedents.

Today, college admissions officers agree that the sons of alumni should not be favored over more gifted applicants who seek admission solely on the basis of their academic record and recommendations. But this amounts to redefining merit to mean the kind of performance and personality that high school teachers and, increasingly, counselors like. Counselors now virtually control many a high school student's future chances, by their decision whether to assign him to a college-preparatory course, and by monitoring his applications for admission. Whether this whole process makes the contest more open, or merely changes the criteria for preferment, is hard to say.[3]

The effect of the high school, and especially of the counselor, on continuity of status between the generations, and hence on the bond between the generations, is the subject of a fascinating study—still little known after five years—by Aaron V. Cicourel and John I. Kitsuse.[4] While the entire work bears on this issue, one particular interview-excerpt is worth quoting here because of the clarity with which it shows a high school student from an upper-status suburban home being punished for his lack of humility in school by restriction of his future chances. This young man had already been classed by his counselor as an "underachiever." Here are some of the counselor's comments to Cicourel and Kitsuse's interviewer:

> Counselor: *His mother says he's a pleasant outgoing boy. His teachers will say he's either a pleasant boy or that he's a pest. I think he's arrogant. He thinks he's handsome. He's nice-looking, but not handsome. He thinks he owns Lakeshore. He talks to his teachers as if they were stupid. He's a good student. He's in biology and algebra honors.*
> Interviewer: *Is he going to college?*
> Counselor: *He plans college. I think he said he plans to go East like MIT, Harvard, etc. He won't make it. He's a candidate for a midwestern school.*[5]

This excerpt, of course, illustrates certain very positive reasons for conflict between youth and older people: the constraint imposed by the school and its basic disrespect for its young captive. But I have introduced it here specifically to call attention to the fact that the school is here destroying the basis for continuity in the home by making it a condition—for higher- as well as for lower-status stu-

---

[3] Christopher Jencks and David Riesman, in *The Academic Revolution* (Garden City, N.Y.: Doubleday, 1968), pp. 146-154, provide a thoughtful, if rather gingerly, discussion of this issue.

[4] Aaron V. Cicourel and John I. Kitsuse, *The Educational Decision-Makers* (Indianapolis: Bobbs-Merrill, 1963).

[5] *Ibid.*, p. 72.

dents—that the student *unlearn* what the home has taught him about himself if he wishes to retain access to his family's present socioeconomic status. In this way, older middle- and upper-class life-patterns are made positively dysfunctional for the young, just as lower-class life-patterns are, in the equalizing process of the school. Unless the tendency of the home is toward docile acceptance of the common-man pattern of life and expectation, the school will run counter to its influence.

The influence of the school itself is, in a matter of this complexity, difficult to isolate and appraise. But it is clear—and, I think, significant—that disaffection in the young is heavily concentrated among both the bright middle-class and upper-middle-class youth, on the one hand, and the lower-class, especially Negro, youth, on the other. The working class, young and old, is, in contrast, much more likely to be hostile to dissent, and especially to demonstrations, and to regard the school as the pathway to opportunity; its children are more willing to put on a clean shirt and tie and await the pleasure of the draft board or the interviewer from industry. For them, the school and family have worked together, and adult role-models retain their quite possibly fatal appeal.

YOUTH AS A DISCRIMINATED-AGAINST CLASS

I have already asserted that conflict between the generations is less a consequence of the ways in which old and young perceive, or misperceive, each other than of structurally created, genuine conflicts of interest. In this, as in other relationships, ideology follows self-interest: we impute to other people and social groups characteristics that justify the use we plan to make of them and the control over them that use requires. The subordinate group, in turn, often develops these very characteristics in response to the conditions that were imposed on them. Slaves, slum-dwellers, "teen-agers," and enlisted men do, indeed, often display a defensive stupidity and irresponsibility, which quickly abates in situations which they feel to be free of officious interference, with which they can deal, by means of their own institutions, in their own way.

For American youth, these occasions are few, and have grown relatively fewer with the escalation of the war in Vietnam. The Dominican intervention, the scale and permanence of our military investment in Southeast Asia, and the hunch that our economic system requires the engagement of its youth at low pay, or none, in a vast military-academic complex, in order to avoid disastrously widespread unemployment—even under present circumstances far greater among youth than among older persons—suggests to thoughtful young people that their bondage may be fundamental to the American political system and incapable of solution within its terms.

That bondage is remarkably complete—and so gross, in comparison to the way in which other members of the society are treated, that I find it difficult to accept the good faith of most adults who declare their sympathy with "the problems of youth" while remaining content to operate within the limits of the coercive system that deals with them, in any official capacity. To search for explanations of the problems of youth in America in primarily psychological terms while suggesting ways of easing the tension between them and the rest of society is rather like approaching the problem of "the American turkey in late autumn" with the same benign attitude. Turkeys would have no problem, except for the use we make of them, though I can imagine clearly enough the arguments that a cadre of specialists in poultry-relations might advance in defense of Thanksgiving, all of them true enough as far as they went: that wild turkeys could not support themselves under the demanding conditions of modern life; that there are now more turkeys than ever before and their general health and nutritional status, if not their life-expectancy, is much more favorable than in the past; that a turkey ought to have a chance to fulfill its obligations and realize the meaning of its life as a responsible member of society; that, despite the sentimental outcries of reformers, most turkeys seem contented with their lot—those that are not content being best treated by individual clinical means and, if necessary, an accelerated program; and that the discontented are not the fattest, anyway, only the brightest.

Young men in America, like most Negroes, are excluded from any opportunity to hold the kind of job or to earn the kind of money without which members of this society committed to affluence are treated with gross contempt. In a sense, the plight of youth is more oppressive, for the means by which they are constrained are held to be lawful, while discrimination against Negroes is now proscribed by law and what remains, though very serious indeed, is the massive toxic residue of past practice rather than current public policy.

Students are not paid for attending school; they are held to be investing in their future—though if, in fact, they invested as capital the difference between the normal wage of an employed adult high school graduate for four to seven years and what little they may have received as stipends during their academic careers for the same length of time, the return accrued to them might easily exceed the increment a degree will bring. But, of course, they have not got it to invest, and are not permitted to get it to live on. The draft siphons off working-class youth, while middle-class youth are constrained to remain in college to avoid it. If there were no draft, their impact on the economy would probably be ruinous. Trade-union restrictions and child-labor laws, in any case, prevent their gaining the kind of experience, prior to the age of eighteen—even as part of a high school program—that would qualify them for employment as adults by the time they reach their legal majority, though young workers could be protected by laws relating to working conditions, hours, and wage-rates, if this protection were indeed the intent of restrictive legislation, without eliminating his opportunity for employment.

Even the concept of a legal majority is itself a social artifact, defining the time at which the social structure is ready to concede a measure of equality to those of its members whom youthfulness has kept powerless, without reference to their real qualifications which, where relevant, could be directly tested. Nature knows no such sharp break in competence associated with maturation, except in the sexual sphere; and comparatively little of our economic and political behavior is overtly sexual. Perhaps if more were, we would be more forthright and less spiteful. Nor is there any general maturational factor, gradual but portentous in its cumulative effect, which is relevant to society's demands.

Neither wisdom nor emotional stability is particularly characteristic of American adults, as compared to the young; and where, in this country, would the electoral process become less rational if children were permitted to vote: southern California? Washington, D.C.? If there should be any age limitation on voting, it ought to apply, surely, to those so old that they may reasonably expect to escape the consequences of their political decisions, rather than to those who will be burdened and perhaps destroyed by them. Certainly, the disfranchisement of youth is impossible to square, morally, with the Selective Service Act—though politically, there is no inconsistency: the second implies the first. But the draft is pure exploitation, in a classical Marxian sense. The question of the need for an army is not the issue. A volunteer army could be raised, according to the conservative economist Milton Friedman,[6] for from four to twenty billion dollars per year; and to argue that even the larger sum is more than the nation can afford is merely to insist that draftees support the nation by paying, in kind, a tax-rate several times greater than the average paid by civilian taxpayers in money, instead of being compensated for their loss in liberty and added risk. To argue that military service is a duty owed to one's country seems quite beside the point: it is not owed more by a young man than by the old or the middle-aged. And, at a time when a large proportion of enlisted military assignments are in clerical and technical specialties identical with those for which civilians are highly paid, the draft seems merely a form of involuntary servitude.

Without a doubt, the Selective Service Act has done more than any other factor not only to exacerbate the conflict between generations, but to make it clear that it is a real conflict of interest. The draft makes those subject to it formally second-class citizens in a way to which no race is subjected any longer. The arrogance and inaccessibility of Selective Service officials, who are neither elected nor appointed for fixed terms subject to review; the fact that it has been necessary to take court action even to make public the names of draft-board members in some communities; the fact that registrants are specifically denied representation by counsel during their dealings with the Selective Service System and can only appeal to the courts after risking prosecution for the felony of refusing induction—all this is without parallel in the American legal process.

But the laws of the land are, after all, what define youth as a discriminated-against class. In fact, it is their discrimination that gives the term "youth" the only operational meaning it has: that of a person who, by reason of age, becomes subject to special constraint and penalties visited upon no other member of the commonwealth—for whom, by reason of age, certain conduct, otherwise lawful, is defined as criminal and to whom special administrative procedures, applicable

[6] Quoted in *Newsweek*, December 19, 1966, p. 100.

to no other member of the commonwealth, are applied. The special characteristics of "youth culture" are derived from these disabilities rather than from any inherent age-graded characteristics. "Youth culture" is composed of individuals whose time is pre-empted by compulsory school attendance or the threat of induction into the Armed Service, who, regardless of their skills, cannot get and hold jobs that will pay enough to permit them to marry and build homes, and who are subject to surveillance at home or in school dormitories if they are detected in any form of sexual activity whatever. Youth and prisoners are the only people in America for whom *all* forms of sexual behavior are defined as illicit. It is absurd to scrutinize people who are forced to live under such extraordinary disabilities for psychological explanations of their resistance or bizarre conduct, except insofar as their state of mind can be related to their real situation.[7]

LAW ENFORCEMENT AND LEGAL PROCESS APPLIED TO YOUTH

In their relationship to the legal structure, youth operate under peculiar disabilities. The educational codes of the several states provide for considerably more restraint even than the compulsory attendance provisions provide—and that provision would be regarded as confiscatory, and hence doubtless unconstitutional, if applied to any member of the commonwealth old enough to be respected as having the right to dispose of his own time. Soldiers are at least paid *something*. But the code does more than pre-empt the students' time. It is usually interpreted by school authorities as giving them power to set standards of dress and grooming—some of which, like those pertaining to hair length, of a kind that cannot be set aside while the student is not in school. It becomes the basis for indoctrination with the values of a petty, clerical social subclass. Regulations on dress, speech, and conduct in school are justified by this subclass as being necessary because school is supposed to be businesslike; it is where you learn to behave like a businessman. This leaves the young with the alternative of becoming little-league businessmen or juvenile delinquents, for refusal to obey school regulations leads to charges of delinquency—which seems a rather narrow choice among the possibilities of youthful life.

But I have written so much more elsewhere[8] about education as a social sanc-

[7] To be sure, as we become more sophisticated in our conception of mental illness, this becomes more and more clearly true of all forms of mental illness. All states of mind have their psychodynamics; but, regardlesss of the school of psychodynamic thought to which one adheres, the most basic possible definition of mental illness seems to be "a chronic or recurring mental or emotional state which disturbs other people more powerful than the victim." Sometimes, of course, as in the case of certain kinds of paranoid schizophrenics, with good reason.

As a corollary to this, it seems to follow that the head of a modern, centralized, national state—unlike his poor, royal predecessors—can never go officially mad until his government is overthrown.

[8] Edgar Z. Friedenberg is the author of *The Vanishing Adolescent* (1959), *Coming of Age in America* (1965), and *The Dignity of Youth and Other Atavisms*, as well as coauthor (with F. Carl Nordstrom and Hilary Gold) of *Society's Children* (1967). Eds.

tion that it seems inappropriate to devote more space to the functioning of the school as such. I have introduced the topic here simply to point out that the educational code, from the viewpoint of those subject to it, constitutes the most pervasive *legal* constraint on the movements and behavior of youth. It is not, however, from the viewpoint of legal theory, the most fundamental. The juvenile code and the juvenile court system provide even more direct contradictions to the standard of due process afforded adults in American courts.

For the juvenile court is, ostensibly, not a criminal court. It is technically a court of chancery before which a respondent is brought as a presumptive ward—not as an adversary, but as a dependent. It is assumed—the language is preserved in the legal documentation used in preparing juvenile court cases—that the authorities intervene *on behalf of the minor,* and with the purpose of setting up, where necessary, a regime designed to correct his wayward tendencies. The court may restrict; it may, as a condition of probation, insist that a respondent submit to a public spanking; it may detain and incarcerate in a reformatory indistinguishable from a prison for a period of years—but it may not punish. It is authorized only to correct.

Because action in juvenile court is not, therefore, regarded as an adversary proceeding, the juvenile courts provide few of the legal safeguards of a criminal court. There is considerable public misunderstanding about this, because the effect of recent Supreme Court decisions on the juvenile court process has been widely exaggerated, both by people who endorse and by people who deplore what the Court has done. What it *has* done, in effect, is to require the juvenile court to provide the usual safeguards if its actions are ever to become part of an adversary proceeding in a regular criminal court. Since the state may at its discretion, try as adults rather than as juveniles youngsters over a certain minimum age who are accused of actions that violate the criminal code, and since the more serious offenses are usually committed by older adolescents, it may choose to provide these accused with the safeguards granted adults from the time of arrest rather than impair its chances for subsequent successful prosecution. It is, therefore, becoming usual, for example, to provide counsel for juveniles in serious cases; to exclude, in the event of a subsequent criminal prosecution, statements taken by probation officers or youth-squad members in a legally improper manner; and to permit juvenile respondents to summon and cross-examine witnesses —procedures which have not been part of juvenile court practice in the past.

These are improvements, but they leave untouched the much vaster potential for intergenerational conflict afforded by the summary treatment of casual offenders, and, particularly, of those youngsters of whose behavior the law could take no cognizance if they were older; for example, truants, loiterers, runaways, curfew-violators, and twenty-year-olds who buy beer in a tavern. For such as these, there is no question of compromising future prosecution in a formal court, and their treatment has been affected very little, if at all, by high-court decisions. The law still presumes that its intervention in their lives is beneficial *per se,* and they have few enforceable civil rights with respect to it. If young people are "troublemakers," they are punished for it—that is all. Step out of line, and the police "take you away," as the Buffalo Springfield described it—on the occasion of a Los Angeles police roundup of the youngsters strolling on the Sunset Strip in the autumn of 1968—in the song, "For What It's Worth," that gained them a national reputation among teen-agers.

It is quite clear that one's moral judgment of the legal position of youth in American society depends very largely on the degree to which one shares the fundamental assumption on which juvenile proceedings are based: that they are designed to help; that the adults who carry them out will, by and large, have the wisdom and the resources, and the intent to help rather than to punish. Legal authorities have caviled at this assumption for some time. Thus, Paul W. Alexander writes in a paper on "Constitutional Rights in Juvenile Court":

> In the area of the child's constitutional rights the last decade has seen a minor but interesting revolt on the part of some highly distinguished judges. So repellent were some of the juvenile court practices that the judges were moved to repudiate the widely held majority rule that a delinquency hearing in a juvenile court is a civil, not a criminal action. . . . This doctrine appeared so distasteful to a California appellate court that the following language appeared in the opinion: "While the juvenile court law provides that adjudication of a minor to be a ward of the court should not be deemed to be a conviction of crime, nevertheless, for all practical purposes, this is a legal fiction, presenting a challenge to credulity and doing violence to reason."[9]

YOUTH TODAY HAVE NO RESPECT FOR THE LAW

The kind of legal structure which youth face would appear to be, of itself, sufficient to explain why young people are often inclined to be skeptical rather than enthusiastic about law and order—and about those of their number who are enthusiasts for law, as student leaders and prominent athletes tend to be. Yet, the hostile relations that develop between youth and law-enforcement agencies are, even so, probably more attributable to the way in which police generally respond to young people than to the oppressive character of the legal system itself—though the two factors are, of course, causally related, because the fact that youth have few rights and many liabilities before the law also makes it possible for law-enforcement agencies to behave more oppressively.

With respect to youth, law-enforcement agencies assume the role of enforcers of morals and proper social attitudes, as well as of the law, and—having few rights—there is not much the young can do about it. Police forces, moreover, provide a manpower-pool by "moonlighting," while off duty, as members of private enforcement squads hired to keep young people from getting out of hand, a task

[9] Included in Margaret K. Rosenheim (ed.), *Justice for the Child* (New York: Free Press of Glencoe, 1962), p. 83.

which they often try to perform by making themselves as conspicuous as possible in order to keep the young people from starting anything—exactly what police would *not* do in monitoring a group of orderly adults in a public place.

My own observations at folk-rock concerts and dances, for example, which are among the best places for learning how young people express themselves and communicate with one another, confirm that surveillance on these occasions is characteristically officious and oppressive. It often expresses a real contempt for the customs of the youngsters, even when these are appropriate to the occasion. Police, clubs in hand, will rush onstage or into the pit at any sign that the performers are about to mingle with the dancers or audience—if a soloist jumps down from the stage, say, or if members of the audience attempt to mount it; or they will have the lights turned up to interrupt a jam session or freakout that has gone on too long, or with too great intensity, for their taste; or insist on ruining a carefully designed and well-equipped light-show by requiring that the house-lights be kept bright. All this is done smirkingly, as if the youngsters at the concert knew that they were "getting out of line" in behaving differently from a philharmonic audience. It should be borne in mind, considering the fiscal basis for rights in our culture, that tickets for the Beach Boys or Jefferson Airplane are now likely to cost more than tickets for a symphony concert, and the youngsters are poorer than symphony subscribers, but they rarely enjoy the same right to listen to their music in their own way, unmolested.

The music itself provides some of the best evidence of the response of the "further-out" youngsters to police action, which, indeed, sometimes inflicts on them more serious damage than the annoyance of having a concert ruined. In Watts, San Francisco, and Memphis, the civil disorders associated with each city in recent years were triggered by the slaying of a Negro youth by a police officer. "Pot busts" are directed primarily against young people, among whom the use of marijuana has become something of a moral principle evoked by the destructive hostility of the legal means used to suppress it: thirty students at the State University of New York at Stony Brook, for example, were handcuffed and herded from their dormitories before dawn last winter, before the lenses of television cameras manned by news agencies which the Suffolk County police had thoughtfully notified of the impending raid.[10] Rock artists, speaking to, and to some degree for, youth, respond to the social climate which such incidents, often repeated, have established. I have already cited the Buffalo Springfield's song "For What It's Worth." The Mothers of Invention are even more direct in their new album, *We're Only In It for the Money*, where they represent the typical parent as believing that police brutality is justified toward teen-agers who look "too weird" and make "some noise."[11]

---

[10] *The New York Times*, January 18, 1968.
[11] Copyright by Frank Zappa Music Company, Inc., a subsidiary of Third Story Music, Inc. (BMI)

BRINGING IT ALL BACK HOME

Finally, exacerbating the confrontations between youth and adults is the fact that the control of youth has largely been entrusted to lower-status elements of the society. Custodial and control functions usually are so entrusted, for those in subjection have even lower status themselves, and do not command the services of the higher grades of personnel that their society affords. Having low status, moreover, prevents their being taken seriously as moral human beings. Society tends to assume that the moral demands made on the criminal, the mad, and the young by their respective wardens are for their own good and to reinforce those demands while limiting the subjects' opportunities for redress to those situations in which the grossest violations of the most fundamental human rights have occurred. The reader's moral evaluation of the conflict that I have described will, therefore, depend very largely, I believe, on the degree to which he shares society's assumption.

As has surely been obvious, I do not share it. The process by which youth is brought into line in American society is almost wholly destructive of the dignity and creative potential of the young, and the condition of the middle-aged and the old in America seems to me, on the whole, to make this proposition quite plausible. Nevertheless, the violation of the young in the process of socialization fulfills an essential function in making our society cohesive. And curiously—and rather perversely—this function depends on the fact that custody and indoctrination—education is not, after all, a very precise term for it—are lower-status functions.

American democracy depends, I believe, on the systematic humiliation of potential elites to keep it going. There is, perhaps, no other way in which an increasingly educated middle class, whose technical services cannot be spared, can be induced to acquiesce in the political demands of a deracinated and invidious populace, reluctant to accept any measure of social improvement, however generally advantageous, which might bring any segment of the society slightly more benefits than would accrue to it. Teachers, police, and parents in America are jointly in the business of rearing the young to be frightened of the vast majority who have been too scarred and embittered by the losses and compromises which they have endured in the process of becoming respectable to be treated in a way that would enrage them. Anything generous—or perhaps merely civil, like welcoming a Negro family into a previously white community, or letting your neighbor "blow a little grass" in peace—does enrage them, and so severely as to threaten the fabric of society. A conference of recent American leaders associated with a greater measure of generosity toward the deprived—John and Robert Kennedy, Martin Luther King, Jr., and Malcolm X, for a start—might, perhaps, agree, if it could be convened.

Many of today's middle-class youth, however—having been spared, by the prevailing affluence, the deprivations that make intimidation more effective in later life—are talking back; and some are even finding support, rather than betrayal, in their elders—the spectacle of older folks helping their radical sons to adjust their identifying armbands during the spring protests at Columbia University is said to have been both moving and fairly common. The protest, in any case, continues and mounts. So does the rage against the young. If the confrontation between the generations does pose, as many portentous civic leaders and upper-case "Educators" fear, a lethal threat to the integrity of the American social system, that threat may perhaps be accepted with graceful irony. Is there, after all, so much to lose? The American social system has never been noted for its integrity. In fact, it would be rather like depriving the Swiss of their surfing.

THE GENERATION GAP IN THE EYES OF YOUTH

ELIZABETH HERZOG and CECELIA E. SUDIA

In my group of friends, the generation gap is the main topic of conversation; we just don't refer to it by that name, but it all boils down to the same thing.

To teenagers the problem is, "I just can't talk to my parents—they don't even try to understand." And to Mom and Dad it's "Billy just doesn't make sense. Some of the ideas he has are so radical!"

These remarks illustrate two major themes in the responses received by the Children's Bureau from high school students to the following questions:

We hear a lot these days about the generation gap. We'd like to know what your friends think about it, and whether they think about it at all. If so, what are the main things that adults do or say or fail to understand that bother teenagers so much?

What about the other side of the coin? Do your friends think that some of the problems come from the teenagers? If so, what are the main things young people do or don't do that make things worse?

In the spring of 1969 these questions were mailed to a panel of 407 high school students randomly selected from students in college preparatory courses in metropolitan areas situated in the four regions of the United States—North, South, Midwest, West. Replies were received from 251 students in 53 schools in

From *Children,* 17 (March 1970), 53-58.

Elizabeth Herzog is Project Director of the Social Research Group, The George Washington University. Cecelia E. Sudia is with the Research Division Office of Child Development, HEW.

12 cities. The purpose was to find the main patterning of opinions among such young people rather than to obtain an exact count.

The complete results are being published in detail by the Office of Child Development as the first in a series of *Youth Reports*.[1] Here we will present only an outline of the general patterns that emerged—along with some illustrative excerpts.

Experience with analogous studies gives ground for confidence that the opinion profile obtained in the Children's Bureau study validly reflects the views of urban high school students enrolled in college preparatory courses.

Teenagers are no more unanimous than their elders on most subjects. In their comments about the generation gap, for every complaint against parents and adults generally, there are conflicting or qualified responses. Some say that their complaint holds for some adults but not all, or for teenagers as well as adults. Often a single response covers a range of opinions, in an effort to say which kinds of teenagers are likely to hold the various views expressed, or to explain that the writer and his friends do not share a particular view. Nevertheless, the main lines of prevalent opinions are clear, and it is possible to differentiate between broad consensus, evenly divided opinions, and views voiced only by a few.

IS THERE A PROBLEM GAP?

A wide range of opinions emerges about the existence and nature of a generation gap. About half the correspondents report that it is viewed as a real problem, and a few add that it is worse than in former years. The other half divides rather evenly between those who say it is not viewed as a problem at all and those who say it is seen as a problem by some young people but not by others.

In some instances the correspondent reports that it is not a problem for "me personally," or for "me and my friends," but that many young people find it a problem. Occasionally the latter are characterized as young people whose relations with their parents are not close, who do not appreciate what they receive, or who have been "brought up wrong."

> We don't talk about the generation gap, as such, because we all recognize it and accept it. Thus, it isn't a topic, but an assumption behind conversation. For example, the remark, "I had a pretty good talk with my Dad last night," is taken to mean that there has been a rare occurrence.

The substantial minority of the young people who dismiss the generation gap as a problem do so on various grounds. Over half report the opinion that a generation gap is normal and no worse now than in the past. Almost as many say it is seen as a problem mainly because it is "blown up by the media."

[1] Herzog, E.; Sudia, C.; Rosengard, B.; Harwood, J.: Teenagers discuss the generation gap. U.S. Department of Health, Education, and Welfare, Office of Child Development, Children's Bureau. Youth Report No. 1. 1970.

From the way my grandparents talk, I'm pretty sure that my parents weren't understood. Of course, I probably won't understand my kids either.

Some who downgrade the importance of the generation gap add that other problems are much more important—for instance, poor quality education, racism, poverty; that difficulties between people are a matter of individuals, not of generations. What we have, they say, is a "people gap" or a "love gap." And a few see the generation gap as an excuse made up by adults as "a blind" for avoiding the "real" problems.

The generation gap is, according to many kids—who have good relationships with their parents—an overemphasized, over-generalized, over-coined phrase, used to describe a rebelliousness occurring during the adolescent years accompanied by friction in the home.

A few, but very few, have a good word to say for the generation gap. Without it, they hold, there would be no progress. It forces teenagers to think for themselves, reach their own conclusions "so we will be a very determined people."

The nature and causes of the generation gap are discussed by many of the young people. By far the majority see it as a gap in understanding or communication. The most common complaint is that "they don't understand" or "we just can't communicate," sometimes because "they" (parents, or adults generally) don't want to, sometimes because they can't. Four out of five refer to failures of communication or understanding, or both.

Often the point is made with intense resentment against the failure of adults to try to understand, communicate, and explain. At the same time, a substantial minority view the communication failure more philosophically, as natural, inevitable, and probably chronic. And a few display sympathetic indulgence. "They can't help it," "they have their own problems."

Our parents are both reticent and communicative and they always seem to be one when it should be the other.

They don't listen. If we try to talk to them about a problem, they are either so involved in giving advice that they don't hear us at all or they aren't listening in the first place.

Most of the kids feel that it is just a lack of interest by both parties to talk to each other.

PARENTAL SINS

Lagging behind the failure to understand and communicate, but nevertheless bulking larger than other complaints, is a cluster of protests against the failure of parents to grant the teenager full status as a person entitled to respect and trust.

Parents, the complaints go, do not respect the teenager's opinions, fail to recognize that his problems are important to him, and do not trust him.

On the one hand such shortcomings are associated with adults' failure to recognize that the teenager is partly grown up and worthy of certain responsibilities. On the other hand, adults are occasionally charged with not making allowances for the teenager's youth and expecting him to be more grown up than he is. Either way, the individual and his growth phase are felt to be belittled or ignored.

I just wish that sometimes they would give us a chance to show them what we have learned.

A less salient part of the sins-of-omission cluster is failure to give teenagers attention and love. Attention, however, is clearly not to be confused with the widely resented "nosiness." "They're too busy," "they don't take time," "they're too wrapped up in their own problems and fights," "it takes time to be a good parent," "kids rebel in order to get attention," "they don't give enough love."

Objections to what parents do stand out almost as much as objections to what they do not do.

Leading all sins of commission is the dual charge of rigidity and strictness: parents are always sure they are right; they refuse to reconsider what they have said, once they have said it; they are given to arbitrary rules and punishments.

The main thing adults do wrong is that they think things are either black or white, only positive or negative. No compromising. Having this attitude, just makes teens kind of "burn" inside, almost until they explode.

On the other hand, a few teenagers complain that many parents spoil children by being overindulgent and overpermissive. One or two associate such indulgence with an effort to "buy love," adding that this only breeds disrespect.

Parents mean well when they try to give you all the things that they never had. They want your life to be better than theirs was. But they don't realize that they might be forcing something onto you, and when you "fail them" or "rebel," they immediately hit you with, "we've given you everything you've ever wanted," or "where did we go wrong?"

A number of parental sins of omission are seen as contributing to sins of commission: lack of understanding, refusal to listen, lack of trust and respect for the teenager as an individual, lead parents to become "nosy," suspicious, and inconsiderate.

A different kind of objection to parental behavior is reported by about one correspondent in 10, but always with intense feeling. This concerns parents who set a poor example for their children, who "say one thing and do another." Such parents are described with biting scorn as being "hypocritical," "phoney," "setting a bad example." They drink, they smoke, they tell half truths, they practice "loose morality," and at the same time urge their children not to do these things.

A small, equally vehement number of respondents report complaints of parents who nag, "yell at their kids," and embarrass them in front of others.

For both boys and girls, lack of understanding and communication leads all complaints by a wide margin. Girls put most emphasis on lack of respect and trust, often perceived as prying and interfering with social activities. Boys also put most emphasis on rigidity and strictness but without specifying the context. Lack of attention and love ranks higher among girls' complaints than among boys'.

CONFLICT IN VALUES

Over one-third of the teenage reporters explicitly refer to value clashes between the generations, and many more discuss value-related points in connection with other complaints. Often the references are general: "We don't have the same values." "We have two opposing philosophies." But more often the conflict is specified: "They" are accused of insufficient interest in the overriding problems of our day, including war, poverty, and racism. "They" are accused of materialism—over-emphasis on money, possessions, economic security, status, individual achievement.

Corollary to both these accusations is the charge that "They" emphasize trivia at the expense of really important things, insist on conformity in matters of dress and grooming, and judge people by externals.

Disapproval of parents' emphasis on nonessentials is linked with indignant protests against adult objections to teenage preferences in hair styles, dress, and grooming. Over one-fourth of the correspondents report such objections. "Parents don't understand fashions are changing" or they think teenagers are "not responsible" if they are not dressed conservatively. Among both boys and girls the subject frequently concerns the hair styles of boys.

A very few of the young people criticize long-haired boys. One goes so far as to agree with his parents that "long hair is disgusting." On the whole, however, the teenagers defend their right to self-determination in dress and grooming, even though the defenders themselves may not exercise that right in ways deplored by their elders.

The teenagers tend to condemn the adults' "over-concern with external appearance" on two grounds: as reflecting a distorted sense of values; and as a violation of individual autonomy. Because of this dual significance, the reporters imply, teenage costume and grooming have taken on the attributes of symbol, of language, of badge, and of weapon—thus acquiring for the young an importance which may seem somewhat at odds with their objections to emphasizing external appearance.

For the first quarter of the school year I kept my hair short and very conservative—I made straight A's. Now that's what they wanted me to do and

I did it (make the grades, not the hair). But, nevertheless, I did what they wanted me to, without any qualms, but I ask them to let me let my hair grow long and the answer is an emphatic "no!" I got the grades, either way (and that gives them satisfaction)—why not let me have my way?

Sometimes the correspondents try to explain the value differences they report. Some of these discussions are bitter, some dispassionate, a few indulgent. The chief excuse offered for their parents is that because they grew up during the depression they attach greater significance to economic security than their children.

Today's young people do not have to worry like their parents did about money and making a living. They can be concerned with other things . . .

Such comments are made by less than one in 15, and certainly not by those who report the views of the nonaffluent.

Nearly half the correspondents explain the value conflicts with adults in such statements as: "The world is changing too fast for them." Often the statement is made without explicit criticism. But more often it accompanies criticism of adults as resistant to change. The adults, it is said, not only fail to understand change but they definitely do not want it, while the younger generation definitely does. Thus, in a sense, change itself becomes a value—positive for the young and negative for adults.

They have carved their own little niche in society and are fearful lest change will destroy it. We understand such fear. We can foresee the same fear ourselves when the next generation wants change.

Most bitter of all is the reported resentment against parents who want to make their children "into a carbon copy of themselves." "When I was your age" is a particularly detested phrase.

SOME PARENTS ARE O.K.

While the wording of our questions tended to invite criticism of adults, the responses do not picture parents and other adults in wholly negative terms. Some respondents—nearly one in 10—explicitly state that they share the values of their own parents. Very few of these correspondents describe themselves as "conservative." They more commonly describe their parents as progressive in their thinking, understanding of young people, and keeping up with the times.

Sometimes the correspondents contrast their own parents with the parents of friends or acquaintances—that is, they view their parents as nice but unusual.

I am thought to be extremely lucky because I get along with my parents . . . I am the exception.

THE WORLD "MESS"

Nearly a third of the correspondents confine their responses to a general consideration of whether there is or is not a generation gap. The remainder divide rather evenly into three groups: those who refer only to intrafamily relations and issues; those who refer only to social problems and issues; and those who talk about both.

Those who do mention society or social problems blame adults for allowing the world to get into "this mess." The positive social goals attributed to youth are pictured with varying degrees of specificity: to end war, to cure poverty, to "stop evils," to promote "spiritual and mental welfare," to reform political processes, to further peace, love, and brotherhood, to engage in community service.

> We are very much concerned about many grave problems, which threaten to destroy the advantages that civilization has given us. We are concerned about overpopulation, racism, poverty, pollution, and most of all, oppression and the stifling of the individual in what is supposed to be a democratic society. The reactions that we have seen to these concerns are very frustrating. School desegregation guidelines are relaxed . . . ; poverty programs are stifled because they might hurt the taxpayer; industry successfully blocks pollution control; and those who wish to democratize America are labeled Communist and suppressed, often violently.

The inevitable counter-point is presented by a very few dissenters who say teenagers are not really so idealistic themselves, but are in fact materialistic and lack positive goals. However, not one correspondent reports that teenagers are content with society as it is.

The specific problems of society most frequently mentioned concern riots, protests and disorders, war, race, and poverty.

> . . . what really annoys many teenagers is the "accepting" view adults have. They accept war, poverty, hunger as unchangeable. The teenagers look at war for what it is—man killing man senselessly. They see race riots, starvation and campus trouble. No wonder they're disgusted.

Comments about forms of protest more frequently disapprove than approve violent and disruptive dissent. Nevertheless, those who are moved to discuss such matters are obviously in sympathy with the reasons for active efforts to bring about change. About one in 20 reports the view that "shock treatment" in the form of violence and disruption may be necessary in order to "awaken the sleeping generation." Almost twice as many, however, see a need to keep violent dissidents within bounds.

> Also, violent marches and occupation of college buildings seems to be carrying things too far. However, many of my friends feel that at times, a peace-

ful march can be important to make grievances known. The inability of peaceful marches to remain peaceful is a major problem . . .

A college is a place to learn—if the students don't like it, they can go some- place else!

All comments concerning war in general and most of those concerning the Vietnam war are strongly negative.

We have to fill out c.o. forms to explain to you why we shouldn't kill, but you're the ones who should have to fill out forms telling us why we should kill.

That these views are not necessarily unanimous is suggested by the fact that the majority of the correspondents make no mention of war at all.

Many correspondents make no mention of race problems, but all who do are emphatic about the need to eliminate prejudice, discrimination, and inequalities. Not one reports endorsement of a "go-slow" policy. Little regional difference in views is perceptible. Among the very few who refer to interracial dating, all de- fend the practice as quite acceptable to youth though not to parents.

I, as a teenager, think that because the older generations have tolerated racism and other forms of human cruelty, their concepts are wrong and should be abandoned.

On the whole, the views of black teenagers resemble those of white teenagers with regard to the existence and nature of the generation gap, although the em- phasis is clearly influenced by keen awareness of their special problems. The pro- portions of those affirming or denying a generation gap are comparable. How- ever, those who belittle the problem do so with special scorn, pointing out that the real gaps are between "Uncle Toms" and all the others, regardless of age.

The gap between aware blacks and unaware blacks is not necessarily one of age. In most cases it involves the extent to which one has been brainwashed by white America . . . Some people as young as junior high school age have proven to be more stubborn to the "de-brainwashing" process than some grandparents.

Some reports from black students include poignant discussions of problems that dwarf such considerations as the generation gap.

I am one of the twelve Negroes who attends a predominantly white school of about 3,000 or more . . . I'm just like a walking test at school. Now the Negro is on stage, performing before an all white audience, trying to sway and correct their opinion of blacks.

The subject of poverty is among the least frequently mentioned in comments about specific social problems. To some extent, however, economic inequalities are implied in references to social problems generally and to race problems.

TEENAGERS ON TEENAGERS

In response to the specific inquiry about "the other side of the coin," over half of the reporters find some readiness to concede that there is fault on the part of both generations. About one-third did not respond to the question.

A number of teenage "sins" are specified, some of them mirror-images of those ascribed to the older generation. Teenagers, like adults, are accused of not listening and not communicating. About two out of five acknowledge that the obligation to give understanding, trust, and respect to their elders is often unfulfilled. About one in seven criticizes the young for not realizing that after all "they are still kids" and can learn from adults—although half as many report belief that teenagers really do know more about today's world than their parents.

Some kids think it's all the parents' fault, but I think it's half and half.

I think both sides need to do less talking and more listening.

In frequency and vehemence, criticisms of the older generation far outweigh criticisms of teenagers, and are less often qualified or restricted to an unrepresentative few. The prevailing view is definitely that the teenagers are not chiefly to blame for the generation gap; about one in 10 exonerates them altogether.

But I just happen to think that the older generations are far more mistake prone, and will not face the reality when they are wrong.

Among the most indignant protests reported are objections to prejudice against teenagers as a group, levied in some form by about one in three, against parents, adults generally, and the "mass media." Nearly a fourth of all the correspondents concede that "some teenagers are really bad," but they usually add that the great majority are O.K. and should not suffer for the misdeeds of the misguided few. They maintain that adults expect the worst and act in such a way as to invite it.

It seems they feel if one girl goes around with every boy in town and doesn't care what she does, that their daughter will do the same. They don't have enough faith in their own child-raising.

The media, it is charged, aggravate such attitudes, by playing up only the bad and ignoring the good.

There are just that small minority of "weirdos" that there has always been, but, with the more publicity, they seem to be a larger group.

Mention of drugs comes in only incidentally, as an occasional specific under broader issues. Use of marijuana receives little support, and heavier drugs none at all. While drug users are sometimes described as "really bad," some sympathetic reference is made to the pressures that drive some young people to drugs.

These kids are looking for something better like maybe through drugs, boy you can't find it that way.

Hippies and Yippies are referred to by about one in 10 correspondents, chiefly in connection with the tendency of adults to blame all teenagers for the misguided deviance of only a few. Less than one in 20 reflect a neutral attitude toward or sympathy with hippie motives and aims although not necessarily with their behavior.

A minority group such as hippies, militants, drug addicts, draft dodgers ruin the reputation of the majority of good teenagers and terrify responsible parents.

Maybe that is why hippies dress as they do. They want to bring to their parents' attention that no matter how unkempt they are they can still love their fellow man.

AUTONOMY AND IDENTITY

In one form or another, the drive for autonomy is conspicuous throughout the responses. Boys especially report a generalized protest against interference with "doing their own thing."

Adults' effort to control teenagers' appearance is regarded, on the one hand, as a defect in values—overemphasizing the trivial, judging the outward appearance rather than the inner man—and, on the other hand, as undue interference with individual autonomy. There is a tendency to contrast adults' emphasis on trivia and externals with teenagers' interest in broad positive goals and essential individual worth.

Parents are always looking after their teenagers like their parents looked after them. But times are changing and this brings more freedom and independence to the teenager. He wants to lead his own life and not the one that his parents try to force him into. Parents, WAKE UP!!! He has his own life to live.

Since the questions were focused on adults' behavior lapses, it is probably not surprising that direct or indirect references to teenage identity problems were rare in the responses. Nevertheless, there are occasional reminders that young people are changing and groping, that one aim of young people is to "find themselves."

> I still have 2 years of high school left, and I intend to keep struggling in that time to be able to live the life and learn the things I need to, as it is necessary if I wish to be the type of person I think I am.

A number of our correspondents are very explicit about their future opportunity to improve our society, and their determination to make the most of it. "We are the leaders of tomorrow," they declare, adding that they hope to improve on what their elders have done. They clearly believe in their own moral superiority.

> We all know what kind of shape the world is in today, after the older generation had charge of it. Today's teenagers want to try and fix it, their own way, and if we don't succeed, it will be through our own mistakes, not through the mistakes of our parents. And we'll be the ones to have the power of changing the world soon.

EAGERNESS TO HELP

The correspondents' wish for understanding and communication between the generations is underscored by the nature of their response to the invitation to communicate with their Government. The response rate (63 percent) in itself is remarkably high for mail interviews, which as a rule evoke less than a 33-percent response.

Not many comment directly on the request to contribute to *Youth Reports,* but among those who do only three comment negatively while 20 are strongly positive.

> This questionnaire is just the typical kind of ineffectual thing the "older generation" would do—pardon my criticism—perhaps you'll get the new communication.

> Thank you, great impersonal governmental edifice—for the first chance I've had to express myself.

> I don't think it is a problem that can ever be solved, but Good Luck anyway. Maybe the government is good for something, and you can at least ease the pressure.

CONFORMITY, REBELLION, AND LEARNING: CONFRONTATION OF YOUTH WITH SOCIETY

IRVING PHILIPS, M.D., and STANISLAUS A. SZUREK, M.D.

This paper describes clinical experience related to the confrontation of youth with society. Its thesis is that in our society the pleasure and satisfaction associated with early successful learning, in all areas of everyday living, is much reduced and distorted during each developmental phase, so that subsequent and continued learning is similarly affected. The inevitable frustration may be expressed by youth in the context of rebellion, alienation, and over-conformity.

In the current confrontation of youth with society, conformity has been construed as an evil of our age. Rebellion has been chosen by youth as the path to solution of problems; and withdrawal, disengagement, and alienation are the defense against submission to and participation in the failures of society. Those engaged in the openly rebellious struggle today, as impatient as their predecessors, intransigently demand complete solutions to current dilemmas, *now*. The widespread conflict in which the present generation of adolescents and youth is engaged elicits the interest of clinicians to try to understand the deeper motivation of those youths involved in such struggles. In the writings of some, sociological factors are stressed.[4, 5, 7, 10, 11, 15]

Sociological factors, however, do not always seem sufficient to account for the behavior of many participant young individuals who are not obviously deprived by a long-standing poverty, racist-ethnic oppression, or discrimination. Even their apparent idealistic empathy with the oppressed seems to require further examination, especially when in the more violent aspects of such militancy there is gross destructiveness, crude obscenity in word and deed, and at times utter disregard of the rights of the majority. Although careful comparative surveys are needed, the question may be raised whether the minority of overtly rebellious youth not belonging in the category of culturally or socioeconomically deprived or oppressed really differs by the usual demographic criteria from the nonparticipating majority. For the rebellious minority, the clinician needs additional biographic information to understand more completely the psychodynamic factors involved in the individual's experiences with his family that impel him to what often seems self-destructive activity.

By Irving Philips, M.D. and Stanislaus A. Szurek, M.D. From *American Journal of Orthopsychiatry*, 40 (April, 1970), 463-472. Copyright ©, the American Orthopsychiatric Association, Inc. Reproduced by permission of the senior author and the publisher. First presented at the 1969 annual meeting of the American Orthopsychiatric Association, New York, N.Y.

Irving Philips, M.D., is Clinical Professor of Psychiatry, and S. A. Szurek, M.D., is Professor of Psychiatry, University of California School of Medicine, San Francisco.

The thesis of this paper is that the pleasure or satisfaction that is part of successful learning in all areas of everyday living either does not occur or is much decreased and distorted in the psychic context of rebellion, alienation, or neurotic overconformity. Learning that leads to creativity does not usually grow out of violence; nor is conformity always a generalized attitude of timid submission without the capacity for new ideas. Conformity is often used today as meaning a slavish submissiveness to prevailing ideas, with little opportunity for modification of custom and norm and consequent inhibition of personal innovation. It often is construed as implying a response only to external coercion. Clinicians, however, recognize a psychological state characterized by a feeling of coercion that in fact results from internal conflict and anxiety about impulses associated with self-expression. Such feelings often are projected outward and seen as coercion by society to force the individual into a predetermined mold.

In contrast, young people who have been fortunate enough to have had the satisfactions of mastery from each preceding developmental phase experience and express a feeling of excitement and anticipation about accepting an increasingly broader and more responsible role in society. Such feelings have a quality of eagerness to do and to learn more and to assume responsibility for oneself and others in an ever-widening social context. To some, such attitudes may be seen as conformity, but what may appear on the surface as conformity in this context is an acceptance of developing social opportunities for one's own satisfaction. Such development is in harmony with the fundamentally just ideals and mores of a generally imperfect society that is nevertheless continually engaged in an effort to provide for the welfare of more and more of its citizens.

The pursuit of one's own satisfactions may appear to be egocentric, but unambivalent altruistic impulses can only flow as a result of the fulfillment and resolution of one's own inner needs. One may say, "my satisfactions are not consonant with others not achieving theirs; mine are part of his." This is similar to Sullivan's[13] concept of expansive humanization that describes a stage in individual personality development as movement from the egocentric position to concern about the world outside the self: "Validation of personal worth requires a type of relationship which I call collaboration, by which I mean clearly formulated adjustments of one's behavior to the expressed needs of the other person in the pursuit of increasingly identical—that is, more and more nearly mutual —satisfactions. . . ." The inculcation of moral imperatives without the fulfillment of one's own satisfactions is, at best, likely to be ambivalent.

For the adolescent, such personal integration is the result of progressively more thorough mastery of new skills. It includes an inner integration of thought, feeling, and action. It expresses a continuity of a personal sense of autonomy that is based upon continued learning from lessons of the past and the application and adaptation of old principles to new problems. It implies the ability to accept new ideas only after thoughtful contemplation and regard of their substance and relationship to self and others. Thus, such integration allows for a minimum of inner conflict, for a choice of vocation, and for intimacy with peer and mate. As

Erikson[2] has stated: "identity formation . . . is a configuration gradually integrating *constitutional givens, idiosyncratic libidinal needs, favored capacities, significant identifications, effective defenses, successful subliminations, and consistent roles.*"

Such abilities develop a sense of identity that is consonant with creative endeavor. It involves the utilization of the past to solve everyday problems of living by means of a consistent and persistent search for what is true about each situation, what is to be assimilated or rejected, what is to be changed or integrated into one's personal world.

Creativity, in this sense, is not limited to such episodes as those in which inductive leaps have occurred to revolutionize aspects of our understanding of nature or human experience. It is accessible to most of us through the persistent utilization of thoroughly integrated learning to solve those everyday problems that are not constant with inner harmony. Thus, whenever there is disaffection and conflict in one's inner or outer world, anxiety results, signaling a need for closer attention to those situations that demand resolution without destruction or alienation. A progressive process ensues that may never be complete but moves toward solutions that may bring satisfactions for a greater number as soon as possible. Creativity in this sense "brings with it a sense of fullness of living, a keen and vivid satisfaction from any activity, and an exuberant eagerness for every variety of possible nondestructive experience in every phase of our finite lives."[14]

No individual matures in a vacuum. The influence on any growing organism of an environment undergoing rapid change is marked. Social factors frequently mentioned in the current literature are relevant. Since the end of World War II there has been a period of unprecedented economic growth, with relatively full employment for the majority, astonishing technologic development, and the rapid accumulation of material goods and wealth. Coincident with such progress toward the good life, there has been growing concern about overpopulation and pollution of air and water, the spectre of progressively more dangerous economic inflation, and the threat of recession or depression. A minority in our country continues to suffer from such inequities in opportunity for employment, housing, and civil rights as to pose serious threats to the integrative forces of society. Finally, the unspeakably destructive power of our weapons remains a threat to the survival of the world, especially as we are engaged in a seemingly unendable war.

The historical relationship of the child to society is that of a miniature adult whose passions and sins are to be curbed, tamed, and formed into the cultural configuration of the adult model as soon as possible. Adolescence is that period prior to adulthood during which rebellion is tolerated only to the extent that the gap between generations is not too disruptive to society or too disorganizing to the young.

The time is fast approaching when 50% of our population will be under 25 years of age. The voting age in some states already has been lowered to 18 years, and other states are contemplating a similar change. Youth is the consumer in a multibillion-dollar market aimed at him, that often develops, shapes, or influences his taste and morality. The young have been instrumental in formulating directions in art, music, and dress, both as direct participants and as audience. All major political persuasions seek their support.

Only a few decades ago the period of an adolescent's dependence on his family was limited. The need to work and to support a new family dictated his course. He sought his vocation, secured employment, and by the end of the second or beginning of the third decade of life achieved an adult status supported by tradition and cultural rituals.

> In times past, the common man's child was often a household head at 16, a valiant soldier in the king's army at 14 or 15, a responsible guild apprentice at 13 or 14. Today his middle-class counterpart, endlessly scheduled and ferried from one supervised activity to another throughout the later years of childhood, and finally thirsting for some autonomy, seeks some daring adventure, some sphere of independent activity.[12]

In recent years, the period of parental support has lengthened. The number and proportion of youths enrolling for higher education has increased considerably, as growing affluence has made possible financial support for these students. Technologic development has demanded new skills; vocational and professional training has extended into the third decade of life.

Thus, full status of manhood is delayed, with resulting ambivalence about the dependent position. Many a father may not feel able to claim fully his rights of manhood while depending upon his own parents for support of his sons and daughters. A parent, in turn, may feel resentment that funds needed for his own self-sufficiency in his later years are eroded by "doing everything for the children," even though this may be done in order to give the children everything the parent missed in his own deprived youth.

The parents of today are children of a great depression who have participated in the greatest period of economic and technologic growth known to man. Many grew up in harsh surroundings, suffered want and privation, fought a terrible war. They dreamed that their progeny would share in better times, would be given opportunities not available to the givers, the new generation would benefit from the harvest of their own hard labor. Despite such genuine parental wishes —some of which might have been neurotically distorted—some have been discontented with their role in life. Work produced little satisfaction; economic gain was eroded by excessive material acquisition, growing debt, and inflation, so that there never seemed to be enough. The highly prized intimacy with mate and family often was a thinly veiled masquerade. These discontents and anxieties led to isolation, fear, and emptiness.

Such parents may turn to the child to seek their reward. Thus, what is given to the child may be accompanied by demands for achievement and success, in a futile attempt, inevitably doomed to failure, to insure a satisfaction to the parent that he himself had not secured in his own life. If satisfaction is not forthcoming from the child, as it had not been from material gain, disappointment and guilt occur. This may be expressed by symptomatic manifestations of depression resulting from internalized aggression or by externalization in further demands upon the young.

Ambivalent attitudes do not help the child achieve success in the learning of needed skills nor, therefore, obtain the satisfaction that accompanies the development of his own integration. In all this parental demand, there is little realistic held to the child in learning, little praise for or satisfaction in his actual achievement. Such parental attitudes do not enhance the adolescent's self-esteem but may hurt his self-regard and evoke feelings of guilt for failures and resentment at the ungratifiable expectations. Even when the child does achieve some success in making good grades, the durable satisfaction is thin because of tension. He feels whatever success he gains is exacted by anxious, continual demands for production, awards, and fame, reinforced by parental exhortation for their own self-glorification. Such repeated experiences tend to lead to adolescent depression with symptomatic behavior expressed externally by destructive behavior in militant activism, or by an alienation from peers and family as a compromise solution, and often a futile attempt to seek some immediately gratifiable goal. Thus, satisfaction is elusive for both parent and child—"What could not remain integrated in the parent's personality because of *his* experience is not available to facilitate the integrated development of his child."[14]

The following case examples may illustrate these processes:

1. Mr. and Mrs. W, the parents of John, age 9, and Jean, age 12, sought help for the younger child. Mr. W was a schoolteacher and Mrs. W was a part-time civil rights attorney. Both received their college educations during the depression years. Mr. W chose his occupation because of its financial security, but now found little zest in his work. He often felt unchallenged by his job, unfulfilled in his tasks, and somewhat inferior to his more ambitious wife. His paycheck never seemed to make ends meet; his wife's employment allowed for "keeping up with the liberal middle-class Joneses." Mrs. W was active in community affairs, often defending "underdog" causes and the civil liberties of her clients. She felt disappointed in her life with her husband, finding him somewhat lacklustre in fulfilling his great potential. She herself experienced somatic complaints as well as recurrent fatigue. She never experienced the pleasure she expected from her vocation: "The job never seemed done and there were always insurmountable obstacles ahead."

The parents consulted the psychiatrist because of John's learning problems. He was often compared unfavorably to his gifted sister. The mother responded to each school failure as her own and reacted with feelings of inadequacy and depression. She demanded more of her son, as she did of herself in her work. The father accepted his son's plight more resignedly,

but felt the boy's troubles to be a recapitulation of his own supposed failure. In the course of weekly interviews for the next nine months, John
began to try harder at his school work and developed a sense of confidence and enthusiasm, with resulting improvement. Each parent was seen
weekly as well. The father began to take greater interest in his work with
his students and consequently had more respect for himself. Although Mrs.
W seemed less tense in her work, she continued to feel anxious about her
family's financial situation. She expressed the thought that perhaps they
were sending the wrong child since the older one was more moody, with
outbursts of temper at the slightest criticism.

Three years later, the daughter, Jean, came to us on the advice of her parents. She quickly assured the therapist that, "I am only here because my
parents asked that I see you." Nevertheless, she agreed to continue in
therapeutic work once a week. She was seen for the next three years, rarely
missing an appointment. Her parents were seen infrequently, at moments
of crisis. Jean was a brilliant student with high academic achievement. At
the time of referral, she was threatened with suspension from school
because of defiance of school rules. She had called the local civil liberties
union and was prepared to make this a civil rights issue. The dean of
women patiently discussed the situation with her until an acceptable compromise was reached. In relating and discussing her past experience she
underplayed her intellectual achievement. She insisted on telling of her
efforts on behalf of the oppressed, which during the previous year resulted
in an arrest at a sit-in, which seemed to be an identification with her
mother's way of dealing with her own troubles. She frequently was involved in radical causes. She was committed to many extracurricular activities and there were always hectic efforts to get everything done. Her school
work was of high caliber, but each test of her skill was accompanied by
frantic efforts to overcram, lest she fail, and each success was accompanied
by belittlement of her own achievement.

In her senior year, Jean threatened to leave home and live in the Haight-
Ashbury area. At this time, her father was transferred to a very conservative school district and was frightened that his position on Vietnam, not
yet a popular one, would be dangerous to his security. Financial worries
were heightened. Her parents feared that if they did not comply with
Jean's demands she would run away. The tension in the family became
acute. The mother remarked, "It would really be cute, if it were someone
else's daughter." Finally, after much discussion, but with great apprehension, they allowed her to leave home and live with a friend. Jean engaged
in all sorts of hippie activity, from drugs to sexual promiscuity, without
resolving her depression. Sexual experiences with her "brothers" in the
commune were described as anesthetic and sometimes distasteful. During
the next two years she slowly began to discuss her present life, and began
to see some of its limitations on her continued growth. She began to
understand how her feelings about not attaining something that was satisfying led to self-blame and feelings of guilt. She gave up drugs and became

more discreet in her relationships. She discontinued her involvement with an older man and moved to an apartment of her own. She became a file clerk and did very well in her routine job, achieving promotions during her brief tenure and some satisfaction in doing well and in earning funds for her college tuition.

As a result of all this, her depression lessened. Although she remained unsure of her abilities and fearful of undertaking advanced study, she nevertheless began to pursue this goal and made plans to apply to college. Her parents became less anxious as she performed better and could tolerate her wishes and aspirations with less tensions. They began to talk together about her future and career with less discontent. The daughter visited home more frequently and stayed for longer periods.

2. Bill W., a 20-year-old college boy, was seen at the clinic because of fatigue, poor school performance, and feelings of depression. "I don't know where I'm going. School is a drag, and it hardly seems worthwhile." He was seen twice weekly for three years. Information concerning his family was garnered during the course of his visits.

His father, a successful attorney and now a county judge, rose from modest circumstances to independent wealth through land speculation. His activity in politics led to his appointment as judge. He was described by his son as a "crude gross man who could smell opportunity and jump on the bandwagon, but possessed little learning or scholarship." His mother married his father after a brief courtship. She had been his secretary and always felt inferior in her role as mother and housewife to her domineering husband. She often expressed to her children her wish that she could have done more for them.

Bill was always pushed to do more by his father—to choose a career that was "useful and promised affluence." His mother acted as a buffer to her husband's demands on their children, encouraging "that we take it easy because average was good enough." After high school, Bill spent a year working on a tanker, jumping ship in Europe and living alone on meager funds. Whenever he needed money he would obtain it from his mother. Despite his father's protestations about the life of his hippie son, the father would write him occasionally and suggest that he visit places that he himself had longed to see in the fantasies of his own youth.

On his return, Bill entered college. Even though he did little work, he obtained average grades. He joined a series of radical campus political groups, but was unable to maintain a sustained interest. He said that he felt alternately frozen in his work and outwardly hostile and ready to explode. In his second year there occurred a student strike against the school administration. He readily joined the student protest, which escalated to a sit-in and finally with a confrontation with the police in which Bill was arrested for resisting an officer. He described this week in his life as exciting and fulfilling, "the first time I really felt worthwhile. I suddenly felt important."

After this incident, he continued to be active in student affairs but suffered periodic depression.

As his therapy continued, Bill became more interested in working with minority group children and developed a tutorial program in the local schools as well as one on his own campus for failing students. He became interested in teaching and chose education as his major area of study. He sought a primary school education credential. Although his father protested his choice of vocation because of its lack of prestige, he continued in his work.

Slowly and persistently, he became more certain of himself and the pursuit of his career. He was able to deal with his father more constructively and with less conflict. They were able to talk together about what each secretly felt about himself and the other. When his son was given a gift by the students in the community for his work, the father expressed pride in the accomplishment and for the first time stated that he himself had longed for some recognition that was equally meaningful and sincere.

As a postscript, near the end of the therapy, when Bill was appointed a graduate teaching assistant, another confrontation occurred on the campus. Hesitantly, he did not participate but counseled his students on how to avoid destructive and violent action as well as how to maintain a persistent and effective dialogue with school administrators. He related how pleased he felt when the student demands were considered and for the most part accepted without any personal injury to anyone.

Youth sees inconsistencies not only in his family but also in his culture—decaying cities and black rebellion contrasted to the good life manufactured by screen and tube. He sees war and poverty in the midst of unprecedented affluence. He sees his world "shooting for the moon" but unable to solve dilemmas at home. He sees the preaching of honesty and trust and the practice in the free enterprise system of "get yours while the getting is good." He sees tax advantage to corporations to spur initiative and the cutting of health budgets in our larger and richer states. He sees the good life as coming through material acquisition, portrayed so vividly by advertising in the communications media. "Buy now, pay later" (with no regard to an interest rate of 12-18%), yet a truth-in-advertising law is almost impossible to achieve. He hears of fidelity while the frequency of divorce and illegitimacy rises precipitously. He listens as the schools indoctrinate the young with "America the Beautiful" while he helplessly observes the increasing pollution of air and stream. "The good life is at hand, and yet we are unable to grasp, understand, or utilize its fruits. The young observe our failings and try to adapt to them by expressing in action much of the discontent that is felt, but not fully comprehended, by their elders."[9] Youth confronts his society with his activism by vividly dramatizing the sado-masochistic distortions of his culture—the inconsistencies, the half truths, and the emptiness of the striving. Such conflicts expressed by a minority of youth mirror the discontents of contemporary society, Noshpitz[8] has suggested a wider application of the Johnson-Szurek clinical observations: in effect, that youth is expressing in "exaggerated and caricatured form . . . the essential failure that his parents experience in their culture coping attempts."

Where a familial atmosphere exists such as sketched above, with a continuous discrepancy between preaching and practice, there may be the introjection of similar poorly integrated parental and societal regard about fundamental values. When the child, and later the adolescent, begins to follow a similar course and his performance becomes inconsistent and erratic about what he is trying to learn in each developmental phase, a painful disappointment is experienced. He may not see clearly that his own performance is the source of his discontent, but is ready to indict his parents and society as the guilty ones, at the same time protesting anxiously his own innocence. Such youths attack and depreciate others, as they themselves feel depreciated by pervasive conflicted feelings, difficult to experience consciously. They have a gnawing feeling that they are not honest or convinced of any goal or ideal consistent with any value system subscribed to by their parents or society. Such a young person may become fearful that he may be enveloped in situations that signify acceptance of and dishonest identification with the Establishment (parent and society), or he may align himself with attitudes that are hostile and destructive toward prevailing cultural mores. Authority is the target and "is then rarely seen clearly as special competence and a particular responsibility which one can progressively acquire through steady learning. . . . Hence a constant fear of, and rebelliousness against, all authority or competence makes satisfying learning in collaborative effort with teachers difficult if not impossible—yet constantly the object of strenuous striving. On the other hand, any exercise of competence by oneself is similarly fantasied as a dangerously placed omnipotent authority whose omniscience is absolutely essential and clearly and obviously impossible."[14]

We do not mean to deny that among this participant minority there may be a few or perhaps many who are thoughtful in their concern, persistent in their query, and peaceful in their quest, who after careful consideration of their consciences, "assume a terrible burden . . . a fearful moral as well as legal responsibility."[3] to violate a law as an expression of nonviolent protest and dissent and accept the punishment for the offense without flight or deceit. This group, nonviolent and not provoking others to invoke counteraggression, are not considered in this discussion.

The young people we have described demand a reexamination of the fundamental values implicit in our society. They have demonstrated with defiance that on occasion has erupted into violence, repression, and counterviolence. The result has been to reaffirm for them the solution to bring down the old, destroy the present fabric of society, and begin anew. Such nihilistic response does not recognize the validity of the suppositions of our society nor does it recognize that there is not now nor may never have been sufficient integration of such fundamental values by sufficient numbers at any one time in our present or past history. The virtues ambivalently observed only lead to a distortion in such values. Such practice does not negate the ethos.

In such reevaluation youth may consider his relationship to himself, his family, and society. Kennan[6] has aptly remarked: "And one would like to warn these young people that in distancing themselves so recklessly not only from the wisdom but from the feelings of parents, they are hacking at their own underpinnings—and even those of people as yet unborn. There could be no greater illusion than the belief that one can treat one's parents unfeelingly and with contempt and yet expect that one's own children will someday treat one otherwise; for such people break the golden chain of affection that binds the generations and gives continuity and meaning to life."

In another context, Whitehorn[16] has stated that the individual must solve his vertical relationships before he is able to deal with his horizontal ones. Normal integrated development of youth requires the resolution of conflict between generations. The gap between generations is not an inevitable concomitant of adolescence (although it often occurs) but is often indicative of the degree of individual psychopathology and familial troubles. The failure of resolution of intrafamilial conflict is often expressed by youth in such distorted forms as alienation or rebellion. When such behaviors in youth occur, the conflicted parent may respond with anger and repression; or, with guilt vicariously encourage in the child the continuation of such actions; or, withdraw from the child in his own alienation and allow him to go on to further destructive activity. The result is the subsequent interference with the psychological processes of the child for creative solutions to his problems.

On the other hand, parents are less likely to contribute to vertical conflicts when they are relatively less conflicted in their own everyday lives. Then, they are more able to provide firm and consistent influence to each episode of development of the child that is satisfying and integrative to both themselves and the child. In periods of so-called rapid social change, it is not only the speed of change that deserves consideration but elements of the total situation that add to parental frustration and lead to exacerbation of latent neuroticisms. When change occurs and is not destructive to society or individual, secure and satisfying living may result. In contrast, the destructiveness to the human condition that often is considered the result of rapid social change more likely reflects a personal integration insufficient to meet the often insufferable obstacles that are present in our changing society such as creeping inflation, increasing population, and crowding, frequent transfers of home and job, growing debt, deteriorating cities with higher incidence of crime and violence, overburdened schools, and so forth. Under such conditions, parents brought up during periods of privation such as depression and war are more likely to respond with anxiety when their financial and social security is threatened, with such inevitable human reactions as greed, exploitation, suspicion, and aggression as consequences.

The cause of parental trouble is not in social innovation itself but in the ways new inventions or technologies are used by men. Innovation for the benefit of society can be the outcome when inventions are suitably applied by fully integrated persons with adequate attention to transitional periods.

We have attempted to delineate some aspects of the situation of youth in conflict that have appeared in our clinical experience. If such factors are confirmed by other clinical observers as being always or almost always present in destructive and alienated youth, then we may regard the present struggle as evidence of increasing internalized conflict in parental figures and their children. Such conflicts may be similar to those in other periods of history and renewed now with only the form changed, consistent with the present cultural mode. It is relevant to quote Clark's[1] comment:

> It is the Irish who wrote the script for American urban violence and the black terrorists have not added anything particularly new. . . . In 1839, the mayor of New York wrote: "The city is infected by gangs of hardened wretches born in the haunts of infamy, brought up in taverns . . . these fellows patrol the streets making night hideous . . . [they] are the most ignorant and consequently the most obstinate white men in the world."

These were not the initialed societies of today but the Fenians, the Molly Maguires, and the Ancient Order of Hibernians. There was demand by Protestant leaders to foster "greater missionary efforts to Christianize the mixed multitudes of the downtown city," and as late as 1906 the New York Gaelic American wanted Irish history taught in the City's schools.[1]

The problems in the current confrontation are great. They cry out for solutions to reduce current and real frustrations of parents and youth with reduction of internal conflict. Upon such solutions we may build a society wherein learning and creativity are enhanced, leading to mastery and productivity so that more of us may labor in a fully participant society.

References

[1] Clark, D. 1968. Urban violence. *Reflections*, 3:2-5. (Reprinted from *America, The National Catholic Weekly Review*, June 1, 1968).

[2] Erikson, E. 1959. Identity and the life cycle. *Psychol. Issues*, 1(1): Monograph 1. International Universities Press, New York.

[3] Fortas, A. 1968. *Concerning Dissent and Civil Disobedience*. World Publishing Co., Cleveland and New York.

[4] Goodman, P. 1960. *Growing Up Absurd*. Random House, New York.

[5] Keniston, K. 1968. *The Young Radicals*. Harcourt, Brace and World, New York.

[6] Kennan, G. 1968. Rebels without a program. *New York Times*, Sunday Magazine Section, Jan. 21, 1968.

[7] Marcuse, H. 1964. *One Dimensional Man*. Beacon Press, Boston.

[8] Noshpitz, J. 1968. Alienation and youth. Paper read before Amer. Acad. Child Psychiat. Philadelphia.

[9] Philips, I. 1968. An adolescent message: happenings on the hip scene. *Ment. Hyg.* 52: 337-340.

[10] Ruesch, J. 1967. The old world and the new world. *Amer. J. Psychiat.* 124:225-226.

[11] Smith, M., Haan, N., and Block, J. 1970. Social-psychological aspects of student activism. In *Rebels and the Campus Revolt,* B. Rubenstein and M. Levitt, eds. Prentice-Hall, Englewood Cliffs, N.J.

[12] Soskin, W., Duhl, L., and Leopold, R. 1955. Chapter in *Pre-Congress Book,* 1966 Cong., Int. Assn. Child Psychiat. and Allied Professions.

[13] Sullivan, H., 1953. *The Interpersonal Theory of Psychiatry.* W. W. Norton, New York.

[14] Szurek, S. 1959. Playfulness, creativity and schisis. *Amer. J. Orthopsychiat.* 29:667-683.

[15] The Changing American People. 1968. *Ann. Amer. Acad. Pol. Soc. Sci.*:378.

[16] Whitehorn, J. Personal communication.

GENERATION OF TYRANTS

HARRIET VAN HORNE

In five years of unremitting stump rhetoric about student power, black power, flower power and all the rest, has anybody besides me ever wondered, "Whatever happened to *parent* power?"

It often seems that the fury of youth in rebellion is exceeded only by the meekness of parents in accepting that rebellion. "My daughter's morals shock me," a mother confesses, "but I hold my tongue because she'd have a fit if I didn't." A lot of parents are failing to speak up, too—which, surely, is one reason for our much-discussed generation gap.

Put yourself in the middle of that gap and you're bound to feel pity in both directions. I certainly do. But I also feel that certain facts must be faced. The child-centered households of the past 25 years have produced too many scruffy, self-centered, quirky kids—young tyrants with unweeded hair, infant gypsies in bizarre clothes, "doing their own thing," venting a naked, unshamed hostility in their hard-rock music . . . then seeking soft answers in opiates.

I am always saddened to hear of those children, usually from "nice" homes, who discover sex too soon and respect for themselves too late. I am sickened by the prevalence of marijuana. And, like a sheltered maiden aunt—which I'm definitely not—I can only gasp when lovely young girls salt their small talk with old, ugly words from the verbal arsenal of the streets.

But these are *our* children. These are the heirs of *our* traditions, *our* fortunes, *our* hopes, *our* genes. And who, if not ourselves, has turned so many of them into what they are: a generation that demands instant answers to tangled, difficult questions—a generation of tyrants?

One suspects that too many of their "nice" homes must have been committed to the idea that sparing the rod is serving the child. But is it really? To me, being

Harriet Van Horne is a free-lance writer and syndicated columnist.

a parent means providing discipline, advice and firmness, no less than love. "Whom the Lord loveth, He chasteneth," the Bible says.

And next time you read of college freshmen invading the dean's office and smoking his cigars, you'd better believe in the Bible.

I recall a newspaper interview of several years ago, in which the late playwright, Moss Hart, was asked to account for the good manners of his two children, who had impressed the reporter by going off to bed, without setting up a howl. "It's simple," Hart said. "They know we're bigger than they are. And besides, they know it's our house."

Isn't it time to return to the "good old days" of parental authority? Couldn't the children now please shut up for a bit and listen to the parents? In other words, isn't it time "parent power" came back into style?

I'm not alone in this view. In recent months a number of distinguished educators have fired off some strong statements about young people, their preoccupations and their "hang-ups." Listen to what Professor John W. Aldridge, of the University of Michigan, has to say on the subject.

In his new book, *The Country of the Young,* he writes: "If . . . parents had given their children a legitimate and useful function in the household, instead of allowing them to believe that they were privileged guests; if they had been made to work for their pleasures, or at least required to wait for them, they might not be quite as dogmatically certain as they now are that solutions must come at once and are *given* rather than achieved. . . ."

The sad truth is that too many post-World War II children were not disciplined. Instead, they were negotiated with. The young quickly learned to outmaneuver their parents at the negotiating table. Thus they grew up with a sense of omnipotence. If parents could be conned, cowed and ridiculed, they reasoned, why, so could institutions.

This is not to say that the young do not have just cause for disapproving of large chunks of the world they are about to inherit. I believe the Vietnam War is every bit as ugly, brutal and immoral as young people proclaim it to be. I also believe that the young may be forgiven for judging many of the men who sit in Congress and in state legislatures as incompetent and corrupt. I believe they are right about the materialistic bent of our society, the hypocrisy, the scarred and eroded land, the air-and-water pollution, the slums, the crime in the streets, the inequities of the tax laws, and the callousness of the new Justice Department toward the young and the blacks. These are all sound reasons for feelings of bitterness in our young. More often than not, I share their indignation, and I have been deeply touched, more than once, by their concern and their passion for peace.

But to improve our society, to right old wrongs and lift up the lowly, we shall need young people who have steeped themselves in learning and acquired political skills and absorbed the standards of the great men who founded this country. What we don't need are young people who spend much of their student time in agitation. "Relevant" courses may be all very well, but not when they are offered as substitutes for the humanities and classics—the disciplines that produce good minds and good citizens.

Education, then, must share with parents the responsibility for the mess we're in. We have failed, in the opinion of Judge Charles Wyzanski, Jr., of the U.S. District Court, to pass on to young people the core of humanistic learning.

The judge writes: "In their early primary and secondary stages we allowed them to have the kind of education from their school and their peers which *they wanted,* because we were not sufficiently convinced of our own beliefs. And they knew it."

If our permissiveness has been as damaging as it seems to have been, one must then ask, "Very well, what caused it? How does it happen that so many parents and educators have fallen down on their jobs?"

To find the answer, we must recall the mood of the country in the aftermath of World War II. Young people then were eager to set up homes and raise families. All other functions of life seemed secondary—a normal response to long months of separation and uncertainty—and the population was on its way to explosion.

We all recall those frantic days: returned soldiers, supported by the GI Bill of Rights, started to rebuild their lives. With their brides they moved into Quonset huts and converted garages. The quarters were cramped—but there was room for the millions of children who were born. And, out of their joy that lives had been spared, that the earth was still good, parents tended to consider each infant a miracle.

The early group of those babies is out of college by now and into adult life. From the viewpoint of college administrators, they were a somewhat sturdier lot, emotionally, than their current counterparts. It's the children who came later, the group now between the ages of 17 and 24, who seem to have the most quirks, the least purpose—and the toughest time scholastically. Not surprisingly, these children have known greater prosperity—and even greater permissiveness.

Today, this is the group most conspicuously in rebellion; this is the group—despite their parents' ambitions for them—most conspicuously lacking in motivation. They do not have that sense of involvement in society that propels a youngster upward and onward toward independence and fulfillment.

The tragedy of these can't-make-the-grade young people is twofold. For one thing, they will never experience so many of life's finer satisfactions: understanding great literature, music, art. Thus, they will feel inferior—and with cause. Secondly, because of their loss, we lose. For the nation needs more people with education, taste and professional skill.

Interestingly, the parents of some spoiled children—the dropouts from school who later become dropouts from life—will try to excuse their failures with "I guess we just loved him too much." A psychiatrist of my acquaintance says, "These parents don't love the child—they love themselves. If you love a child, you prepare him for adult life. It's easier, when a child is small, to treat him as a toy, a puppy, something to show off. It takes a great deal of character and discipline to raise a normal, moderately adjusted child."

Other parents justify their failures on grounds of having themselves been immobilized by their own inner conflicts. Or of wanting to spare their offspring the suffering and privation they had known. This, of course, is understandable—perhaps even laudable. Still, the fact remains that other generations have also had their problems and have managed not to use them as a crutch. I heard recently about a man who told his doctor, "My children despise me because they know how insecure I am." "My father was more insecure than you'll ever be," replied the doctor, "but I was 25 before he let me know it."

I suspect there's never been a time when the wisdom—and experience—of the tribal elders have been so little regarded by the young. It is Dr. Aldridge's thought that the young are unconsciously hoping "that some benevolent catastrophe will destroy adult society before they are obliged to enter it." A strong statement, but it suggests that the young are not unaware of their ineptitude. It may even have struck some of them that the warm cocoon in which they grow up did not really prepare them for the gritty realities of America at mid-century. By having spared him "the pain I suffered," parents may well have diminished their child's capacity to cope with life.

What about the modern habit of treating a child as if he were the parents' equal?

"There's no even exchange between generations," writes Dr. Thomas J. Cottle of the Harvard Medical School, "nor is there even a possibility for it. Parents are by definition *not* peers of their children. For some young people, a quiet, inner strength vanishes when their parents trespass on the property of time."

Authority is a complicated business. One of the strengths of our American past was that authority knew its place, demanded its due, and kept itself above compromise.

"Parents simply cannot break down or retreat," Dr. Cottle warns. Nor can parents confide their troubles to a child, nor attribute to him a wisdom or cleverness he could not, in the nature of things, possibly possess.

An old friend of mine, married to a lawyer, tells me how she used to dread going to the home of a certain judge and his wife. "They were sweet, gentle people," she recalls, "but their son was a terror." At the age of fourteen the son was telling his father how he had erred on the bench. "Isn't he a bright lad?" the judge would beam. Now and again my friend would suggest that boys of fourteen ought to be more respectful of their fathers. "Please," the mother would interrupt. "The boy is brilliant. We must allow him to express himself." That brilliant boy went far for a time. He made lots of money and dabbled in politics. Not so long ago, still a young man, he was indicted on charges which included bribery and conspiracy. During his trial, he continued to "express himself." His interruptions were the despair of the judge who sat on his case and of the lawyer who successfully defended him.

In every generation, parents and children have problems accepting on another. Every society, down through the ages, worries that the upcoming generation isn't worthy of the culture it is inheriting. Nonetheless, in times past most parents were inclined to forgive youth its follies. "Wild colts make the finest horses," and "wanton lads the truest husbands," ran the old notions. "For God's sake," wrote Robert Louis Stevenson, "give me the young man with brains enough to make a fool of himself."

But today, in their follies, the young are not making fools of themselves—at least not as individuals. Rather they are conformists in their very nonconformity. Despite their talk of "doing your own thing," there is a depressing sameness about the things they do. Their personalities lack the vibrant, thrusting quality we used to admire—and envy—in the young; their performance seems to me stage-managed to the point of boredom.

I think it unlikely that we shall greatly change the basic character of our present generation of young people. They will continue to wear their hair long until —as one of them wrote to me recently—"Richard Nixon and Ronald Reagan start wearing their hair long."

But what about their little brothers and sisters? What are we to do to restore "parent power" to *their* lives? First, start practicing it. Don't be afraid to say, "We're bigger and it's our house." Give love, be gentle, be firm. Have the courage to believe in principles and to stick up for them. That's what we *can* do.

But there's one thing, we *must not* do—or at least *should not* do. We should not go overboard in the other direction. If we've produced a generation of tyrants, we should not then become tyrants ourselves, in the old authoritarian ways. Let's not become Moms with Iron Fists producing a band of brutal neo-Nazis who torture puppies and stock-pile guns in the garage.

If that were our only alternative, most of us would happily settle for the boys and girls we've got. And wish them luck in their next demonstration.

But there *is* another alternative. Let's call it parent power.

THE TIMES THEY ARE A-CHANGIN': THE MUSIC OF PROTEST

ROBERT A. ROSENSTONE

At the beginning of the 1960s, nobody took popular music very seriously. Adults only knew that rock n' roll, which had flooded the airways in the 1950s, had a strong beat and was terribly loud; it was generally believed that teen-agers alone

A revised version of an article from *The Annals of the American Academy of Political and Social Science,* No. 382 (March, 1969), 131-144. Reprinted with the permission of the author and the publisher.

Robert A. Rosenstone is Associate Professor of History at the California Institute of Technology.

had thick enough eardrums, or insensitive enough souls, to enjoy it. Certainly, no critics thought of a popular star like the writhing Elvis Presley as being in any way a serious artist. Such a teen-age idol was simply considered a manifestation of a sub-culture that the young happily and inevitably outgrew—and, any parent would have added, the sooner the better.

In recent years this view of popular music has drastically changed. Some parents may still wonder about the "noise" that their children listen to, but important segments of American society have come to recognize popular musicians as artists saying serious things.[1] An indication of this change can be seen in magazine attitudes. In 1964, the *Saturday Evening Post* derided the Beatles— recognized giants of modern popular music—as "corny," and *Reporter* claimed: "They have debased Rock 'n Roll to its ultimate absurdity." Three years later the *Saturday Review* solemnly discussed a new Beatles record as a "highly ironic declaration of disaffection" with modern society, while in 1968 *Life* devoted a whole, laudatory section to "The New Rock," calling it music "that challenges the joys and ills of the . . . world."[2] Even in the intellectual community, popular music has found warm friends. Such sober journals as *The Listener, Columbia University Forum, New American Review,* and *Commentary* have sympathetically surveyed aspects of the "pop" scene, while *The New York Review of Books*—a kind of house organ for American academia—composer Ned Rorem has declared that, at their best, the Beatles "compare with those composers from great eras of song; Monteverdi, Schumann, Poulenc."[3]

The reasons for such changes in attitude are not difficult to find: there is no doubt that popular music has become more complex, and at the same time more serious, than it ever was before. Musically, it has broken down some of the old forms in which it was for a long time straight-jacketed. With a wide-ranging

[1] The definition of "popular music" being used in this article is a broad one. It encompasses a multitude of styles, including folk, folk-rock, acid-rock, hard-rock, and blues, to give just a few names being used in the musical world today. It does so because the old musical classifications have been totally smashed and the forms now overlap in a way that makes meaningful distinction between them impossible. Though not every group or song referred to will have been popular in the sense of selling a million records, all of them are part of a broad, variegated scene termed "pop." Some of the groups, like Buffalo Springfield, Strawberry Alarm Clock, or the Byrds, have sold millions of records. Others, like the Fugs or Mothers of Invention, have never had a real hit, though they are played on radio stations allied to the "underground." Still, such groups do sell respectable numbers of records and do perform regularly at teen-age concerts.

[2] *Saturday Evening Post,* Vol. 237, March 21, 1964, p. 30; *Reporter,* Vol. 30, Feb. 27, 1964, p. 18; *Saturday Review,* Vol. 50, August 19, 1967, p. 18; *Life,* Vol. 64, June 28, 1968, p. 51.

[3] "The Music of the Beatles," *New York Review of Books,* Jan. 15, 1968, pp. 23-27. See also "The New Music," *The Listener,* Vol. 78, August 3, 1967, pp. 129-130; *Columbia University Forum* (Fall 1967), pp. 16-22; *New American Review,* Vol. 1 (April 1968), pp. 118-139; Ellen Willis, "The Sound of Bob Dylan," *Commentary,* Vol. 44 (November 1967), pp. 71-80. Many of these articles deal with English as well as American popular groups, and, in fact, the music of the two countries cannot, in any meaningful sense, be separated. This article will only survey American musical groups, though a look at English music would reveal the prevalence of the themes explored here.

eclecticism, popular music has adapted to itself a bewildering variety of musical traditions and instruments, from the classic Indian sitar to the most recent electronic synthesizers favored by composers of "serious" concert music.

As the music has been revolutionized, so has the subject matter of the songs. In preceding decades, popular music was almost exclusively about love, and, in the words of poet Thomas Gunn, "a very limited kind [of love], constituting a sort of fag-end of the Petrarchan tradition."[4] The stories told in song were largely about lovers yearning for one another in some vaguely unreal world where nobody ever seemed to work or get married. All this changed in the 1960s. Suddenly, popular music began to deal with civil rights demonstrations and drug experiences, with interracial dating and war and explicit sexual encounters, with, in short, the real world in which people live. For perhaps the first time, popular songs became relevant to the lives of the teenage audience that largely constitutes the record-buying public. The success of some of these works prompted others to be written, and from the second half of the decade on there was a full efflorescence of such topical songs; written by young people for their peers. These works may be grouped under the label of "protest" songs, for taken together, they provide a wide-ranging critique of American life. Listening to them, one can get a full-blown picture of the antipathy that the young song writers have toward many American institutions.

Serious concerns entered popular music early in the 1960s, when a great revival of folk singing spread out from college campuses, engulfed the mass media, and created a wave of new "pop" stars, the best known of whom was Joan Baez. Yet, though the concerns of these folk songs were often serious, they were hardly contemporary. Popular were numbers about organizing unions, which might date from the 1930s or the late nineteenth century, or about the trials of escaping Negro slaves, or celebrating the cause of the defeated Republicans in the Spanish Civil War. Occasionally there was something like "Talking A-Bomb Blues," but this was the rare exception rather than the rule.[5]

A change of focus came when performers began to write their own songs, rather than relying on the traditional folk repertoire. Chief among them, and destined to become the best known, was Bob Dylan. Consciously modeling himself on that wandering minstrel of the 1930s, Woody Guthrie, Dylan began by writing songs that often had little to do with the contemporary environment. Rather, his early ballads like "Masters of War" echoed the leftist concerns and rhetoric of an eariler era. Yet, simultaneously, Dylan was writing songs like "Blowin' In the Wind," "A Hard Rains' A-Gonna Fall," and "The Times They Are A-Changin'," which dealt with civil rights, nuclear war, and the changing world of youth that parents and educators were not prepared to understand. Acclaimed as the best of protest-songwriters, Dylan in mid-decade shifted gears, and in the song "My Back Pages," he denounced his former moral fervor. In an ironic

---

[4] "The New Music," p. 129.
[5] *Time,* Vol. 80, Nov. 23, 1962, pp. 54-60, gives a brief survey of the folk revival.

chorus claiming that he was much younger than he had been, Dylan specifically made social problems the worry of sober, serious, older men; presumably, youths had more important things than injustice to think about. After that, any social comment by Dylan came encapsulated in a series of surrealistic images; for the most part, he escaped into worlds of aestheticism, psychedelic drugs, and personal love relationships. Apparently attempting to come to grips in art with his own personality, Dylan was content to forget about the problems of other men.[6]

The development of Dylan is important not only because he is the leading song writer, but also because it parallels the concerns of popular music in recent years. Starting out with traditional liberal positions on war, discrimination, segregation, and exploitation, song writers have turned increasingly to descriptions of the private worlds of drugs, sexual experience, and personal freedom. Though social concerns have never entirely faded, the private realm has been increasingly seen as the only one in which people can lead meaningful lives. Today the realms of social protest and private indulgence exist side by side in the popular music, with the latter perceived as the only viable alternative to the world described in the former songs.[7]

In turning to recent protest songs, one finds many of the traditional characters and concerns of such music missing. Gone are exploited, impoverished people, labor leaders, "finks," and company spies.[8] This seems natural in affluent times, with youths from middle-class backgrounds writing songs. Of course, there has been one increasingly visible victim of exploitation, the Negro; and the songsters have not been blind to his plight. But egalitarian as they are, the white musicians have not been able to describe the reality of the black man's situation. Rather, they have chronicled Northern liberal attitudes towards the problem. Thus, composer-performer Phil Ochs penned works criticizing Southern attitudes towards Negroes, and containing stock portraits of corrupt politicians, law officials, and churchmen trembling before the Ku Klux Klan, while Paul Simon wrote a lament for a freedom rider killed by an angry Southern mob.[9] Similarly white-oriented was Janis Ian's very popular "Society's Child," concerned with the problem of interracial dating. Here a white girl capitulates to society's bigotry and breaks off

---

[6] Willis, "The Sound of Dylan," gives a good analysis of his work.

[7] It must be pointed out that, in spite of the large amount of social criticism, most songs today are still about love.

[8] This article is concerned almost exclusively with music written and performed by white musicians. While popular music by Negroes does contain social criticism, the current forms—loosely termed "soul music"—make comments about oppression similar to those which Negroes have always made. The real change in content has come largely in white music.

[9] Phil Ochs, "Talking Birmingham Jam" and "Here's to the State of Mississippi," *I Ain't Marching Any More* (Elektra, 7237); Simon and Garfunkel, "He Was My Brother," *Wednesday Morning 3 A.M.* (Columbia, CS 9049). (Songs from records will be noted by performer, song title in quotation marks, and album title in italics, followed by record company and number in parentheses.)

a relationship with a Negro boy with the vague hope that someday "things may change."[10]

Increasingly central to white-Negro relationships have been the ghetto and urban riots, and a taste of this entered the popular music. Phil Ochs, always on top of current events, produced "In the Heat of the Summer" shortly after the first major riot in Harlem in 1964. Partially sympathetic to the ghetto-dwellers' actions, he still misjudged their attitudes by ascribing to them feelings of shame —rather than satisfaction—in the aftermath of the destruction.[11] A later attempt, by Country Joe and the Fish, to describe Harlem ironically as a colorful vacation spot, verged on patronizing blacks, even while it poked fun at white stereotypes. Still, it was followed by sounds of explosion that thrust home what indifference to the ghetto is doing to America.[12] The most successful song depicting the situation of the Negro was "Trouble Coming Everyday," written by Frank Zappa during the Watts uprising in 1965. Though the song does not go so far as to approve of rioting, it paints a brutal picture of exploitation by merchants, bad schooling, miserable housing, and police brutality—all of which affect ghetto-dwellers. Its most significant lines are Zappa's cry, that though he is not black, "there's a whole lots of times I wish I could say I'm not white." No song writer showed more empathy with the black struggle for liberation than that.[13]

While the downtrodden are heroes of many traditional protest songs, the villains are often politicians. Yet, politics rarely enters recent songs. Ochs, an unreconstructed voice from the 1930s, depicts vacillating politicians in some works, and Dylan mentioned corrupt ones early in the sixties. But the typical attitude is to ignore politics, or, perhaps, to describe it in passing as "A yardstick for lunatics."[14] Even those who call for political commitment, caution against trying "to get yourself elected," because to do so you will have to compromise principles— what's worse, you'll have to cut your hair.

It is true that the death of President Kennedy inspired more than one song, but these were tributes to a martyr, not a politician.[15] If Kennedy in death could inspire music, Lyndon Johnson in life was incapable of inspiring anything, except perhaps contempt. In a portrait of him, Country Joe and the Fish pictured the, then, President as flying through the sky like an "insane" Superman. Then they fantasized a Western setting with "Lyndon" outgunned and sent back to his Texas ranch.[16]

On traditional area, antiwar protest, does figure significantly in the music. With America's involvement in Vietnam and mounting draftcalls, this seems natural

[10] Dialogue Music, Inc.

[11] Ochs, *I Ain't Marching Any More.*

[12] "The Harlem Song," *Together* (Vanguard, VSD 79277).

[13] Mothers of Invention, *Freak Out* (Verve, 65005).

[14] Strawberry Alarm Clock, "Incense and Peppermints," *Strawberry Alarm Clock* (Uni., 73014); "Long Time Gone," *Crosby, Stills and Nash* (Atlantic, SD 8229).

[15] Phil Ochs, "That Was the President," *I Ain't Marching Any More;* the Byrds, "He Was A Friend of Mine," *Turn! Turn!* (Columbia, CS 9254).

[16] "Superbird," *Electric Music for the Mind and Body* (Vanguard, 79244).

enough. Unlike many songs of this genre, however, the current ones rarely assess the causes of war, but dwell almost exclusively with the effect which war has on the individual. Thus, both Love and the Byrds sing about what nuclear war does to children, while the Peanut Butter Conspiracy pictures the effect of nuclear testing on everyone—a "firecracker sky" poisoned with radioactivity.[17] Most popular of the antiwar songs was P. F. Sloan's "Eve of Destruction," which, for a time in 1965, was the best-selling record in the country (and which was banned by some patriotic radio-station directors). The title obviously gives the author's view of the world situation; the content deals mostly with its relationship to young men like himself, as it asks why they tote guns if they don't believe in war.[18] There are alternatives to carrying a gun, and defiance of the draft enters some songs, subtly in Buffy St. Marie's "Universal Soldier" and stridently in Ochs' "I Ain't Marching Any More" and Steppenwolf's "Draft Resister."[19] Perhaps more realistic in its reflection of youthful moods is the Byrds' "Draft Morning," a haunting portrait of a young man reluctantly leaving a warm bed to take up arms and kill "unknown faces." It ends with the poignant and unanswerable question, "Why should it happen?"[20]

If many songs criticize war in general, some have referred to Vietnam in particular. The Fugs give gory details of death and destruction being wreaked on the North by American bombers, which unleash napalm "rotisseries" upon the world.[21] In a similar song, Country Joe and the Fish describe children crying helplessly beneath bombs.[22] No doubt, it is difficult to make music out of the horrors of war, and a kind of black humor is a common response. In a rollicking number, the Fugs, with irony, worry that people may come to "love the Russians" and scream out a method often advocated for avoiding this: "Kill, kill, kill for peace."[23] And one of Country Joe's most popular numbers contains an attack on generals who think that peace will be won "when we blow 'em all to kingdom come."[24]

The injustice and absurdity of America's Asian ventures, perceived by the song writers, does not surprise them for they feel that life at home is much the same. The songs of the 1960s show the United States as a repressive society where people who deviate from the norm are forced into conformity—sometimes at gunpoint; where those who do fit in lead empty, frustrated lives; and where meaningful human experience is ignored in a search for artificial pleasures. Such

[17] Love, "Mushroom Clouds," Love (Elektra, EKL 4001); the Byrds, "I Come and Stand at Every Door," Fifth Dimension (Columbia CS 9349); Peanut Butter Conspiracy, "Wonderment," Great Conspiracy (Columbia, CS 9590).
[18] Trousdale Music Publishers, Inc.
[19] Buffy St. Marie, "Universal Soldier," Southern Publishing, ASCAP; Ochs, I Ain't Marching Any More; Steppenwolf, Monster (Dunhill DS 50066).
[20] The Notorious Byrd Brothers (Columbia, CS 9575).
[21] "War Song," Tenderness Junction (Reprise, S 6280).
[22] "An Untitled Protest," Together.
[23] "Kill for Peace," The Fugs (Esp. 1028).
[24] "I Feel Like I'm Fixin' to Die," I Feel Like I'm Fixin' to Die (Vanguard, 9266).

a picture is hardly attractive, and one might argue that it is not fair. But it is so pervasive in popular music that it must be examined at some length. Indeed, it is the most important part of recent protest music. Here are criticisms, not of exploitation, but of the quality of life in an affluent society: not only of physical oppression but also of the far more subtle mental oppression that a mass society can produce.

YOUTH AS VICTIM

Throughout the decade, young people have often been at odds with established authority, and, repeatedly, songs picture youth in the role of victim. Sometimes the victimization is mental, as when the Mothers of Invention complain of outworn thought patterns and say that children are "victims of lies" which their parents believe.[25] On a much simpler level, Sonny Bono voices his annoyance that older people laugh at the clothes he wears, and he wonders why they enjoy "makin' fun" of him.[26] Now, Bono could musically shrug off the laughs as the price of freedom; but other songs document occasions when Establishment disapproval turned into physical oppression. Thus, Canned Heat tells of being arrested in Denver because the police did not want any "long hairs around."[27] The Buffalo Springfield, in a hit record, describe gun-bearing police rounding up teenagers on Sunset Strip.[28] On the same theme, Dylan ironically shows that adults arbitrarily oppose just about all activities of youths, saying that they should "look out" no matter what they are doing.[29] More bitter is the Mother's description of police killing large numbers of hippies, which is then justified on the grounds that because they looked "weird" it "served them right."[30] A fictional incident when the song was written, the Mothers were clearly prescient in believing Americans capable of shooting down those who engage in deviant behavior.

Though the songs echo the oppression that youngsters have felt, they do not ignore the problems that all humans face in a mass society. Writer Tom Paxton knows that it is not easy to keep one's life from being forced into a predetermined mold. In "Mr. Blue" he has a Big-Brother-like narrator telling the title character, a kind of Everyman, that he is always under surveillance, and that he will never be able to indulge himself in his precious dreams of freedom from society. This is because society needs him to fill a slot, no matter what his personal desires. And Mr. Blue had better learn to love that slot, or "we'll break you."[31] Though no other writer made the message so explicit, a similar fear of being forced into an unwelcome slot underlies many songs of the period:

[25] We're Only in it for the Money (Verve, 65045).
[26] "Laugh at Me," Five West Cotillion, BMI.
[27] "My Crime," Boogie (Liberty, 7541).
[28] "For What It's Worth."
[29] "Subterranean Homesick Blues," Bob Dylan's Greatest Hits (Columbia, KCS 9463).
[30] We're Only in it for the Money.
[31] "Mr. Blue" Clear Light (Elektra, 74011).

The society of slotted people is an empty one, partly described as "TV dinner by the pool."[32] It is one in which people have been robbed of their humanity, receiving in return the "transient treasures" of wealth and the useless gadgets of a technological age. One of these is television, referred to simply as "that rotten box," or, in a more sinister image, as an "electronic shrine." This image of men worshipping gadgets recurs. In the nightmare vision of a McLuhanesque world—where the medium is the message—Simon and Garfunkle sing of men so busy bowing and praying to a "neon god" that they cannot understand or touch one another. Indeed, here electronics seem to hinder the process of communication rather than facilitate it. People talk and hear but never understand, as the "sounds of silence" fill the world.[33] Such lack of communication contributes to the indifference with which men can view the life and death of a neighbor, as in Simon's "A Most Peculiar Man."[34] It also creates the climate of fear which causes people to kill a stranger for no reason other than his unknown origins in Strawberry Alarm Clock's "They Saw the Fat One Coming."[35]

Alienated from his fellows, fearful and alone, modern man has also despoiled the natural world in which he lives, has in Joni Mitchell's words, paved paradise to "put up a parking lot."[36] With anguish in his voice, Jim Morrison of the Doors asks "What have they done to the earth?" and then angrily answers that his "fair sister" has been ravished and plundered.[37] In a lighter tone but with no less serious intent, the Lewis and Clark Expedition describe the way man has cut himself off from nature in the great outdoors, where chains and fences keep him from the flowers and trees. With a final ironic thrust, they add that there's no reason to touch the flowers because they are "plastic anyway."[38]

This brings up a fear that haunts a number of recent songs, the worry that the technological age has created so many artificial things that nothing natural remains. Concerned with authenticity, the songsters are afraid that man himself is becoming an artifact, or in their favorite word, "plastic." Thus, the Jefferson Airplane sing about a "Plastic Fantastic Lover," while the Iron Butterfly warn a girl to stay away from people "made of plastic."[39] The image recurs most frequently in the works of the Mothers of Invention. In one song, they depict the country is being run by a plastic Congress and President.[40] Then, in "Plastic People" they start with complaints about a girl friend who uses "plastic goo" on her face, go on to a picture of teen-agers on the Sunset Strip—who are probably their fans—as being "plastic," too, and finally turn on their listeners and advise them to

---

[32] Mothers of Invention, "Brown Shoes Don't Make It," *Absolutely Free* (Verve, 65013).

[33] "Sounds of Silence," *Sounds of Silence* (Columbia, CS 9269).

[34] *Sounds of Silence.*

[35] *Wake Up . . . It's Tomorrow* (Uni., 73025).

[36] "Big Yellow Taxi," *Ladies of the Canyon* (Reprise, RS 6376).

[37] "When the Music's Over," *Strange Days* (Elektra, 74014).

[38] "Chain Around the Flowers," *The Lewis and Clark Expedition* (Colgems, COS 105).

[39] *Surrealistic Pillow* (Victor, LSP 3766) "Stamped Ideas;" *Heavy* (Atco, S 33-227).

[40] "Uncle Bernie's Farm," *Absolutely Free.*

check themselves, for "you think we're talking about someone else."[41] Such a vision is frightening, for if the audience is plastic, perhaps the Mothers, themselves, are made of the same phony material. And if the whole world is plastic, who can be sure of his own authenticity?

LOVE RELATIONSHIPS

Toward the end of "Plastic People," the Mothers say that "true love" cannot be "a product of plasticity." This brings up the greatest horror, that in a "plastic" society like the United States, love relationships are impossible. For the young song writers, American love is viewed as warped and twisted. Nothing about Establishment society frightens them more than its attitudes towards sex. Tim Buckley is typical in singing that older Americans are "Afraid to trust in their bodies."[42] Others give graphic portraits of deviant behavior. The Fugs tell of a "Dirty Old Man" hanging around high school playgrounds; the Velvet Underground portray a masochist; and the Mothers depict a middle-aged man lusting after his own thirteen-year-old daughter.[43] The fullest indictment of modern love is made by the United States of America, who devote almost an entire album to the subject. Here, in a twisted portrait of "pleasure and pain," is a world of loveless marriages, homosexual relationships in men's rooms, venomous attractions, and overt sadism—all masked by a middle-class, suburban world in which people consider "morality" important. To show that natural relationships are possible elsewhere, the group sings one tender love lyric; interestingly, it is the lament of a Cuban girl for the dead Ché Guevara.[44]

The fact that bourgeois America has warped attitudes towards sex and love is bad enough; the songsters are more worried that such attitudes will infect their own generation. Thus, the Collectors decry the fact that man-woman relationships are too often seen as some kind of contest, with a victor and vanquished and in which violence is more acceptable than tenderness.[45] Perhaps because most of the singers are men, criticisms of female sexual attitudes abound. The Mothers are disgusted with the American woman, who lies in bed gritting her teeth, while the Sopwith Camel object to the traditional kind of purity by singing that they don't want their women "wrapped up in cellophane."[46] This is because such a woman will bring you down with her "talking about sin."[47] All the musicians

---

[41] "Plastic People," *Absolutely Free.*

[42] "Goodbye and Hello," *Goodbye and Hello* (Electra, 7318).

[43] *The Fugs;* "Venus in Furs," *The Velvet Underground and Nico* (Verve, V6-5008); "Brown Shoes Don't Make It," *Absolutely Free.*

[44] *The United States of America* (Columbia, CS 9614).

[45] "What Love," *The Collectors* (Warner Bros.-Seven Arts, WS 1746).

[46] *We're Only in it for the Money,* "Cellophane Woman," *The Sopwith Camel* (Kama Sutra, KLPS 8060).

[47] "Cellophane Woman."

would prefer the girl about whom Moby Grape sings who is "super-powered, deflowered," and over eighteen.[48]

Living in a "plastic" world where honest human relationships are impossible, the song writers might be expected to wrap themselves in a mood of musical despair. But they are young—and often making plenty of money—and such an attitude is foreign to them. Musically, they are hopeful because, as the title of the Dylan song indicates, "The Times They Are A-Changin'." Without describing the changes, Dylan clearly threatens the older generation, as he tells critics, parents, and presumably anyone over thirty, to start swimming or they will drown in the rising flood-waters of social change.[49]

In another work, Dylan exploits the same theme. Here is a portrait of a presumably normal, educated man, faced with a series of bizarre situations, who is made to feel like a freak because he does not understand what is going on. The chorus is the young generation's comment to all adults, as it mocks "Mr. Jones" for not understanding what is happening all around him.[50]

The changes going on are, not surprisingly, associated with the carefree, joyful experiences of youth. As Jefferson Airplane sings, "It's a wild time" one in which people are busy "changing faces."[51] The most full-blown description of the changing world is Tim Buckley's "Goodbye and Hello," a lengthly and explicit portrait of what the youth hope is happening. Throughout the song the author contrasts two kinds of people and their environments. On the one hand are the "antique people"—godless and sexless—of an industrial civilization, living in dark dungeons, working hard, worshipping technology and money, sacrificing their sons to placate "vaudeville" generals, and blinding themselves to the fact that their "masquerade towers" are "riddled by widening cracks." Opposed to them are the "new children," interested in flowers, streams, and the beauty of the sky, who wish to take off their clothes to dance and sing and love one another. What's more, the "antique people are fading away"; in fact, they are already wearing "death masks."[52]

Buckley's vision of the new world that is coming is obviously that of a kind of idyllic Eden before the fall, a world in which men will be free to romp and play and indulge their natural desires for love. It is a pagan world, the antithesis of the Christian ideal that would postpone fulfillment to some afterlife. Elsewhere, Buckley explicitly condemns that part of Christianity which saves pleasure for an afterlife. Similarly, the Door's Jim Morrison wants to cancel his "subscription to

---

[48] "Motorcycle Irene," *Wow* (Columbia, CS 9613).

[49] *Bob Dylan's Greatest Hits.*

[50] "Ballad of a Thin Man/Mr. Jones," *Highway 61 Revisited* (Columbia, CS 9189). Though this song has obvious homosexual overtones, it also stands as youth's criticism of the older generation.

[51] "Wild Tyme (H)," *After Bathing at Baxter's* (Victor, LSO-1511).

[52] "Goodbye and Hello," written by Tim Buckley, *Goodbye and Hello.*

the resurrection," and then shrieks for a whole generation: "We want the world and we want it now."[53]

Though the times may be changed, the songsters are well aware that—despite their brave words and demands—there is plenty of strength left in the old social order. Obviously, they can see the war continuing, Negro demands not being met, and the continuing hostility of society toward their long hair, music; sexual behavior, and experimentation with drugs. Faced with these facts, the musicians have occasionally toyed with the idea of violent revolution. Some, like the Band see it as an inevitable great storm "coming through" the country. Others wish to force the issue. The Doors, claiming "we've got the numbers," call on people to get their guns, for "the time has come," while Jefferson Airplane echoes the same plea in asking for volunteers to change the world.[54]

Yet most musicians have not believed revolution feasible, and more typically they have dealt with the problem of how to live decently within the framework of the old society. Here they tend toward the world of private experience mentioned earlier in connection with Dylan. Many of their songs are almost programs for youth's behavior in a world perceived as being unlivable.

The first element is to forget about the repressive society out there. As Sopwith Camel says, "Stamp out reality . . ." before it stamps you out.[55] Then it is imperative to forget about trying to understand the outside world rationally. In a typical anti-intellectual stance, the Byrds describe such attempts as "scientific delirium madness."[56] Others combine a similar attitude with a strong measure of *carpe diem*. Spirit deride people who are "always asking" for "the reason" when they should be enjoying life, while H. P. Lovecraft admits that the bird is on the wing and states, "You need not know why."[57] What is important is that the moment be seized and life lived to the fullest. As Simon and Garfunkel say, one has to make the "moment last," and this is done best by those who open themselves fully to the pleasures of the world.[58]

The most frequent theme of the song writers is the call to freedom, the total freedom of the individual to "do his own thing." Peanut Butter Conspiracy carry this so far as to hope for a life that can be lived "free of time."[59] Circus Maximus and the Byrds—despite the fact that they are young men—long to recapture some lost freedom that they knew as children.[60] Such freedom can be almost solipsistic; Jimi Hendrix claims that even if the sun did not rise and the mountains

[53] "Pleasant Street," written by Tim Buckley, "When the Music's Over," *Strange Days*.

[54] "Look Out, Cleveland," *The Band* (Capitol, STAO-132); "Five to One," *Waiting for the Sun* (Elektra, EKS 74024); "Tell all the People," *The Soft Parade* (Elektra, EKS 75005).

[55] "Saga of the Low Down Let Down," *The Sopwith Camel*.

[56] "Fifth Dimension," *Fifth Dimension*.

[57] "Topanga Window," *Spirit* (Ode, 212 44004); "Let's Get Together," *H. P. Lovecraft* (Phillips, 600-252).

[58] "Feeling Groovy," *Sounds of Silence*.

[59] "Time Is After You," *West Coast Love-In* (Vault, LP 113).

[60] "Lost Sea Shanty," *Circus Maximus* (Vanguard, 79260); "Going Back," *The Notorious Byrd Brothers*.

fell into the sea, he would not care because he has his "own world to live through."[61] But for others, it can lead to brotherhood. H. P. Lovecraft asks all to "Try and love one another right now."[62]

A desire for freedom is certainly nothing new. Neither is the attempt to find freedom far from smoggy cities in the rural world of nature that Dylan has recently celebrated in his 1970 album *New Morning* and that Joni Mitchell depicts in "Woodstock." What is different in the songs is the conviction that freedom should be used by the individual in an extensive exploration of his own internal world. Central to the vision of the song writers is the idea that the mind must be opened and expanded if the truths of life are to be perceived. Thus, the importance of external reality is subordinated to that of a psychological, even a metaphysical, realm. The most extensive treatment of this subject is by the Amboy Dukes, who devote half of a long-playing record to it. Their theme is stated quite simply: mankind would be happy if only people took the time "to journey to the center of the mind."[63] Like any mystical trip, what happens when one reaches the center of the mind is not easy to describe. Perhaps the best attempt is by the Iron Butterfly, who claim that an unconscious power will be released, flooding the individual with sensations and fusing him with a freedom of thought that will allow him to "see every thing." At this point, man will be blessed with the most supernatural power of knowing "all."[64]

Such a journey is, of course, difficult to make. But youth has discovered a short cut to the mind's center, through the use of hallucinogenic drugs. Indeed, such journeys are almost inconceivable without hallucinogens, and the so-called "head songs" about drug experiences are the most prevalent of works that can be classified as "protest."[65] In this area, the songs carefully distinguish between "mind-expanding," nonaddictive marijuana and LSD, and hard, addictive drugs which destroy the body. Thus, the Velvet Underground and Love both tell of the dangers of heroin, while Canned Heat warn of methedrine use and the Fugs describe the problems of cocaine.[66] But none of the groups hesitate to recommend "grass" and "acid" trips as a prime way of opening oneself to the pleasures and beauties of the universe. As the Byrds claim in a typical "head song," drugs can free the individual from the narrow boundaries of the mundane world, allowing him to open his heart to the quiet joy and eternal love which pervade the whole uni-

---

[61] "If 6 Was 9," *Axis* (Reprise, S 6281).

[62] "Let's Get Together," *H. P. Lovecraft.*

[63] "Journey to the Center of the Mind," *Journey to the Center of the Mind* (Mainstream, S 6112).

[64] "Unconscious Power," *Heavy.*

[65] There are so many "head songs" that listing them would be an impossibly long task. Some of the most popular protest songs of the decade have been such works. They include Jefferson Airplane, "White Rabbit," *Surrealistic Pillow;* the Doors, "Light My Fire," *The Doors* (Elektra EKS 74007); Strawberry Alarm Clock, "Incense and Peppermints," *Incense and Peppermints;* and the Byrds, "Eight Miles High," *Fifth Dimension.*

[66] "Heroin," *Velvet Underground;* "Signed D.C.," *Love* (Elektra, 74001); "Amphetamine Annie," *Boggie;* "Coming Down," *The Fugs.*

verse.[67] Others find the reality of the drug experience more real than the day-to-day world, and some even hope for the possibility of staying "high" permanently. More frequent is the claim that "trips" are of lasting benefit because they improve the quality of life of an individual even after he "comes down."[68] The Peanut Butter Conspiracy, claiming that "everyone has a bomb" in his mind, even dream of some day turning the whole world on with drugs, thus solving mankind's plaguing problems by making the earth a loving place.[69] An extreme desire, perhaps, but one that would find much support among other youths.

This, then is the portrait of America that emerges in recent popular songs which can be labelled as "protest." It is, in the extreme eyes of those like Steppenwolf, a kind of "Monster" gone berserk, a cruel society which makes war on peoples abroad and acts repressively toward helpless minorities like Negroes, youth, and hippies at home. It is a land of people whose lives are devoid of feeling, love, and sexual pleasure. It is a country whose institutions are crumbling away, one which can presumably only be saved by a sort of cultural and spiritual revolution which the young themselves will lead.

Whether one agrees wholly, partly or not at all with such a picture of the United States, the major elements of such a critical portrait are familiar enough. It is only in realizing that all this is being said in popular music, on records that sometimes sell a million copies to teenagers, in songs that youngsters often dance to, that one comes to feel that something strange is happening today. Indeed, if parents fully understand what the youth are saying musically to one another, they must long for the simpler days of Elvis Presley and his blue suede shoes.

If the lyrics of the songs would disturb older people, the musical sound would do so even more. In fact, a good case could be made that the music itself expresses as much protest against the status quo as do the words. Performed in concert with electronic amplification on all instruments—or listened to at home at top volume—the music drowns the individual in waves of sound; sometimes it seems to be pulsating inside the listener. When coupled with a typical light show, where colors flash and swirl on huge screens, the music helps to provide an assault on the senses, creating an overwhelming personal experience of the kind that the songs advise people to seek. This sort of total experience is certainly a protest against the tepid, partial pleasures which other songs describe as the lot of bourgeois America.

Another aspect of the music which might be considered a kind of protest is the attempt of many groups to capture in sound the quality of a drug "trip," to try through melody, rhythm, and volume to—in the vernacular—"blow the mind" of the audience. Of course, youngsters often listen to such music while under the influence of hallucinogens. In such a state, the perceptive experience supposedly can have the quality of putting one in touch with regions of the mind and mani-

[67] "Fifth Dimension," *Fifth Dimension.*
[68] See Country Joe and the Fish, "Bass Strings." *Electric Music for the Mind and Body;* or United States of America, "Coming Down," *United States of America.*
[69] "Living, Loving Life," *Great Conspiracy.*

festations of the universe that can be felt in no other way. Such mysticism, such transcendental attitudes, are certainly a protest against a society in which reality is always pragmatic and truth instrumental.

To try to explain why the jingles and vapid love lyrics of popular music in the 1950s evolved into the social criticism and mystical vision of more recent days is certainly not easy. Part of it is the fact that performers, who have always been young, started writing their own songs, out of their own life experiences, rather than accepting the commercial output of the older members of tin pan alley. But this does not explain the popularity of the new songs. Here one must look to the youthful audience, which decided it preferred buying works of the never kind. For it was the commercial success of some of the new groups which opened the doors of the record companies to the many that flourish today.

Though one cannot make definitive judgments about this record-buying audience, some things seem clear. Certainly, it is true that with increasingly rapid social change, parents—and adults in general—have less and less that they can tell their children about the ways of the world, for adult life experiences are not very relevant to current social conditions. Similarly, institutions like the school and the press suffer from a kind of cultural lag that makes their viewpoints valueless for youth. Into the place of these traditional sources of information have stepped the youth themselves, and through such things as the "underground" press and popular music they are telling each other exactly what is happening. In this way, the music has achieved popularity—at least in part—because it telegraphs important messages to young people and helps to define and codify the mores and standards of their own subculture. A youngster may personally feel that there is no difference between his parents' drinking and his use of marijuana. Certainly, it is comforting to him when his friends feel the same way, and when popular songs selling millions of copies deliver the same message, there are even stronger sanctions for his "turning on." Thus, the lyrics of the music serve a functional role in the world of youth.

It is interesting to note that the popular music also puts youth in touch with serious, intellectual critiques of American life. Perhaps it starts only as a gut reaction in the song writers, but they have put into music the ideas of many American social critics. Without reading Paul Goodman, David Riesman, C. Wright Mills, or Mary McCarthy, youngsters will know that life is a "rat race," that Americans are a "lonely crowd," that "white-collar" lives contain much frustration, and that the war in Vietnam is far from just. And they will have learned this from popular music, as well as from their own observation.

The other side of the coin from criticism of contemporary life is the search for personal experience, primarily of the "mind-expanding" sort. As is obvious by now, such expansion has nothing to do with the intellect, but is a spiritual phenomenon. Here a final critique is definitely implicit. Throughout the music—as in youth culture—there is the search for a kind of mystical unity, an ability to feel a oneness with the universe. This is what drugs are used for; this is what the total environment of the light and music shows is about; and this is what is sought in the sexual experience—often explicitly evident in the orgasmic grunts and moans of performers. Through the search for this unity, the music is implicitly condemning the fragmentation of the individual's life which is endemic in the modern world. The songsters are saying that it is wrong to compartmentalize work and play, wrong to cut men off from the natural rhythms of nature, wrong to stifle sex and love and play in favor of greater productivity, wrong to say man's spiritual needs can be filled by providing him with more material possessions.

This is obviously a criticism that can only be made by an affluent people, but these youth do represent the most affluent of all countries. And rather than wallow in their affluence, they have sensed and expressed much of the malaise that plagues our technological society. The charge may be made against them that they are really utopians, but the feeling increases today that we are in need of more utopian thinking and feeling. And while one might not wish to follow their prescriptions for the good life, they have caught something of the desire for freedom that all men feel. What could be more utopian and yet more inviting than the future painted by the Mothers, a time when all the lonely people—poor or fat or gray-haired—will feel free to take off their clothes "to sing and dance and love."[70] Of course it is difficult to say how close such a time is. But as Plato wrote and the Fugs have echoed, "When the mode of the music changes, the walls of the city shake."[71] Now the mode has changed and the walls are shaking. Perhaps that future is closer than we think.

[70] "Take Your Clothes Off When You Dance," *We're Only In It for the Money*.
[71] "When the Mode of the Music Changes," *It Crawled* (Reprise, IS 6305).

PART TWO

DIMENSIONS OF ALIENATION
AND CONFLICTING VALUES

TWO

ACTIVIST STUDENTS AND THEIR DEMANDS

Given the wide variety of environmental conditions and social-psychological variables present in the lives of adolescents, it is apparent that the schools cannot assume complete responsibility for the fact that some students are distressed about certain conditions and policies related to their lives in school. The obligation of educators is to be certain that they are at least more a part of the solution than of the difficulty. There is good reason to believe that often this has not been the case; schools have indeed contributed to feelings of alienation and to some resulting activist behavior.

One must search in vain for any completely successful definition of "alienation," even among reasonably sophisticated social scientists. After students, parents, journalists, and other commentators add their interpretations, anything like a uniform definition becomes hopeless. Perhaps Melvin Seeman's explanation of alienation is most descriptive of its several negative elements. A feeling of powerlessness, meaninglessness, normlessness, isolation, and self-estrangement were all identified as characteristics common to alienated individuals.[1] Given these psychological propensities, there remains the question of what kind of behavior the individual will exhibit. Conceivably, he could act as a tuned out "hippie" or a practicing revolutionary. In its purer psychological sense, a relatively non-activist or "drop out of society" behavior is usually implied.

This chapter is concerned only with those individuals who are able to turn their feelings of alienation into activist behavior. There is strong evidence to indicate that, at least on the college level, a majority of student activists come from families with upper-middle-class incomes (above $15,000 annually) and comparatively permissive, highly educated parents.[2] An interesting, although not particularly surprising, finding of Richard Flacks was that the parents of activists, as well as the activists themselves, were more liberal than non-activists and their parents. It was hypothesized that liberal attitudes toward a wide range of social issues were assimilated by activist students from their parents while the students were still residing at home.

There is good reason to believe that activist parents are more lenient than the parents of non-activists. In his college student sample, Flacks found that parents

[1] Melvin Seeman, "On the Meaning of Alienation," *American Sociological Review*, 24 (December, 1959): 783-791.
[2] Richard Flacks, "The Liberated Generation: An Exploration of the Roots of Student Protest," *Journal of Social Issues*, 23 (July, 1967): 52-75.

of activist students revealed significantly lower tendencies toward intervention in the lives of their offspring than did the parents of non-activists. This does not suggest that activist students had suffered any adverse psychological damage as a result of their parents' permissiveness. Indeed, there is some evidence that activists are in better psychological health, i.e., they are less neurotic, than the non-activists. To oversimplify, they are less likely to possess authoritarian personalities and be obsessed with socially imposed career worries, but are more likely to be in tune with their natural propensity toward seeking the better life.[3]

On the lower end of the socio-economic spectrum are numerous disenchanted youth whose social experiences have included a protracted period of negative contact with the schools, including unsatisfying learning experiences. Although there is considerable disagreement as to what is really bothering relatively affluent but alienated youth, the bulk of evidence points to the fact that poor urban youth seek entrance into a style of life which has come to be identified with middle-class status. They do not reject middle-class culture for being overly commercial. Their alienation stems more from an inability to come up with the material, social, and psychological resources necessary for middle-class goal attainment than a rejection of those same goals and values.[4]

With one exception, the literature on student demands selected for this section has been reprinted from student publications. Included is the *Chicano Student News,* which reflects both the demands and frustrations of Mexican-American students during the 1968 East Los Angeles "blowout," and the program of the Black Youth Alliance of New York City. Jerry Farber's "Annotated Manifesto" and the Berkeley High School Student Union Program display a comparatively radical point of view. Most of the remaining selections, reflecting student frustrations, defiance, cynicism, humor, and desires for increased freedom, are probably quite typical of activist feelings. The single article not appearing in a student publication is taken from the conservative *National Review.* It represents the smallest minority in the school—the "individualist youth," or conservative activists. With the silent majority generally remaining silent, the conservative student does on occasion speak for a group larger than his own.

Some of the activist dissenters' criticism is aimed at national issues, much at local issues, and a considerable amount at the school structure itself. The absence of flexibility and versatility within the organization is often identified as a problem. Too often alert students with a bent toward liberal views see the school spending too much time in discipline and conformity and showing too little evidence of flexibility. Equally serious is the charge that the secondary schools are not doing well in vocational training programs and academic preparation. A rigid curriculum is seen as part of the problem. According to one adult observer, "our singular pursuit of academic considerations may have improved the aca-

---

[3] Christian Bay, "Political and Apolitical Students: Facts in Search of a Theory," *Journal of Social Issues,* 23 (July, 1967): 79-91.

[4] David Gottlieb, "Poor Youth: A Study in Forced Alienation," *Journal of Social Issues,* 25 (Spring, 1969): 91-120.

demic preparation of some students, but may also have narrowed their sense of competence, limited their self-esteem, and made increasing numbers of them closed to subsequent intellectual growth."[5] The same commentator attributed the problem to the large size of schools, together with the accompanying problems of impersonality, rigidity, bureaucracy, and, frequently, authoritarian atmospheres. At its worst the school can become a fairly representative microcosm of what seems wrong with the social order, a place where one can learn antisystem, and perhaps even antisocietal attitudes.

While administrators as a group are certainly aware of student dissent, and many even agree that school policies must be reformed, some question remains whether or not the system is capable of change. Radical students and some not so radical adults have gone so far as to suggest that the school system as a system is not capable of systematic, intelligent, compassionate change.[6] It has been asserted that the only way improvement can be realized is for the "top down" concept of school administration and organization to be abandoned in favor of a balance of power approach involving student participation. Some of the more interesting proposals for realizing this objective are included in Chapter 9. The student written selections in the present chapter provide a representative sample of the enormity of the problem.

[5] Douglas H. Heath, "Student Alienation and the School," *School Review,* 78 (August, 1970): 515-528.
[6] See Jack R. Frymier, "Why Students Rebel," *Educational Leadership,* 27 (January, 1970): 346-350.

STUDENT DEMANDS

BLOW OUTS were staged by us, Chicano students, in the East Los Angeles High Schools protesting the obvious lack of action on the part of the LA School Board in bringing ELA schools up to par with those in other areas of the city. We, young Chicanos, not only protested but at the same time offered proposals for much needed reforms. Just what did we propose?

To begin with, we want assurance that any student or teacher who took part in the BLOW OUTS—WILL NOT be reprimanded or suspended in any manner. You know the right to protest and demonstrate against injustice is guaranteed to all by the constitution.

We want immediate steps taken to implement bi-lingual and bi-cultural education for Chicanos. WE WANT TO BRING OUR CARNALES HOME. Teachers, administrators, and staff should be educated; they should know our language (Spanish), and understand the history, traditions and contributions of the Mexican culture. HOW CAN THEY EXPECT TO TEACH US IF THEY DO NOT KNOW US? We also want the school books revised to reflect the contributions of Mexicans and Mexican-Americans to the U.S. society, and to make us aware of the in-

From *Chicano Student News* [East Los Angeles], 15 (March, 1968), 3.

justices that we, Chicanos, as a people have suffered in a "gabacho" dominated society. Furthermore, we want any member of the school system who displays prejudice or fails to recognize, understand, and appreciate us, our culture, or our heritage removed from ELA schools.

Classes should be smaller in size, say about 20 student to 1 teacher, to insure more effectiveness. We want new teachers and administrators to live in the community their first year and that parents from the community be trained as teacher's aides. We want assurances, that a teacher who may disagree politically or philosophically with administrators will not be dismissed or transferred because of it. The school belongs to the community and as such should be made available for community activities under supervision of Parents' Councils.

There should be a manager in charge of janitorial work and maintenance details and the performance of such duties should be restricted to employees hired for that purpose. IN OTHER WORDS NO MORE STUDENTS DOING JANITORIAL WORK.

And more than this, we want RIGHTS—RIGHTS—STUDENT RIGHTS—OUR RIGHTS. We want a free speech area plus the right to have speakers of our own choice at our club meetings. Being civic minded citizens we want to know what the happenings are in our community so we demand the right to have access to all types of literature and to be able to bring it on campus.

The type of dress that we wear should not be dictated to us by "gabachos," but it should be a group of Chicano parents and students who establish dress and grooming standards for Chicano students in Chicano schools.

Getting down to facilities. WE WANT THE BUILDINGS OPEN TO STUDENTS AT ALL TIMES, especially the HEADS. Yeah, we want access to the Heads at all times. . . . . . . When you get right down to it, WE ONLY DEMAND WHAT OTHERS HAVE. Things like lighting at all ELA football fields, swimming pools. Sport events are an important part of school activity and we want FREE ADMISSION for all students. We, CHICANO STUDENTS, BLEW OUT in protest. Our proposals have been made. The big question is will the School Board take positive action. If so, WHEN?

IF NOT———BLOW OUTS—BABY—BLOW OUTS!!

THE PROGRAM OF THE BLACK YOUTH ALLIANCE

We of the BYA are a dedicated group of students who have come to the realization that the so-called "Negroes," our Black brothers still, are lost, blind, debased, demoralized, and brainwashed to the point that the only salvation for them lies in the Black youth to come. We have come to realize that the white world will MEET ITS END at the hands of Black Youth!!

Revolutionaries? Only to the extent that we advocate a radical change in the relations between the white man, and the Black human being!

Activists? Only in the sense that it is the Black activity of the Black youth that will be the telling factor in the trying days that lie ahead in the Black man's life!

Militants? To the point where militancy is necessary to bring about the badly needed changes in the lives of *all* men.

Dedicated? We are *DETERMINED* to liberate our lost brothers and sisters whose minds are entrapped by the white man's BRAIN WASHING!!

The following program which we have developed is one which we know to be detrimental to *us*, in that it envelops the needs of *every* Black individual, in particular, the Black student. It is also evident that this program is the *only* program which offers the Black student a definite plan towards the survival of the Black race in a country that seeks, at every turn, to completely annihilate him.

We know that the student needs this program, and we also know that the Black man, collectively, has the wisdom to recognize his brother's efforts to pull him out of the gutter of debased morality and slime that the white man's striknology has put him into. It is now a clearly defined case of Black Survival Through Black Identity that is set before us. There is only *one* way in which we can accomplish this survival: We MUST ACT!!

The Black high school student supports the *Black Youth Alliance* and its program, because he realizes he has obligations to fight for *power*—financially, physically, mentally and spiritually. He supports us because we support *him*, with a program that he *knows* is the only means for his survival; the program of the BYA.

THE PROGRAM . . .

1. We feel the need to install with the Black Youth a sense of political awareness in a hope to end the terrible plague of *Black Apathy* that has been forced upon us.

2. We feel the need to declare unto ourselves a full and complete realization of Black Pride, hence we conclusively draw unto ourselves the conception "Black Is Beautiful"!!

3. We feel and sense the need to prepare Black students for the time to come, the "near future," when we the youth shall become the dominant factor in the mainstream of Black current events. We wish to prepare ourselves for the time when we must make the same decisions our foreparents made—*without making the same mistakes!!!*

We want to know for ourselves the time to be militant, and the time to be pacific; the time to remain on the outside and the time to get involved; the time to *stand up* and the time to remain underground. We want to be able to define for ourselves the conditions under which we as the center of Black political life of the next decade shall exist.

4. We also orient the *Black Action Movement* because we wish to satisfy our de-

sire to measure the degree of unity exhibited by the student in New York's high schools.

5. We wish to conclusively establish for once and for all the *maximum* power which the Black community can exhibit when called upon to mobilize.

6. We wish to establish a precedent for a *true* mobilization of Youth to help further the cause of Black Beauty and Black Identity in the community, the city, the nation, and the world.

7. We feel that the proposed "Afro-American History" and "Afro-American Culture" classes and courses will not be substantial to the needs that will arise from the desire of Black youth to learn more concerning our heritage, beauty, kind, and identity.

8. We realize that the said courses will only be "token" courses, in that they will not reflect the *true* instillment of a *self-image* into the student in regard to his heritage.

9. We *know* that these same courses will be taught by *white* teachers who will teach the lessons from a *white* point of view, thereby *whitening* the images of our already little known heroes, and then establishing as "fanatical" the works of such dedicated Black men as W. E. B. DuBois, Marcus Garvey, and Al Hajj Shabazz Al Malik (to the Uninformed, Malcolm X).

10. It is already evidenced that these same *white* teachers will proceed to "glorify" the deeds of Portugal, Spain, Germany, France, and especially England and America, in relation to the rape, and continued exploitation of *Africa, Asia,* and other Non-White domains.

11. We realize that the net results of this *reverse education* will be: THE WHITENING OF THE BLACK MAN'S WORLD, THE DEGRADING OF THE BLACK MAN'S SELF-IMAGE, and a reduction in the Black Man's physical and mental prowess; a weakening and total destruction of his personal drives for BLACK BEAUTY AND SURVIVAL, THROUGH BLACK IDENTITY.

12. We aim to work for the complete and total unification of Black Peoples in an effort to improve the standing of the Black man in this nation so that he is no longer a parasite, dependent on the white man, but that he stands as a completely separate, *independent,* and distinct personality.

13. We aim to advocate the furtherance of the "revolutionary" idea of an independent *Black economy,* recognizing the need for *unity,* not only in Black Ideals, but also in the *Black dollar.*

14. We aim to promote and perpetuate *unity* among the Black Youth, showing the need for an *alliance of ALL Black Organizations!!*

15. To advocate the establishment of a HIGH SCHOOL IN HARLEM, a LIBERATION SCHOOL that will be controlled by the Black People, taught by the Black People, and to establish a MUSEUM OF AFRO-AMERICAN CULTURE in correlation with the LIBERATION HIGH SCHOOL.

16. To establish such schools in EVERY BLACK COMMUNITY.

17. TO PROVIDE A MOBILIZED BLACK YOUTH FORCE TO OFFER DEFENSE TO THE BLACK COMMUNITY IN TIMES SO NEEDED, AND the same force, upon a majority decision TO COME TO THE AID OF ANY COMMUNITY OR ORGANIZATION FOLLOWING THE IDEALS OF BLACK IDENTITY AND LIBERATION!!

18. TO GIVE A TOTAL AND LASTING SUPPORT TO BLACK STUDENT ORGANIZATIONS, with the goal of educating our brothers in the art of fighting off the white man's trick bag.

19. To provide guidance for those *awakened* brothers who realize that their fight IS NOT IN VIETNAM, BUT RATHER IT IS AGAINST THE ENEMY WHOSE TANKS ARE ROAMING THE DETROIT, WATTS, NEWARK, HARLEM AND CLEVELAND STREETS.

20. To provide for our lost brothers, who are hooked on the fishline of the oppressor, in an effort to relieve them of the total schizophrenia which the "pigs's" dope and liquor has brought upon them.

21. Finally, we dedicate our whole spiritual, physical, and intellectual being to EXPOSING THE RACIST PIG FOR WHAT HE IS!! WE WANT THE WORLD TO KNOW THAT THE AMERICAN INFORMATION AGENCIES ARE *LYING* WHEN THEY SAY THAT RACE PROBLEMS ARE ON THE UP AND UP!!! WE WANT THEM TO KNOW THAT AMERICA IS GOING D-O-W-N—at the hands of the BLACK YOUTH!!

BLACK-YOUTH ALLIANCE NEWSLETTER
New York City

AN ANNOTATED MANIFESTO

JERRY FARBER

School is where you let the dying society put its trip on you. Our schools may seem useful; to make children into doctors, sociologists, engineers—to discover things. But they're poisonous as well. They exploit and enslave students; they petrify society; they make democracy unlikely. And it's not what you're taught that does the harm but how you're taught. Our schools teach you by pushing you around, by making timid square apathetic slaves out of you—authority addicts.

Schooling doesn't have to be this destructive. If it weren't compulsory, if schools were autonomous and were run by the people in them, then we could learn without being subdued and stupefied in the process. And, perhaps, we could regain control of our own society.

From *YIP* (Culver City Student Union), 1 (May 29, 1970).

Students can change things if they want to because they have the power to say "no." When you go to school, you're doing society a favor. And when you say "no," you withhold much more than your attendance. You deny continuity to the dying society; you put the future on strike. Students can have the kind of school they want—or even something else entirely if they want—because there isn't going to be any school at all without them.

BERKELEY HIGH SCHOOL STUDENT UNION PROGRAM

The HSSU has a Program which we feel relates to the needs of all students. We think that people should form chapters of the HSSU in every school so that, when we move on issues which affect all of us we'll be together. The Program is flexible. It can be changed as our needs change. As it now stands, the Program is as follows:

1. WE WILL CREATE A STUDENT UNION. Some of us last year learned that it is impossible to fight for real change as individuals. We've got to be together. We must recognize our relationship as students to a bad system. We must then realize our need to move together to fight it. The HSSU will be the banding together of all students who want to see radical change in the schools. We believe in organization which brings out the leadership and creativity existing in everyone. The basic issue is getting ourselves together, uniting, and fighting for common goals.

2. WE WILL EXERCISE OUR RIGHTS. The only way that students can gain power over their own lives is to organize. All students have the right to get themselves together for their own needs. This means we will exercise our rights of free speech, our right to leaflet, our right to have independent newspapers (like PACK RAT), and our right to take political action in our own interests in the schools without censorship, restriction, or penalty. Our rights, like this Program, will become a reality, and not just words on this piece of paper, through practice.

From *Pack Rat* [Berkeley Underground Student Newspaper], 1 (October, 1969).

3. WE WILL HAVE A JOYOUS MOVEMENT. Everyone should be able to express themselves through art—work, dance, sculpture, drama, music, and all means open to the imagination. Materials should be made available to all students free. We will defy all puritanical restraints on what we can or cannot do. We shall have media—newspapers, films, posters, leaflets, and music—to express our student community and culture. We shall set up festivals, fairs, and happenings where people can meet for fun, expression, and communication.

4. WE WILL STRUGGLE AGAINST RACISM. We oppose and will resist all forms of racism existing in the school, in others, and in ourselves. We support the right of all students to get themselves together for their own needs. We support the Black Student Union and the Chicano Student Union. Racism is being used by the system to keep us apart; to divide and conquer—to keep us from seeing who the real enemy is. We will fight racism with solidarity—the solidarity of all peoples in the world, and the unity of all students—as brothers and sisters.

5. WE WILL FIGHT FOR THE LIBERATION OF WOMEN. The role of the women in this society is defined as a passive one. The schools serve to perpetuate the society's image of women as unintelligent, silly men-chasers, as sexual objects bearing babies, and as frantic consumers. This is a corrupt image, used too long to manipulate women. The schools discourage women, from preparing for well-paying jobs by channeling them into home-economics and secretarial classes. There is a lack of respect for women, for the simple fact that they are women. As women—and high school students—we must realize our real position as equal, intelligent human beings, capable of sharing the same responsibilities as men. The HSSU will struggle together against male supremacy and for the liberation of women.

6. WE WILL END OPPRESSIVE PHYSICAL EDUCATION. We object to and will resist the military-like regimentation of P.E. and the drill sergeant mentality of the gym teachers. We do not recognize and will resist the false authority of gym teachers who seek to indoctrinate an attitude of unquestioning conformity in their students. We recognize the right of any student to refuse to participate in P.E. without penalty. We will resist the shit that we have all had to take in the past. We will create and develop new P.E. courses which will respect the individual.

7. WE WILL END ADMINISTRATIVE CONTROL OF STUDENT ACTIVITIES. The administration has no business in either trying to control or influence student elections and student government. We will return student elections and student government to the students. We have the right to control the destinies of our own lives. We have the right to develop our own politics and organizations regardless of administrative opinion and approval. We are determined to use this right.

8. WE WILL END THE PRINCIPAL'S VETO POWERS. We will resist the powers and rule of one man who can overrule the wishes of the students. This denial of democracy by a school system which says it wants to develop in its students "an appreciation of our democratic tradition," must be ended. We will turn the schools into genuine people's schools where decisions are made collectively.

9. WE WILL END SUSPENSIONS AND EXPULSIONS. The barbaric system of "corrective" punishment for such "crimes" as cutting, smoking, and other similar "offenses" must be ended. Such practices have no place in a people's school. New methods of dealing with so-called "disciplinary" problems will be instituted. We will sever the long arm of the administration which serves to slap every "troublemaker" and every would be "troublemaker" back into the line of the unquestioning and submissive student. We will no longer tolerate suspensions or expulsions of a political or asinine nature.

10. WE WILL END THE REPRESSION OF HIGH SCHOOL STUDENTS. The political repression of high school students takes many forms. Last year, it went from administrators giving warnings to students, to attempting to disqualify a legitimate student election, to suspensions on false charges, to the gestapo-like tactic of ordering a student arrested and dragged from his home by the police. This year two active members of the HSSU have been busted by the pigs. One for disturbing the peace (he was advising a student of his rights in the Park), and the other on the bullshit charge of loitering. We will actively resist and will end such uncalled for political repression by any means necessary.

11. WE WILL UNITE WITH OTHER MOVEMENTS. We will unite with other movements throughout the country to attain our mutual liberation and equal rights. In the final analysis, Berkeley High School will not be free until the rest of America is also free. It is to our mutual benefit and survival that we unite with other movements throughout the community and the country. Our struggle is theirs, and their struggle is ours. We must be prepared to support the struggles of high school students everywhere. If we support each other, we can win. The key to ultimate victory lies in our ability to unite in a common struggle for common goals.

The HSSU recognizes that above all "the important thing is to pull yourself up by your own hair; to turn yourself inside out and see the world with fresh eyes."

COTTON WOOL

Once upon a time, you see, there was a young girl who believed, who or what she believed *in* is of no importance now . . . she believed. She went to a kingdom, unfortunately a communistic-like dictatorship, and attempted to relate to the poor, downtrodden subjects of the kingdom her believes. But the awful ogre who repressed the basic human freedoms there attacked the girl and banished her. Several of the girl's friends and fellow-believers picketed the kingdom and were informed that as long as they did not approach any closer than the sidewalks that they could carry their "Turn On to Jesus" signs.

"Preparing students for life" is one of the supposed goals of the benevolent Long Beach Unified School District . . . but the very nature of the system only

From *The Loudmouth* [Long Beach Underground Student Newspaper], III [n.d.]. Unedited, including misspellings.

serves to insulate us in cotton wool from the realities of life. It may be argued that religious dogma is best taught in churchs . . . yet, who can deny that the quest for the "true" religion is a vital portion of man's existance?

Obviously, we are concerned with the *Loudmouth,* so now consider the proposal of allowing it and the *Truth* (and any others) on campus. Except for a few feeble-minded idiots who themselves are insulated from reality, no person today can deny that the believes, plans, and actions of the varied political groupings concern every American. To believe otherwise is to ignore Watts, Chicago, Century City, the Minutemen, the John Birchers, and the Students for a Democratic Society . . . and to ignore these is tantamount to suicide as a nation. Further, if a person believes that the graduate from this institution is not going to encounter people who will attempt to sway him to the "Left" or "Right" it would be obvious that he too was an idiot. It further follows logically that if the student is going to "be prepared for life" he must be faced with these, and myriad other problems currently suppressed by the rigid system of this school district.

Consider, if you will, experimental animals. They are raised in germ-free environments where their every need is cared for. There is no question that these animals are among the healthiest in the world and literally never suffer from illness except for old age and the scapel of the experimenter. However, if the animals are released from their stirle, sanitary environment and placed in the "outside world," they die. Away from the elaborate precautions against germs the rats do not even have an opportunity to starve to death . . . they fall victim to absurd little illnesses to which they had never before been exposed. In other words, their bodies have had no opportunity to create what is laughingly refered to as a "natural immunity." These animals could survive *only* in their sterile, protected, and artificial environment. Even this "Utopia" for rats has its drawbacks. In fact, their environment is a negative utopia in the best Orwellian fashion. These rats who are product of generations of experimental animals are developing genetic differences from their free-running kin . . . their claws are becoming more rounded, better adapted for clinging to the wire mesh of their cages. It is exactly this situation that the School Board now places the student . . . an artificial environment protected from the "outside world." Damn it! I don't want my "claws to become rounded, better adapted for clinging to the wire mesh of my cage!" I don't want to fear going into the "outside world" because I may become exposed to "heretofore unknown microbes." The Board of Education and all of the rest of the feeble idiots who seek to "protect" me may (or may not) hold the best of intentions but they smother me in their clumbsy attempts . . . and I plan to survive.

Picture this imaginary situation. A person has gone through the Long Beach Unified School District; through elementary, junior, and senior high school years. Although he was always insulated from the world, our educators assure him that he is ready for "life."

The student has been trained for the outside world with no dope present, no sex, no outside speakers, and certainly not controversial issues! In other words, he has been trained for a nice, orderly world dreamed up by the nice, orderly minds of those who control the schools . . . minds who choose to ignore the mush and mire and crap that is the reality of the screwed-up world they have handed us. Minds incapable of dealing with the reality of the world because of their guilt over it.

This is the big night! Graduation has come! The student goes through the ceremony, the all-night dance, and wakes up the next morning.

Shock! There, in the middle of the "outside world" are several men speaking on controversial issues. The student, unable to draw on similar experiences in the past, cannot seperate the liars and hypocrites from those who are sincere. The student is seduced, duped, drafted, married, divorced, bought alive and sold again before he finally develops what is called a "natural immunity" to the world that is nothing more than experiencing it.

The Loudspeaker never mentioned the draft, because that didn't affect our now drafted student. The Loudspeaker never mentioned con artists . . . so the student buys the Queen Mary. The Loudspeaker never mentioned racism . . . so the student joins the American Independent Party and Wallace. The Speaker never mentioned the Minutemen so the student buys a .44 magnum to protect himself against the black hordes of Africa. The Speaker never mentioned issues other than how to clean up the campus, so the student in dispair with the mess that his country is in, joins the S.D.S. and turns his talents toward destruction. Speaking of our local fish-wrapper, we would like to (again) state that we don't want to provide the answers or even ask the questions above . . . we sure as hell don't get grades for doing so . . . we don't get credit in college for "Underground Newspaper 1-A" taken in high school . . . what we do get is a lot of our time and effort taken up in doing what is the Speakers job . . . to inform and educate (just like they themselves teach in Journalism that newspapers should do . . . to say nothing of the role of the Fourth Estate towards proposing ideas for benefiting the community.) In fact, we're damned sick and tired of having to do another groups job for them in order to make the school a little more real . . . and are infuriated at the Board of Education for asphyxiating good journalists on the Speaker staff with censorship and forcing them to write on trivialities.

Look. In psychology, in zoology, in biology, in medicine, in politics, in history, in every phase of human endeavor and life, there is a generality that stands out . . . "Those who are over-protected suffer and die when that protection is removed"; (or if it remains, never achieve their full potential.)

If the present system of education is allowed to continue, students will either suffer when thrust into the "outside world" or worse, they will develop "rounded claws" and be suited only for life in a tiny, confined cage. The solution is simple; inculate the students by allowing such things as the Loudmouth, the Truth, outside speakers, controversial issues, and the world onto campus.

But that solution assumes that the Board of Education wishes the student to be inoculated against the world . . . but it seems that they would prefer the students to "develop rounded claws" so we fit their nice, sterile confining cages. So that this generation does not show them just how badly they have screwed this culture.

But my claws are still straight, and my sons claws *will be straight*. I do not intend to stand idley by and be pounded into fitting someone elses sterile dream world.

Look, you decrepent, hypocritical, controlling fossils . . . I have my own dream.

A general question may be asked. Does Wilson practise improvement ...or appeasement?

IF....

You turn the W.W. of Woodrow Wilson Up Side down... you get the MM of Mickey Mouse.

but that's not much of a change now... is it?

If the School Board Gets More Money...
by Waleed S. Al-Fadhly

The Los Angeles School Board is greatly in need of money for increased salaries, reductions in class size, and necessary educational innovations. New Improved Tide reporters have uncovered a list of top-priority innovations to improve the educational process. Below, we present a sneak preview of what the Los Angeles City high school may have in 1971 if the School Board gets more money.

The Automatic Disposal Unit

To help solve the environmental crisis in our schools.

The No-Bra Detector

For those periodic checks in the Girls' Gym.

Student Government Machine

Comes with plastic-coated Student Congress reports that can be used semester after semester.

Automatic Noon-Aids

Keeps students in; agitators out.

Electronic Programmer

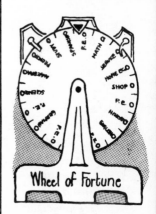

Wheel of Fortune

Relieves teachers and administrators of bothersome, time-consuming duties.

Instant Grade Computer

From *New Improved Tide* [John Marshall High School Underground Student Newspaper], III (February 18, 1970).

```
┌──────────────────────────────────────────────────────────┐
│  I was screwed by my school                               │
│                                                           │
│  on _____ (date)                   │
│                                                           │
│  The claim I was _____     │
│                                                           │
│            ____True-so what?                              │
│            ____Completely False        ╭──╮               │
│            ____Otherwise                                  │
│      They  ____Suspended Me                               │
│            ____Expelled Me                               │
│            ____Excluded Me                               │
│            ____Called My Parents                         │
│                                                           │
│  My name is _____     │
│                                                           │
│  My school is _____     │
└──────────────────────────────────────────────────────────┘
```

From *New Improved Tide* [John Marshall High School Underground Student Newspaper], III (February 18, 1970).

THE STORY OF THE POSTING OF THE THESES
M-DAY AT IRONDEQUOIT HIGH

RICHARD BROOKHISER

How Martin Luther II, Age 14, beat back the Moratorium-makers and their mimeograph machines—armed only with a typewriter—and how, on the way home from school, experienced an epiphany of sorts.

For centuries, the pamphlet has been one of the most powerful weapons in the great wars of words. In the hands of men like Swift, Burke and Thomas Paine, it

From *National Review* (150 East 35 Street, New York, N.Y. 10016), 22 (February, 1970), 196-98. Reprinted with the permission of the publisher.

has changed the course of history. The following account shows how this ancient device was once again put to good use—and how the Moratorium at IHS did not go undefied.

The first thing I noticed Tuesday morning was that a large crowd was entering the northwest door of IHS at an unusually slow rate. The cause of this delay was two students who were passing out some sheet or other, probably related to Homecoming Weekend. But then I realized that this was The Week, the week of the Fifteenth. Already, the leaflet was thrust in my hand, I was reading the first sentence. My worst suspicions were confirmed; the sale of indulgences had begun. Tetzel had arrived in Irondequoit.

The flaws of this leaflet are perhaps not as numerous as one might expect; it is such a vapid document. But in my book, it still rates a nosegay. "We have been turned down in efforts for outside speakers. . . ." In other words, turned down in efforts for outside liberals. The Moratorium "encourages a broad cross-section of Americans to work against the war. . . ." That is to say, it encourages the left-wing, which though numerous, is hardly a broad cross-section. And the word "leafletting." Good heavens! when a writer has at his disposal the most subtle and varied language in the world, one might think he could avoid such monstrosities as "leafletting"! But what galled me most about the pass-out was just its air of smug cockiness: "We, as concerned students," "The program . . . is an individual expression of your moral views," "We . . . must educate the community," and most odious of all, "You may stay in school. . . ." Oh, how uncommonly good of them to say so.

By first period, I was already sufficiently wrought up to do something. It seemed that I was a voice crying in the wilderness. Everywhere I went, I saw the blue Moratorium buttons, I could hear the Moratorium being praised—the war was being cursed by bell, book and candle and no one realized that the Mass was being recited backwards. Similar pass-outs that afternoon only served to rile me more. By the time I got home, my choler had not subsided, but I had given it a definite purpose; the Moratorium would not go unchallenged.

And so, all that night, I typed. I did not have access to the resources of the other pamphleteers—they were so organized, there had to be a teacher behind them. So for two hours, I made do with carbon paper, cranking out four sheets at a time. And the end result: "The 95 Theses of the Vietnam War entitled *I Protest!*"

Looking back on it all, I am often startled. At one point, I borrowed dangerously from the rhetoric of the Left: . . . "the enemies of the people of South Vietnam." I consider the bit about bluejays inspired, though it must seem rather bitchy in print. The eleventh thesis is almost a direct quote from an appraisal of Eleanor Roosevelt by James Burnham, and the closing of the last thesis could have been lifted from *The Prisoner*. Also, upon reflection, I must agree with Wm. F. Buckley Jr., that a true Moratorium, devoted to serious thought on the war, would be welcome. But the Moratorium, as it was, amounted to nothing more than an intellectual Saturnalia (you see, we do learn something from mythology), so that Thesis Number Six should remain unchanged.

So it was that after two hours of furious activity, I had one measly pile of papers and no idea what to do with them. The Moratorium people could drown IHS in pass-outs (on two days, at least four different antiwar pamphlets were distributed); I had only 33 typewritten sheets, including duds (joke's on me, I put the carbon paper in backwards). I decided to call the principal, Dr. Davis, to check on regulations concerning the dissemination of propaganda. I was informed that his mother was ill and in the hospital, and that he might be back in ten minutes or at 3 A.M. That was bad; Doc might have been sympathetic to my position. I would have to call Mr. Wilson, Dean of Students; I did not know what he thought. In the meantime, however, one of our neighbors had seized the line; the Moratorium might be over before she stopped talking. I amused myself by playing a Bach "Intrata." The neighbor hung up. Wilson was busy; I thought of calling Dave Stevenson, resident conservative of the senior class. Mother suggested that we creep into the school at night, post our manifestos and softly fade away. It was getting late ("Ricky, it's *bed*-time!"). But finally, Mr. Wilson answered. This was the first test. I would have to proceed gingerly.

BEARDING BUREAUCRACY

I stated my question: What were the regulations of IHS, as I had a Moratorium message? He asked for a name. I gave it; it was all in the open now. I sounded him out carefully.

"I believe my pamphlet . . . supplements those passed out today." Well, in that case, Lester Maddox "supplements" the SDS.

"What position do you take?"

"Uh . . . I believe my leaflet . . . calls into question . . . certain points . . . raised in the other leaflet." I could have said: "My leaflet attacks the entire structure of leftist orthodoxy," but it did not seem appropriate. With fear and trembling, I listened as Mr. Wilson outlined the rules—I could pass out anything to my heart's content, so long as it neither advocated the overthrow of the government nor was obscene; anything put on the walls, however, would have to be okayed by a Power—himself, or the Doc.

I had heard The Word. Tomorrow, I would set to work.

I arrived at school half an hour early. The very first thing, I accosted Mr. Wilson in the halls. We adjourned to his inner sanctum; he read my paper. "Well . . . that's very good." Relief, relief. The night before, he had mentioned something about initialing each sheet, but this morning, he waived the requirement. The last hurdle was passed. I was loose in Wittenberg.

One leaflet by the Band room, one by the teacher mailboxes, four surrounding the Large Group Instruction Center (scene of scheduled debates on the war), three by the cafeteria, three on the stairs, two on the doors of the teachers' lounge, one on a blank bulletin board, two by some lavatories, two over drinking fountains, and the most pointed touch of all, one under the plaque honoring veterans of the Korean War. The school was filling with people. One student carrying pro-Moratorium leaflets spotted me busily at work on the LGIC. His features lit up. "Oh, you have pamphlets too!" I put on a most disarmingly liberal face.

"Sure. I'll trade you one of mine for one of yours." The exchange was made. I scuttled around a corner before the explosion took place.

THE TRUTH DAWNS

I had used every paper, keeping one for myself. Already, I could see small knots of people collecting around my work. Let the leftists "leaflet" away, they didn't have anything posted. School had begun; I had finished just in time. I went off to Band, my first period.

The only subject of talk was the Moratorium. A few "concerned students" could be seen outside milling around the bus loop; a flag with the peace sign emblazoned on it had been run up the flagpole. And quite innocently, I passed around a copy of my leaflet (I said I had found it lying on the floor). Mark Spahn, French horn player, read it, among others.

"Mmmm. Must have been written by Hossenfefer [a prominent liberal]."

He read on.

"Guess not. Must be sarcastic."

And finally, the truth dawned on his left-wing mind.

"He's serious!"

Martin Luther II had taken his place in history.

On my way to homeroom, I was held up at the bottom of the stairs. Half a dozen students and teachers were looking at my paper. Delay was never so sweet.

Yet, by second period, the fruits of my labor had been removed. Those little initials, passed over by Mr. Wilson, were near the root of the problem. Though Doc might agree with my position, duty forced his hand. If he let thirty notices stay up now, by next month the halls would be completely papered over.

OF SHREWS AND CYCLISTS

Even so, it appears that my message reached more people than I had hoped. Someone had scrawled at the bottom of one leaflet: "If your to chicken to sign your name why write this?" I feel critics who spell like that deserve no rebuttal. Several teachers made favorable remarks—how they guessed my identity might be a question that Mr. Wilson could shed some light on.

But there was more to the Moratorium story. Sixth period, my Social Studies class trooped down to the LGIC to hear a debate on the subject of the war. The school administration, seeking to appease the radicals and head them off, had set aside the Fifteenth as a day for a "panel discussion" of the war each period. A lot of thanks they got for their efforts. I was also somewhat wary of the debate itself—we might hear anything from black-armbanded Maoists to the Christian Anti-Communist Crusade. The teacher sitting across the aisle from me had an armband; it took nearly ten minutes to quiet the room down. I wondered rather vaguely if this was the way they did things in the UN.

Finally, the debate began. The conservatives were represented by Stevenson and Smith, meticulous in their suits and ties—it was a good sign. Opposing them were two sophomore girls. Behind the debaters, a monstrous portrait glared over their shoulders, executed by some student. The subject of the painting looked like a cross between Mahatma Gandhi and Ho Chi Minh.

The arguments flew back and forth. I was impressed by the good taste that the debaters were exercising. Of course, the Left spouted off its usual quota of gaffes, viz. that American terrorism is like Nazi Germany. But to this, Smith gamely responded that the parallel with the Nazis was very good—when applied to North Vietnam. The debate was dominated by the conservatives, not only because their position was superior, which went without saying, but because they expressed it with more skill. At this point, questions from the floor were solicited.

All during the liberal exposition, I had been taking notes, and now I was faced with a dilemma. There was such a wealth of logical errors at which to fire away that I was hard pressed to pick. But finally, I made my choice. My hand was raised. A friend behind me whispered: "Make it good, Rick."

The last question had been from an antiwar student, some shrew in the front row had vented her spite on Tom Smith. I hoped to profit by contrast. Rising slowly from my seat, trying to look for all the world like Wm. F. Buckley, Jr. and hoping that my red and yellow turtleneck sweater did not detract from that impression, I spoke.

"We have heard of corruption and delays in the elections in South Vietnam," I addressed the antiwar party, "do you have any statistics on the free and open elections that have been held in North Vietnam?"

I sat down, gloating over my wit—and heaven save us all, the sophomores proceeded to prate on about elections in South Vietnam! My irony had been completely over their heads! It was left to Tom Smith to restate my point when he replied to their answer. My golden opportunity had been lost because the Diet of Worms had been taking stupid-pills! The debate meandered to its conclusion.

But there is one more incident to relate, perhaps more important than Tom Smith or Martin Luther II or anything that I have seen before.

It was after school; I was walking home. First, however, I decided to make a detour to the front lawn where the names of the American war dead were read. I had left school somewhat late; not many people were there. The sign announcing that you were looking at Irondequoit High School had been covered by Moratorium posters. A "concerned student" read the list, a hood sat at his feet (anything to get out of school). Before them on the grass were perhaps half a dozen people, all girls. A few cyclists gaped in curiosity from the sidewalk.

BLASPHEMY

I had a few nasty thoughts about pasting my last paper to the reader's nose. But it did not seem to be worth the trouble. The names came on.

"Foster, John . . ."

And this was the way of it, I reflected—the Left, shedding its tears when thoughts were needed, unwittingly aiding those very dictators who had not a trace of tears in them.

"Foster, William . . ."

Drearily the reading proceeded. It would make as much sense, I thought, to read the names in a fifty-year-old telephone book—they, too, were all dead.

"Fowler, David . . ."

At once, I was shocked out of my reverie. The reader had stumbled over a name. I looked at him closely. He kept on going. The hood, the girls—none of them had noticed. And suddenly, I saw the truth of it all. He had stumbled over a name and gone right on. I had been wrong all along. The reader, the students, the Left—they did not *care*, how could they care? David Fowler was only a name to them, a word on paper, a stop to be pulled in the organ of human emotions, a pawn in the ideological spasms of their minds. If only they realized the magnitude of that list they were reading, if only they could sense the horror of one death, much less of thousands. But they could not sense this; the reading of the names, the whole Moratorium itself was only a selfish act, a forum from which they could announce their existence to the world. Those names being read, the whole idea of names being read—it was not tragedy, it was blasphemy. The Left had become like the insensate brutes it had defended for so long.

I have no more to say. The Moratorium is over. If it comes again in April, I shall be strongly tempted to ignore it.

The Ninety-Five Theses of the Vietnam War

I PROTEST against the leaflet passed out yesterday as being an emotional and grotesque distortion of the truth.

I PROTEST against the use of such words as "leafletting."

I PROTEST against that leaflet as a thinly veiled invitation to students to boycott school on Moratorium Day.

I PROTEST against the idea that the authors of that leaflet could educate anybody about anything, much less "educate the community and local industry" on the subject of the war in Vietnam.

I PROTEST against the idea that a student, because of his conscience, may refuse to attend school. This idea is conducive to hypocrisy and is plainly illegal.

I PROTEST against the entire Moratorium itself, which will only give moral aid and comfort to the enemies of South Vietnam.

I PROTEST against the idea that only a person who opposes the war in Vietnam may have a conscience.

I PROTEST against those who would withdraw from Vietnam, leaving it open to Communist subjugation.

I PROTEST against the use of the word "dove" to describe the anti-war members of the left-wing. A much more accurate symbol would be the bluejay, a bird which is both raucous and shrill.

I PROTEST against the use of the word "liberal" to describe the left-wing, because this word implies a degree of tolerance and broad-mindedness, while in reality, the Left is often characterized by the most repugnant self-righteousness.

I PROTEST against the rhetoric of the Left in which all distinctions are blurred, all reason done away with and which covers the issues in a cloud of emotion which makes sane analysis impossible.

FINALLY, I PROTEST against those who say that coexistence with Communism is either possible or desirable.

BECAUSE Communism is, of its very nature, a militant and aggressive faith

AND even in its most ideal form, Communism is based on the subordination of the individual to the State, an idea which is repulsive to all free men.

If I can be shown, by logic and reasoning, that my statements are false, I will recant. Until then, I can not—I will not recant. *Here I stand.*

MARTIN LUTHER II

White Rabbit

One pill makes you larger and one pill makes you small,
And the ones that Mother gives you don't do anything at all,
Go ask Alice when she's ten feet tall.

And if you go chasing rabbits and you know you're going to fall,
Tell them all who got silken colored hair has given you the call,
Call Alice when she was just-small.

When the men on the chess-board get up and tell you where to go,
And you'll just have some kind of mushroom and your mind is moving low,
Go ask Alice—I think she'll know—

When the logic and proportion have fallen so I'll be dead,
And the white knight is talking backwards and the red queens are ahead,
Remember what the door-mouse said;
"Heed your head—heed your head."

THREE

THE DRUG PROBLEM

The appropriateness of including in this volume a chapter on drug use is debatable. While turning on to drugs is certainly an all too common pattern followed by alienated adolescents, it represents a problem quite different from the several dimensions of activist behavior discussed elsewhere in Part Two. Clearly, drug use does not appear to represent the same kind of problem as underground newspapers, dress codes, or riots. From one perspective, however, drug use can be seen as a type of adolescent response to the larger problems of society and to the individual's own internal stresses and strains.

It might be useful to think of potential student responses to stress as falling along a continuum—from extrapunitive to intropunitive. In extrapunitive responses the adolescent lashes out at the offending agent by some actual, physical, protest, e.g., he defies the authorities with respect to dress, develops an underground newspaper, riots, etc. Intropunitive responders turn inward with their problems—they drop out physically, i.e., leave the school prior to graduation, or psychologically, i.e., withdraw in a neurotic way, turn on to drugs, etc. Those in the latter category are well described by the catch phrase of the drug set: "Tune in, turn on, drop out."

Sections on alcohol and tobacco might well have been included. Drug use, however, has been more closely tied to the issues of dissent running throughout the present volume. Within the context of drug use, Irving Philips has captured well the concerns of youth:

> Today youth sees in our society horror and growing impotence; a war and
> no way to stop it, a black rebellion and no way to join it; and institutions
> of reform that are dormant and have no ideology or direction. For some,
> the only alternative to participating in this society is complete disengage-
> ment and withdrawal.[1]

How widespread is drug use among adolescents? How grave is the problem? The magnitude and depth of drug use have been well described in a variety of documents and reports. Witness these facts and observations:

[1] Irving Philips, "An Adolescent Message: Happenings on the Hip Scene," *Mental Hygiene*, 52 (July, 1968): 337.

—20 to 40 percent of high school and college students have tried marijuana at least once, according to Dr. Stanley Jolles, former director of the National Institute of Mental Health.

—counselors in one school district put drug abuse among their students at 75 percent, among whom an estimated one third are habitual users.

—a marijuana sale took place in a classroom "before the astonished sixth grade classroom teacher."[2]

—one California community has hired a full-time narcotics-education officer and set up a twenty-four hour hot-line which parents or children can use to call for assistance.[3]

—from 1960 to 1967, the arrests of youth under eighteen for narcotic drug law violations rose 778.3 percent.[4]

—heroin was responsible for the deaths of 224 teenagers in New York City during 1969; 20 were below the age of fifteen.[5]

—a survey of 11,356 pupils in grades 6, 8, 10, and 12 in one Western community revealed that 0.3 percent of the sixth graders used marijuana but that 10 percent had friends who used marijuana, and 12.5 percent had friends who used other drugs.[6]

Drug use and drug abuse are emotional topics and in most discussions needed distinctions between use and abuse are not drawn. This failure to differentiate between the terms helps to explain the cry of hypocrisy raised by adolescents when presented with information about drug use. Many adolescents are quick to point out that tobacco and alcohol are used much more extensively than the "mind drugs" and consequently any discussion of drug use should include these agents.

A clear distinction has been made between the use and abuse of alcohol. Abuse has been defined as "a pattern of use which interferes with the psychological, social, academic, or vocational functioning of a given individual." With respect to other drugs, however, abuse is legally defined as "any use of a non-medically approved drug, of a medically approved drug for non-medically approved purposes."[7]

Justification for legally defining abuse as stated above centers around the harmful effects of the drugs. One apparent problem, and the basis upon which adolescents and others see a credibility gap, is the failure to classify categorically

---

[2] Editorial, *Phi Delta Kappan,* 50 (December, 1968): 213.

[3] *Ibid.*

[4] Institute for Development of Educational Activities, Inc., *High School Students and Drugs* (Dayton, Ohio: Institute for Development of Educational Activities, Inc. [n.d.]), p. 14.

[5] *New York Times Supplement,* March 6, 1970.

[6] Glenn Leach, "Drug Abuse is Hitting Younger Children," *Instructor,* 79 (August, 1969): 60-61.

[7] Helen H. Nowlis, "Student Drug Use," Invited Address, Div. 7, Annual Meeting of the American Psychological Association, Washington, D.C., September 2, 1969. EDRS Document ED 035 025/CG004738.

alcohol and tobacco with the mind drugs, and the failure, based upon their own personal experiences, to suffer the harmful effects said to be a consequence of certain drugs—particularly marijuana. Unfortunately, we know little about the long term effects of marijuana because of its short history of prolonged use in this country. Research in India and Egypt, however, does suggest some physical debilitation associated with long-term use.[8] Obviously this is an area needing considerable further investigation.

There is some evidence to suggest that experimentation and even addiction are occurring at younger ages than has been true in the past. (Indeed, one of the editor's children, now in the second grade, has already been exposed to drug education.) One report has alleged that Cub Scouts in one community can "discuss the pros and cons of pot with savvy."[9] When this information is considered in light of the number of drug induced deaths of youths under fifteen, the basis for concern is understandable.

Easy generalizations about the causes and effects of drugs abuse are not possible. There simply are too many complex factors operating in individual circumstances, for as Helen Nowlis writes:

> If one wants to understand drug effect and drug use one must look, not solely at the pharmacological agent, but at the person who chooses to use drugs, how much he uses, when and where and how, and what he expects, wants, or believes will result from that use."[10]

The diversity among drug users is aptly illustrated by excerpts from two case histories.

Case I

> I have used all types of drugs from hash, pot, and acid to hard stuff. It's all a bad scene. The people who push it don't use it because they know it's bad stuff. All you are doing is ruining your life and letting people make money through you . . .
>
> "Man if you're on the stuff please—for your sake get off it. If you can't fight it by yourself, then get help from someone. It may be rough trying to straighten yourself out, but it's never too late. Man at least try . . . you don't know me but, I needed help and someone helped me.
>
> "If someone offers drugs, be more of a man than I was and say no. Learn from my mistakes. I don't want anyone to go through the hell I went through and am still going through."[11]

---

[8] William H. McGlothlin, "Marijuana," in Margaret O. Hyde, ed., *Mind Drugs* (New York: Pocket Books, 1969), pp. 19-40.
[9] Editorial, *Phi Delta Kappan*, 50 (December, 1968): 213.
[10] Nowlis, "Student Drug Use," p. 7.
[11] Riverside [California] *Press*, November 11, 1970.

Case II

. . . I was in the sixth grade and 10 years old when my experience with drugs began. My first exposure was with tranquilizers and sleeping pills in the bathroom of my home. I didn't know what they were and I really don't know why I did it, but I took them to my room and took four of them.

In about an hour or so I got a . . . I don't know if it was physical or mental . . . but I got a lift from them. I felt good. I just felt good. I felt like I could do things I could never have done before . . . I had a powerful command over things. So I thought that if I felt that good, another pill would make me feel better. Anyhow, within a few days all 20 pills were gone except two. I saved two of them and showed them to a friend of mine who said he could get me more. He said they were sleeping pills or tranquilizers. That was the beginning and I went on the search for more.[12]

Excerpts from Case I represent part of the content of a suicide note left by a distraught user who felt his life had been ruined by drug use. His addition apparently was encouraged by peers and others outside the home.

Case II was successfully rehabilitated. In contrast to that of the first case, Case II's experience with drugs began at home. In both instances we have no information about personality makeup, home situations, or other internal and external factors which may have predisposed the youths to drugs. As suggested above, it is entirely likely that there was no one predisposing factor or set of factors which led to drug use.

There apparently is little reliable information about personality patterns of drug users as opposed to non-users. Take the case of a marijuana user, for example. With respect to heavy users, W. H. McGlothlin's summary of the research suggests that the user is more introverted and tends to be more present oriented than future oriented. Further, "the heavy user drifts along with little concern for adjustment to anything other than his immediate needs and impulses. The individual pothead tends to use primitive, magical thinking as opposed to rationality or objective, factually determined thinking."[13] A definition of "heavy user" is missing. Missing too is information about the occasional user or about patterns of use. Obviously there is much to be known. Where shall we begin? Given the current state of our knowledge about drug use and drug abuse, what information is critical for the educator? There is widespread agreement that factual information about drugs and their effects is a *sine qua non* of a program of education.

The first article of the present chapter, "Drugs of Abuse and Their Effects," presents factual information on drugs, including, particularly, what is currently known about their effects on the human organism. There is general agreement

---

[12] Institute for Development of Educational Activities, Inc., *High School Students and Drugs*, p. 14.
[13] McGlothlin, "Marijuana," p. 30.

that factual information devoid of emotionalism is needed most at this time. Any discussion of drug use and abuse should begin from a factual base.

The second paper, "Marijuana: Three Viewpoints," supports what many already know or suspect—that perceptions of the problems of marijuana use vary. Included are brief looks at drug use as seen by a parent, student, and narcotics agent.

Who uses drugs and why? These are questions for which there are no hard and fast answers. While there is considerable clinical information about drug use and their effects, empirical and data oriented research are in short supply. These are concerns of the article by Dr. Simon Auster, "Some Observations on Adolescent Drug Use." Dr. Auster makes clear early the fact that adolescent drug users are not a homogeneous group. Four groups of adolescent drug users are delineated, and considerations in planning drug education programs are briefly highlighted.

Nowlis has written similarly about subcategories of drug users:

> There is no doubt that some young people use drugs to escape from pressure, from anxiety, from impulses which threaten them, from the stresses and strains of growing up. There is also no doubt that some people who are ill use drugs. But unless one defines doing anything that is not socially approved as illness, the great majority of young people who use drugs illegally are not ill and are not in need of psychiatric treatment. Many use them because they think it is fun. Many try them out of curiosity. Many use marijuana much as we use alcohol to facilitate social interaction. Some use them as occasional respite from the pressures of increasing academic demands.[14]

A glossary of terms frequently used in the drug culture is presented in the next article. Information about the various terms and language of drug users is useful to teachers, counselors, administrators and other school personnel having direct contact with adolescents. Those who would communicate with and understand adolescents would do well to familiarize themselves with this terminology. As will be apparent, the listing is not exhaustive. Undoubtedly, there are many other terms and local variants for many of the words given.

In the final article, David Lewis outlines a program of drug education. While this program is intuitively sound, there is little research which would establish or refute the validity of any specific drug education program. For the reader whose interest in the subject extends beyond the data presented here, a selective list of additional sources follows this headnote.

[14] Nowlis, "Student Drug Use," p. 8.

BIBLIOGRAPHY ON THE DRUG PROBLEM

Ackerly, W. C. and Gibson, G. "Lighter Fluid Sniffing." *American Journal of Psychiatry,* 120 (May, 1964): 1056.

Allen, E. J. *Merchants of Menace.* Springfield, Ill.: Charles C Thomas, 1961.

Anslinger, Harry J. and Gregory, J. D. *The Protectors.* New York: Farrar, Straus and Co., 1964.

Anslinger, H. J. and Oursler, W. C. *The Murders.* New York: Farrar, Straus, 1961.

Ausubel, David P. *Drug Addiction: Physiological, Psychological and Social Aspects.* New York: Random House, 1958.

Barber, B. *Drugs and Society.* New York: Russell Sage Foundation, 1967.

Barbiturates as Addicting Drugs. Public Health Service Publication, No. 545 (revised June, 1964).

Barron, F. et al. "The Hallucinogenic Drugs." *Scientific American,* 210 (April, 1964): pp. 24, 29-37.

Blum, R. H. et al. *Society and Drugs,* Vol. I. San Francisco: Jossey-Bass, 1969.

————. *Students and Drugs.* San Francisco: Jossey-Bass, 1969.

————. *Utopiates: The Use and Users of LSD-25.* New York: Atherton Press, 1964.

Board of Education of the City of New York. *Teenage Narcotics Addiction— Abuse of Chemical Products.* Curriculum Bulletin 1963-64, Series No. 12.

Buckwalter, J. A. *Merchants of Misery.* Mountain View, Calif.: Pacific Press Publishing Co., 1956.

Casriel, Daniel H. *So Fair a House: The Story of Synanon.* Englewood Cliffs, N.J.: Prentice-Hall, 1963.

Chapman, Kenneth, M.D. *The Addict and the Community.* Washington, D.C.: U.S. Department of Health, Education and Welfare, 1957.

Chein, I. et al. *The Road to H.* New York: Basic Books, 1964.

Cohen, S. "A Classification of LSD Complications." *Psychosomatics* (May-June, 1966): pp. 182-186.

Cohen, S. *The Beyond Within: The LSD Story.* New York: Atheneum, 1964.

Dalrymple, W., "A Doctor Speaks of Marijuana and Other 'Drugs'." *Journal of American Colleges Health Association,* February, 1966, p. 218.

Demos, G., Shainline, J., and Thomas, W. *Drug Abuse and You.* New York: Chronicle Guidance Publications, 1968.

DeRopp, R. S. *Drugs and the Minds.* New York: St. Martin's Press, 1957. (Also in paperback, Evergreen E218, 1960.)

The Drug Takers. New York: Time-Life Books, 1964.

Eddy, Norman, *Different Approaches to Drug Addiction.* New York: Fordham University Press, 1959.

Eddy, N. B. et al. "Drug Dependence: Its Significance and Characteristics." *Bulletin, World Health Organization,* 32 (1965): 721.

Essig, C. F. "Addiction to Nonbarbiturate Sedative and Tranquilizing Drugs." *Clinical Pharmacology and Therapy,* 5 (May-June, 1964): 334.

Evin, D., ed. *The Drug Experience.* New York: Arion Press, 1961.

Fort, J. "The Problem of Barbiturates in the USA." *Narcotics,* January-March, 1964, pp. 17-35.

Goldstein, Richard. *1 in 7.* New York: Walker, 1966.

Harney, Malachi L. *Narcotics and Crime.* Springfield, Ill.: Department of Public Safety, Division of Narcotics Control, 1960.

Hoffer, A. "D-lysergic Acid Diethylamide (LSD), A Review of Its Present Status." *Clinical Pharmacology Therapy,* March-April, 1965, p. 183.

Howe, Hubert Shattuck. *Narcotics and Youth.* West Orange, N.J.: Brook Foundation, 1953. (Address: 51 Lakeside Avenue, West Orange, N.J.)

Kolb, Lawrence. *Drug Addiction as a Medical Problem.* Springfield, Ill.: Thomas Press, 1962.

Laurie, Peter. *Drugs.* Baltimore: Penguin Books, 1967.

Lawton, J. J., and Malmquist, C. P. "Gasoline Addiction in Children." *Psychiatric Quarterly,* 35 (July, 1961): 335.

Lerner, Jeremy. *The Addict in the Street.* New York: Grove Press, 1964.

Lindesmith, Alfred R. *The Addict and the Law.* Bloomington, Ind.: Indiana University Press, 1965.

Louria, Donald. *Nightmare Drugs.* New York: Pocket Books, 1966.

Lowen, Alexander. *The Betrayal of the Body.* New York: MacMillan, 1966.

Lowry, James, M.D. *Hospital Treatment of the Narcotic Addict.* Washington, D.C.: U.S. Department of Health, Education and Welfare, 1956.

Maurer, David W., and Vogel, Victor H. *Narcotics and Narcotic Addiction.* 2d ed. Springfield, Ill.: Charles C Thomas, 1962.

Mayor's Committee on Marijuana. *The Marijuana Problem in the City of New York: Sociological, Medical, Psychological and Pharmacological Studies.* Lancaster, Pa.: Jacques Cattel Press, 1964.

McGlothin, W. H. "Hallucinogenic Drugs: A Perspective." *Psychedelic Review,* no. 6, 1965.

McGlothlin, W. H., and Cohen, S. "The Use of Hallucinogenic Drugs Among College Students." *American Journal of Psychiatry,* 122 (November, 1965): pp. 572-574.

Mills, J. "Drug Addiction," *Life,* February 26, March 5, 1965.

Mills, James. *Panic in Needle Park.* New York: Farrar, Straus and Giroux, 1966.

Murtagh, John M., and Harris, Sara. *Who Live in Shadow.* New York: McGraw-Hill, 1959.

Narcotics Education, Inc. *Really Living.* Washington, D.C.: Narcotics Education, Inc., 1960.

New Jersey Drug Study Commission. *Interim Report 1965.* Trenton, N.J.: New Jersey Drug Study Commission.

New York City Board of Education. *What Secondary Schools Can Do About Teen-Age Narcotics Addiction.* New York: New York City Board of Education, 1956-57.

New York Police Department. *The Scourge of Narcotics.* New York: The Department, 1958.

Pharmaceutical Manufacturers Association. *Medicinal Narcotics.* Washington, D.C.: Pharmaceutical Manufacturers Association, 1965.

The President's Advisory Commission on Narcotic Drug Abuse. *Final Report.* Washington, D.C.: Government Printing Office, 1963.

Ross, Barney, and Abramson, Martin. *No Man Stands Alone: The True Story of Barney Ross.* Philadelphia: Lippincott, 1957.

Saltzman, Jules. *What We Can Do About Drug Abuse.* New York: Public Affairs Committee, 1966.

Schmidt, J. E. *Narcotics, Lingo and Lore.* Springfield, Ill.: Charles C Thomas, 1959.

Seevers, M. H. "Abuse of Barbiturates and Amphetamines." *Postgraduate Medical Journal,* January, 1965, pp. 45-51.

Shepard, Jack. "I Popped in the Pill. I'm Off." *Look,* 31 (August 23, 1967), pp. 22-23.

Smith, D. R. Drug Intoxication: Barbiturates and Tranquilizers." *Applied Therapy,* March, 1964, pp. 219-222.

Smith, Justin E. "Drug Habit." *World Book Encyclopedia.* 1961. Vol. IV. "Narcotic." World Book Encyclopedia. 1961. Vol. XIII.

Solomon, David, ed. *LSD: The Consciousness Expanding Drug.* New York: G. P. Putnam's, 1964.

————. *The Marijuana Papers.* Indianapolis: Bobbs-Merrill, 1966.

The United Nations and Narcotic Drugs. New York: United Nations Office of Public Information [n.d.].

U.S. Department of Health, Education, and Welfare. Food and Drug Administration. *First Facts about Drugs.* Washington, D.C.: Government Printing Office, 1963.

U.S. Department of Health, Education, and Welfare. Food and Drug Administration. *Student Reference Sheet: Hallucinogenic Drugs.* Washington, D.C.: Government Printing Office, 1965.

U.S. Department of Health, Education, and Welfare. Vocational Rehabilitation Administration. *Rehabilitating the Narcotic Addict.* Washington, D.C.: Government Printing Office, 1967.

U.S. Department of Health, Education, and Welfare. *Narcotic Drug Addiction.* Mental Health Monograph 2, Public Health Service Publication No. 1021. Washington, D.C.: Government Printing Office, 1963.

U.S. Department of Health, Education, and Welfare. *What to Know About Drug Addiction,* by Harris Isbell. Public Health Service Publication No. 94, Washington, D.C.: Government Printing Office, 1958.

U.S. Interdepartmental Committee on Narcotics. *Report to the President.* Washington, D.C.: Government Printing Office, 1956.

U.S. Treasury Department. Bureau of Narcotics. *Prevention and Control of Narcotics Addiction.* Washington, D.C.: Government Printing Office, 1962.

U.S. Treasury Department. Bureau of Narcotics. *Living Death, The Truth About Drug Addiction.* Washington, D.C.: Government Printing Office, 1956.

U.S. Treasury Department. Bureau of Narcotics. *Prevention and Control of Drug Addiction.* Washington, D.C.: Government Printing Office, 1960.

Vogel, Victor H., and Vogel, Virginia E. *Facts About Narcotics and Other Dangerous Drugs."* Chicago, Ill.: Science Research Associates, 1967.

————. *Facts About Narcotics.* Chicago, Ill.: Science Research Associates, 1960.

Wakefield, Dan. *The Addict.* New York: Fawcett, 1963.

Wilkerson, David. *The Cross and the Switchblade.* New York: Pyramid Publications, 1970.

Williamson, Henry. *Hustler! The Autobiography of a Thief.* New York: Doubleday, 1965.

Wilner, D., and Kassebaum, G. *Narcotics.* New York: McGraw-Hill, 1965.

Winick, Charles. *The Narcotic Addiction Problem.* New York: The American Social Health Association [n.d.].

World Health Organization. Expert Committee on Addiction-Producing Drugs, 13th Report. 1964.

Yablonsky, Lewis. *The Tunnel Back.* New York: Macmillan and Co., 1965.

DRUGS OF ABUSE AND THEIR EFFECTS

PREPARED BY SMITH KLINE AND FRENCH LABORATORIES AND THE NATIONAL
EDUCATION ASSOCIATION

Substances with abuse potential range from simple kitchen spices through common flowers and weeds to highly sophisticated drugs. All these substances may be divided into five categories: 1) narcotics, 2) sedatives, 3) tranquilizers, 4) stimulants, and 5) hallucinogens.

Medically defined, narcotics are drugs which produce insensibility or stupor due to their depressant effect on the central nervous system. Included in this definition are opium, opium derivatives (morphine, codeine, heroin) and syn-

From *Drug Awareness,* Richard E. Horman and Allen M. Fox, eds. (New York: Avon Books, 1970), pp. 23-43. Reprinted with the permission of the senior editor and Smith Kline and French Laboratories.

thetic opiates (meperidine, methadone). As regulated by Federal narcotic laws, however, the term "narcotics" also embraces the coca leaf and its derivative, cocaine. Pharmacologically, this drug is a stimulant, not a depressant, but for law enforcement purposes it is considered a narcotic. All other drugs susceptible to abuse are non-narcotics.*

Whatever their classification, most of these drugs have important legitimate applications. Narcotic, sedative, tranquilizing and stimulant drugs are essential to the practice of modern medicine. Hallucinogens are used in medical research. To the abuser, though, these same medically useful drugs have a compelling attribute: they affect the nervous system, producing a change in his emotional responses or reactions. The abuser may feel intoxicated, relaxed, happy or detached from a world that is painful and unacceptable to him.

With repeated use, many drugs cause *physical dependence*. This is an adaptation whereby the body learns to live with the drug, tolerates ever-increasing doses, and reacts with certain withdrawal symptoms when deprived of it. The total reaction to deprivation is known clinically as an abstinence syndrome. The symptoms that appear depend on the amount and kind of drug used. Withdrawal symptoms disappear as the body once again adjusts to being without the drug— or if the drug is reintroduced.

With many drugs, the chronic user finds he must constantly increase the dose in order to obtain an effect equal to that from the initial dose. This phenomenon, called *tolerance*, represents the body's ability to adapt to the presence of a foreign substance. Tolerance does not develop for all drugs or in all individuals; but with drugs such as morphine, addicts have been known to build up great tolerance very quickly. It is interesting to note, however, that tolerance does not develop for all the possible effects of a given drug. For example, tolerance develops to the euphoric-like effects of heroin, but only slightly to the constricting effects on the pupil of the eye. *Complete* tolerance may not develop to a drug's toxic effects; accordingly, no matter how high his tolerance, an addict may still administer a lethal dose to himself. Tolerance can occur without physical dependence.

A more important factor in keeping the abuser enslaved by his habit is the *psychic* or *psychological dependence* present in most cases of drug abuse. Psychic dependence is an emotional or mental adaptation to the effects of the drug. The abuser not only likes the feeling from the drug and wants to reexperience it—he feels he cannot function normally without the drug. It enables him to escape from reality—from his problems and frustrations. The drug and its effects seem to provide the answer to everything, including disenchantment and boredom. With the drug, all seems well. It is the *psychological* factor which

This article first appeared as chapter 2 of the book entitled *Drug Abuse: escape to nowhere*, 1967.

* This includes marijuana. Popularly regarded as a narcotic drug, it is not so considered either medically or under law. The confusion, in part, stems from the fact that the drug is controlled by the Federal Bureau of Narcotics.

causes an addict who has been withdrawn from his physical dependence to return to drug abuse.

All substances with abuse potential can produce changes in behavior, particularly when large amounts are improperly used. The abuser may be withdrawn and solitary, or sociable and talkative. He may be easily moved to tears or laughter. He may be quick to argue or believe that "someone is out to get him." These changes in behavior may be harmless or may constitute a danger to both the abuser and society. Much of the public concern about drug abuse stems from widely publicized changes in behavior accompanying the use of drugs.

Three frequently confused terms encountered in drug abuse discussions are "addiction," "habituation" and "drug dependence." *Addiction* has been defined as a state of periodic or chronic intoxication produced by the repeated consumption of a drug and involves tolerance, psychological dependence, usually physical dependence, an overwhelming compulsion to continue using the drug, and detrimental effects on both the individual and society. *Habituation* has been defined as a condition, resulting from the repeated consumption of a drug, which involves little or no evidence of tolerance, some psychological dependence, no physical dependence, and a desire (but not a compulsion) to continue taking the drug for the feeling of well-being that it engenders. Detrimental effects, if any, are primarily on the individual.

Through the years, the terms addiction and habituation have frequently been used interchangeably — and erroneously so, with the result that discussions of drug abuse have been fraught with semantic difficulties. Accordingly, the World Health Organization (WHO) recently recommended that these terms be replaced by a single and more general term—"drug dependence." *Drug dependence* is described as "a state arising from repeated administration of a drug on a periodic or continuous basis." Since many different kinds of drugs can be involved in drug dependence, the term is further qualified in accordance with the particular drug being used: Examples: "drug dependence of the morphine type," "drug dependence of the barbiturate type."

Although it was hoped that the newer terminology involving "drug dependence" and its various qualifiers would eventually replace the older terms of "addiction" and "habituation," from a practical standpoint this is not possible. The language of laws (international, national and local) which governs drugs subject to abuse encompasses the terms "addiction" and "habituation." As it would be difficult to set these laws aside, it appears that all three terms will become a part of drug abuse terminology, with "drug dependence" being favored by medically oriented groups and "addiction" and "habituation" being favored in legislative and law enforcement circles.

MORPHINE-LIKE NARCOTICS (OPIATES)

Medical Use.   Natural and synthetic morphine-like drugs are the most effective pain relievers in existence and are among the most valuable drugs available to the physician. They are widely used for short-term acute pain resulting from surgery, fractures, burns, etc., and in the latter stages of terminal illnesses such as cancer. Morphine is the standard of pain relief by which other narcotic analgesics are evaluated.

The depressant effect of opiates produces drowsiness, sleep and a reduction in physical activity. Side effects can include nausea and vomiting, constipation, itching, flushing, constriction of pupils and respiratory depression.

Manufacture and distribution of medicinal opiates are stringently controlled by the Federal government through laws designed to keep these products available only for legitimate medical use. One aspect of the controls is that those who distribute these products are registered with Federal authorities and must comply with specific record-keeping and drug security requirements.

Abuse. The appeal of morphine-like drugs lies in their ability to reduce sensitivity to both psychological and physical stimuli and to produce a sense of euphoria. These drugs dull fear, tension or anxiety. Under the influence of morphine-like narcotics, the addict is usually lethargic and indifferent to his environment and personal situation. For example, a pregnant addict will usually continue drug abuse despite the fact that her baby will likewise be addicted—and probably die shortly after birth unless medical treatment is undertaken at once.

The price tag on the abuse of these drugs is high. Chronic use may lead to both physical and psychological dependence. Psychological dependence is the more serious of the two, since it is still operative after drug use has been discontinued. With chronic use, tolerance develops and ever-increasing doses are required in order to achieve a desired effect. As the need for the drug increases, the addict's activities become increasingly drug-centered. When drug supplies are cut off, characteristic withdrawal symptoms may develop.

Symptoms of withdrawal from narcotic analgesics include:

Nervousness, anxiety, sleeplessness.

Yawning, running eyes and nose, sweating.

Enlargement of the pupils, "gooseflesh," muscle twitching.

Severe aches of back and legs, hot and cold flashes.

Vomiting and diarrhea.

Increase in breathing rate, blood pressure and temperature.

A feeling of desperation and an obsessional desire to secure a "fix."

The intensity of withdrawal symptoms varies with the degree of physical dependence. This, in turn, is related to the amount of drug customarily used. Typically, the onset of symptoms occurs about 8-12 hours after the last close. Thereafter, symptoms increase in intensity, reach a peak between 36-72 hours, and then gradually diminish over the next 5-10 days. However, weakness, insomnia, nervousness, and muscle aches and pains may persist for several weeks. In extreme cases, death may result.

Because increasing pressure by law enforcement authorities has made traffic in heroin more difficult, "street" supplies have tended to contain increasingly low percentages of active ingredient. (The heroin content of a "bag" now ranges between 3 and 10%. Pure heroin is "cut"—diluted—with milk sugar.) As a consequence, many present-day narcotic addicts experience relatively mild withdrawal symptoms unless they are consuming many bags per day. On the other hand, narcotic addicts can die from overdosage when the supplies they buy in the "street" contain more than the customary low percentage of heroin. (Addict deaths from over-dosage at a rate of one a day have been reported in New York City.)

EXEMPT NARCOTIC PREPARATIONS

Under Federal law, some preparations containing small amounts of narcotics are exempt from the prescription requirement. The reason for their exemption lies in the fact that very large quantities of such preparations would have to be consumed regularly for a considerable time to produce significant dependence. These products include certain cough medicines and paregoric remedies which may be sold in pharmacies without a doctor's prescription. Pharmacists selling exempt preparations must have a Federal narcotics stamp.

Paregoric: *Medical Use.* Paregoric, a liquid preparation containing an extract of opium, is used to counteract diarrhea and to relieve abdominal pain.

Cough Syrup: *Medical Use.* Exempt cough formulas which contain codeine are used to combat the symptoms of respiratory disorders. While the chief use of codeine is for pain relief, it is also an effective cough suppressant when taken in small doses.

Abuse. Although these preparations are reasonably safe and free of addiction liability when used as directed, they can be abused. Addicts will sometimes turn to paregoric or cough syrups—as well as other drugs—when heroin is in short supply. (Very large quantities of these exempt preparations are consumed by addicts when abused as inferior substitutes for more potent drugs.)

In some areas, high school students are known to abuse paregoric medicines and codeine cought remedies. Of the formulas which have been abused, a number have a high alcohol content—which very probably has much to do with their popularity. (The alcohol content in some of these products is as high as 40%.)

DEPRESSANTS (SEDATIVES)

This group includes a variety of old and new drugs which have a depressant effect on the nervous system. Within this group, the most commonly abused products are the barbiturates. The "street" term for this type of product is "goof-ball."

Medical Use.   The first barbituric acid derivative, barbital, was introduced to medicine shortly after the turn of the century. Since that time, over 2,500 barbiturates have been synthesized. Today, only about 30 are widely used medically. The barbiturates are among the most versatile depressant drugs available. They are used for epilepsy, high blood pressure, insomnia and in the treatment and diagnosis of mental disorders. They are used before and during surgery. Alone or in combination with other drugs, they are prescribed for almost every kind of illness or special situation requiring sedation. Used under medical supervision, barbiturates are impressively safe and effective.

Abuse.   The abuser takes barbiturates orally, intravenously or rectally. Although barbiturate intoxication closely resembles alcoholic intoxication, barbiturate abuse is far more dangerous than alcohol abuse or even narcotic abuse. Unintentional overdosage can easily occur. Convulsions, which may follow withdrawal, can be fatal. Overindulgence in alcohol before barbiturate ingestion may result in fatal depression of respiratory and cardiovascular systems.

The barbiturate abuser exhibits slurred speech and staggering gait. His reactions are sluggish. He is emotionally erratic and may be easily moved to tears or laughter. Frequently, he is irritable and antagonistic. Sometimes, he has impressions of euphoria. Because he is prone to stumble or drop objects, he often is bruised and has cigarette burns.

Chronic misuse of barbiturates is accompanied by the development of tolerance and both psychological and physical dependence. Physical dependence appears to develop only with continued use of doses much greater than those customarily used in the practice of medicine. In a physically dependent barbiturate abuser, abrupt withdrawal is extremely dangerous. Withdrawal from the drug should *always* be supervised by a physician.

In withdrawal, during the first 8-12 hours after the last dose, the barbiturate abuser who has become physically dependent appears to improve. After this, there are signs of increasing nervousness, headache, anxiety, muscle twitching, tremor, weakness, insomnia, nausea and a sudden drop in blood pressure when the person stands abruptly (he often faints). These symptoms are quite severe at about 24 hours. There are changes in the electroencephalographic readings and, within 36-72 hours, convulsions resembling epileptic seizures may develop. Such convulsions occasionally occur as early as the sixteenth hour of withdrawal or as late as the eighth day.

Convulsions, which can be fatal, are an ever-present danger with barbiturate withdrawal and distinguish barbiturate from narcotic withdrawal. (Narcotic addiction is not characterized by a failure of muscular coordination or by convulsions upon drug withdrawal.) Whether or not convulsions occur, there may be a period of mental confusion. Delirium and hallucinations similar to the delirium tremens (DT's) of alcoholism may develop. Delirium may be accompanied by an extreme agitation that contributes to exhaustion. The delirium may persist for several days followed by a long period of sleep. (Delirium may also develop early in the course of withdrawal.)

MISCELLANEOUS DEPRESSANTS

A number of nonbarbiturate depressants used medically to induce sleep and for sedation are also capable of being abused. With chronic use of high doses, tolerance, physical dependence and psychological dependence can develop. Withdrawal phenomena occur following abrupt discontinuation of drug use. Clinical symptoms and patterns of abuse resemble those observed for barbiturates.

Because of their abuse potential, several of these drugs have become subject to the regulations of the Drug Abuse Control Amendments of 1965. Glutethimide, ethchlorvynol, ethinamate and methyprylon are examples of the newer sedatives which are now controlled.

TRANQUILIZERS

The term "tranquilizer" refers to a rather large group of drugs intoduced since the early 1950's. Unlike barbiturate-type sedatives, tranquilizers can be used to counteract tension and anxiety without producing sleep or significantly impairing mental and physical function.

All tranquilizers are not alike. In general, they may be divided into two groups —"major" or "minor"—based on their usefulness in severe mental disorders (psychoses). "Major" tranquilizers are those with antipsychotic activity. These include primarily the phenothiazine and reserpine-type drugs. Reserpine also is used to treat high blood pressure. The antipsychotic tranquilizers are not known to produce physical dependence. Abuse of this type of tranquilizer is practically nonexistent.

The "minor" group of tranquilizers includes a number of chemically quite different drugs. For the most part, they are not effective in psychotic conditions. They are widely used, however, in the treatment of emotional disorders characterized by anxiety and tension. Many are useful as muscle relaxants.

Through the years, it has been found that some members of this second group of tranquilizers occasionally have been abused. The two drugs most often reported have been meprobamate and chlordiazepoxide. Chronic abuse of these drugs, involving increasingly larger daily doses, may result in the development of physical and/or psychological dependence. Symptoms during misuse and following abrupt withdrawal closely resemble those seen with barbiturates. Chronic use of high doses can result in convulsions if the drugs are suddenly withdrawn. In order to combat abuse of this category of tranquilizers, the FDA has requested more stringent controls on meprobamate, chlordiazepoxide and diazepam. To date, abuse of tranquilizers has been infrequent and has not become a "street" problem. Abuse supplies usually are obtained by having prescriptions refilled in excess of normal needs.

STIMULANTS

This group includes drugs which directly stimulate the central nervous system. The most widely known stimulant in this country is caffeine, an ingredient of coffee, tea, cola and other beverages. Since the effects of caffeine are relatively mild, its usage is socially acceptable and not an abuse problem. The synthetic stimulants such as amphetamine and other closely related drugs are more potent and can be abused. Another dangerous stimulant is cocaine.

COCAINE

Cocaine is obtained from the leaves of the coca bush found in certain South American countries. It is an odorless, white crystalline powder with a bitter taste, producing numbness of the tongue. (The word "coca" is often confused with "cacao." The two are not related. Cacao is the name of a tree from which cocoa and chocolate are derived.)

Medical Use.   Cocaine was once widely used as a local anesthetic. Its place in medicine, however, has been largely taken by newer, less toxic drugs.

The stimulant effect of cocaine results in excitability, talkativeness and a reduction in the feeling of fatigue. Cocaine may produce a sense of euphoria, a sense of increased muscular strength, anxiety, fear and hallucinations. Cocaine dilates the pupils and increases the heart-beat and blood pressure. Stimulation is followed by a period of depression. In overdosage, cocaine may so depress respiratory and heart function that death results.

Abuse.   International control measures have greatly reduced the abuse of cocaine, although the chewing of coca leaves in some South American countries is still common. Cocaine is either sniffed or injected directly into a vein. The abuse of cocaine tends to be more sporadic than the abuse of heroin. The intense stimulatory effects usually result in the abuser voluntarily seeking sedation. This need for sedation has given rise to a practice of combining a depressant drug such as heroin with a drug such as cocaine ("speedball") or alternating a drug such as cocaine with a depressant. In some persons, cocaine produces violent behavior. Cocaine does not produce physical dependence. Tolerance does not develop and abusers seldom increase their customary dose. When drug supplies are cut off, the cocaine user does not experience withdrawal symptoms, but he does feel deeply depressed and hallucinations may persist for some time. Strong psychological dependence on the drug and a desire to reexperience the intense stimulation and hallucinations cocaine produces lead to its chronic misuse.

AMPHETAMINE

Medical Use. Amphetamine has been available since the early 1930's. First used medically as a nasal vasoconstrictor in treatment of colds and hay fever, amphetamine was later found to stimulate the nervous system. This stimulating activity is the primary basis for its uses in medicine today. Amphetamine is used for narcolepsy (a disease characterized by involuntary attacks of sleep) and to counteract excessive drowsiness caused by sedative drugs. But in the main, amphetamine is used in obesity, where the drug exerts an anti-appetite effect, and to relieve mild depression such as that accompanying menopause, convalescence, grief and senility. Paradoxically, this drug tends to calm hyperactive, noisy, aggressive children, thus producing more normal behavior.

Amphetamine may produce a temporary rise in blood pressure, palpitations, dry mouth, sweating, headache, diarrhea, pallor and dilation of the pupils. Such effects are generally seen only with high doses or as occasional side effects with therapeutic doses. Amphetamine drugs seldom cause death, even in acute overdosage.

Abuse. Amphetamine is a stimulant. It increases alertness, dispels depression and superimposes excitability over feelings of fatigue. It also produces an elevation of mood and a feeling of well-being. All these are factors underlying amphetamine abuse—and explain its popular name, "pep pill."

Amphetamine usually is taken orally in the form of tablets or capsules. However, there have been reports of intravenous use in which amphetamine is dissolved in water and then injected. With this route of administration, the effects of the drug are felt almost immediately.

Most medical authorities agree that amphetamine does not produce physical dependence, and there is no characteristic abstinence syndrome upon abrupt discontinuation of drug use. Mental depression and fatigue, however, are frequently experienced after the drug has been withdrawn. Psychological dependence is common and is an important factor in continuance of and relapse to amphetamine abuse. The development of tolerance permits the use of many times the usual therapeutic dose.

An acute psychotic episode may occur with intravenous use, or a drug psychosis may develop with the chronic use of large doses. Symptoms include extreme hyperactivity, hallucinations and feelings of persecution. These bizarre mental effects usually disappear after withdrawal of the drug.

Generally, misuse is associated with milder symptoms. The abuser is talkative, excitable and restless, and experiences a "high." He suffers from insomnia, perspires profusely, has urinary frequency and exhibits a tremor of the hands.

MISCELLANEOUS STIMULANTS

There are a number of other stimulant drugs which, while not closely related to amphetamine chemically, do have similar uses and effects. (A typical drug of this type is phenmetrazine, used medically in the treatment of obesity.)

When abused, such drugs can produce all of the effects associated with the abuse of amphetamine, including hallucinations. Nevertheless, such drugs are not as widely misused as amphetamine drugs, and only phenmetrazine has been placed under the same controls imposed upon amphetamine.

HALLUCINOGENS

Distortions of perception, dream images and hallucinations are characteristic effects of a group of drugs variously called, hallucinogens, psychotomimetics, dysleptics or psychedelics. These drugs include mescaline, d-lysergic acid diethylamide (LSD), psilocybin and dimethyltryptamine (DMT). At present, they have no general clinical medical use—except for research applications. However, they are being encountered with increasing frequency as drugs of abuse.

Marijuana, while chemically distinct from the foregoing, is also considered a hallucinogen. Pharmacologically, it is *not* a narcotic although its control under the Marijuana Tax Act of 1937—and later laws—is somewhat similar to the control imposed on narcotics. Also, like narcotic law enforcement, marijuana law enforcement is handled by the Federal Bureau of Narcotics as well as certain state and local law enforcement agencies.

MARIJUANA (CANNABIS)

According to the Commission on Narcotic Drugs of the Economic and Social Council of the United Nations, marijuana abuse is more widespread, from a geographical standpoint, than abuse of any other dangerous drug. Widely encountered in North and South America, Africa, Southeast Asia and the Middle East, it is known as bhang or ganja in India, hashish in the Middle East, dagga in South Africa and maconha or djamba in South America.

The intoxicating substance which gives marijuana its activity is found primarily in a resin from the flowering tops and leaves of the female plant. The potency of marijuana varies with the geographical location in which the plant grows, time of harvest, and the plant parts used. For example, hashish is stronger than Amercian marijuana because the former contains more resin.

Medical Use.   At one time, marijuana had a minor place in the practice of medicine. But because the safety and effectiveness of newer drugs so outweigh the limited utility of marijuana, it is no longer considered medically respectable in the United States. In a few countries of the world (such as India and Pakistan), it still may be encountered as a local remedy.

Abuse.   Marijuana may be smoked, sniffed or ingested, but effects are experienced most quickly with smoking. The mental effects include a feeling of euphoria, exaltation and a dreamy sensation accompanied by a free flow of ideas. Senses of time, distance, vision and hearing are distorted. Sometimes panic and fear are experienced. Hallucinations may develop with large doses. In the company of others, the marijuana user is talkative and laughs easily. When alone, he is more often drowsy and quiet. The initial period of stimulation is frequently followed by a moody reverie and drowsiness. The user's ability to perform many tasks normally or safely—particularly automobile driving—is seriously impaired.

Other effects of marijuana include dizziness, dry mouth, dilated pupils and burning eyes, urinary frequency, diarrhea, nausea and vomiting, and hunger, particularly for sweets.

Marijuana does not produce physical dependence or an abstinence syndrome. Once the user has established the amount of marijuana needed to achieve his particular "high," there is little tendency to increase the dose, indicating that tolerance doesn't develop. Moderate to strong psychic dependence can develop in accordance with the user's appreciation of the drug's effects.

In terms of some effects on behavior, use of marijuana is roughly comparable to moderate abuse of alcohol (also a drug). Like alcohol, it tends to loosen inhibitions and increase suggestibility, which explains why an individual under the influence of marijuana may engage in activities he would not ordinarily consider. Although the marijuana smoker sometimes feels himself capable of extraordinary physical and mental feats, he seldom acts to accomplish them for fear of disrupting his "euphoric" state. But what he does not realize is that the drug can have unpredictable effects—even on persons accustomed to its use.

To date, available information indicates that marijuana has few detrimental effects on an individual's *physical* health. Psychic dependence and the drug's effects, however, may lead to extreme lethargy, self-neglect and preoccupation with use of marijuana to a degree that precludes constructive activity. Additionally, the use of marijuana may precipitate psychotic episodes or cause impulsive behavior in reaction to fear or panic. According to a 1965 report on drug dependence in the Bulletin of the World Health Organization: "Abuse of cannabis (marijuana) facilitates the association with social groups and subcultures involved with more dangerous drugs, such as opiates or barbiturates. Transition to the use of such drugs would be a consequence of this association rather than an inherent effect of cannabis. The harm to society derived from abuse of cannabis rests in the economic consequences of the impairment of the individual's social functions and his enhanced proneness to asocial and antisocial behavior."

MESCALINE, PSILOCYBIN, DMT

For centuries, various Indian tribes have used mescaline (derived from the Mexican cactus, peyote) in religious ceremonies. Mescaline is available on the illicit market as a crystalline powder in capsules or as a liquid in ampuls or vials. It may also be obtained as whole cactus "buttons," chopped "buttons" in capsules, or as a brownish-gray cloudy liquid. The drug is generally taken orally, but may be injected. Because of its bitter taste, the drug is often ingested with tea, coffee, milk, orange juice or some other common beverage.

Psilocybin is derived from certain mushrooms found in Mexico. It has been used in Indian religious rites as far back as pre-Columbian times. It is not nearly as potent as LSD, but with adequate doses, similar hallucinogenic effects are produced. Psilocybin is available in crystalline, powdered or liquid form.

DMT (dimethyltryptamine) is a more recent addition to the list of presently abused hallucinogenic agents. Although prepared synthetically, it is a natural constituent of the seeds of certain plants found in the West Indies and South America. Powder made from these seeds is known to have been used as a snuff as far back as the arrival of Columbus in the New World—and is still used by some Indian tribes of South America. DMT produces effects similar to those of LSD, but much larger doses are required.

Some varieties of morning glory seeds are also abused for their hallucinogenic effects. The bizarre behavioral effects produced upon ingestion are probably attributable to LSD-like components.

LSD

LSD (lysergic acid diethylamide) was synthesized in 1938 from lysergic acid present in ergot, a fungus that grows on rye. LSD is the most potent of the hallucinogens. On the illicit market, the drug may be obtained as a small white pill, as a crystalline powder in capsules, or as a tasteless, colorless or odorless liquid in ampuls. Frequently, it is offered in the form of impregnated sugar cubes, cookies or crackers. LSD is usually taken orally, but may be injected.

LSD primarily affects the central nervous system, producing changes in mood and behavior. The user may also exhibit dilated pupils, tremor, elevated temperature and blood pressure, and hyperactive reflexes. Tolerance to the behavioral effects of LSD may develop with several days of continued use, but physical dependence does not occur. Although psychic dependence may develop, it is seldom intense. Accordingly, most LSD devotees will use the drug when available, but do not seem to experience a serious craving when LSD cannot be obtained.

In general, the LSD experience consists of changes in perception, thought, mood and activity. Perceptual changes involve senses of sight, hearing, touch, body image and time. Colors seem to intensify or change, shape and spatial relation appear distorted, objects seem to pulsate, two-dimensional objects appear to become three dimensional and inanimate objects seem to assume emotional import. Sensitivity to sound increases but the source of the sound is elusive. Conversations can be heard but may not be comprehended. There may be auditory hallucinations of music and voices. There may be changes in taste and food may feel gritty. Cloth seems to change texture, becoming coarse and dry or fine and velvety. The subject may feel cold or sweaty. There are sensations of light-headedness, emptiness, shaking, vibrations, fogginess. Subjects lose awareness of their bodies with a resultant floating feeling. Arms or legs may be held in one position for extended periods of time. Time seems to race, stop, slow down or even go backwards. Changes in thought include a free flow of bizarre ideas including notions of persecution. Trivial events assume unusual significance and importance. An inspiration or insight phenomenon is claimed by some LSD adherents.

The mood effects of LSD run the gamut. There may be bursts of tears, of laughter, or the subject may feel no emotion at all. A state of complete relaxation and happiness, not apparent to an observer, may be experienced. A feeling of being alone and cut off from the world may lead to anxiety, fear and panic. Accordingly, the LSD session is frequently monitored by an abstaining LSD-experienced friend to prevent flight, suicidal attempts, dangerous reaction to panic states, and impulsive behavior, such as disrobing. There may be a feeling of enhanced creativity, but this subjective feeling rarely seems to produce objective results.

After a number of hours, the effects of LSD begin to wear off. Waves of the LSD experience, diminishing in intensity, alternate with periods of no effects at all, until all symptoms disappear. Some fatigue, tension, and recurrent hallucinations may persist long after ingestion of the drug. Psychological changes induced by the drug can persist for indefinite periods.

There is, at present, no approved general medical use for LSD. Some interesting results have been obtained with the drug in certain medically supervised research programs—particularly in the treatment of chronic alcoholism and terminal illness. However, the Food and Drug Administration now takes the position that LSD has insufficient clinical utility to warrant either prescription or nonprescription use. Consequently, LSD is now subject to controls similar to those for any unproven investigational drug.

Medical warnings notwithstanding, large quantities of the drug have become available on an illicit basis for use in "mind expansion"—an application not even contemplated in medical research programs undertaken to date. Those using LSD for this purpose advocate unrestricted use of the product. They state that the drug is not inherently dangerous, claiming either personal use without complication or citing safe use by various notables from many fields. Although it may be true that some individuals have had LSD experiences without apparent ill effect, growing medical evidence shows the drug can cause very serious, and often damaging reactions in many. Hospital admissions of persons with acute LSD induced psychoses are on the increase. Bizarre behavior in public, panic, fear, and homicidal and suicidal urges have been reported. Psychotic states have been induced through use of the drug—both with emotionally unstable individuals and with persons in whom no sign of emotional instability had been evident. Although most LSD-induced psychotic episodes have occurred in persons initially experimenting with the drug, untoward results have also occurred with "experienced" abusers. What's more, "casualties" have happened even when the drug has been taken under supervision, both medical and nonmedical. LSD also can produce delayed psychotic reactions in some individuals. In some instances, hallucinations have recurred for weeks after the drug was taken. In the opinion of Dr.

James L. Goddard, Commissioner of Food and Drugs, medically unsupervised use of LSD is analogous to playing "chemical Russian roulette."

SOLVENTS

Among non-drug substances frequently encountered in drug abuse situations are various solvents. For example, the inhalation of solvent fumes from glue, gasoline, paint thinner and lighter fluid will produce a form of intoxication. Inhalation is practiced most frequently by youngsters between 10 and 15 and occasionally up to 18 years. Glue usually is squeezed into a handkerchief or bag which is placed over the nose and mouth. Gasoline and paint thinner fumes may be inhaled directly from tanks and cans.

After a number of "drags," the individual experiences excitation, exhilaration and excitement resembling the initial effects of alcoholic intoxication. Blurring of vision, ringing ears, slurred speech and staggering are common, as are hallucinations. This phase of intoxication lasts from 30-45 minutes after inhalation, followed by drowsiness, stupor and even unconsciousness of about an hour's duration. Upon recovery, the individual usually does not recall what happened during the period of intoxication.

Present knowledge concerning solvent inhalation indicates that physical dependence does not develop with the abuse of these agents, although a tendency to increase the amount inhaled suggests tolerance. Repeated use and relapse to use indicate the development of psychic dependence.

Some medical problems can attend solvent inhalation. The chief dangers of inhaling these substances are death by suffocation, the development of psychotic behavior, and the state of intoxication these substances produce. Additionally, a severe type of anemia has been observed in glue-sniffers who have an inherited defect of the blood cells (sickle-cell disease). It is known that many solvents and the ingredients of some types of glue can damage the kidneys, liver, heart, blood and nervous system. Although such adverse effects as a result of *inhalation* have not been established, they remain a distinct possibility.

Protecting the Home Front

MARIJUANA: THREE VIEWPOINTS

PARENT

"I am perfectly aware that we have a drug problem in this country, especially in the colleges and in the high schools. My son's high school newspaper said in an

From *Revelation Now:* A National Student Journalism Review, 1 (November, 1969), 1. Reprinted with the permission of Barry Glassner, Coordinator-Publisher.

article that at least 35 per cent of the students at his school have smoked marijuana.

"When I was in college some of the students had smoked marijuana. But now it's getting out of hand.

"I must admit, however, that some of the laws on marijuana are too harsh; but that makes no difference, they are the laws of this country and they should be obeyed. If you don't obey them, then you should be prepared to suffer the consequences.

"All I know is that kids are really crazy if they experiment with anything like L.S.D., and I'm sure my son hasn't experimented with drugs.

"Anyone who does is running away from reality."

STUDENT

"I have smoked several times. I'd use the word drugs, but it has a sinister connotation. Besides, grass and hash are hardly drugs.

"My parents get . . . my mother anyways . . . gets hysterical when she talks about drugs. She keeps telling me that everyone thought cigarettes were harmless 20 years ago, and now they found out it causes lung cancer. 'So stay away from drugs because who knows what it may cause!'

"I was surprised how many kids have tried it. I've admitted smoking to about three people, and two of them who I would have never suspected smoked too.

"The funny thing is how easy it is to get. All these middle class types like me try to get it and everyone is willing to give it away.

"As for police, they can break up smoking like they can break up all the old men's Thursday night poker games."

NARCOTICS AGENT

"Despite any claims that Nixon has stopped the amount of marijuana in the United States, it is still readily accessible to anyone that wants it.

"The amount of busts made this year by the Chicago Police is 1,087 (as of October 27), and that doesn't include specific raids made by individual policemen.

"The main problem is not in the use of drugs, but in the abuse of drugs. Now, I carry out the laws, I don't make them; but I see too many kids gradually go from marijuana to other drugs. You've got to realize that laws are here to protect other people and yourself. The laws are made by the people.

"We've got six million alcoholics and we have laws against alcoholism . . . just think what would happen if we legalize marijuana."

SOME OBSERVATIONS ON ADOLESCENT DRUG USE

SIMON L. AUSTER, M.D.

The sufferer is tremulous and loses his self-command; he is subject to fits of agitation and depression. He has a haggard appearance . . . as with other such agents, a renewed dose . . . gives temporary relief, but at the cost of future misery.

This description of the effects of coffee was written at the beginning of this century by a professor at Cambridge University, the most distinguished pharmacologist of the time, in a standard medical textbook. In any analysis of the use of drugs, because of the intense passions aroused, it is useful to keep close to the forefront of one's attention the radical change in attitude towards this now-common beverage that the most informed medical opinion has undergone in the past 50 years. Hopefully, it will provide a perspective that will engender a more thoughtful and less emotional consideration of these substances.

The observations and conclusions which follow are based on experience with a large number of adolescent drug users, most, but not all, middle class. The majority were seen in a clinical setting, some over an extended period of time. Many others were speaking in wide-ranging, informal discussions and not in the role of patient.

The discussion will be concerned with most of the spectrum usually considered subject to abuse, save one. This includes both those totally prohibited, such as the opiates, cocaine, the hallucinogens and cannabis derivatives, and those in general use, but subject to control, mainly the amphetamines and barbiturates. It will also touch on the almost infinite range of volatile organic solvents used for sniffing; e.g., glue, gasoline, cleaning fluid, etc. The lone exception referred to is alcohol. Although its use is increasingly associated with that of other drugs, it is in a secondary position; the primary abuse of alcohol in this population does not fit the patterns described.

Users distinguish between two general classes, the "ups" and the "downs." In the former group are cocaine, the hallucinogens, amphetamines, solvents, and usually, cannabis. In the latter group are the opiates, the barbiturates, tranquilizers, and for some people, cannabis derivatives. Within these two general categories, users, even "garbage collectors" who will take anything, are generally aware of differences between the drugs. Thus opiates are referred to as "hard

Revised version of "Some Observations on Adolescent Drug Use," *Educational Leadership*, 27 (December, 1970): 281-86. Reprinted with permission of the Association for Supervision and Curriculum Development and Simon L. Auster, M.D. Copyright © 1970 by the Association for Supervision and Curriculum Development.

Simon L. Auster, M.D., is Director of Fairfax—Falls Church Mental Health Center, Falls Church, Virginia.

stuff" and the popular button reading "SPEED KILLS" is a reference to the danger of the amphetamines. Barbiturates are known not to mix with alcohol, even in small amounts. The absence of any established long or short-term ill effects from cannabis is recognized and frequently quoted, and the latest findings of LSD research are generally known and discussed. It is generally unwise to attempt to deter kids from drug use by scare tactics; any audience will invariably contain at least one listener who is as knowledgeable as the speaker, if not more so. Further, this scare approach can itself be held at least partially responsible for some of the experimentation with these drugs; many of the kids see friends and acquaintances taking them without the predicted deleterious results, and come to disbelieve all the dire warnings they have been given about drugs. This absence of apparent consequence perhaps more than any other factor, has made many youngsters skeptical of warnings about the dangers of drug abuse. This can even be true with "hard" drugs, for any large metropolitan community will have more than a few adolescents who have used opiates fairly heavily for extended periods of time without encountering difficulty in stopping when the drug was no longer available, or became too difficult to obtain.

Drug usage cuts across population barriers, although the pattern of usage differs among social groups. The use of cannabis and the opiates among the lower class ghetto resident is an old phenomenon and has been extensively described. Its use in middle and upper class youth is relatively new and is probably the single factor most responsible for the current upsurge in community concern about drugs and their effects. Until recently, it was generally accepted as strictly a matter for the police and the Narcotics Bureau; now, more people are growing concerned as the issue becomes more immediate with their children becoming involved in drug use.

Adolescent users seem to fall into several different categories. In the ghetto population, while the heavy use of opiates and cannabis have led to the conclusion that drugs are mainly used to escape from the miserable reality of the users' lives, careful study has revealed consistent differences between the personalities of true addicts and non-addicts (who may be casual users). Briefly summarized, the former have a significant degree of shortsightedness in their judgment; their capacity for decision-making and purposeful action is seriously limited; they see themselves mainly in negative terms; they are unable to form genuinely intimate relationships; they are closely tied to their mothers; and they are often badly confused about their sexual feelings. That the sociological aspects of drug use in this class have been emphasized in relative contrast to the individual aspects is perhaps a reflection of the broader society's appreciation of the close, almost causal, tie between the central elements of lower class ghetto life and the significant areas of disturbance in the personality of the addict, as well as in some appreciation of the greater "need" for escape from the misery of this kind of life.

This emphasis, however, should not lead us to overlook some of the similarities between users from this group and those from other social classes. In the middle and upper class population, adolescent users seem to fall into one of four categories.

The first group consists of those who, with or without the use of drugs would be readily recognized as psychologically disturbed, whether or not themselves addicted; members of this group show the greatest similarity in personality characteristics to the more carefully studied lower class addicts. These are youngsters whose difficulties, should one trouble to look closely, clearly antedated any exposure to drugs, who on close examination show fairly disturbed patterns of family relationships and for whom the drugs often represent an effort at restitution. For them the drug usage is almost incidental and is not likely to be terminated until the underlying disturbance begins to be altered. The "garbage collectors" almost invariably come from this group, as they frantically try anything in the medicine chest—or outside of it—for the sought-after effect.

The major element that drugs provide for this group is a sense of vitality. The ordinary experience of self for these youth is one of an inner void. Any of these drugs, to the extent that they alter internal perceptions, replace this void with some kind of feeling, so necessary for the sense of being alive. While this can be readily mistaken as a search for "kicks," there is an urgency to it that belies such a limited interpretation, that suggests a more profound role for these substances in the individual's functioning, perhaps analogous to that of the medically prescribed tranquilizers in another situation. This is one reason why exhortation isn't very successful with them. When it comes to the difference between feeling alive and feeling dead, they, along with most of us, opt to feel alive.

The second group, and probably the largest, is composed of the faddists, those who will take almost any drug in a social situation because that is what everyone else is doing, because it is the "in" thing to do. This group is composed mainly of cannabis users, with some trying the hallucinogens and amphetamines and occasionally even heroin. They use the drug as an avenue of gaining and reinforcing group acceptance and they are relatively indifferent to the particular chemical or its distinctive effect. Their parents went on panty raids when they were in college and their grandparents swallowed live goldfish and patronized speakeasys. With this group it is important to note that while the "kick" obtained from the drug is appreciated, and even rhapsodized, it is a distinctly secondary factor in its use. It is the group pressure that determines the use and even much of the praise sung about it. If caught once, members of this group are likely to discontinue use, for fear of the consequences of being caught again. If not, use is likely to be self-limited anyway.

If these youth have any psychological handicap, it is in their generally narrow view of life and sheep-like tendency to follow the flock. Occasionally, one of them becomes profoundly depressed as a result of such experimentation with an hallucinogen, the effect of which was to make him aware of there being much more to life than his constricted, limiting perspective had allowed him to see until then. The depression was a result of the realization of how much living he had missed and how much work he would have to do to make up for it. For these kids, the drug provided a therapeutic experience, despite themselves.

The third group, perhaps the next largest, is made up of those that use primarily cannabis and the hallucinogens. They often start using them out of curiosity and continue to use them intermittently because they find them helpful in clarifying personal questions with which they might be wrestling. They do not come to rely on these drugs to find answers or to resolve the developmental challenges of their adolescence; rather, the drugs are used as an occasional adjunct in this process. While adequate and satisfying friendships are consistently characteristic of members of this group, with their parents they may be cordial and friendly or in a state of armed truce with occasional skirmishes. Their academic performance ranges from outstanding to failing and usually parallels the tolerance of the school for experimentation and deviance, and the quality of its teachers. Most of the adolescents in this category seen clinically have been referred only because someone, usually their parents, panicked at the discovery that they were using drugs.

A final group of drug users, although constituted mainly of adults with relatively few adolescents, warrants mention, if only to complete the picture. This group is mainly composed of more mature people, to all appearances healthy and functioning well in the society both in their personal and occupational lives. Members of this group may or may not use cannabis and are focused mainly on the hallucinogens which they take occasionally. For these people, the drug appears to have provided an introduction to a transcendant dimension, foreign to ordinary experience.

The "hippie" group is a conglomerate, rather than a single type. It contains a large representation of the first, more disturbed, group. Many members of the second, faddist, group may present themselves as "hippie" for the same reasons they use drugs; it is the "in" thing. Occasionally members of the third group go through a personal crisis, often over philosophical issues, that leads to a temporary withdrawal into the hippie community; it has been reported that after about a year or two, they return to their previous state, often with more insight and maturity. For many, this may be an unavoidable stage in their development, similar to the perhaps more familiar and readily understood need of other youth in a similar state of crisis for a period of military service or for a routine, mindless job; both kinds of experience provide breathing spells, the "hippie" unstructured, the others clearly structured.

As with earlier thinking about lower class drug use, understanding of the upsurge in drug usage among the middle and upper class adolescent population must be sought in the context of contemporary American society at least as much as in the individual psychology of the users. Furthermore, any explanation must also take into account why, for many, the movement has been in the direction of certain specific drugs, particularly cannabis and the hallucinogens, rather than alcohol. The first, more disturbed, group of users delineated earlier is relatively small and the use of drugs by those constituting this group is merely one item in a spectrum of deviant and disordered behavior; for them, the societal factors, while present, are secondary. For the second, faddist group, drug use is itself secondary to a simple group phenomenon and the choice of a drug other than alcohol for this purpose is primarily a function of the ready availability of the drugs and the shock and horror with which these substances, in contrast to alcohol, are regarded by a large segment of the adult authorities, against whom at least some of the behavior is directed.

It is for the third group that an understanding of the primary factors in drug use is to be found in the context of the broader society. In this third group, the use of drugs can be related to a phenomenon widespread in the population, namely, a search for greater self-understanding and significance in living, an effort to escape the alienation, the confusion, and the uncertainty so rampant in contemporary society, and a wish to become able to grasp the presence of the moment and live their lives, even the most prosaic moments of them, fully and with immediacy. While the extraordinary vogue experienced by psychoanalysis during the past two decades was, in part, a prelude to this, then phenomenon has exploded in the past few years with the development of a wide range of activities, all of which have as a goal, increased self-awareness. One factor which may account for the current increased need for this kind of experience is that, despite the constants of human existence and relatedness, the contemporary world, the world in which the present adolescent and young adult generation grew up, and which helped shape their mode of living, has undergone such massive structural change during the past decades, as Marshall McLuhan has attempted to describe, that the context in which these constants are lived out is qualitatively different from that which the older generation experienced in its development. The technology which has led to a threshold offering the alternatives of annihilation or abundance has radically changed life styles, and more subtly, the structure of the environment. And to the extent that all organisms in part are products of their environments, these youth and young adults are qualitatively different from the older generation. As a consequence, the reference standards applied in earlier years to assess situations are no longer felt to be relevant or even at all to have meaning for analyzing a contemporary problem.

In the confusion and uncertainty that ensue, anything will be welcomed that may intensify internal experience so as to bring into awareness heretofore unrecognized responses that may help in making an assessment of a complex and puzzling situation. Since self-awareness and understanding are their defined tasks, psychoanalysis and psychotherapy have been, in the recent past, a major direction in which people turned for help in these areas; however they were, and continue to be rejected by many because of the label of sickness associated with their use. More recently, other avenues have been explored for their self-discovery potential. Drugs, through their direct effects of heightening internal perceptions of sensation, thought, and feeling represent one such avenue, albeit one condemned by the social order. Group experiences represent another, more acceptable route, traveled as much, if not more, by adults, as by youth. These groups, known variously as T-groups, encounter groups, sensory awareness training, etc., are usually considered under the heading of "affective education" or "the human potential movement." They provide a setting in which a person can experience highly intensified and occasionally new, but otherwise appropriate reactions to a variety of prototypical situations. When he is angry, he is intensely so, and knows it; when he is anxious, when he is loving, when he is happy, he feels it so strongly that he cannot be mistaken. This enables the person to clarify his feelings and responses to these situations and to begin to generalize them to situations arising in the course of ordinary living. Eastern forms of meditation and related practices, of which yoga is probably the best known, through the insights and understanding to be gained from the conscious direction of attention inward, are other avenues to this same goal. More lonely and more difficult, demanding exceptional self-discipline, they have attracted many youth as well as adults. Much of the recent popular interest in Eastern philosophy may be consequent to a recognition of the potential of these teachings for enabling the practitioner to achieve this sought-after clarity.

These various approaches may also give direction to many of those who are distressed by the contrast between the values they have been taught and the quality of life they experience in their families and communities. For these people, in addition to the self-understanding, the immediacy of the group experience provides a person with some sense of significance and worth in his human encounters, and meditation and drugs, by turning attention inward, provide some orientation in the search for answers to the eternal questions of meaning.

It is important to realize that there is not necessarily any change in values inherent in this situation; quite the contrary, the problem may be most acute when traditional values are clear and accepted, but the relative uniqueness of the situation creates uncertainty about how they should be applied. This dilemma is perhaps best illustrated by the issue of achievement, so often a focus of intergenerational conflict. As a value, achievement has been one of the keystones of the American social order, yet many contemporary youth, by their disinterest, appear to be rejecting it in all areas, academic, economic, whatever. Even among many of those who are achieving, the question, "achievement for what?" is frequently heard—and a source of distress to many parents. This is a deceptive phenomenon, as underlying that question, and indeed the entire issue, can be found the question, "achievement at the expense of what?" They are not rejecting achievement; rather, aware of Donne's injunction that "No man is an island unto himself," they are concerned about the isolation which in their observation of the adult world has all too often been a direct and inevitable consequence of it. When added to this is their perception of the potential of technology for either enhancing the fulfillment of the individual or for increasing his isolation, increasingly being applied in the latter direction, the state of their personal relationships demands greater attention and efforts to avoid isolation become a matter of greater urgency. Thus, their initial test of anyone whom they meet is concerned with the degree to which he has transcended the pressures towards personal isolation so pervasive in our society and which they have almost invariably observed and experienced in their own families. They turn to those who have passed this test and have also achieved excellence in their chosen fields, who have been able to maintain both values, as it were, in the face of a cultural pattern that maintains them in opposition to each other. For those people, each of whom is "doing his own thing" in the deepest sense, their respect is of the highest order.

Compared to the members of the third group, the seekers, who may use drugs occasionally but primarily look to their peer group for assistance in these areas, the problem with the more disturbed youngsters of the first group who exclusively rely on drugs for these purposes, is that they have so little sense of self and consequently, are so unable to "get with" a peer group, to bounce the experiences off them, that they can't make use of such relationships. They are pervaded by a sense of futility about life and relationships which leads them to mistrust all relationships, even those with their contemporaries, and turn inward for answers and relief. To the extent that drugs assist in this process through their pharmacological effects, they will be used with little hesitation by these youth. The others have developed sufficient separateness from their families and have enough of an identity to enable them to enter into some kind of relationship with peers, although they too may use these drugs as occasional adjuncts.

These considerations have important implication for those concerned with controlling drug usage. Members of the first, more disturbed, group will respond only as the underlying disturbance is alleviated; not only is education ineffective, but even in the face of threats they may not trouble themselves to attempt to hide their continuing usage. A good education program can be expected to have its maximum impact on members of the second, faddist, group, some of whom it will reach, not unlike the effects of a good education program on the danger of tobacco. Needless to say, it must be good; a bad program is worse than worthless insofar as it creates a "credibility gap." At the same time, members of this group are likely to be deterred from drug use by the threat of legal sanctions to the same degree that such a threat will be a deterrent to any prohibited behavior. In the last two groups, in which use is intermittent and controlled, any fact provided by an education program will be considered in a decision about use, as would any significant data with which they were provided, and the threat of legal sanctions may have some effect; nevertheless, real success in limitation will depend on the development of the kinds of social programs and activities that establish an alternate pathway to the insights being reached through the drugs.

But it is the creation of just such a pathway that poses the greatest challenge. It would need to incorporate those elements leading to the goals the youth are seeking, understanding and self-awareness, participation and involvement, passion and commitment. To no small degree would the creation of this pathway mean opening an avenue running counter to the prevailing patterns of relationship in American society. This poses a problem, not because of the unacceptability of such approaches, but rather because of the paucity of people capable of providing leadership; a society characterized by alienation is not likely to produce a plethora of people capable of involvement.

While it has been suggested that this will require the creation of new social institutions, the analysis presented also has implications for preventive programs that can be implemented through those already established. Most important among these is the school, which, as the primary institution with which all children articulate, has the greatest potential for this development. The above considerations suggest that an effective education program could enable it to achieve this potential. Although such a program should naturally include a strong basic syllabus on drugs themselves for both student and teacher, the greater emphasis must be on educating the teacher and administrator to an understanding of the circumstances leading to drug use among youth. It is only after being confronted by the experience which the youth are undergoing that generates the vacuum so readily filled by drugs, that the teacher is in a position to develop those non-drug avenues available to fill it, or better, structure a curriculum free of such a vacuum. If the formulation developed earlier is valid, this would mean building into the curriculum the opportunity for students to experience directness and immediacy and their emotional concommitants, with the areas under study, with each other, and with the teacher. This is the real challenge.

"... especially efficient in producing nightmares with hallucinations which may be alarming in their intensity. . . . Another peculiar quality . . . is to produce a strange and extreme degree of physical depression . . . a grevious sinking . . . may seize upon a sufferer so that to speak is an effort . . . the speech may become weak and vague . . . by miseries such as these, the best years of life may be spoiled." This was written by the same authors responsible for the comments on coffee quoted earlier in this paper, but here they were describing the effects of tea.

These two statements should remind us that, as the Advisory Committee on Drug Dependence of the British Government remarked in its report, "The gradation of danger between consuming tea and coffee at one end of the scale and injecting heroin intravenously at the other may not be permanently those which we now ascribe to particular drugs."

GLOSSARY OF TERMS

Bag—Small packet of narcotics
Bagman—The dealer, the pusher
Bang—Injection of narcotics
Bean—Capsule

Bennies—Benzedrine tablets
Bindle—Small amount of narcotics packaged in folded paper or envelope

From *Drug Abuse* (1968, revised; Trenton: N. J. State Department of Education, 1969), pp. 68-71. Reprinted with permission of the publisher.

Bombito—Vial of Desoxyn

Blast Party—Group of marijuana smokers smoking together

Blast a Stick—Smoke a marijuana cigarette

Blow a Stick—Same as above

Blue Heavens—Sodium Amytal tablets

Boy—Heroin

Bread—Money

Burn—To take money for heroin with no plans to deliver, stuff or phony drugs

Busted—Arrested

C—Cocaine

Caballo—Heroin

Cap—Capsules of narcotics

Champ—Junkie who won't inform no matter how sick he is

Charged Up—Under effect of narcotics

Chippy—Potential addict

Coke—Cocaine

Coked Up—Under influence of cocaine

Cokie—Cocaine addict

Cold Turkey—Abrupt withdrawal without medication

Connect—Make purchase of narcotics

Connection—Dealer in narcotics

Cook Up a Pill—Smoke opium

Cooker—Any spoon or bottle cap used in the preparation of heroin

Cop—Buy narcotics

Cotton Top, Cottonhead—User who recooks the cotton fibers found in cookers when their supply is used up and they are in need of an injection.

Cut—Adulterate narcotics

Deck—Small packet of narcotics

Dollies—Dolophine pills

DooJee—Heroin

Dope—Any narcotics

Dynamite—Narcotics of high potency

Eighth—Eighth of an ounce

Ends—Money

Fix—An injection

Fly—Take narcotics

Fuzz—Police, the law

Gimmicks—Equipment for injection by hypo needle

Goof Ball—Barbiturate

Grass—Marijuana in raw state

Gun—Hypodermic needle

H—Heroin

Hand-to-hand—Person-to-person delivery

Happy Dust—Cocaine

Hay—Marijuana

Heeled—Having narcotics

Hemp—Marijuana

High—Under the effect of narcotics

Holding—Possessing narcotics

Hooked—Addicted

Hop-head—Addict

Horse—Heroin

Hot Shot—Injection of poison which user believes to be good drugs

Joint—Marijuana cigarette

Jones—The habit, an addict

Joy Pop—A now and then injection, usually a skin injection

Junk—Narcotics

Junkie—Narcotics user

Kick—Break the dependence on a drug

Kilo—Large amount of narcotics

M—Morphine

Man—Policman or detective

Main Liner—Addict who injects directly into veins

Manicure—Clean and prepare marijuana for rolling into cigarettes

Member—Negro or some other than white person

Monkey—Expensive habit

Off—No longer a user

Outfit—Eye dropper, cooker (spoon or bottle cap) used to prepare fix. (See *Tools or Works*)

Pad—Drug user's home

Pack—Heroin

Piece—One ounce

Plant—Cache of narcotics

Pure—Pure narcotics of very good grade

Pop—An injection

Pot—Marijuana

Pusher—Narcotic seller

Quill—Folded matchbox cover or a paper soda straw for sniffing narcotics through the nose.

Rainbows—Tuinal capsules

Red Devils—Seconal capsules

Reefers—Marijuana cigarettes

Roach—Butt of a marijuana cigarette

Rumble—Police in the neighborhood; a shake-down or search

Satch Cotton—Cotton saturated with heroin

Scat—Heroin

Schmeck—Heroin

Scoring—Making a purchase of a drug

Script—Doctor's prescription

Set Up—An arrangement to have someone caught dealing in illegal drugs

Shoot Up—Take an injection

Shooting Gallery—Place where addicts congregate to take injection

Shot—Injection

Silk—A white person

Sixteenth—Sixteenth of an ounce

Sleigh Ride—Cocaine

Sniffing—Sniffing narcotics through nose, usually heroin or cocaine

Snorting—Same as sniffing

Snow—Cocaine

Speedball—A mixture of heroin and cocaine

Spike—Hypodermic needle

Spoon—Sixteenth of an ounce of heroin

Stash—Cache of narcotics

Stool—Informer

Stuff—Narcotics

Supplier—Drug source

Tecata—Heroin

Take a Band—Take drugs

Take-off—Take drugs

Taste—Small quantity of narcotics usually given as sample or as reward

Tea—Marijuana

Thoroughbred—Higher-type sellers who won't reveal anything about operation, one who sells pure narcotics

Tooies—Tuinal capsules

Tools or Works—Equipment used for injection by hypodermic

Toss—Search

Toxy—The smallest container of prepared opium

Weed—Marijuana

Weed-head—Addict

White Stuff—Heroin

Vic—One who has been given a hot shot, a victim

Yellow Jackets—Nembutal capsules

Yen Hook (Hock)—Instrument used in opium smoking

Yen Shee—Opium ash

Yen Shee Suey—Opium wine

DRUG EDUCATION

DAVID C. LEWIS, M.D.

This paper suggests an approach to discussing drug problems with young people which the author has gained, as he says, by trial and error as he has participated in and observed the implementation of drug education programs in colleges, high schools, and junior high schools. Lewis discusses such a program's goals, methods, and content in clear detail and with rare understanding.

As a physician and an educator, I have had the opportunity to participate in several drug education programs in colleges, high schools, and junior high schools and, by trial and error, have developed an approach to discussing drug problems with young people that I feel is effective. In addition, I have observed how various school systems have approached the implementation of this area of education.

I was struck by the large number of schools that have added drug education programs to their curricula without any clear notion of what they want to accomplish and, consequently, without any means of evaluating the programs. There is a vague idea: "We should have one." In this paper we shall examine both the goals and the methods of such programs, and describe in practical terms an approach that has shown some promise in my experience.

Some schools have decided that the primary goal is to eliminate the use of drugs. While this seems to be a desirable and sensible aim, it has led to programs designed to discourage drug use directly by portraying the worst fates that might befall the user. Such scare techniques have produced a very real credibility gap, and the goal of across-the-board abstinence has created more problems than it has solved.

The discussion of marihuana use is an example. A teacher may present the arguments for total abstinence rather strongly to a class in which 10 to 20 percent of the students have already experimented with the drug. The class might feel compelled to confront the teacher with a different set of facts and values—which are often based on personal experience and are well-articulated. The teacher in this impossible position could well fail to be convincing in his efforts to present an alternate viewpoint, and he will have diminished his effectiveness as a source of information and guidance in this area.

While it is exceedingly difficult to determine whether a school program increases or decreases drug use, it is quite possible that a sensational program can cause an increase; the students' reaction is to rebel and show the "Establish-

From *National Association of Secondary School Principals Bulletin*, 53 (December, 1969), 87-89. Reprinted with the permission of the author and the publisher.

David C. Lewis, M.D., is Assistant Professor of Medicine at Harvard Medical School.

ment" how wrong it is. Recently, I participated in a drug-education program in a well-known suburban school system. The high school cancelled all classes and held a day-long drug symposium. A congeries of experts spoke on drugs. No one advocated the use of drugs. Yet, two weeks later, two students who had just tried marihuana for the first time told me, "We figured if it was worth calling off classes to talk about drugs for a whole day, it's certainly worth trying."

This kind of experience suggests that the drug education program should be incorporated into the ongoing curriculum, not sensationalized or condensed into a massive one-day session. Unless a believable discussion of drug use and the motivations for it can be conducted in the classroom, it would be far better to have no program at all.

GOALS

The goal of a drug education program in the secondary school should be to provide information in such a manner that students can understand the social, medical, moral, and legal implications of drug use in *personal* terms. To accomplish this goal, drug education can be organized into two categories: topical, or concerned with giving information, and dynamic, dealing with decision-making.

There is a significant body of information now available for presentation in a topical manner. The justification for this information-giving approach is twofold: first, the subject of drugs is very much on the minds of students, and second, drug use is a matter of great social, medical, moral, and legal concern in our society at the present time. Therefore, it is a topic that should properly be a matter of discussion in the schools, just as racism, pollution, and violence are valid subjects for inclusion in the curriculum.

The dynamic approach to drug education focuses on how a young person arrives at the decision to use or not use drugs. It requires an examination of the motivational forces and situations that lead students to seek this form of experience over others. And it requires the imparting of a feeling for what drug use would mean in *personal* terms: What would drugs do *to* me? What would drugs do *for* me? This is the *critical feature* of the entire effort, because in the last analysis the choice of using drugs or not using them is in the hands of the student. One cannot imagine a form of legal or parental control that would separate young people from the literally hundreds of drugs that can alter their moods and also be of harm.

This presents the greatest challenge to the educator. For, if it is essential for young people to have a feeling for what drug use would mean in personal terms, what form of educational experience will young people accept, short of actual experimentation? The answer to this question is the key to designing a really meaningful educational program. It will be considered in practical terms in our discussion of the design of curriculum materials.

METHODS

Setting up the Program: Who Plans?   Because the school establishment is viewed by many young people as alien to their needs when drugs are discussed, credibility is one sticky problem that arises in the preparation of a program. Many students actually know more than their teachers about drugs and, as noted above, damaging confrontations can occur. My first plea, therefore, is that students have a part in the planning of any drug education program. Because credibility is crucial, student involvement is essential.

The involvement of students at the planning stage will help to avoid another kind of confrontation as well—that which occurs on issues that are peripheral to the ones under discussion. For instance, I have found it best not to get hung up in a discussion which is commonly introduced by the question, "How can you tell me what to do about drugs when you have made such a mess of society with the war, poverty, and so forth?" This question reflects the students' constant effort to shift responsibility away from themselves and onto the older generation. If I accept this shift, much of the credibility that I can offer in discussing drugs is wiped out. I try to counter this by telling them that I agree with their concerns and am personally working to fight against the same injustices that they are attacking. Then I put it back to them: "What are *you* doing to correct the wrongs you see in society?" I then focus on drugs, with comments designed to make it clear that the responsibility for drug-taking does not rest with society in general, but squarely with them. The inclusion of students in the planning of the program can bring this same focus to the program from the beginning.

Setting up the Program: Who Teaches?   The teachers should teach the program. The current practice of bringing in outside professionals to lecture about drugs in the school is not desirable: it produces an unhealthy degree of sensationalism, and it does not provide the continuity and depth that an ongoing program in the curriculum can offer.

However, it will be some time before classroom teachers are adequately trained to field the subject of drugs, which is a complex and continually changing area. Teachers should not be put at the disadvantage of having to carry the entire program unless first-rate source material on the pharmacological, psychological, and legal effects of drugs is available to them. Assembling such materials is a necessary early step in planning a drug education program. Another step is the development of a system whereby the teachers can work with the experts in teacher workshops and in their classrooms, rather than in the assembly hall.

A WAY TO GET STARTED

Pre-Test: What do young people know about drugs? It is easy to overestimate or underestimate the students' level of sophistication on this subject, and the teacher must have a realistic notion of the class's knowledge in order either to plan a credible program or to evaluate the program's effectiveness at the conclusion.

One who overestimates the students' knowledge finds that what appeared to be understanding and sophistication was, in fact, the mouthing of rumor, hearsay, and often outright false information about drugs and the laws that control their use. This teacher runs the risk of omitting or treating briefly topics about which the students need real information.

The teacher who underestimates the students' knowledge, on the other hand, risks presenting material that is "old stuff," or talking down to the class, or being too simplistic—any of which can produce the reaction, "We know more than our teacher about this," and severely damage the teacher's role in the program.

The plea here, then, is to check the receiver before transmitting, to determine the level of student expertise and understanding and to provide a starting-point against which the program can be checked in the evaluation stage.

Questions on page 125 illustrate the type of pre-test that could be undertaken as a preliminary step. The availability of this type of information, coupled with a sounding of what the students perceive as their educational needs from a drug education program, puts the school in a much stronger position to present material that is pertinent.

CONTENT

The actual content of a drug education program should not be limited to a discussion of marihuana, LSD, amphetamines, and heroin: one should not talk about this group without discussing alcohol and tobacco. This is not simply to afford a comparison between legal and illegal drugs, but also to point out that from a medical viewpoint, excessive alcohol use and cigarette smoking are major health problems that many feel are a greater threat to young people and their future health than the use—albeit increasing use—of psychedelics, stimulants, and narcotics.

Topical information in the following categories should be provided about each drug:

- Indications for medical use
- History of non-prescribed use
- Physical effects
- Mental effects
- Medical and social complications of repeated and excessive use
- Treatment of drug dependence
- Data on the relationship of drug use to job and school performance and to crime
- Relevant laws and their enforcement.

Pre-Test

(This is a sample of the kinds of questions that can be used.)

Usage: Have you or any of your friends used the following drugs?

	once	more than once
marihuana		
LSD (acid)		
amphetamines (diet pills, "speed")		
opiates (heroin, opium)		
sedatives (barbituates, tranquilizers)		
glue		
alcohol		
cigarettes		

Law: Check the *maximum* federal penalty for illegal possession of marihuana (first offence).

    a. none

    b. fine only

    c. 1 year in prison

    d. 10 years in prison

Medical: Check the appropriate column.

	T	F	Don't know
1. A common cause of death in heroin users is overdose.			
2. Alcohol causes direct damage to the body.			
3. You can become physically dependent on marihuana.			
4. LSD leads to chromosome damage which has been shown to cause leukemia.			
5. Hepatitis is common in drug-using young people.			

Answers:

LAW: d

MEDICAL: 1-T; 2-T; 3-F; 4-F; 5-T

The dynamic discussion of how young people arrive at their decision to use or not to use drugs can start with a class' building a list of motivational and social forces such as the ones listed below:

Motivational Forces (Pro and Con)

1. Experimentation
2. Pleasure
3. Aesthetic experience
4. Self-revelation
5. Religious experience
6. Defiance of authority
7. Depression

1. Concern about the immediate physical and emotional effects
2. Concern with the long-term effects
3. Respect for the law
4. Lack of interest in drugs
5. Available alternatives to the drug experience

Social Forces

- Group pressure
- Loneliness
- Family Relationships
- Friendships

The format for such class discussion is crucial. Education is experience. How can drug experience be discussed without an individual's having the experience? We certainly can't hand out drugs for experimentation in the classroom. And teachers have probably had less experience than students have. The challenge of imparting a feeling for what drug experience would mean in personal terms is what was referred to earlier as the critical feature of the drug education effort. The means that I have found most effective in approaching this goal is the inclusion of drug experienced young people in the educational process. This can be done in three ways:

1. In person. This method has been described and evaluated in a previous article in the *Bulletin,* "Utilizing Drug-Experienced Youth in Drug Education Programs," September, 1969.

2. By means of media. I have found audio tapes and interviews to be far superior to movies.

3. Through case reports. These are third best, but also useful and especially convincing when coupled with a tape or movie.

The following is offered as a concrete example. It is selected from the amphetamine section of a comprehensive drug curriculum designed by the author for junior and senior high school students. The material selected for illustration is from the dynamic section of the curriculum, and includes excerpts from taped interviews with drug users, excerpts from a section discussing motivations, and one case study. Questions to stimulate class discussion are included. These questions are handled best by a class that has already studied the physical and mental effects of the drugs.

On Stimulant Drugs—The Amphetamines

Jill, aged 16:

> I used to take one tablet of Dexedrine a day. I really felt it improved my school work. Then I had some trouble with history, and I started to take more. The next thing I knew, I was on speed.

What do you think about Jill's decision to take more Dexedrine?

Susan, aged 18:

> When I started doing it (speed*), I was over 180 pounds. I started doing it to lose weight, and then I lost 50 pounds. Then I got hepatitis, and when I got hepatitis, I kept eating, and I gained back 20 pounds. Now I can't do that anymore 'cause I started seeing cockroaches that weren't there.

What does Susan's statement tell us about the physical and mental effects of repeated amphetamine use? If hepatitis didn't motivate Susan to stop, why do you suppose seeing "cockroaches that weren't there" did?

John, aged 18:

> "I was at this party at a girl's house. She had some diet pills, and she gave me five of them, and I took them, and I dug it. And then I was really into diet pills for a while, and then somebody offered me crystal meth, and I did up a hit of that, and I just got into doing crystal meth. Just kept on doing it.

How much drug taking do you think is a passive decision—because drugs are available? How much drug taking is influenced by social pressure as might be present at a party where drugs are used?

Frank, aged 15:

> I had two jobs and took amphetamines to stay awake. I needed the money. What's wrong with that?

Do you think there is anything wrong with that?

---

* Methamphetamine, or Methedrine, is a stimulant that has a particularly powerful effect on the mind. It is now sold through illicit channels along with marihuana, LSD and heroin. It is called "speed" or "crystal meth" on the street.

Motivation

What are the reasons young people give for using these drugs without a physician's prescription

"To get high. For kicks."

Most youthful experimenters try amphetamines for these reasons. If the experience is pleasurable, there can be psychological craving to repeat it and sometimes the desire is to remain high all the time. When the drug methamphetamine, which produces the most vivid high, is used repeatedly, its user is given the unappealing title of "speed freak" by his peers.

Why do you think a person would want to remain high all the time?

"To improve my performance."

The desire to improve school work or athletic performance is the reason some young people give for taking amphetamines. Many merely seek to stay awake longer; others believe that these drugs increase alertness and physical stamina. You will be better able to evaluate the validity of this reasoning after you have studied the mind and body effects of these drugs.

"Because my friends do it."

Social pressure is an important ingredient in drug taking and this is recognized by the youthful user. Many cannot articulate a reason why they tried a drug and refer instead to the social situation in which it was used. "I did it because I was at a party," or "My buddy told me to try it." This kind of reasoning is quite typical of the one-time user who seeks more to be a part of a group and has no real commitment to the drug.

"Because I can't do without it."

A small group of young people become so dependent on amphetamines that they feel that they cannot function without them. They might not even seek the euphoric, or high effects, but rather state that their amphetamines prevent depression.

Case Study

Early in the evening, a 20-year-old young man arrived in the doctor's office, dirty from head to toe, his eyes bloodshot, and holding his head down to hide his face. He had spent the summer living in the city park, having left home about a year before. He rather sheepishly asked for something to cover up the marks on his face. Examination revealed multiple gouged-out areas about his face. He had come to find out if he could get something to hide the sores that was less irritating than the grease makeup he was already using. He was advised to wash his face and leave the sores open to the air. He accepted this after some discussion about what it takes to help wounds heal without infection. Then, almost in passing, although it was the heart of the issue, he was asked about the origin of the wounds on his face. Ostensibly ignoring the question, he rose to leave. As he put his hand on the doorknob, he turned and said curtly, "I did it to myself." Asked whether he wanted to talk about it, he left the room as if he didn't hear. The doctor had just begun to write a note in his chart when he looked up and saw the young man had come back. He said in a sarcastic tone, "Well, if you really want to know, I'll tell you. I've taken speed twice in my life, and the first time, a month ago, I just got all hopped up; nothing much happened. This time I was alone. I took the same amount of speed, and a little while later, I found myself standing in front of the mirror, staring at myself. I just looked and looked, and I remember taking my hands up to my face and picking open the skin. I can remember picking open every spot with my own hands, and then I went to sleep. When I woke up in the morning, I had trouble remembering exactly how it happened; it was like a nightmare. I can just remember myself in front of that mirror."

At this point he went into some detail on his past experiences with drugs. Although he'd used marihuana episodically for about three years, his experience with speed was relatively new. He was thoroughly frightened now and stated with some credibility that he wasn't going to try speed again for fear of hurting himself. Once confidence was established, this young man was able to relate an episode from his early adolescence that seemed relevant. He had become very depressed about his social life and his inability to date the prettiest girls. On a day when his family was away, he remembers standing in the bathroom before the mirror and picking at his face. Less severe damage had been done on that occasion than on the current one.

As he left the office, he added that he didn't want to talk about this with a psychiatrist; however, as kind of an afterthought, he turned and asked whether it would be all right if he came back to see the physician again.

Class Discussion

What do you think was the most frightening part of the drug experience for this young man? Why do you suppose he was so reluctant to tell the doctor?

Why do you think he took speed a second time? Why do you suppose he took the drug when he was alone? Do you think most drugs are taken alone or in groups? What are the differences between taking a drug alone and taking it with other people?

Do you think that the episode described when he was younger is relevant to the way he reacted to a drug at age 20?

SUMMARY

In this discussion of current and proposed drug education programs for schools, the following suggestions were made:

1. Articulate at the outset the goals of a drug education program applicable to the school's situation.

2. Evaluate the level of student sophistication about drugs and the expectations the students have for a drug education program.

3. Include students in planning the program.

4. Attempt an honest dissemination of information rather than a moralistic or punitive polemic.

5. Try to include the drug experienced young person in the educational process, either directly or by means of tapes, movies, or case reports.

6. Recognize—and bring the students to recognize—that the ultimate decisions about drug use rest with the students.

This sixth point is basic to the program and crucial for its effectiveness. As I recently said to the sophomore class at Newton South High School:

> Meaningful control rests not with the law, the Federal Bureau of Narcotics and Dangerous Drugs, the police; nor is it the ultimate responsibility of your doctor, your parents, or your teachers. The on-the-spot decision of whether or not to take drugs is clearly yours. The drugs go into you. The responsibility is yours. It is with a respect for your good judgment that I detail the effects of these agents. To make a rational choice, you must have respect for yourselves, your mind, your body, and your future.

References

[1] Lewis, David C., Freedman, Marion, and Stolow, Arthur. "Utilizing Drug-Experienced Youth in Drug Education Programs." The Bulletin of the National Association of Secondary School Principals, Vol. 53, No. 338, September 1969, pp. 45-51.

[2] Lewis, David C. The Drug Experience: Data for Decision-Making. CSCS, Inc., Boston, 1970. 320 pages and 4 cassette audiotapes.

FOUR

STUDENT RIGHTS AND RESPONSIBILITIES

Only recently has much attention been directed toward the rights of students. Historically, it was assumed that First Amendment rights really did not apply to minors in a school setting. Because of immaturity, lack of financing, and lack of interest, students have not been in a position to organize and support influential lobbies and organizations which could serve their interests. The result in part has been delayed recognition of their rights. Until very recently, student rights have been assessed as being at a level slightly superior to that of patients in mental institutions and inmates in jails, and roughly comparable to that of members of the armed forces.

Ira Glasser, executive director of the New York Civil Liberties Union, describes the status of student rights as scandalous in the course of reviewing several case studies and judicial decisions relevant to the issue. His title, "Schools for Scandal . . . ," may be taken as a fair representation of his point of view. Among adult organizations, the American Civil Liberties Union has been the most active in seeking to advance the cause of student rights. Their well publicized pamphlet, *Academic Freedom in the Secondary Schools,* includes a carefully argued case for student rights in the areas of free expression and communication, freedom of association, freedom of assembly and the right to petition, student government, student discipline, personal appearance, freedom from discrimination, the rights of married and/or pregnant students and academic freedom. At base, the argument of the ACLU is that all of the Bill of Rights, plus the fourteenth amendment guaranteeing the equal protection of the laws to all citizens, have full applicability to students.

As with the civil rights movement, the courts have provided the legal basis for advances in the area of student rights. Rights have been won; in most cases they have not been freely granted by schoolmen. In recent years courts have helped to remind school officials and other authorities that students need not await the magic age of 21—or even 18—before experiencing constitutionally guaranteed liberties. Frequently the courts have been asked to rule on the reasonableness of limitations and restrictions which have been imposed on students by school authorities. Occasionally their decisions have even served to remind the public that education itself is a right and that the capricious expulsion of pupils denies them that right.

In fairness to contemporary school authorities, all of whom are as much a part of their cultural milieu as other citizens, it must be acknowledged that the history of denying student rights has its own origin in cultural and legal precedents. Schools, by serving as the guides and guardians of young people, have enjoyed a special moral and legal role in society, rather analogous to that of the family. Such a relationship quite naturally places a strain on the personal and civil liberties of those who are guided and guarded. Legally, the arrangement has been known as *in loco parentis*, meaning that school officials have been permitted to make many of the same kinds of arbitrary decisions enjoyed by parents, and without the need to defend their actions.

It has only been in the last several years that the concept of *in loco parentis* has given ground to the concept that students enjoy full legal rights to citizenship. The article by C. Michael Abbot, "Demonstrations, Dismissals, Due Process, and the High School . . . ," contains a detailed commentary on the legal limits of dissent and disruption. One may infer, to express it perhaps too simply, that the courts have affirmed the legality of dissent but continue to find disruption illegal. In practical terms, they are requiring school systems to demonstrate more clearly than before just how a given protest activity disrupts an instructional activity.[1]

There is now ample legal affirmation of the right to wear freedom buttons (*Burnside* v. *Byars,* 1966) and black armbands (*Tinker* v. *Des Moines Independent Community School District,* 1969). Similarly, virtually all forms of non-disruptive behavior can expect legal sanction. Included in this category are parades and the criticism of policy decisions made by public officials, including school officials. Disruption, or the absence thereof, still remains the key differentiating criterion between illegal and legal acts.[2] The right of an individual to address a group at any time or place convenient to the speaker is still considered an act of disruption (*Cox* v. *Louisiana,* 1965). Similarly, disruption need not be politically engendered to be declared illegal. In the case of *Fitzpatrick* v. *Board of Education of Central School District No. 2* (1967), the New York Supreme Court affirmed a school district's right to suspend a student for walking home for lunch on the grounds that since not all pupils could eat at the same time, permitting some to leave the campus would result in undue commotion and noise disruptive to other students.

In the U.S. Supreme Court landmark *Gault* decision (1967), the right of a juvenile to enjoy the same legal protections enjoyed by adult defendants was affirmed, including the right to notice, a hearing, counsel, and confrontation—all the rights of due process. An earlier case, *Dixon* v. *Alabama State Board of*

[1] See Richard L. Berkman, "Students in Court: Free Speech and the Functions of Schooling in America," *Harvard Educational Review,* 40 (November, 1970): 567-595.
[2] It is clear that school authorities still possess the necessary legal support to handle disruptive students. In California, the guidelines were published in Robert R. Granucci [Deputy Attorney General], *Protecting the Schools; Legal Remedies for Disruptive Conduct,* reproduced by permission of the Office of the Attorney General (Burlingame: California Teachers Association, 1969), 13 pp.

Education (1961), went a long way toward establishing student procedural rights, including adequate notice prior to a lengthy suspension or expulsion, notice of the charges, and some kind of hearing. After a lengthy court process in New York, however, the Second Circuit Court of Appeals failed to affirm a district court's judgment on the right of a student to have counsel present in a guidance conference *(Madera v. Board of Education,* 1967). The rationale of the court was that a guidance conference between counselors, parents, teachers, and administrators was not a criminal proceeding; thus the demands of due process did not apply.

The litigation of the past five years has helped clarify the legal boundaries within which a school district must work in its effort to maintain discipline. It has also helped to make administrators wary of arbitrary disciplinary actions against students. The article by Laurence W. Knowles, "Keeping Out of Court," helps to point out the wisdom of always trying to "out fair" students. There is evidence that some educators are developing a growing desire to do just that.

In 1970 a special task force of the National Education Association proposed a twenty-four page code intended as a kind of bill of rights for students. Effective September, 1970, another powerful group, the New York City Board of Education, put into effect a "Resolution Stating the Rights and Responsibilities of Senior High School Students," the particulars of which are included in this chapter. While both the action itself and the terms of the resolution were criticized by some administrators and teachers, the response was generally favorable, to wit the short article by student Jeff Summer taken from *Revelation Now.*

Obviously not all of the problems are being solved with dispatch. Unwed mothers have only recently won the right to attend public school following the birth of their children,[3] while a majority of school systems still deny pregnant girls of school age the right to continue schooling. The article by Frances Wurtz and Geraldine Fergen, "Boards Still Duck Problem of Pregnant Schoolgirls," is addressed to this problem.

Although the bulk of attention would appear to be directed at student rights rather than at their responsibilities, it may be quite reasonable to expect the latter quality to grow out of their successful experiences in asserting their rights. It would be surprising if the successful expression of rights did not also lead to a practical realization of limits and an awareness of responsibilities to themselves and others. As one commentator has asserted, "responsibility grows out of respect for one's self and an understanding of the meaning of personal freedom"; it cannot develop before freedom is granted.[4]

---

[3] Leo O. Garber, "Unwed Mothers Win Right to Attend Public School," *Nations Schools,* 85 (April, 1970): 81-82.

[4] Morrel, J. Clute, "Rights and Responsibilities of Students," *Educational Leadership,* 26 (December, 1968): 240-242.

SCHOOLS FOR SCANDAL —
THE BILL OF RIGHTS AND PUBLIC EDUCATION

IRA GLASSER

There are only two public institutions in the United States which steadfastly deny that the Bill of Rights applies to them. One is the military and the other is the public schools. Both are compulsory. Taken together, they are the chief socializing institutions of our society. Everyone goes through our schools. What they learn—not from what they are formally taught but from the way the institution is organized to treat them—is that authority is more important than freedom, order more precious than liberty, and discipline a higher value than individual expression. That is a lesson which is inappropriate to a free society—and certainly inappropriate to its schools.

I. PROCEDURAL RIGHTS

Walter Crump is a slim, 18-year-old, esthetic-looking Negro college student. On first impression he is talented, articulate, and gentle, and further meetings do not alter that impression. Until May 4, 1969, he attended the High School of Music and Art, a special school in New York City, compiling a satisfactory academic and disciplinary record. With graduation only a few weeks away, Walter Crump was looking ahead to college in the fall and from there to a career in the theater. On May 4 all that very nearly came to an end.

Early in the day, Mr. Crump was involved in a minor verbal altercation with a teacher. The facts of the disagreement are unimportant; the incident at worst appears to have involved an undetermined amount of rudeness and discourtesy on both sides. No violence or threat of violence occurred. It was the kind of a verbal flare-up that occurs daily in almost every imaginable setting, and which usually passes without damage to either party.

Later that afternoon, however, Mr. Crump was summarily suspended and told to go home until further notice. (That procedure was unambiguously in violation of the New York City Board of Education's own rules, which require that a suspended student be kept in school until a parent is informed prior to sending the student out of the school.)

Further notice did not come until 12 days later, at which time Mr. Crump's foster mother was told to come with Walter to a hearing—the board called it a "guidance conference"—eight days later on May 22, at the office of an assistant superintendent of schools. (That procedure also was in violation of the board's

From *Phi Delta Kappan*, 51 (December, 1969), 190-94. Reprinted with the permission of the author and the publisher.

Ira Glasser is Executive Director of the New York Civil Liberties Union.

own rules. The maximum period that a principal may suspend a child is five days, and a "guidance conference" with prior notification to the parent by certified mail must occur within that period.)

Mr. Crump was unable to persuade his foster mother to attend the hearing, so he went himself. When he arrived, approximately 45 minutes late, he discovered that the hearing had been held without him. Before the hearing began, two separate requests were made by parents of two fellow students at the High School of Music and Art to attend the hearing in support of Mr. Crump. Both requests were denied, despite the fact that a state law had been passed and signed by Governor Rockefeller that very month granting the right of students to be represented—even by a lawyer if they wished—at hearings arising out of suspensions of more than five days. The denial of these requests, therefore, was in violation of state law.

At the "hearing," Mr. Crump was summarily "convicted" (of what, nobody knows) and, just a few weeks short of graduation, dismissed from the school. On May 23, Mr. Crump's foster mother received a letter from the assistant superintendent curtly informing her that a "guidance conference" had been held in absentia and that Walter had been discharged from school, effective immediately.

The expulsion of Mr. Crump from full-time public education was totally lacking in even the minimal rudiments of due process of law. He never received a meaningful hearing; he was never informed of his right to be represented by counsel; he was never informed of the charges against him; and his supporters were not permitted to speak in his behalf.

But that was not the end of it. A few days later, Mr. Crump's foster mother received another letter, this time from the Bureau of Child Welfare. The letter informed her that since Mr. Crump was over 18 and now out of school (the Board of Education had been thoughtful enough to allow a bureau caseworker to attend the "guidance conference" and to send his supervisor a copy of the dismissal letter), board payments to his foster parents would soon end.

At that point, one of the High School of Music and Art parents who had been refused admission to the guidance conference arranged an appointment for Mr. Crump with an attorney from the New York Civil Liberties Union. NYCLU immediately informed the Bureau of Child Welfare that the dismissal from school was being contested, that in their judgment the dismissal was illegal, and that a federal suit was being prepared that very afternoon. To no avail: The Bureau cut off board payments the next day, also without a hearing and without even the courtesy of a reply.

Mr. Crump's attorney subsequently filed suit in federal court, obtained a new hearing (which he was allowed to attend), and, not surprisingly, Walter Crump was reinstated, more than a month after the initial suspension. He was graduated without incident three weeks later.

If what happened to Walter Crump had been an isolated instance, it would be no less outrageous; but at least one could not easily draw inferences about an entire school system. In fact, however, the procedures which governed Walter Crump's case govern other cases as well. The frightening thing about the procedures followed by school officials in the Crump case is precisely that they were *routine*. The independent experiences of several respected agencies in New York—the NAACP Legal Defense and Education Fund, Citizens Committee for Children, the New York Civil Liberties Union, the Metropolitan Applied Research Center, Mobilization for Youth, and several parents associations—suggest that what happened to Mr. Crump happens regularly and widely to anyone facing suspension. Two things may be said about the procedures governing student suspensions in New York (and there is no reason to believe that New York is unique; although some other cities may enjoy better procedures, cases raising the same issues have arisen all over the United States):

1. The procedures represent a gross denial of the constitutional right to due process, including the right to a fair hearing.

2. Even those inadequate procedures are regularly violated by school officials.*

If Mr. Crump had not had a friend knowledgeable enough and aggressive enough to seek legal help, it is difficult to say where he would be today. Certainly he wouldn't be in college. Other students, perhaps I should say other *children,* have not been so fortunate.

Even when legal redress is possible to obtain, it may not be possible to undo the damage inflicted in the meantime. Nothing illustrates that better than the mass expulsions that occurred at Franklin K. Lane High School in New York last January.

On January 27, 1969, 670 students, most of them black or Puerto Rican, were summarily expelled from Lane. They received no notice of, nor any opportunity to contest, the action taken against them. Letters were sent out on January 24 informing parents that they had a week to contest the expulsions, but only three days later all 670 were expelled and informed that there was no chance at all to reverse the decision. Moreover, January 24 turns out to have been a Friday and January 27 the following Monday, so actually parents received no notice whatsoever.

The alleged reason for the expulsion was to relieve overcrowded conditions at Lane by eliminating multiple sessions and by putting the school on a single session. Yet two-thirds of the 61 academic high schools in New York City were more overcrowded than Lane, some of them substantially so, and only one operated on a single session. The truth is that what happened at Lane was the result of severe pressures arising out of the bitter teachers' strike during the fall; those pressures finally resulted in an agreement by the powerful—teachers, administrators, and politicians—against the powerless—students and their parents. It is precisely to protect the powerless against the excesses of the powerful that

---

* A startling fact in the Crump case was the extent to which school authorities broke even their own rules and regulations.

the Bill of Rights was invented. Yet here that protection did not exist. It is ironic indeed that a city which was capable of being whipped into a frenzy over the issue of due process during the strike was conspicuously silent during what was surely the single most stunning denial of due process ever to have occurred in the New York City school system.

Once the decision was made to expel the students, a mechanical rule was devised: All students who were absent 30 days or more during the fall semester and who had maintained an unsatisfactory academic record in the fall semester were to be expelled.

The decision to expel based on student attendance records and academic achievement during the 1968 fall semester seemed peculiar indeed. After all, it was during that semester that Lane was struck for 36 days as part of the city-wide teachers' strike. In addition, there were several brief boycotts by students and parents over dissatisfaction with the strike settlement. Finally, there was a severe flu epidemic in New York that fall, causing widespread absenteeism among both students and teachers. Hardly a typical semester by which to measure either attendance or achievement!

Although we hear much these days about procedures which supposedly protect the guilty, it is ultimately out of a concern for the innocent that fair procedures were developed. Consider what happened to a few of those caught in Frank K. Lane's net:

1. *Arthur Knight.* Mr. Knight was expelled on January 27 as he attempted to re-register for the spring, 1969, semester. Prior to the fall, 1968, semester, Knight had maintained a satisfactory academic record. He was legitimately absent for the entire fall semester due to a serious kidney ailment. On his first day back he was expelled.

Later by more than a month, during which he was out of school entirely, he was directed to report to a special annex to continue his "education." (Inexplicably, some of the expelled students were ultimately assigned to this annex instead of being expelled completely.) But the "annex" offered no grades, no examinations, and no homework. There were few if any books, and only three teachers. The entire annex was only open from 9 a.m. to 12 noon. It was clearly a custodial institution, not an educational one.

What had Arthur Knight done to deserve such punishment? Why wasn't he allowed to contest the punishment at a hearing?

2. *Oscar Gonzalus.* Mr. Gonzalus was notified of his expulsion by mail. He had no chance to challenge it. Yet the criteria by which students were expelled did not apply to him, because he had been absent less than 30 days during the fall, 1968, semester. Furthermore, most of those absences were due to an attack of the flu. Finally, Gonzalus had maintained a satisfactory academic record before the fall semester. All these facts could have been proven at a fair hearing *before* expulsion. But no fair hearing was allowed.

3. *Marcine Chestnut.* Miss Chestnut was expelled because of an allegedly de-

ficient attendance record. Yet despite her poor attendance, partly due to a severe case of the flu, she maintained a satisfactory academic record during the fall, 1968, semester, as she had during previous semesters. Like the others, however, she had no chance.

More than two months later, a complaint was filed in federal court in behalf of all 670 students. In late April, 1969, almost three months to the day after the initial expulsion, Federal Judge Jack B. Weinstein reinstated all 670 students and ordered the school to provide remedial work to make up for the lost time. Judge Weinstein found that the action against the 670 had denied them their constitutional right to due process.

Beyond the legal question, of course, is the larger morality of what happened at Lane. Though many students were innocently caught up in the action, and all were denied due process, many others were indeed absent for more than 30 days and did have failing academic records. For these students, the penalties were even greater, for these were students in grave trouble. For such students, the legal victory was meaningless because the educational damage was irremediable. At this writing (August, 1969), ongoing attempts to retrieve what was lost during the three months are reaching only a few of the 670, and helping even fewer. It says a great deal about a school system whose response to students hanging on by the slimmest thread is to cut that thread for reasons of administrative convenience.

II. 1st AMENDMENT RIGHTS

Procedural rights are not the only rights denied to students by public schools. Attitudes toward individual rights are indivisible; institutions that do not protect the right to a fair hearing are not likely to protect free speech either. The schools are no exception.

Indeed, the most publicized conflicts between school authorities and students involve First Amendment rights: free speech, freedom of the press, freedom of assembly. All across the country, from New York to Mississippi, from Iowa to Texas, from California to Alabama, courts are being asked, for the first time in many cases, to consider the demands of students for freedoms normally guaranteed to adults but traditionally denied to students. Like soldiers in the military, students are suggesting that the Bill of Rights applies to them.

In 1965, a group of black students in Mississippi were suspended for wearing buttons saying "Freedom Now." The suspension was challenged in federal court and eventually resulted in a landmark decision by the U.S. Court of Appeals for the Fifth Circuit. The court reinstated the students on the ground that no significant disruption of the educational process had taken place as a result of the wearing of the buttons, and that therefore there was no legal basis for suspending the students.

It is instructive to note that on the same day the same court decided a similar case *against* another group of suspended students. In that case, school officials were upheld because there was clear evidence that the students wearing the buttons harassed students who did not wear them and created a variety of other substantial disturbances.

Thus the court sought to limit the power of school officials to prevent the free expression of views, but nonetheless upheld the power of school officials to regulate disruptive conduct. In effect, the court constructed a factual standard which requires school officials to provide conclusive evidence of substantial interference with the educational functioning of the school before they may prevent political expression by students. In the absence of such a factual determination one way or the other, implied the court, we are simply granting public school officials a blank check to suppress political speech arbitrarily, a right no other civilian public official has.

Despite this decision, students all over the country have been regularly denied the right to peaceful political expression during the past few years, whether or not such expression involved substantial disruption. In 1967, John Tinker, then a 15-year-old high school student in Des Moines, Iowa; his sister Mary Beth, 13; and a friend, Christopher Eckhardt, 16, decided to publicize their opposition to the war in Vietnam by wearing black armbands to school. The form of expression seemed to fall well within the standard enunciated in the Mississippi case: What could be a more passive, less disruptive form of expression than the wearing of armbands!

The principals of the Des Moines schools responded by first banning the wearing of armbands and then suspending the Tinkers and their friend. Parents of the students filed suit in federal court, and the case eventually reached the U.S. Court of Appeals for the Eighth Circuit, which upheld the principals' action. That decision was in clear conflict with the earlier decision by the Fifth Circuit Court of Appeals in the Mississippi case, and no one could resolve the conflict except the U.S. Supreme Court, which agreed to hear the case.

On February 24, 1969, the Supreme Court reversed the lower court's decision and upheld the students' right to wear the armbands. The court made the following points:

1. The wearing of an armband for the purpose of expressing views is clearly within the protection of the First Amendment.

2. Both students and teachers are entitled to the protections of the First Amendment. "It can hardly be argued," said the court, "that either students or teachers shed their constitutional rights to freedom of speech or expression at the schoolhouse gate. This has been the unmistakable holding of this court for almost 50 years."

3. While actual disturbance which intrudes upon the work of the school or the rights of other students may be banned, the mere *fear* that such a disturbance might occur is not sufficient. As the court said, ". . . in our system, undifferentiated fear or apprehension of disturbance is not enough to overcome the right to freedom of expression. Any departure from absolute regimentation may cause

trouble. Any variation from the majority's opinion may inspire fear. Any word spoken, in class, in the lunchroom, or on the campus, that deviates from the views of another person may start an argument or cause a disturbance. But our Constitution says we we must take this risk; and our history says that it is this sort of hazardous freedom—this kind of openness—that is the basis of our national strength. . . ."

4. The standard of the Mississippi button case was upheld; that is, before an expression of views may be prohibited, school officials must show that the exercise of the forbidden right would "materially and substantially interfere with the requirements of appropriate discipline in the operation of the school."

5. Students are constitutionally entitled to freedom of expression not only in the classroom but also elsewhere in the school hours. Freedom of expression, said the court, "is not confined to the supervised and ordained discussion which takes place in the classroom. . . . A student's rights . . . do not embrace merely the classroom hours. When he is in the cafeteria, or on the playing field, or on the campus during the authorized hours, he may express his opinions. . . ."

While the *Tinker* case appears to settle the problem of wearing buttons, arm-bands, or other symbols in school, other First Amendment rights are still in dispute, and some are currently in court. These chiefly involve the right of students to distribute political leaflets and other material such as unauthorized newspapers in the school. In one case in Jamaica High School in New York City, Jeffrey Schwartz, a senior, was suspended for *mere possession* of an unauthorized newspaper which in previous issues had been harshly critical of that school's principal, particularly with respect to students' rights.

When the suspension was challenged by the student's parents and their lawyer, the school decided to waive Jeffrey's remaining requirements and graduate him about six months ahead of time. When his parents went into court to contest the action, the Board of Education lawyers argued that the case was moot because the boy was graduated; his diploma was available to him anytime, they insisted. But after making that argument for six months, the principal refused to grant him his diploma in June on the grounds that he had not fulfilled the requirements which the principal had waived months before! Subsequently, after being out of school for an entire semester, Mr. Schwartz had to attend summer school in order to be able to get into college in the fall. Along the way, the principal caused a New York State scholarship, won by Mr. Schwartz in a competitive examination, to be revoked for failing to graduate on time in June!

The issues raised in the *Schwartz* case are typical of those being raised in high schools all over the country.

It is particularly difficult for students to reconcile what they learn in their social studies classes about James Madison and free speech and John Peter Zenger and freedom of the press with what they confront when they try to exercise those rights in school. It is even more difficult to reconcile what they learn about fair trials with what they are subjected to at "guidance conferences." In the end, students learn less about American values from formal classroom instruction than from the way the school is organized to treat them. Unfortunately, what they do learn is that when individual rights collide with discipline and authority, individual rights inevitably recede. That such lessons are taught by our public schools is an educational scandal of major dimensions.

III. PERSONAL RIGHTS

No discussion of students' rights is complete without mentioning the widespread attempt by school officials to regulate the dress and personal appearance of students. Nothing illustrates the repressiveness of public schools more. All across the United States, thousands of students have been suspended or otherwise excluded from classes for the style of their dress or the length of their hair. In almost all cases, questions of offensiveness, health, or safety were not present. Such cases have arisen practically everywhere and have been decided differently in different places. In New York, the Commissioner of Education has clearly upheld the right of students to wear their hair or their clothes as they please within limits of safety. In Texas, the U.S. Court of Appeals has upheld the power of school officials to regulate the length of a student's hair, and similar rulings have occurred in Connecticut. In Wisconsin a federal court recently declared such actions by school officials to be unconstitutional. And in Massachusetts federal judge Charles Wyzanski has written an eloquent opinion in support of a student's right "to look like himself." The U.S. Supreme Court has so far considered the issue too trivial to deserve its attention.

Beyond the legal questions, however, consider the social significance of the attempt by school authorities to regulate personal appearance so closely. Consider the institutions of our society which insist on regulating dress: prisons, mental hospitals, convents, and the military. All these institutions depend for their existence on maintenance of a rigid system of authority and discipline. The slightest expression of individualism represents a threat to the structure of authority. These institutions recognize that the strict regulation of personal appearance is an important social mechanism to maintain control by creating a climate in which unquestioning obedience to authority will flourish. Whatever justification for such a practice may exist in prisons or in the military—or for that matter in political dictatorships whose first official acts usually involve the rounding up of "hippies"—what possible justification is there for such repression in the schools of a free society? In fact, the denial of personal rights must be seen as part of a pattern which included the denial of First Amendment rights and procedural rights as well.

It is not the students who are radical. They seek completely traditional American rights, rights which are guaranteed in the Constitution but denied to them. Rather, I think, it is the principals who violate students' rights who are the radicals. They are the ones who deny the traditional protections of the Bill of Rights to students, and they are the ones who are subverting the traditional balance between freedom and authority by perpetuating rules which sacrifice individual rights at almost every opportunity.

As the U.S. Supreme Court said in the case of *West Virginia* v. *Barnette:*

> *The Fourteenth Amendment, as now applied to the states, protects the citizen against the state itself and all of its creatures—boards of education not excepted. These are, of course, important, delicate, and highly discretionary functions, but none that they may not perform within the limits of the Bill of Rights. That they are educating the young for citizenship is reason for scrupulous protection of constitutional freedoms of the individual, if we are not to strangle the free mind at its source and teach youth to discount important principles of our government as mere platitudes.*

That was 26 years ago.

STUDENTS' RIGHTS

If secondary school students are to become citizens trained in the democratic process, they must be given every opportunity to participate in the school and in the community with rights broadly analogous to those of adult citizens. In this basic sense, students are entitled to freedom of expression, of assembly, of petition, and of conscience, and to due process and equal treatment under the law. The American Civil Liberties Union has already described how such freedoms appertain to college students in its pamphlet on "Academic Freedom and Civil Liberties for Students in Colleges and Universities." But the difference in the age range between secondary school and college students suggests the need for a greater degree of advice, counsel, and supervision by the faculty in the high schools than is appropriate for the colleges or universities. From the standpoint of academic freedom and civil liberties, an essential problem in the secondary schools is how best to maintain and encourage freedom of expression and assembly while simultaneously inculcating a sense of responsibility and good citizenship with awareness of the excesses into which the immaturity of the students might lead.

It is the responsibility of faculty and administration to decide when a situation requires a limit on freedom for the purpose of protecting the students and the school from harsh consequences. In exercising that responsibility, certain fundamental principles should be accepted in order to prevent the use of administra-

From *Academic Freedom in the Secondary Schools* (September, 1968; reprinted, New York: American Civil Liberties Union, December, 1969), pp. 9-20. Reprinted with the permission of the publisher.

tive discretion to eliminate legitimate controversy and legitimate freedom. The principles are:

1. A recognition that freedom implies the right to make mistakes and that students must therefore sometimes be permitted to act in ways which are predictably unwise so long as the consequences of their acts are not dangerous to life and property, and do not seriously disrupt the academic process.

2. A recognition that students in their schools should have the right to live under the principle of "rule by law" as opposed to "rule by personality." To protect this right, rules and regulations should be in writing. Students have the right to know the extent and limits of the faculty's authority and, therefore, the powers that are reserved for the students and the responsibilities that they should accept. Their rights should not be compromised by faculty members who while ostensibly acting as consultants or counsellors are, in fact, exercising authority to censor student expression and inquiry.

3. A recognition that deviation from the opinions and standards deemed desirable by the faculty is not *ipso facto* a danger to the educational process.

FREEDOM OF EXPRESSION AND COMMUNICATION

Primary liberties in a student's life have to do with the processes of inquiry and of learning, of acquiring and imparting knowledge, of exchanging ideas. There must be no interference in the school with his access to, or expression of, controversial points of view. No student should suffer any hurt or penalty for any idea he expresses in the course of participation in class or school activities.

The right of every student to have access to varied points of view, to confront and study controversial issues, to be treated without prejudice or penalty for what he reads or writes, and to have facilities for learning available in the school library and the classroom may not be derogated or denied.

1. LEARNING MATERIALS

Toward these ends policies should be adopted in writing establishing solely educational criteria for the selection and purchase of class and library materials including books, magazines, pamphlets, films, records, tapes and other media. These policies should provide principles and procedures for the selection of materials and for the handling of complaints and grievances about these materials.

The removal from the school library or the banning of material alleged to be improper imposes a grave responsibility. It should be exercised, if at all, with the utmost of circumspection and only in accordance with carefully established and publicly promulgated procedures. (Such procedures are detailed in the ACLU pamphlet, "Combatting Undemocratic Pressures on Schools and Libraries —A Guide for Local Communities.")

2. FORUMS

Generally speaking, students have the right to express publicly and to hear any opinion on any subject which they believe is worthy of consideration. Assemblies and extra-curricular organizations are the more obvious, appropriate forums for the oral exchange of ideas and offer the opportunity for students to hear views on topics of relatively specialized interest. Whatever the forum, the faculty should defend the right of students to hear and participate in discussions of controversial issues. Restrictions may be tolerated only when they are employed to forestall events which would clearly endanger the health or safety of members of the school community or clearly and imminently disrupt the educational process. Education, it may be noted, should enable individuals to react to ideas, however distasteful, in rational and constructive ways.

The education of young people to participate in public presentations of opinions and to choose wisely among those that are offered suggests that they help plan assembly programs. The students should have the responsibility for planning other forums, especially those offered by extracurricular organizations: for selecting the topics, choosing the speakers, and determining the method of presentation.

Students may choose speakers from their own ranks, from the faculty, and from outside the school. The community at large may provide speakers who have knowledge and insights that might not otherwise be available to students; it may introduce to the school persons whose presence enriches the educational experience. Controversies that are sometimes involved in inviting outside speakers should not deter faculty advisers from encouraging their presence at school.

Every student has the right to state freely his own views when he participates in a discussion program. Faculty members may advise the students on such matters as style, appropriateness to the occasion, and the length of their presentations and on the avoidance of slander, but they must not censor the expression of ideas. To foster the free expression of opinions, students participating on panels should have wide latitude to state the differences in their views. For the same reason, questions from members of student audiences are ordinarily desirable and should be encouraged by arranging question periods of reasonable length at the end of talks.

3. STUDENT PUBLICATIONS

The preparation and publication of newspapers and magazines is an exercise in freedom of the press. Generally speaking, students should be permitted and encouraged to join together to produce such publications as they wish. Faculty advisors should serve as consultants on style, grammar, format and suitability of the materials. Neither the faculty advisors nor the principal should prohibit the publication or distribution of material except when such publication or distribution would clearly endanger the health or safety of the students, or clearly and imminently threaten to disrupt the educational process, or might be of a libelous nature. Such judgment, however, should never be exercised because of disapproval or disagreement with the article in question.

The school administration and faculty should ensure that students and faculty may have their views represented in the columns of the school newspaper. Where feasible, they should permit the publication of multiple and competing periodicals. These might be produced by the student government, by various clubs, by a class or group of classes, or by individuals banded together for this specific purpose. The material and equipment for publication such as duplicating machines, paper and ink should be available to students in such quantity as budget may permit.

The freedom to express one's opinion goes hand in hand with the responsibility for the published statement. The onus of decision as to the content of a publication should be placed clearly on the student editorial board of the particular publication. The editors should be encouraged through practice, to learn to judge literary value, newsworthiness, and propriety.

The right to offer copies of their work to fellow students should be accorded equally to those who have received school aid, and to those whose publications have relied on their own resources.

The student press should be considered a learning device. Its pages should not be looked upon as an official image of the school, always required to present a polished appearance to the extramural world. Learning effectively proceeds through trial and error, and as much or more may sometimes be gained from reactions to a poor article or a tasteless publication as from the traditional pieces, groomed carefully for external inspection.

4. SCHOOL COMMUNICATIONS

Guarantees of free expression should be extended also to other media of communication: the public address system, closed-circuit television, bulletin boards, handbills, personal contact. Reasonable access should be afforded to student groups for announcements and statements to the school community. This should include the provision of space, both indoor and outdoor, for meetings and rallies.

The school community, i.e., the administration, faculty and the student organization, has the right to make reasonable regulations as to matter, place and time of using these communication media.

The electronic media are monopolistic by nature, and their audiences are captive. When these are used as vehicles for the presentation of opinions, the guarantees and procedures applied to school assemblies should similarly be invoked with respect to choice of topics, balance of participants and freedom of expression.

5. RESTRICTIONS ON POLITICAL THOUGHT

Not only should the student be guaranteed freedom to inquire and to express his thoughts while in the school; he should also be assured that he will be free from coercion or improper disclosure which may have ill effects on his career.

a. Loyalty Oaths. Loyalty oaths are, by their inherent nature, a denial of the basic premises of American democracy. Whether imposed by the school itself, or by an external political authority, oaths required as a condition for enrollment, promotion, graduation, or for financial aid, violate the basic freedoms guaranteed to every individual by the Bill of Rights.

b. Inquiries by Outside Agencies. The solicitation by prospective private, governmental or other outside agencies or persons of information about students is a practice in which there are inherent dangers to academic freedom. To answer questions on a student's character, reliability, conduct, and academic performance is part of the school's responsibility. But questions about a student's values and opinions may be deemed invasions of educational privacy and impingements on academic freedom. A teacher's ability to resist such invasions of privacy will be strengthened if the school proscribes the recording of student opinions and adopts policies on responding to outsiders' questions that safeguard academic freedom.

Even in schools that have adopted policies to prevent the recording and disclosure of individuals' beliefs, there will be times when the teacher has to rely on his own judgment in deciding to reply or not to reply to questions about students. Both educational and personal liberty considerations should help guide the faculty member faced with inquiries that may invite the disclosure of religious, political, social, and other opinions and beliefs. Education often calls for probing, hypothesizing, and thinking out loud. Reports to persons outside the school on students' opinions therefore threaten the learning process. Moreover, an atmosphere conducive to an understanding of freedom and of the need for an interplay of ideas in a free society will hardly prevail if teachers report to outsiders on opinions expressed by their students.

The opinions and beliefs of secondary school students, although often stated with great enthusiasm, are highly subject to change. Many youths have great eagerness, exuberance, idealism, and propensity for adventure, but limited experience. The community, its laws, its parents, and the schools themselves therefore recognize that students are not as accountable for their actions as adults. Consistent with this attitude, schools should understand this difference and refrain from answering questions about students' beliefs.

6. FREEDOM OF RELIGION AND CONSCIENCE

All students are entitled to the First Amendment guarantees of the right to practice their own religion or no religion. Under the terms of the amendment, as repeatedly interpreted by the Supreme Court, any federal, state, or local law or practice is unconstitutional if it has the effect of extending to religion the mantle of public sponsorship, either through declaration of public policy or use of public funds or facilities.

Students' rights in this area are protected by judicial decisions which have found the following practices unconstitutional:

a. The recitation of any form of prayer as a group exercise,

b. The reading of the Bible as a form of worship; mandatory Bible instruction; use of schools for Bible distribution,

c. Sectarian holiday observances,

d. The showing of religious movies in class or assembly exercises,

e. The use of public school facilities for religious instruction, either within school hours or for after-school classes, whether by church or lay groups.

The teaching of religion should be distinguished from teaching factually about religion as, for example, an aspect of world history or of social sciences. Even in teaching about religion, the younger the child, the more wary the teacher must be of indoctrination. Certainly, public schools may explain the meaning of a religious holiday, as viewed by adherents of the religion of which it is a part, but may not seek to foster a religious view in the classroom or otherwise.

Although a salute to the flag and oath of allegiance are commonly accepted practices in school assembly exercises, exemptions should be granted to a student whose religious scruples or other principled convictions lead him to refuse to participate in such exercises. The Supreme Court has held that the protection of freedom of religion under the First Amendment encompasses such exemption on grounds of religious belief. There should be no distinction in this respect between student objection based on religious conviction and that based on non-religious grounds of conscience.

FREEDOM OF ASSOCIATION

The right to individual free expression implies in a democracy the right to associate for the exchange of opinion or the statement of ideas held in common.

1. EXTRACURRICULAR ACTIVITIES

Students should be free to organize associations within the school for political, social, athletic, and other proper and lawful purposes, provided that no such group denies membership to any student because of race, religion or nationality, or for any reasons other than those related to the purpose of the organization (i.e., a French club requirement for competence in French). The fact of affiliation with any extramural association should not in itself bar a group from recognition, but disclosure of such fact may be required. Any group which plans political action or discussion, of whatever purpose or complexion and whether or not affiliated with a particular legal party, should be allowed to organize and be recognized in any educational institution. The administration should not discriminate against a student because of membership in any such organization.

Student organizations are entitled to faculty advisors of their own selection. If no volunteer is available, a faculty member should be assigned to provide the required supervision, in order that the organization may exercise its right to function in the school.

The use of rooms and other facilities should be made available, as far as their primary use for instructional purposes permits, to recognized student organizations. Bulletin boards and access to school-wide communications systems should be provided for the use of student organizations, and they should be permitted to circulate notices and leaflets. The legitimate power of school authorities to safeguard school property should not be misused to suppress a poster or piece of literature by reason of objections to its content.

The nature and type of programs, projects and procedures of any student organization should be within the province of student decision, subject only to emergency ban by student government or principal in the event that a proposed activity clearly threatens the health and safety of the students, or clearly and immediately threatens to disrupt the educational process. Such a ban should not become permanent unless its justification is established through open hearings and argument.

A student organization should be permitted to use the name of the school as part of its own name, and to use this name in all activities consistent with its constitution. The school may adopt such regulations as will prevent any student organization from representing overtly or by inference that its views are sanctioned by the school. Restrictions may fairly be placed on the use of the school name in extramural activities (such as participation in public demonstrations or parades), but any such restrictions should be without discrimination in respect to all student organizations.

The administration and the faculty should not discriminate against any student because of his membership or participation in the activities of any extracurricular student association.

2. OUT-OF-SCHOOL ACTIVITIES

The school has no jurisdiction over its students non-school activities, their conduct, their movements, their dress and the expression of their ideas. No disciplinary action should be taken by the school against a student for participation in such out-of-school activities as political parties and campaigns, picketing and public demonstrations, circulation of leaflets and petitions, provided the student does not claim without authorization to speak or act as a representative of the school or one of its organizations. When a student chooses to participate in out-of-school activities that result in police action, it is an infringement of his liberty for the school to punish such activity, or to enter it on school records or report it to prospective employers or other agencies, unless authorized or requested by the student. A student who violates any law risks the legal penalties prescribed by civil authorities. He should not be placed in jeopardy at school for an offense which is not concerned with the educational institution.

FREEDOM OF ASSEMBLY AND THE RIGHT TO PETITION

The right "peaceably to assemble" is constitutionally bracketed with the right to "petition the government for a redress of grievances." Accordingly, individual students and student organizations should be permitted to hold meetings in school rooms or auditoriums, or at outdoor locations on school grounds, at which they should be free to discuss, pass resolutions, and take other lawful action respecting any matter which directly or indirectly concerns or affects them, whether it relates to school or to the extramural world. Nor should such assemblages be limited to the form of audience meetings; any variety of demonstration, whether it be a picketline, a "walk," or any other *peaceful* type, should be permissible. The school administration is justified in requiring that demonstrations or meetings be held at times that will not disrupt classes or other school activities and in places where there will be no hazards to persons or property; it also may require advance notice when necessary to avoid conflicts and to arrange for proper protection by faculty or police.

The right to distribute printed material, whether produced within or outside the school, should always be recognized, subject only to limitations designed to prevent littering, except when such distribution would clearly endanger the health or safety of the students, or clearly and imminently threaten to disrupt the educational process, or might be of a libelous nature. But the administration may require that the distributor be a student enrolled in the school.

In general, subject only to reasonable restrictions of time and place, students should be free also to collect signatures on petitions concerning either school or out-of-school issues. Neither the administration nor the faculty should have the right to screen either the contents or the wording of the petitions; they should receive them when presented and give their fullest consideration to the proposals therein.

Similarly, the wearing of buttons or badges, armbands or insignia bearing slogans or admonitions of any sort should generally be permitted as another form of expression.[1] No teacher or administrator should attempt to interfere with this practice on the grounds that the message may be unpopular with any students or faculty, or even with the majority of either group. The exercise of one or another of these techniques of expression may, under certain circumstances, clearly and imminently constitute a danger to peace or clearly and imminently threaten to disrupt the educational process. Such a situation might require staying action by

[1] In 1966, a U.S. Court of Appeals upheld the right of Mississippi high school students to wear "freedom buttons" in school "as a means of silently communicating an idea" and therefore legally protected by the First Amendment. (*Burnside v. Byars* 363 F.2d 744 1966).

the administration, similar to a temporary injunction, and subject to revocation if and when a hearing determines that the facts no longer warrant it. Interference in this way with the exercise of student rights should seldom occur, and should be undertaken with the greatest reluctance and only when accompanied by careful explanation.

STUDENT GOVERNMENT

The functions and powers of student government organizations, and the manner of selection of their officers, as well as the qualifications for office, are matters to be determined as the respective school communities think desirable, but certain rights should be guaranteed within the structure of any student government, if it is to fulfill its role as an educational device for living in a democracy.

1. The organization, operation and scope of the student government should be specified in a written constitution, formulated with effective student participation.

2. The government should function with scrupulous regard for all constitutional provisions, which should be changed only by a prescribed process of amendment in which there should be effective student participation.

3. No constitutional provision, by-law or practice should permit decisions, including expenditures of student organization funds, to be made exclusively by the faculty or administration.

4. All students should have the right to vote and to hold office.

5. The statements, votes, decisions or actions of a student incident to his role in student government should be judged solely within the sphere of the school civic life, through the medium of electoral action by his peers, or through pre-established constitutional process. Full and free participation in student government should be encouraged by an understanding that neither marks, course credits, graduation, college recommendations, nor other aspects of scholastic life will ever be adversely affected as a consequence of a stand or action with which faculty or administration may disagree. Nor should such penalties ever be invoked for failure to make financial contribution in support of any school activity.

6. In respect to the selection of officers of the student organization:

   a. All students who meet the qualifications fixed by the school constitution should be permitted to be candidates. However, disqualification for a specified period from participation in extracurricular activities, including student government, might in appropriate cases be imposed as a penalty for serious or repeated infractions of school rules.

   b. Candidates should be free to speak without censorship, subject only to equally enforced rules as to the time and place of their speeches.

   c. All candidates should have equal opportunity to publicize their campaigns.

   d. Candidates should be permitted to group into slates or parties, if they so desire.

e. Voting and vote-counting procedures should make provision for scrutiny by representatives of all candidates.

f. The candidate chosen by vote of the students should be declared elected, with no faculty veto.

g. Any electoral rules which may be adopted should apply equally, without discrimination, to all candidates.

STUDENT DISCIPLINE

The regulations concerning appropriate student behavior in the school at large should preferably be formulated by a student-faculty committee. Regulations governing the school as a whole should be fully and clearly formulated, published, and made available to all members of the school community. They should be reasonable. Specific definitions are preferable to such general criteria as "conduct unbecoming a student" and "against the best interests of the school," which allow for a wide latitude of interpretation.

1. THE RIGHT OF DUE PROCESS

To maintain the orderly administration of the school, minor infractions of school discipline may be handled in a summary fashion. In every case a student should be informed of the nature of the infraction with which he is charged. The teacher and/or administrator should bear in mind that an accusation is not the equivalent of guilt, and he should therefore be satisfied of the guilt of the accused student prior to subjecting such student to disciplinary action.

A student's locker should not be opened without his consent except in conformity with the spirit of the Fourth Amendment which requires that a warrant first be obtained on a showing of probable cause, supported by oath or affirmation, and particularly describing the things to be seized. An exception may be made in cases involving a clear danger to health or safety.

The penalties meted out for breaches of school regulations should be commensurate with the offense. They should never take the form of corporal punishment. Punishment for infractions of the code of behavior should bear no relation to courses, credits, marks, graduation or similar academic areas, except in cases where they relate to academic dishonesty.

Those infractions which may lead to more serious penalties, such as suspension or expulsion from school, or a notation on the record, require the utilization of a comprehensive and formal procedure in order to prevent a miscarriage of justice that could have serious effects on the student and his future. Such hearings should therefore be approached not in terms of meting out punishment but rather as an attempt to find the best solution for the student's needs consistent with the maintenance of order in the school.

The procedure should include a formal hearing and the right of appeal. Regulations and proceedings governing the operation of the hearing panel and the appeal procedure should be predetermined in consultation with the students, published and disseminated or otherwise made available to the student body. Responsibility for the decision reached as a result of the hearing rests solely with the administration. It may seek the opinions and participation of teachers and students in reaching its conclusion.

Prior to the hearing, the student (and his parent or guardian) should be:

a. Advised in writing of the charges against him, including a summary of the evidence upon which the charges are based.

b. Advised that he is entitled to be represented and/or advised at all times during the course of the proceedings by a person of his choosing who may or may not be connected with the faculty or administration of the school and may include a member of the student body.

c. Advised of the procedure to be followed at the hearing.

d. Given a reasonable time to prepare his defense.

At the hearing, the student (his parent, guardian or other representative) and the administrator should have the right to examine and cross-examine witnesses and to present documentary and other evidence in support of their respective contentions. The student should be advised of his privilege to remain silent, and should not be disciplined for claiming this privilege. The administration should make available to the student such authority as it may possess to require the presence of witnesses at the hearing. A full record should be taken at the hearing and it should be made available in identical form to the hearing panel, the administration and the student. The cost thereof should be met by the school.

In those instances where the student is being exposed to a serious penalty because of an accumulation of minor infractions which had been handled in summary fashion, or any instance where evidence of prior infractions so handled is presented at the hearing by the administration, the student (his parent, guardian, or other representative) should be permitted to reopen those charges and present evidence in support of the contention that he was wrongfully accused and/or convicted of the minor infraction.

After the hearing is closed, the panel should adjudicate the matter before it with reasonable promptness and make its findings and conclusions in writing, and make copies thereof available in identical form and at the same time, to the administration and the student. The cost thereof should be met by the school. Punishments should so far as possible avoid public humiliation or embarrassment. Group punishment should be used only if every member of the group is guilty of the infraction. Cruel and unusual punishment should never be imposed.

2. THE ROLE OF THE POLICE IN THE SECONDARY SCHOOLS

Where disciplinary problems involving breaches of law are rampant, schools cannot be considered sacrosanct against policemen and the proper function of law officers cannot be impeded in crime detection. Whenever the police are in-

volved in the schools, their activities should not consist of harassment or intimidation. If a student is to be questioned by the police, it is the responsibility of the
school administration to see that the interrogation takes place privately in the
office of a school official, in the presence of the principal or his representative.
Every effort should be made to give a parent the opportunity to be present. All
procedural safeguards prescribed by law must be strictly observed. When the
interrogation takes place in school, as elsewhere, the student is entitled to be
advised of his rights, which should include the right to counsel and the right to
remain silent.

PERSONAL APPEARANCE

The matter of acceptable dress and grooming is a frequent issue in schools.
Education is too important to be granted or denied on the basis of standards of
personal appearance. As long as a student's appearance does not, in fact, disrupt
the educational process, or constitute a threat to safety, it should be no concern
of the school.

Dress and personal adornment are forms of self-expression; the freedom of
personal preference should be guaranteed along with other liberties. The reconciliation of the rights of the individual with the needs of the group was well
expressed in the decision by California Superior Court Judge W. G. Watson in
the case of Myers v. Arcata Union High School District. (1966)[2]

> The limits within which regulations can be made by the school are that
> there be some reasonable connection to school matters, deportment, disci-
> pline, etc., or to the health and safety of the students. . . . The Court has
> too high a regard for the school system . . . to think that they are aiming at
> uniformity or blind conformity as a means of achieving their stated goal in
> educating for responsible citizenship. . . . [If there are to be some regula-
> tions, they] must reasonably pertain to the health and safety of the students
> or to the orderly conduct of school business. In this regard, consideration
> should be given to what is really health and safety . . . and what is merely
> personal preference. Certainly, the school would be the first to concede
> that in a society as advanced as that in which we live there is room for
> many personal preferences and great care should be exercised insuring that
> what are mere personal preferences of one are not forced upon another
> for mere convenience since absolute uniformity among our citizens should
> be our last desire.

FREEDOM FROM DISCRIMINATION

No student should be granted any preference nor denied any privilege or right
in any aspect of school life because of race, religion, color, national origin, or

[2] Superior Court of California, Humboldt County (unreported)

any other reason not related to his individual capabilities. It is the duty of the administration to prevent discrimination and to avoid situations which may lead to discrimination or the appearance thereof, in all aspects of school life, including the classroom, the lunchroom, the assembly, honors, disciplinary systems, athletics, clubs and social activities.

THE RIGHTS OF MARRIED AND/OR PREGNANT STUDENTS

The right to an education provided for all students by law should not be abrogated for a particular student because of marriage or pregnancy unless there is compelling evidence that his or her presence in the classroom or school does, in fact, disrupt or impair the educational process for other students. This includes the right to participate in all the activities of the school. If temporary or permanent separation from the school should be warranted, the education provided elsewhere should be qualitatively and quantitatively equivalent to that of the regular school, so far as is practicable.

ACADEMIC FREEDOM AND EDUCATION

The academic freedoms set forth in the student section of this pamphlet must be looked upon as more than a line of defense; they are positive elements in the educational process of a democracy. The spirit of these freedoms should permeate the school and their expression should be actively encouraged by faculty and administration. A school which does not respect civil liberties has failed the community, its students and itself.

In 1943, the Supreme Court, in the case of *West Virginia Board of Education* v. *Barnette*[3] affirmed the basic concept that no agent of a school board can compel a student to surrender his constitutional rights as a privilege of attending school. The majority opinion stated:

> The Fourteenth Amendment, as now applied to the States, protects the citizen against the State itself and all of its creatures—the Board of Education not excepted. These have of course, important, delicate and highly discretionary functions, but none that they may not perform within the limits of the Bill of Rights. That they are educating the young for citizenship is reason for scrupulous protection of Constitutional freedoms of the individual, if we are not to strangle the free mind at its source and teach youth to discount important principles of our government and mere platitudes.

In 1967, the Supreme Court held, in an 8-1 decision, *In re Gault*,[4] that: ". . . Neither the Fourteenth Amendment nor the Bill of Rights is for adults alone."

---

[3] *West Virginia Board of Education v. Barnette*, 319 U.S. 624 (1943)
[4] *In re Gault*, 87 S. Ct. 1428 (1967)

DEMONSTRATIONS, DISMISSALS, DUE PROCESS, AND THE HIGH SCHOOL: AN OVERVIEW

C. MICHAEL ABBOTT

The Fourteenth Amendment, as now applied to the States, protects the citizen against the State itself and all of its creatures—Boards of Education not excepted. These have, of course, important, delicate, and highly discretionary functions, but none that they may not perform within the limits of the Bill of Rights.[1]

INTRODUCTION

While much has recently been written of the prerogatives of students on the college and university level,[2] their secondary school counterpart[3] has to date been largely ignored. This no doubt explains, in part, why the history of that body of case law concerning the requirements of due process of law in administrative hearings for high school students indicates that a pupil may be expelled from a public school without notice or a formal hearing;[4] or why it has only too recently been stated that the application of the First Amendment to public school students is "of questionable relevance."[5]

Perhaps this is not surprising, for unlike teachers and professors who have large and influential lobbies to give needed support,[6] students on the secondary level do not boast such organizations, while only in recent years have college and university groups begun to wield power commensurate with the size of their potential membership.

Notwithstanding the causes of this indifference toward the secondary school, however, its obvious consequence has been to leave largely unexplored any differences that may exist in the legal principles underlying the administrative handling of demonstrations or dismissals at the high school level. Yet, in the light of recent events, it is evident that there is a need for their enunciation. For, as Justice Jackson so aptly remarked, "[school boards] are numerous and their territorial jurisdiction often small. But small and local authority may feel less sense of responsibility to the constitution, and agencies of publicity may be less vigilant in calling it to account."[7]

It does not follow that, because the high school student is less likely to receive the protection to which he is entitled, he is less likely to need it. Thus, a number of recent cases indicate an inchoate body of law applicable to student demon-

From *School Review*, 77 (June, 1969), 128-43. Copyright © 1969 by The University of Chicago. All Rights Reserved. Printed in the U.S.A. Reprinted with the permission of the author and the publisher.

C. Michael Abbott is an attorney with the Neighborhood Legal Services Center, Detroit, Michigan.

strations and dismissals that is only beginning to be felt by school administrators in this long-neglected area. It will be the purpose of this article to explore the present strength of student prerogatives on the secondary level—the result of which will indicate that we are beyond the point of no return in guaranteeing the applicability of the Fourteenth Amendment and the Bill of Rights to all, regardless of age or status. The Supreme Court brought the point home quite clearly in spelling out the due process requirements in the treatment of juvenile offenders when it said, "Whatever may be their precise impact neither the Fourteenth Amendment nor the Bill of Rights is for adults alone."[8]

THE PROBLEM

Demonstrations are a symbol of our times. The clamor of group involvement in direct action confrontations with the establishment power structures has, by virtue of the mass media, brought an unequaled awareness of social reform movements into every American living room.

The effectiveness of acting in concert has not been missed by the young. Student demonstrations may be viewed, in part, as a microcosm of the greater malaise that afflicts our society. Thus, the strength of student sit-ins, boycotts, and mass rallies has assumed heretofore unknown proportions.[9] Likewise, the racial overtones and the pleas for equal educational opportunities have been accompanied by lawlessness and violence. And there is little question that the problem is a growing one.

In addition, the difficulties in handling this type of student activity become compounded when met with hasty or arbitrary action that will affect those involved far more than is necessary, prudent, or even legally permissible. The recentness of such events has no doubt caught many administrators unaware of how to react to demonstrations or how to handle school dismissals. Yet it is important that they do so in a way that comports with the "fundamental fairness" that has long been a part of our constitutional scheme. Certainly, it would be anomalous should conduct of students be regulated by concepts of justice that differ from those taught in the classroom.

And such a fear is magnified because of the nature of the group most often involved. In New York State, the problem was recently described in this manner:

> As the Director of the Bureau of Child Guidance testified, most of the pupils [suspended for misconduct] are members of "multi-problem families." The expression "multi-problem families" appears to be a euphemism for the new aliens in our midst—the urban poor. . . . These children emerge, in the main, from the quagmire of urban poverty and the vast social distortions which now infect the inner city.[10]

In addition, the very reasons that have compelled these students to make demands on the establishment in the only way known to them[11] prevent them from being able to defend themselves before it when they are required to do so. The same problems which the middle-class citizen might feel to be routine matters may strike a chord of genuine intimidation among those in the ghettos who are not used to dealing directly with principals, school counselors, or judges. Nor are they apt to have the funds for a lawyer—that protective buffer that the more affluent instinctively seek.

The problem can be put in greater perspective by considering the importance of fair procedure to the student involved. That he has much to fear from the arbitrary use of power may be as true on the secondary level as at a college or university. This is particularly so where misconduct may result in an expulsion or a lengthy suspension. The stigma of compulsory withdrawal is likely to follow even the high school student for many years after the incident has been settled in the mind of the institution concerned. Such a procedure almost always involves a permanent notation on the student's record which may have long-lasting effects on his entrance into college or the job market. And if the child is unable to return to school, the economics of a premature withdrawal are just as startling, but more tangible, evidence of the burden that he must shoulder. The Supreme Court observed as much almost fifteen years ago when it proclaimed: "In these days, it is doubtful that any [person] may reasonably be expected to succeed in life if he is denied the opportunity of a high school education."[12] And that a student should be expelled for exercising fundamental notions of freedom of speech or association without a showing that this action was detrimental to the functioning of the school, or without his having an opportunity to appear in order to attempt to demonstrate his innocence, may leave psychological scars on his attitude and personality.[13] Further, such punishment is calculated to encourage that conformity and dependence that is the antithesis of education.

Finally, the "culturally deprived" student most likely to feel the consequences of a dismissal from school is also apt to be the least able to afford it, thus reinforcing the helplessness that is likely to have motivated his conduct. A federal district court recently summed it up this way: "Difficult as the problems thus presented might be, they are not a reason for setting aside constitutional guarantees. For most of these children, perhaps the one state conferred benefit which they have of greatest monetary value is the right which has been given them by state law to attend the public schools without charge."[14]

However, the courts have been traditionally reticent about exercising their power in the educational sphere. Relatively few cases have been brought, and of those that have, many go no further than the trial court, where there is often no official report. But there are other reasons. In the past, courts have maintained that they had no power to entertain student suits "except where fraud, corruption, oppression or gross injustice is palpably shown,"[15] that public education is a matter reserved for state administrative control,[16] or that the Fourteenth Amendment is not applicable to the prerogative of a school to discipline its students.[17] Too, there is a natural inclination to consider such matters as only within the special competence of school administrators and teachers. However, these notions have since been laid to rest where students face expulsion or suspension for misconduct.[18]

Procedural difficulties have also played their part. The use of mandamus in an attempt to compel affirmative action on the part of the school or university was often considered inapposite and, because of its discretionary nature, may still be ineffectual. Jurisdiction was still another problem prior to *Monroe v. Pape*[19] in 1961. There, the Supreme Court gave an expanded interpretation of 42 U.S.C. sec. 1983, which has since allowed student suits to be brought under that statute in a due process proceeding.

THE SPECIAL ROLE OF IN LOCO PARENTIS

One of the more significant reasons for judicial inaction, however, stems from the peculiar legal relationship between student and school. Although the commonly applied theories on the university level of "privilege" or "contract"[20] are unsuitable to the secondary school, a third proposition, that the school stands *in loco parentis*, has achieved historical popularity on both college and high school levels.[21]

This doctrine, emphasizing the role of the school in the upbringing of the child, is an extension of the concept of the state as *parens patriae*—the state succeeding to the duties of the parent wherever the latter is unable to attend to them.[22] However, even on the secondary level, an examination of the *in loco parentis* concept demonstrates that it is ill-suited to the realities of the relationship it describes and does not present a rational basis for judicial review. Although the theory on its face imposes no self-evident restrictions, it is clear that some are required because of the harm that may result from an expulsion or a lengthy suspension from school. A state court exposed the more obvious difficulties of *in loco parentis* over a century ago:

> From the intimacy and nature of the relation, and the necessary character of family government, the law suffers no intrusion upon the authority of the parent, and the privacy of domestic life, unless in extreme cases of cruelty and injustice. This parental power is little liable to abuse, for it is continually restrained by natural affection, the tenderness which the parent feels for his offspring, an affection ever on the alert, and acting rather by instinct than reasoning.
>
> The schoolmaster has no such natural restraint. Hence he may not safely be trusted with all a parent's authority, for he does not act from the instinct of parental affection. He should be guided and restrained by judgment and wise discretion and hence is responsible for their reasonable exercise.[23]

Functionally, the role of the secondary school as a disseminator of established cultural values makes it less concerned with the creative development and research germane to the university. Too, while many university students are reaching a leveling-off period in academic and emotional maturity, the high school student may be only emerging from adolescence. Nevertheless, the unrest of today's student is but one indication of the increased sophistication and knowledge that mark the American teenager and which render him much less susceptible to the attitude symbolized by the switch-carrying schoolmaster of past times. In addition, the currently popular theory in regard to the breakdown of the family unit does not necessarily imply an obligation on the part of the state to pre-empt the parental role, and certainly not in an arbitrary manner. Further, the power that the school must have to deal with distracting elements in the classroom, even subjecting them to expulsion if necessary,[24] scarcely resembles the duty of a parent to care for his child until emancipation:

> In the case of a minor son, the circumstances would be rare, which could demand an expulsion from the parental roof and the hospitalities and associations of home. Nor even if such circumstances existed, would any prudent parent impose so serious a penalty, without first consulting the primary sources of his information, and freely communicating them to his accused son, and according to him the amplest time and opportunity to exculpate himself.[25]

Nor does the doctrine of in loco parentis allow for those times when the pupil may be acting with parental consent, while violating a rule of the school. And finally, it is argued that for those teachers in the slum-centered school, there is a special need to assume parental responsibility by means of compensatory education. However, such a theory adds little weight to the utility of in loco parentis as a standard of review where arbitrary action is alleged. In fact, it may also be urged that it is for these students that the analogy truly breaks down, for the extent to which a white middle-class teacher can veritably be considered to stand in loco parentis to a black student from the ghetto is dubious indeed, and is apt to be so perceived by teacher and pupil alike. Particularly in light of the recent movement toward the desegregation of teachers,[26] as well as students, is this likely to be a significant factor.

One suspects that the concept of in loco parentis is too easily used as a mask or shield to cover a variety of situations in which pupil control is sought, without the concomitant responsibilities that must necessarily flow from such a proposition. Taken literally, it is a misguided analogy to the relationship that one assumes should exist between parent and child. As a guide to the evaluation of teacher-pupil relationships, it serves to obfuscate the problem rather than enlighten the court. It would seem that the demise of in loco parentis on all levels would indeed be welcome.

STUDENT DEMONSTRATIONS

It is irrefutable that high school students, like others, are fully protected by the Fourteenth Amendment[27] in their right to demonstrate.[28] Thus, in *Edwards* v. *South Carolina*,[29] Negro high school and college students were allowed to assemble at the site of the state government to express their "feelings and . . . dissatisfaction with the present condition of discriminatory actions against Negroes."[30] In striking down a breach of the peace conviction, the Supreme Court went on to point out the strength underlying the precepts of the First Amendment:

> A function of free speech under our system of government is to invite dispute. It may indeed best serve its high purpose when it induces a condition of unrest, creates dissatisfaction with conditions as they are, or even stirs people to anger. Speech is often provocative and challenging. It may strike at prejudices and preconceptions and have profound unsettling effects as it presses for acceptance of an idea. That is why freedom of speech . . . is . . . protected against censorship or punishment, unless shown likely to produce a clear and present danger of a serious substantive evil that rises far above public inconvenience, annoyance, or unrest. . . . There is no room under our constitution for a more restrictive view. For the alternative would lead to standardization of ideas either by legislatures, courts, or dominant political or community groups.[31]

More recently, in *Hammond* v. *South Carolina State College*,[32] a federal district court held that a rule requiring prior administrative approval of all public demonstrations was an unconstitutional restraint on the student's First Amendment rights, requiring a reversal of their unlawful suspensions. The court was also of the opinion that a college campus was a sufficient analogy to the "site of State government" protected in *Edwards*.[33] The decision seems a sound one since it is difficult to conceive of a place better suited to the free discussion or dissemination of ideas than a college, university, or, under proper conditions, a high school.[34] However, where a student rally displays objectionable signs and broadcasts obscene expressions which threaten to disrupt the maintenance of order on campus,[35] or where students block access to school buildings,[36] expulsions by the institution will be upheld. Similarly, a sit-in by students in campus buildings after hours may result in criminal convictions of trespass or unlawful assembly.[37] Such results are consistent with providing a forum for all within narrow and reasonable restrictions that do no more than proscribe conduct unreasonable in terms of time, place, or manner.

Accordingly, in *Burnside* v. *Byars*[38] a high school regulation prohibiting students from wearing "freedom buttons" was recently struck down as arbitrary and an unnecessary infringement on the student's protected right of free expression. The court recognized that the school requires regulations which are necessary for maintaining an orderly forum for classroom learning and considered a "reasonable regulation" to be one which contributed to that end. However, "mild curiosity" over the wearing of the buttons did not "materially and substantially interfere" with normal school decorum, "nor would it seem likely that the simple wearing of buttons unaccompanied by other conduct would ever do so."[39] In a companion case, the court upheld a regulation forbidding the wearing of similar buttons on the grounds that an "unusual degree" of boisterous conduct and commotion was the result,[40] though without prejudice to the plaintiffs to show that the activity could be carried out without upsetting the school routine.

Recently, the Supreme Court, in *Tinker* v. *Des Moines Independent Community School District*,[41] supported the view of the First Amendment taken by the court in *Burnside*. Officials of the school district passed a regulation prohibiting the wearing of armbands on school facilities, having been informed that several students intended to wear the bands to mourn for those who had died in the Vietnam War. Although conceding that the wearing of the band was a symbolic act of expression that fell within the First Amendment, the eighth Circuit Court had felt that school officials not only had a right but "an obligation to prevent anything which might be disruptive of such an atmosphere." Citing the Vietnam War as a subject of major controversy, the court concluded that "it was not unreasonable in this instance for school officials to anticipate that the wearing of armbands would create some type of classroom disturbance."[42]

In reversing, the Supreme Court closely followed the *Burnside* test:

> In order for the State in the person of school officials to justify prohibition of a particular expression of opinion, it must be able to show that its action was caused by something more than a mere desire to avoid the discomfort and unpleasantness that always accompany an unpopular viewpoint. Certainly where there is no finding and no showing that the exercise of the forbidden right would "materially and substantially interfere with the requirements of appropriate discipline in the operation of the school," the prohibition cannot be sustained (citing Burnside v. Byars).[43]

Here, the Supreme Court pointed out, the record did not disclose that the armbands worn by the students caused, or gave school authorities reason to anticipate they would cause, a disruption in the classroom.

Justice Fortas, writing for a strong majority of seven, made it clear that students have a right to fundamental constitutional guarantees, saying "it can hardly be argued that either students or teachers shed their constitutional rights to freedom of speech or expression at the schoolhouse gate."[44]

This decision of the high court need not be considered an extreme position in the protection afforded student dissidents. Certainly there is sufficient force in the guidelines of *Burnside* and *Tinker* to curb the activities of those who insist on being destructive. The lower court decision in *Tinker*, however, would have allowed unlimited discretion to school administrators if the test were whether in their opinion a certain regulation is necessary to prevent *future* reactions and comments from *other* students likely to disturb the classroom. The argument that the state may be able to impose more severe restrictions on demonstrative activity occurring during school hours is well taken, but goes too far when it becomes a prophylactic measure designed to suppress any attempt at freedom of expression without regard to its relation to the necessary atmosphere required for classroom learning.[45] Although factors of immaturity may indeed be relevant in determining the extent to which free discourse is permitted in the secondary school classroom—and to that extent the doctrine of a "free marketplace of ideas"[46] may be somewhat altered—the argument is too facile that it has no application whatsoever or that school administrators in their unrestricted wisdom will always handle delicate constitutional rights with the greatest care so that guideposts are neither required nor desirable. Where it can be done in a reasonable and non-disruptive fashion, secondary school students should be able to "ridicule the governor, argue for the admission of Red China to the United Nations, sign a petition urging a general blockade of Cuba or participate in orderly demonstrations to promote any lawful end"[47] just as their college counterparts may do.[48] Whether they will choose to do so is yet another matter.

It would seem self-evident that it is incumbent upon the state to show the compelling state interest that will justify an abridgment of freedom of expression when dealing with minors as with any other group. For it is precisely at the lower levels of government that freedom of expression is more likely to occur,[49] and so it is here that we should be most chary. This is not to say that local officials should have no discretion, but rather that the importance of their work demands the closest attention to traditional constitutional freedoms. In the words of the Supreme Court: "That they are educating the young for citizenship is reason for scrupulous protection of Constitutional freedoms of the individual, if we are not to strangle the free mind at its source and teach youth to discount important principles of our government as mere platitudes."[50]

THE ADMINISTRATIVE HEARING AND STUDENT MISCONDUCT

Dixon v. *Alabama State Board of Education*[51] firmly established the modern-day precedent that has greatly influenced the expansion of student procedural rights. Since that fifth circuit decision, the proposition seems unassailable that, before students at a tax-supported institution of learning can be expelled or given a lengthy suspension for misconduct, they must be afforded notice of the charges against them and some type of hearing that will at least comport with minimum due process standards.[52] Such a position would seem sound and necessary even at the secondary level where such disciplinary action will be a part of the student's permanent record, may well have a bearing on his acceptance at the college of his choice, and in any case is but a recognition that students, as well as adults have a right to be treated fairly. It is doubtful that lesser punishment would merit such a proceeding, particularly since the child's age and the discretion inherent in the teacher's role become increasingly important factors as the educational level of the student decreases.

Many of the issues yet to be resolved are the specifics that need be afforded in any particular case, and there is no doubt room for a flexible approach. It is generally conceded that a full trial, identical to that of a court of law, need not be provided. *Dixon* indicates that the hearing provided must be more than an "informal interview" and that the "rudiments of an adversary proceeding" should be preserved.[53] Thus, it would seem that the student should be allowed to compel the use of witnesses, and where those involved are other students or faculty, this should pose no problem. Otherwise, it may be difficult for a student to adduce the evidence he feels should be before the court. Such a procedure should also obviate any untoward feelings concerning "tattling." Although some risk of perjury may exist even at the lower levels, the right to the aid of witnesses is sufficiently important to outweigh such a possibility, and the opportunity to cross-examine will further reduce the chance of false testimony. Important as cross-examination may be in other contexts, however, it will no doubt be largely ineffectual for the high school student unless the more obvious need of *some form* of counsel is met. Thus, a high school senior was held to have the right to counsel in order to face a charge of cheating where the consequences would have been the denial of a state diploma and of certain scholarship and qualifying-exam privileges.[54] But the second circuit held that a mere "guidance conference" to determine whether a child suspended for misconduct may return to the school he had been attending or must be transferred to another does not require the presence of a lawyer.[55] While the procedure followed in that case seems sufficiently circumspect,[56] one might not feel as easy in other situations. And though a lawyer at the secondary level may be more intimidating to school administrators than to college personnel, it is also true that the former are more apt to be oblivious to constitutional safeguards, thus indicating a greater need for an attorney or his equivalent at that level.[57] In addition, the public school student, perhaps unlike his college counterparts, most of whom are over twenty-one,[58] may be unable to articulate a defense or even spell out mitigating circumstances. And, as we have observed, this is most likely to be true of the "urban poor." If one can assert that the "liberty" of the Fourteenth Amendment encompasses the right to pursue a public education,[59] it does not seem to be a libertarian invention to suggest that the indefinite suspension of a pupil may be equivalent to a deprivation of that liberty. Where this follows as a *direct* result of a disciplinary hearing, counsel should be permitted. For those not able to afford an attorney and where a legal services center is not available, there is no reason that the school should not provide some form of counsel, even if not a trained lawyer, to represent the child.[60]

Strict rules of evidence should not be mandatory, particularly where the presence of counsel could insure that a fair balance is struck in the evidence received, even though his opinion would not be binding. But there is little reason why a transcript could not be furnished where desired by either party. Such a requirement could be met in its simplest form by the use of a tape recorder and would thus require little, if any, administrative inconvenience. Some form of review by the governing board of the institution concerned would impact a healthy atmosphere of accountability.

It has been suggested that the privilege against self-incrimination may be applicable to expulsion proceedings and the like, and while it is not likely to be a problem in most cases, there is no reason why it should not be honored, for coercive intimidation is most likely to occur, if at all, at the lower levels. On the other hand, the inconvenience and formality attached to warnings of a right to counsel or to keep silent and the interest in preserving a rehabilitative atmosphere would not seem to warrant those elements of criminal procedure. Similarly, an extensive behavioral code typical of the criminal laws is not required. However, the regulation in question should not be "so vague that men of common intelligence must necessarily guess at its meaning and differ as to its application."[61] Finally, the burden of proof should rest upon those bringing the charge.

CONCLUSION

Hopefully, school administrators will recognize the opportunity that now exists to effectively channel traditional concepts of freedom of speech and association and of due process of law into lessons of how a democratic society should function. This would seem to be a far wiser course than resisting the implementation of due process standards. For certainly there is a warning implicit in the growing number of cases that even public school students will not be satisfied with less than their just demand for constitutional protection, whether conceived as "fundamental fairness" or a "fair shake" or by some other label. The point was well made recently by a federal court and should not be ignored by those responsible for the direction of the secondary schools:

> From the standpoint of administering justice, we strongly urge that this State, in its own wisdom, encourage their educational institutions to review their existing procedures to insure that they have adequate procedural machinery to implement the minimum standards already in force. As an enlargement on previous decisions, we strongly recommend that disciplinary rules and regulations adopted by a school board be set forth in writing and promulgated in such manner as to reach all parties subjected to their effects. In colleges and universities this can easily be accomplished through distribution of handbooks or catalogues. Moreover, we recommend that each disciplinary procedure incorporate some system of appeal. . . . The practicality of this suggestion lies in the fact that this would evidence one more sign of the particular institution taking initiative to safe-

guard the basic rights of the student as well as its own position, prior to disciplining him for misconduct.[62]

This is particularly important where there are racial overtones present, for one can hardly overlook the fact that many of the procedures that are now guaranteed as a result of court action arose out of such incidents. And with the growing pains that will inevitably come with the increased integration of the public schools, the fairness of administrative procedures—if history is a guide—will no doubt assume even greater importance.

It is past time for the school administrator to take the lead in recognizing that students as well as adults have the right to fair treatment. Similarly, it can be urged that the long-used shibboleth of *in loco parentis* as it applies to disciplinary measures should be exchanged for one of "procedural fairness." As the federal district court pointed in *Madera:*

> The need for procedural fairness in the state's dealing with college students' rights to public education, where in many instances students are adults and have already attained at least a high school diploma, should be no greater than the need for such fairness when one is dealing with the expulsion or suspension of juveniles from the public schools. Such fairness seems especially required when the child involved has yet to acquire even the fundamental educational prerequisites that would allow him to go on to college.[63]

It is not surprising that the first of the due process cases to reach the Supreme Court dealing with student rights has come down on the side of the students.[64] It may be well to remember the words of Justice Frankfurter, who was of the opinion that "the history of American freedom is in no small measure the history of procedure."[65] It is clear by the recent decisions of his contemporary brethren that they, too, have studied their history.[66]

Notes

[1] Board of Education v. Barnette, 319 U.S. 624, 637 (1942); Tinker v. Des Moines Independent School District, 89 S. Ct. 733, 737 (1969).

[2] The exhaustive treatment that has been given this subject on the college level need not be repeated here. For a comprehensive bibliography, see William W. Van Alstyne, "Student Academic Freedom and the Rule-making Powers of Public Universities: Some Constitutional Considerations," 2 Law in Transition Quarterly, 1, 2n. 3 (1965); "Symposium: Legal Aspects of Student-Institutional Relationships," 45 Denver Law Journal 497, at 612, 613 (Special 1968).

[3] As used in this paper, the terms "secondary school" and "high school" refer generally to all grades above the elementary level.

[4] This is said to be the weight of authority at the secondary school level. See Annot., 58

A.L.R. 2d 903 (1958). Eleven states have statutory provisions which require a hearing. See Welf. L. Bull., June 1968, at 18.

[5] "Developments in the Law—Academic Freedom," 81 Harv. L. Rev. 1045, 1053 (1968) (hereinafter cited as Developmental Note). Elsewhere, however, the authors recognized that, "although freedom of speech and thought in the learning situation has been given little emphasis as such at the lower levels, with the recognition of education as indispensable to the welfare of the individual and of society the right of protection from arbitrary treatment by the school has become a principal ingredient of pupil freedom." Id. at 1050.

[6] E.g., at the college level, the American Association of University Professors; and representing the public schools, the National Education Association and the American Federation of Teachers.

[7] Barnette, 319 U.S. at 637-38. In the past, the problem has been no less troublesome at the college level. Over a decade ago, the situation prompted this quote from Harvard law professor Warren Seavey: "It is shocking that the officials of a state educational institution, which can function properly only if our freedoms are preserved, should not understand the elementary principles of fair play. It is equally shocking to find that a court supports them in denying to a student the protection given to a pickpocket." Seavey, "Dismissal of Students: 'Due Process,' " 70 Harv. L. Rev. 1406, 1407 (1957).

[8] In re Gault, 387 U.S. 1, 13 (1967). Section 1 of the Fourteenth Amendment reads in part: "No *State* shall make or enforce any law which shall abridge the privileges or immunities of citizens of the United States; nor shall any *State* deprive any person of life, liberty, or property, without due process of law; nor deny to any person within its jurisdiction the equal protection of the laws." U.S. Const. Amend. XIV, § 1 (emphasis supplied). The italicized words indicate why it is "state action" that must be shown before the Fourteenth Amendment comes into play.

[9] Recent events have included a boycott of 500 high school students to force integration in Hillsborough, North Carolina, and sit-ins in Cincinnati, Ohio, which resulted in the suspension *en masse* of 1,400 students from the public schools. See *Durham Morning Herald* (North Carolina), May 15, 1968, §A, p. 1, col. 4; *New York Times,* May 2, 1968, §C, p. 41, col. 2. Similar acts in South Bend, Indiana, resulted in scores of arrests on trespass charges. *Ibid.* In Camden, New Jersey, junior and senior high students were meeting in executive session with the board of education after they had staged demonstrations asking for the resignations of white principals, coaches, and athletic directors, while in White Plains, New York, an agreement was signed in answer to student demands for the inclusion of courses in Afro-Asian culture and other curriculum changes. *Id.,* May 12, 1968, §1, p. 36, col. 1; Jim Leeson, "The New Mood of Blackness—Theme and Variations," *Southern Education Report* (July/August, 1968), p. 3.

[10] Madera v. Board of Education of City of New York, 267 F. Supp. 356, 374 (S.D. N.Y.), rev'd 386 F. 2d 778 (2d Cir., 1967), cert. denied 390 U.S. 1028 (1968).

[11] A recent study in Washington, D.C., revealed that "the young Negroes in the newspaper headlines—except for small numbers of the ideologically radical and the extremely alienated—are not rioting because they want 'out' from the white world, but because they want 'in.' They share the values of their white peers and want the same privileges. Standing in the margins of a white society that both invites and rejects, the Negro youth is frustrated by the incongruity. Hence anger. Hence violence." Sophia McDowell, "How Anti-White Are Negro Youth?" *American Education* (March, 1968), p. 2.

[12] Brown v. Board of Education, 347 U.S. 483, 493 (1953).

[13] This remark from a federal court would seem to apply equally well to secondary school students: "In the disciplining of college students there are no considerations . . . which should prevent the Board from exercising at least the fundamental principles of fairness by giving the accused students notice of the charges and an opportunity to be heard in their own defense. Indeed, the example set by the Board in failing so to do, if not cor-

rected by the courts, can well break the spirits of the expelled students and of others familiar with the injustice, and do inestimable harm to their education. Dixon v. Alabama State Board of Education, 294 F. 2d 150, 157 (5th Cir.), cert. denied 368 U.S. 930 (1961).

[14] Madera v. Board of Education of City of New York (see n. 10 above).

[15] Smith v. Board of Education, 182 Ill. App. 342, 347 (1913).

[16] Steier v. New York State Education Commissioner, 271 F. 2d 13, 18 (2d Cir. 1959).

[17] State ex rel Sherman v. Hyman, 180 Tenn. 99, 171 S.W. 2d 822, cert. denied 319 U.S. 748 (1942).

[18] See, e.g., Dixon v. Alabama State Board of Education (n. 13 above). It is now well established that students enjoy the protection of the Fourteenth Amendment. See, e.g., Cooper v. Aaron, 358 U.S. 1, 19 (1958): "It is of course, quite true the responsibility for public education is primarily the concern of the States, but it is equally true that such responsibilities, like all other state activity, must be exercised consistently with federal constitutional requirements as they apply to state action."

[19] 365 U.S. 167 (1961).

[20] Unlike a college education, which has sometimes been characterized as a "privilege" rather than a "right," the public schools are generally compulsory until the child reaches a certain age. Likewise, there has been no need for a contractual theory in the public school, though one could urge that it is implied. Even on the university level, however, both theories have been discredited: "Private interests are to be evaluated under the due process clause of the 14th Amendment, not in terms of labels or fictions, but in terms of their true significance and worth." Knight v. State Board of Education, 200 F. Supp. 174, 178 (M.D. Tenn. 1961).

[21] On the college campus there is a growing tendency to reject the theory, and three jurisdictions have recently done so. See Buttny v. Smiley, 281 F. Supp. 280 (1968); Moore v. Student Affairs Committee of Troy State University, 284 F. Supp. 725 (1968); Goldberg v. Regents of the University of California, 57 Cal. Rptr. 463 (D.C.A. 1967).

[22] "Where parental duty for any cause is not performed, the state through its appropriate agencies succeeds thereto, not as an original right, but a resumption of a right delegated to parents as the natural guardians of their children." Wisconsin Industrial School for Girls vs. Clark County, 103 Wis. 651, 79 N.W. 422, 428 (1889). But see in re Gault (n. 8 above) at 16, where the Supreme Court observed that the concept of parens patriae "proved to be of great help to those who sought to rationalize the exclusion of juveniles from the constitutional scheme," adding that "its meaning is murky and its historic credentials are of dubious relevance."

[23] Lander v. Seaver, 32 Vt. 114, 122-23 (1859).

[24] A public school, however, unlike a university, may have an obligation when expelling or suspending a student to provide a program by which he can continue his education elsewhere, particularly if the student is within the compulsory age limits.

[25] Commonwealth ex rel Hill v. McCauley, 3 Pa. County Ct. 77, 87-88 (1887).

[26] See, e.g., Hal R. Lieberman, "Teachers and the Fourteenth Amendment—the Role of the Faculty in the Desegregation Process," 46 N.C. L. Rev. 313 (1968). As of 1966, the Office of Education found that 41 per cent of the teachers of secondary school Negro pupils are white. Office of Education, Equality of Educational Opportunity, Vol. III (Washington, D.C.: Government Printing Office, 1966).

[27] The First Amendment reads in part as follows: "Congress shall make no law . . . abridging the freedom of speech, or of the press, or the right of the people peaceably to assemble, and to petition the Government for a redress of grievances." U.S. Const. Amend. I. First Amendment freedoms are protected from state invasion by the Fourteenth Amendment.

[28] Since demonstrations are not considered to be "pure" speech, they may be afforded less protection than verbal oratory. Nevertheless, a recent Supreme Court decision indicates that only "reasonable" restrictions as to time, place, duration, or manner may be

constitutionally imposed by the state in such cases. See Cox v. Louisiana, 379 U.S. 536 (1965). Note also it has generally been held that the wearing of long hair is not symbolic expression within the First Amendment, and even if it were, it is conduct subject to regulation by school authorities. See, e.g., Ferrel v. Dallas Independent School District, 392 F.2d 697 (5th Cir.), cert. denied 89 S. Ct. 98 (1968). In this regard teachers have been more fortunate than students. See, e.g., Finot v. Pasadena City Board of Education, 58 Cal. Rptr. 520 (2d Dist. C.A. 1967). The Board of Education's assignment of a teacher to an inferior teaching position solely because of his wearing a beard was held to be in violation of the Fourteenth Amendment as a deprivation of "liberty" where there was an absence of any experience as to what effect the beard would have upon the educational process. Recently, however, a Wisconsin federal court became the first to hold that a school regulation forbidding long hair on male students is unconstitutional. See Breen v. Kahl, 37 U.S. Law Week 2506 (March 11, 1969).

[29] 372 U.S. 229 (1963).

[30] *Id.* at 230.

[31] *Id.* at 237.

[32] Hammond v. South Carolina State College, 272 F. Supp. 947 (S. S.C. 1967). See also Brooks v. Auburn, 37 U.S. Law Week 2478 (February 25, 1969) (State University president's guideline for campus speakers designed to prevent address by antidraft advocate, constitutes political censorship that violates students' First Amendment rights).

[33] *Id.* at 950. In upholding the right to protest on campus, the court distinguished Adderly v. Florida, 385 U.S. 39 (1966), where it was held that demonstrations conflicting with the lawfully dedicated use of property, in this case a jailhouse, would not be protected under the First Amendment. *Ibid.*

[34] "The vigilant protection of constitutional freedom is nowhere more vital than in the community of American schools," Shelton v. Tucker, 234 U.S. 479, 487. The classroom is peculiarly the "market-place of ideas," Keyishian v. Board of Regents, 385 U.S. 589, 603 (1967). (See also n. 46 below.)

[35] Goldberg v. Regents of the University of Calif. (See n. 21 above).

[36] See Buttny v. Smiley (n. 21 above).

[37] In re Bacon, 49 Cal. Rptr. 322 (D.C.A. 1966).

[38] Burnside v. Byars, 363 F.2d 744 (5th Cir. 1966).

[39] *Id.* at 748-49.

[40] Blackwell v. Issaquena County Board of Education, 363 F.2d 749 (5th Cir. 1966).

[41] 37 U.S. Law Week 4121 (February 25, 1969).

[42] 258 F. Supp. 971, 973 (1966).

[43] See n. 41 above at 4123.

[44] See n. 41 above at 4122.

[45] Cf. the dissenting opinion of Judge Tuttle in Ferrel v. Dallas Independent School District (see n. 28 above), who finds the wearing of "Beatle type" haircuts to be protected behavior under the First and Fourteenth Amendments, adding, in language applicable to both Blackwell and Tinker cases: "These boys were not barred from school because of any actions carried out by them which were of themselves a disturbance of the peace. They were barred because it was anticipated, by reason of previous experiences, that their fellow students in some instances would do things that would disrupt the serenity or calm of the school. *It is these acts that should be prohibited, not the expressions of individuality by the suspended students"* (italics supplied).

[46] "The best test of truth is the power of the thought to get itself accepted in the market. . . . That at any rate is the theory of our Constitution," Abrams v. United States, 250 U.S. 616, 630 (1919).

[47] Van Alstyne, 2 Law in Transition Quarterly (see n. 2 above) at 22.

[48] Cf. Dickey v. Alabama State Board of Education, 273 F. Supp. 613 (M.D. Ala. 1967) (student editor's right to publish editorial critical of state government upheld).

[49] Thomas I. Emerson, *Toward a General Theory of the First Amendment* (New York:

Random House, Inc., Vintage Books, 1967), p. 45: "Infringement of freedom of expression is the more likely to occur the lower the level of official involved, and local institutions are less capable of maintaining individual rights than the more remote and often better-staffed institutions at the higher levels. The objection that national uniformity in this area constitutes an unwarranted interference with state or local rights is not sufficiently persuasive to outweigh the advantages and the need of federal supervision."

[50] Board of Education v. Barnette, 319 U.S. 624, 637 (1942).

[51] Dixon (see n. 13 above).

[52] *Ibid.* Note also that the distinction between the public and the private sphere insofar as state supported versus privately funded schools are concerned is an increasingly nebulous one. The arguments delineating those factors that have heretofore constituted "state action" and thus rendered a private interest subject to the restraint of the Fourteenth Amendment need not be repeated here. The concept of education as a public function will undoubtedly receive additional impetus in the years to come; and at the elementary and secondary levels, where education is compulsory for all, a dismissal without procedural safeguards is likely to be soon held arbitrary action that is contrary to Fourteenth Amendment limitations, notwithstanding the characterization of the institution as public or private.

[53] *Id.* at 158-59.

[54] Goldwyn v. Allen, 54 Misc. 2d 94, 281 N.Y.S. 2d 899 (S. Ct. 1967).

[55] Madera v. Board of Education of the City of New York (see n. 10 above).

[56] *Ibid.* In Madera, those attending the conference were the child, his parents, the principal, two guidance counselors, the district superintendent and her assistant, and the school court co-ordinator.

[57] One might also adopt procedures that could effectively reduce any threat of intimidation. E.g., by requiring the lawyer to remain seated when addressing witnesses or board personnel (a procedure followed in some state courts) and by requiring him to gain recognition by the head of the panel before speaking, this might be accomplished.

[58] U.S. Bureau of the Census, *Current Population Reports,* Series p-20, No. 110, p. 12, July 24, 1961.

[59] Although the theory of the deprivation inflicted by the state in Dixon and its progeny is not usually spelled out, various Supreme Court decisions indicate that this is not a major obstacle. See, e.g., Bolling v. Sharpe, 347 U.S. 497, 499-500 (1954) ("liberty . . . extends to the full range of conduct which the individual is free to pursue"); Meyer v. Nebraska, 262 U.S. 390, 399 (1923) (liberty includes "right to acquire useful knowledge").

[60] In Madera, the "court co-ordinator" may have been able to fulfil such a representative function. Note, however, that this would involve appearing on *behalf* of the child rather than as a mere intermediary between student and disciplinary board. Too, this form of compromise may provide the best solution in instances where an argument as to the inadvisability of a lawyer can be made on the grounds that his presence would only aggravate the situation and rigidify the positions of both sides.

[61] Dickson v. Sitterson, 280 F. Supp. 486, 498 (M.D.N.C. 1968).

[62] Zanders v. Louisiana State Board of Education, 281 F. Supp. 747, 761 (W.D. La. 1968).

[63] Madera (see n. 10 above) at 373.

[64] Tinker v. Des Moines Independent School District (see n. 41 above).

[65] Malinski v. New York, 324 U.S. 401, 414 (1945) (separate opinion).

[66] Cf.: "But the survival of our society as a free, open, democratic community will be determined not so much by the specific points achieved by the Negroes and the youth generation as by the procedures—the rules of conduct, the methods, the practices—which survive the confrontations. Procedure is the bone structure of a democratic society, and the quality of procedural standards which meet general acceptance—the quality of what is tolerable and permissible and acceptable conduct—determines the durability of the society and the survival possibilities of freedom within the society." Abe Fortas, "The Limits of Civil Disobedience," *New York Times Magazine,* May 12, 1968, p. 95.

HOW MUCH FREEDOM FOR HIGH SCHOOL STUDENTS?

SEYMOUR P. LACHMAN and MURRAY POLNER

Black students want a way into the system; whites want out. All demand expanded student rights and a creative school experience.

The New York City Interim Board of Education was created and took office in May of 1969. A month earlier the so-called Spring Offensive, a blend of violent and nonviolent disturbances, had spread swiftly through many schools. It was the first dramatic revelation in New York City that the confusion of a bewildered and fragmented America had now reached its high schools. Personally committed to civil liberties as well as reconciliation between the warring factions, all of whom felt varying degrees of powerlessness and frustration, we were determined to make an effort, however modest, to deal with the ferment constructively and rationally. This meant not merely to "cool" things but to deal as genuinely as we could with the development of long-range guidelines that would permit peaceful protest, nonviolent dissent, and significant reform within the system. We were also aware that change would have to recognize the legitimate roles of principals and classroom teachers. We were determined, therefore, to select the rational and salvageable in student demands and build upon that.

Above all, we wanted to develop a framework which would allow for growth and change and within which students might be treated as young adults and as a legitimate interest group in the total educational process with a share in the decision-making process. This would involve them in such areas as control of their newspapers, their style of dress, their curriculum and cocurricular activities, and student discipline, among others.

The result was our resolution stating "Rights and Responsibilities of Senior High School Students," a limited and moderate document although, paradoxically, one of the most advanced ever proposed for consideration by any public school body in the United States. We had been working on this resolution for several months, and we considered it a first attempt at bridging the dangerous gulf between students and those in authority that had been developing in New York City's public high schools. We hoped that the resolution would initiate city-

From *New York University Education Quarterly*, 1 (Summer, 1970), 21-23. Copyright © 1970 by New York University. Reprinted with the permission of the senior author and the publisher.

Seymour P. Lachman is Commissioner, New York City Board of Education (on leave as Professor of History at City University of New York). Murray Polner is Executive Assistant to the Chancellor, New York Board of Education, Brooklyn, New York.

wide and national discussion and debate and that the topic of student rights would finally become respectable. After months of consultations with numerous groups and individuals and after it was tentatively and informally approved by the lay Board of Education in the fall of 1969, the resolution was presented to the public in open session.

STUDENT CONCERNS

The outcome of the public meetings on the "Rights and Responsibilities" resolution was hardly a surprise. Two hearings were abruptly suspended because of outbursts from the audience. Black students insisted we deal with issues crucial to *them,* most notably their "15 Demands," which included such things as a call for black and Puerto Rican history courses, ethnic clubs, community control, the banning of police from the schools, and student-faculty councils with the right to hire and fire faculty. We learned quickly that the resolution dealt only in part with *their* priorities. For black students in our high schools increasingly viewed themselves in a dramatically different way from that of their white middle-class peers: as estranged pariahs, struggling for their heritage, dispatched into hostile white neighborhoods, shunted off into what they considered inane and degrading general courses. One of them told us, "I'm less concerned with wearing slacks to school than the white girls are. What's important to me now is getting teachers to relate to us, courses that offer something real, people who treat us with respect. They're fighting for the First Amendment; we're for that too but before that comes our lives, our existence." She wanted, first of all, a way *into* the system.

White students, or at least a sizeable number of them, mounted a different challenge. They wanted a way *out* of the system. And they wanted immediate change. The resolution, they argued, was too limited. "Lachman prefers to leave the function (decision-making role) where it presently lies," said a student on CBS-TV, "in the hands of the Board." One thing desired by virtually all the students with whom we met—despite differences in political views and whether they studied in academic or vocational schools—was expansion of the rights they already exercised. It was also difficult for them to grasp the important aspect of student responsibility and self-discipline that was built into the resolution.

But there was also something more urgently expressed by them than gratification of "demands." Many of the brightest students described their schools as boring and lifeless. The schools, they charged, demanded subservience, emulation, and indoctrination rather than creativity and challenge. A staggering number felt oppressed and indifferent, if not hostile. Even the more conservative students we interviewed expressed a chagrin that at times approached that of their more liberal peers.

THOSE IN AUTHORITY REACT

To all of this, many of their elders and especially many of the principals reacted with alarm and anxiety. Their organization lobbied energetically against the resolution as yet another invasion of their authority and as a possible invitation to chaos. They insisted that the schools were confronting primarily a small minority of troublemakers. They urged that no rights be offered students without a broader program that contained more explicit responsibilities. These included demands that the central board "undertake a full-scale investigation of any individual or outside agency contributing to school unrest," that principals be granted strengthened rights to suspend students, and that alleged disrupters be isolated in specially developed settings until they were no longer "so socially or emotionally immature that they cannot cope with the challenges of large and complex high schools." Disagreeing with their diagnosis and their remedy were many teachers in the city school system as well as citywide organizations such as the United Parents Association, the Citizens Committee for Children, and the Public Education Association. In another context, the State Commissioner of Education suggested instead that student restiveness was an outgrowth of more complex causes:

> The breathless exponential rate of change, technologically and socially . . . conflicts between the races, the war in Vietnam, outmoded curriculum and irrelevant courses . . . depersonalized educational systems . . . authoritarian and paternalistic administrations . . .

In retrospect we think the debate has been worthwhile. We also believe our resolution to be a step forward in the direction of peaceful reform, attempting as it does to formalize what is viable and constructive behavior. Student rights most surely will be a continuing and major concern in this decade, and events may outstrip the document's sentiments. There are those who say that the seventies may well bring far more student participation, among other possibilities perhaps even collective bargaining for students. We think, nonetheless, that at this time in history a clear statement of student rights must be made by those of us in authority roles. We have to earn the right to administer by responding to the felt needs of our constituency. Students are a part of that constituency.

NEW YORK CITY BOARD OF EDUCATION
RESOLUTION STATING RIGHTS AND RESPONSIBILITIES OF SENIOR HIGH SCHOOL STUDENTS (EFFECTIVE SEPTEMBER, 1970)

1. In each high school there should be established an elective and representative student government with offices open to all students. The student government

From *New York University Education Quarterly*, 1 (Summer, 1970), 23-24. Copyright © 1970 by New York University. Reprinted by permission of the publisher.

will establish reasonable standards for candidates for office. All students should be allowed to vote in annual elections designed to promote careful consideration of the issues and candidates.

a. The student government shall have the power to allocate student activity funds, subject to established audit controls and the By-Laws of the Board of Education. Extracurricular activities shall be conducted under guidelines established by the student government. The student government shall be involved in the process of developing curriculum and of establishing disciplinary policies.

b. Representatives selected by the student government shall meet at least monthly with the principal to exchange views, to share in the formulation of school student policies, and to discuss school-student relations and any other matters of student concern.

2. A parent-student-faculty consultative council, as established by previous Board of Education resolutions, shall meet at least monthly to discuss any matter relating to the high school. The consultative council shall organize a subcommittee to consider matters of schoolwide concern submitted by individual students. The subcommittee shall place such problems on the agenda of the consultative council when appropriate. The consultative council shall establish a continuing relationship with the principal to secure information regarding the administration of the school, to make recommendations for the improvement of all school services, and to promote implementation of agreed-upon innovations. Its structure and operating procedures shall be placed on file with the Chancellor.

3. Official school publications shall reflect the policy and judgment of the student editors. This entails the obligation to be governed by the standards of responsible journalism, such as avoidance of libel, obscenity, and defamation. Student publications shall provide as much opportunity as possible for the sincere expression of all shades of student opinion.

4. Students may exercise their constitutionally protected rights of free speech and assembly, as long as they do not interfere with the operations of the regular school program.

a. Students have a right to wear political buttons, arm bands, and other badges of symbolic expression, as long as these do not violate the limits set in 4c, below.

b. Students may distribute political leaflets, newspapers, and other literature at locations adjacent to the school.

c. Students shall be allowed to distribute literature on school property at specified locations and times designated. The principal and the student government shall establish guidelines governing the time and place of distribution at a site that will not interfere with normal school activities. They will also provide for sanctions against those who do not adhere to prescribed procedures. No commercial or obscene material, nothing of a libelous nature or involving the defamation of character, nor anything advocating racial or religious prejudice will be permitted to be distributed within the school. In noting these exceptions it is clearly the intention of the Board of Education to promote the dissemination of diverse viewpoints and to foster discussion of all political and social issues.

d. Students may form political and social organizations, including those that champion unpopular causes. These organizations, however, must be open to all students and must abide by Board of Education policies as developed in guidelines established by the student government acting in concert with the principal. These organizations shall have reasonable access to school facilities.

5. Faculty advisors shall be appointed by the principal after consultation with the student group.

6. Students have the right to determine their own dress, except where such dress is clearly dangerous, or is so distractive as to clearly interfere with the learning and teaching process. This right may not be restricted even by a dress code arrived at by a majority vote of students as Dr. Ewald Nyquist, State Commissioner of Education, held this year in Decisions No. 8022 and 8023.

7. Students shall receive annually upon the opening of school a publication setting forth rules and regulations to which students are subject. This publication shall also include a statement of the rights and responsibilities of students. It shall be distributed to parents as well.

8. A hearing must be held within five school days of any suspension as prescribed by law and the circulars of the Chancellor.

9. The extent and definition of student rights and responsibilities are subject to discussion by the consultative councils. Appeals from the decisions of the head of the school, relating to rights and responsibilities herein enumerated, must first be lodged with the assistant superintendent in charge of the high schools, then the Chancellor, and finally the Central Board of Education. All such appeals shall be decided as quickly as possible.

10. Rights also entail responsibilities. One of the major goals of this document is to establish a new trust, one based on the humane values of self-respect and respect for others. No student has the right to interfere with the education of his fellow students. If dialogue is interrupted or destroyed, then the bonds that hold us together are broken. It is thus the responsibility of each student to respect the rights of all who are involved in the educational process.

KEEPING OUT OF COURT

LAURENCE W. KNOWLES

A distressing effect of student dissent has been an increase in litigation by students, parents, and institutional watchdogs.

Increasing litigation by students, parents and community organizations has added some formidable and unfamiliar new pressures to the administrator's workload: legal headaches.

The Oliver Browns (school desegregation), the Mrs. Murrays (Bible reading), and most recently, the Tinkers (black armbands) have helped pave the path to the courtroom, together with the increasingly active institutional watchdogs, such as the American Civil Liberties Union and the NAACP. Moreover, court victories by parents encourage others, and the litigation seems to feed on itself.

Since legal problems with students are increasing in number and complexity and official reactions and solutions to these problems are likely to be subjected to judicial review, a wrong step can land the school administrator in court— with the accompanying expense, notoriety, and often embarrassment.

Litigation cannot be avoided entirely, but school systems can minimize it, and increase their chances of success in suits that are filed, by anticipating problems and taking precautionary steps. Here are some methods:

Don't get caught with your policies down. If a school waits until a difficult situation arises, the administrator is likely to find himself subjected to some highly emotional pressure from his community which may lead to a rash and illegal decision on his part.

He should keep in mind that this decision may well be reviewed later in the clinical atmosphere of the courtroom, with the superintendent and board members as defendants in a civil suit for damages.

The superintendent should anticipate difficult situations and draft and formally adopt comprehensive policies before such situations materialize. That way, before the situations arise, they can be dispassionately assessed and a cool, legal judgment obtained.

An example: Three boys are indicted for rape, outside the school grounds, and released on bond. What should the school do? A policy drawn prior to this event might very well provide that "No student shall be suspended from

---

Laurence W. Knowles is Professor of Law at the University of Louisville School of Law.

classes or otherwise treated differently solely by reason of being charged with a crime."

With no prior regulation at all, it is easy to imagine the community pressures on the administrator and school board.

On the other hand, if the board had acted before the crisis, it could counter the pressure by pointing to a "long-standing policy" of nonaction until the students are determined guilty by the proper tribunal.[1]

Of course, the pressures of the moment may force a reversal of a rational regulation adopted before the crisis arose. But it takes a lot of pressure to change a "long-standing policy" for the worse.

Clearly define policy. Policies designed to punish certain conduct must be clearly worded and adopted in advance. Expulsion and suspension are obviously punitive, and as such, can be constitutionally applied only to acts clearly proscribed in published school regulations.

The idea is simply that persons cannot be punished for acts that were not distinctly defined as criminal when committed. A very recent California case[2] applied this doctrine to a haircut regulation. The rule in question provided: Excessive tightness in clothes as well as extremes in shirttails and, similarly, extremes of hair styles are not acceptable."

The court agonized for several pages before concluding that the word "extreme" is unconstitutionally vague. Presumably, if school officials redrafted the regulation to read "not over ten inches in length" it would have survived at least an attack on vagueness grounds (but perhaps not on free speech grounds[3]).

When investigating crime or breaches of school regulations, act as if the school is a policeman and the student is a citizen. The purpose of these suggestions is to prevent a lawsuit—to play it safe. There is no better way than to accord students all the safeguards available to adults. A partial list follows:

1. *Confessions:* In serious matters, advise the student he need not say anything until he talks with his parents, or someone they select as his representative.

The sweeping language of the Supreme Court in *In re Gault*[4] seems to make this imperative. The Court there said: "It would indeed be surprising if the privilege against self-incrimination were available to hardened criminals but not to children. The language of the Fifth Amendment . . . is unequivocal and without exception."

---

[1] Howard v. Clark, 299 N.Y. Supp. 2nd 65 (Sup. Ct. 1969). It is not certain that the school can exclude students even after conviction.
[2] Myers v. Areata Union High School District, 78 Cal. Rptr. 68 (Cal. App. 1969). See also Buttny v. Smiley, 281 F. Supp. 280 (D. Colo., 1968).
[3] Breen v. Kahl, 296 F. Supp. 702 (W. D. Wisc. 1969); contra, Ferrell v. Dallas Independent School District 392 F. 2nd 697 (5th Cir. 1968), cert. den. 393 U.S. 856 (1968).
[4] 387 U.S. 1, 47-8 (1957).

What this means is that an overly aggressive school administrator may foreclose any possibility of criminal or juvenile proceedings based on statements he extracts from a student—or, for that matter, any other evidence procured as a result of the statements. The prosecution's case is stillborn,[5] because of misinformed zealousness on the schoolman's part.

2. *Searches of the student's person:* If a student is reasonably suspected of carrying a dangerous weapon, an administrator can probably pat him down in a cursory search.[6] If he is suspected of possessing less patently dangerous materials, such as marijuana or pornography, even a cursory search may be illegal.[7]

The precedents cited for these rules are precedents involving police treatment of adults, not students. Significantly, however, recent judicial accommodation of young people's rights has not been limited to the U.S. Supreme Court, but is appearing in lower federal and state courts. In a very recent haircut case,[8] a federal judge reasoned that because haircut regulations would be obviously unconstitutional if applied to adults, they are a *fortiori* unconstitutional if applied to younger people.

Painting with a broad brush the court remarked: "Cautious counsel to avoid judicial issues merely because they concern younger people . . . is neither prudent, expedient, or just. It is time to broaden the constitutional community by including with its protections young people whose claim to dignity matches that of their elders."

If this view wins the fore, treating children like adults in the school will not only be judicious, but constitutionally imperative.

3. *Searches of lockers:* Before a locker is leased, the student should be required to acknowledge an agreement that the locker is purely school property, and that the school reserves the right to inspect it at any time and for any reason. Without such classification, a locker may well be considered to be a private compartment of a student.[9]

Try always to "out-fair" students. Can you really be too fair in investigating and procedurally processing student suspensions? If a student wants a lawyer, the names of witnesses against him, the right to crossexamine, a public hearing—what danger is there in granting these requests? A little time and expense, maybe, but nothing compared to the time, expense and anxieties of lawsuit following a suspension where such requests were denied. Is it any comfort after a legal trial

[5] Cf. Freman v. Wilcox, 167 S.E. 2nd 163 (Ga. 1969), rejecting the confession of a 14 year-old who was given his Fifth Amendment warnings, while his parents were not so advised.
[6] Terry v. Ohio, 392 U.S. 1 (1968); Matter of Lang. 44 Misc. 2d 900, 255 N.Y.S. 2d 987 (1965); State v. Lowry, 95 N.J. Super. 307, 230 A. 2d 907 (1967).
[7] Sibron v. New York, 392 U.S. 40 (1968).
[8] Breen v. Kahl.
[9] Katz v. U.S., 398 U.S. 347 (1967), People v. Overton, 283 N.Y. S. 2d 22 (1967), vacated and remanded, 89 S. Ct. 252 (1969).

and several appeals to learn that the school administration really has the right to refuse a public hearing? And what if the school administration learns that it didn't have this right after all?[10]

These axioms may well allow some students to avoid punishment. Indeed, a skillful lawyer may demolish the testimony of witnesses against a student.

Again, if a student is not forced to remove his shoes or empty his pockets, some marijuana may not be found. And students will go unpunished because the administration was too fair.

On the other hand, being solicitous of student dignity, and mindful of fair play will prove far more effective in "selling" the establishment and keeping its representatives out of the courtroom.

[10] See generally, Abbott, Due Process and Secondary School Dismissals, 20 Case W. Rev. L. Rev. 378 (1969).

BOARD OF EDUCATION ACTS
N.Y. STUDENTS GAIN RIGHTS

JEFF SUMMER, New York, N.Y.

The New York City Board of Education's recent resolutions of "Rights and Responsibilities For Senior High School Students" will have massive repercussions in the city's schools.

Last year's student disorders will probably be replaced by meaningful activity within the school structure. The Board of Education has proved to be responsive to students' legitimate grievances, while the High School Principal's Association appears to fear the new youthful activism.

The Board's resolution would abolish the General Organization Council and replace it with an organization elected by all school members. Students would be allowed to distribute literature outside the school and in specified places within the building. Censorship of student publications would be outlawed. Suspended students would have the right to counsel and the right to cross examine witnesses. Machinery would be created for the purpose of evaluating complaints about alleged violations of student rights.

Many of the Board's proposals were originally stated by the now defunct N.Y.C. High School Student Union. Many of these issues last year's fuel for student strikes, have been transformed to assets by the new Board. The Board's bold action on these sensitive areas should establish more stability within the school system and give students a forum for meaningful action.

From Revelation Now: A National Student Journalism Review, 1 (January, 1970), 4. Reprinted with the permission of Barry Glassner, Coordinator-Publisher.

Changes in the school climate can already be seen in the failure of most of last year's underground newspapers. The greater freedom allowed the "establishment press," has reduced the need for underground publications.

Independent journalism, however, will once again be practiced by the *High School Free Press*, the largest of last year's underground papers. The *Press* printed its first edition on Dec. 6, and will again be a gadfly in the side of the school establishment. Even the *Free Press* admitted that the new Board has made some significant steps.

The liberalism of the new Board is rivaled by the conservatism of the School Principals Association. The Association has come out against increased student rights, claiming that the Board is stripping a school administration of tools necessary for orderliness.

The United Federation of Teachers has generally supported the reforms. Future school tensions may result in a student-faculty alliance against a repressive administration.

The dismal outlook of a system struggling back to normal after a crippling strike has been completely altered since last year. Never before did students possess their present degree of freedom. Cynical high school students, taught by experience to distrust optimism, can again look towards an era of hope.

BOARDS STILL DUCK THE PROBLEM OF PREGNANT SCHOOLGIRLS

FRANCES WURTZ and GERALDINE FERGEN

Scarcely one school district in three makes any educational provisions at all for its unmarried, pregnant school-age girls. The statistic becomes the more appalling in face of the fact that nearly 150,000 girls of school age become pregnant out of wedlock each year.

So contends a new study conducted to investigate what school districts across the nation are doing to educate increasing numbers of pregnant girls. Aim of the study was to find answers to questions such as these: Are pregnant girls excluded from educational programs in local public school districts? Are they at least permitted to participate in a limited school arrangement? Do school boards make special educational facilities available to these girls? What role do state departments of education assume in behalf of pregnant schoolgirls?

Frances Wurtz is a registered nurse serving as coordinator of the associate degree nursing program at Mineral Area College, Flatriver, Mississippi. Geraldine Fergen is Professor of Special Education, Illinois State University, Normal, Illinois.

At a time when attainment of a high school diploma never has been more important to society and to the welfare of the adult, pregnancy creates stumbling blocks to the continuing education of thousands of unmarried school-age girls. Illegitimacy has tripled in the past 25 years, and an annual increase of 30,000 unmarried, pregnant schoolage girls is anticipated. (New Jersey's special education officials indicate 4,500 public school girls become pregnant each year; Maryland indicates 2,000 girls 16 years old and younger; San Francisco estimates 400; Detroit reports 800; and St. Louis estimates 1,000 each year.)

The fact that virtually anyone can obtain a high school diploma these days and that curriculums are diverse enough to please everyone sheds suspicion on girls who are not high school graduates. More importantly, career advancement and further education are predicated on ownership of a high school diploma—all of which seems to indicate school boards that dismiss girls known to be pregnant or that don't specify a program of instruction for pregnant girls are being extremely short-sighted, if not cruel.

Information leading to these conclusions was supplied by 48 state departments of education, which responded to a comprehensive questionnaire. Returns indicated that 33 states provide special reimbursement to local school districts for the education of pregnant school-age girls. An additional 12 states offer no money but provide consultative assistance in planning programs. Only three states have no educational programming for pregnant students, while opinions disallowing special funding have been rendered by attorney generals in two states.

All states providing financial assistance to local districts to educate pregnant girls allocate the funds as part of their special education programs. The funding categories, however, vary from state to state, with some states including education of pregnant students under programs for the physically handicapped, others under programs for the maladjusted, and still others under programs for the emotionally disturbed.

Increases in their allotments for schooling pregnant girls are anticipated by 30 states. Of the 12 states that offer only planning consultation, nine disclosed plans to reimburse local districts through state special education funds.

Number of operating school districts reported as providing special educational services for pregnant girls was 5,450 out of an approximate potential of 17,000. Rapid district reorganization and establishment of special education cooperative units already may have changed the figures, but it is clear that, in spite of the availability of state reimbursement, a great many districts are not utilizing the funds and, one may suppose, not providing for the educational needs of pregnant girls.

Programs for continuing the education of pregnant girls in the 5,450 districts run the gamut from home-bound instruction to continuation in the regular school program, to transference to homes for unwed mothers or other residence institutions, to attendance at special classes, to home-school telephone teaching and part-time participation in regular classes (see policies on page 23).

Four distinct trends were spotted by the study: (1) School districts are moving away from home instruction for pregnant girls toward special classes or attendance in regular programs. (2) States are providing increased financial assistance to local districts with some kind of continuing education for expectant mothers. (3) State departments of education are assuming larger leadership in establishing and maintaining such programs. (4) Rehabilitation of the individual has become the keynote in long-range planning of educational programs for pregnant school-age girls.

Although all these trends are indeed positive, still to be answered are questions about why some states continue to buck the trend toward increased establishment of programs for pregnant girls and, perhaps more importantly, why many school districts have not moved forward in this area when their states stand ready to reimburse every penny of the cost.

How Five Board Policies Look at It

To pinpoint what school boards are saying right now about educating pregnant students, The American School Board Journal requested reference assistance from the EPS/NSBA Clearinghouse in Connecticut. The reply: A definite need exists for many school boards to update their policies on student pregnancy; forward-looking policies are rare; comprehensive ones, virtually nonexistent.

A handful of happenings indicate, however, that school boards cannot avoid updating policies on student pregnancy much longer: Students are beginning to flex some Due Process muscles over the issue of pregnancy in school; court suits have been brought against school boards and administrators who assume the roles of physicians by setting arbitrary time periods specifying when a pregnant student may return to school; and the National Council on Illegitimacy advocates the legal right to continued schooling in regular school classes for pregnant girls and young mothers.

But what do school boards say? Little enough. Here is a representative sampling of board policy positions on pregnant students and young mothers:

East Orange, N.J.—"Unwed mothers will be admitted unless their health does not permit it or unless they are needed at home to care for the baby. If and when the girl's health improves and arrangements are made for the care of the baby, she must attend school if she is under sixteen years of age."

Towson, Md.—"The enrollment of unmarried mothers and pregnant girls of school age cannot be legally denied. Either the parent or the pupil must write to the principal requesting permission for the pupil to enroll. The visiting teacher shall be requested to investigate the case. The team conference technique shall be used in making the final recommendations regarding the educational program of these pupils . . ."

Charlotte, N.C.—"The board of education does not condone early marriage and/ or pregnancy among high school students and their beginning of families at an early age. Neverthless, it is the intent of the board of education to aid these young people in the continuation of their education within the limits of reasonable safe-guards both for the school and the young people."

Aberdeen, Wash.—"A pregnant girl (married) shall withdraw from school at a time set in consultation with the principal, girls' advisor and parent, and before her condition becomes obvious. In most cases a pregnant girl may be allowed to complete a quarter if this will aid in setting a time of re-entry or completion of her education . . . Pregnant girls who are confined to a maternity home that has access to a public school program may continue their high school studies and transfer back to high school at an appropriate time set in a conference with the high school principal and counselor . . ."

Goldsboro, N.C.—"The board of education does not uphold or condone the socially unacceptable behavior of students who are the parents of a child born out of wedlock. The board does, however, recognize its responsibility to educate each student in order that he may accept the responsibility of citizenship in a democracy and be a contributor, rather than a deterrent, to society. An unwed, expectant mother shall report her condition to the girls' counselor and withdraw from school when the fact is known. An unwed mother may be readmitted to school at the beginning of the school year following the birth of the child. Upon re-entry, the school staff shall make every effort to help rehabilitate her toward a successful life . . . as long as her conduct is acceptable and her presence is compatible with the welfare of the group."

FIVE

DRESS CODES AND GROOMING STANDARDS

The matter of student dress and grooming is to many the most trivial of student rights issues. Ironically, it has also aroused the most participants and produced the most confrontations between students and school officials, at least in middle-class schools. What that implies about the values, concerns, and obligations of school officials and the public at large will be left to the reader's judgment. Regardless of where one's values lie, it is becoming apparent that of all the issues discussed, this is the one most nearly resolved.

Beyond a doubt, there has been a substantial relaxation of rigid standards in recent years. Nevertheless, in spite of a full range of opinion concerning the limits of specific regulations, support for some kind of school enforced dress and grooming standards remains high. A small opinion sample of *Instructor Magazine* subscribers conducted in spring, 1969, revealed both an overwhelming acceptance of a "reasonable dress code," and a diversity of opinion concerning the parameters of the term "reasonableness."

Activist students have been every bit as distressed about school imposed dress and grooming standards as they have about the seemingly more important aspects of free expression. Their central point is that dress is an irrelevant consideration in the learning process, and that the school would do well to shift its emphasis from concern over petty conformity to serious education. Both of the articles by students in this chapter emphasize this point of view with conviction.

As a group, school administrators have been reluctant to surrender what seems to them to be a societally imposed obligation to enforce society's traditional standards. When athletics is involved the situation becomes a bit more complex. On a number of occasions administrators have been forced into a "back the coach" stance following a coach's insistence that his players adhere to a certain grooming norm as a necessary sign of team discipline. In such a case the assumed rights of the individual and the assumed right of a coach to establish authority over "his" athletes clash head on. Chances are that the responses of four administrators on the hypothetical issue of a coach suspending his star athlete, as posed by the editors of *School Management*, fairly represent the attitude of public secondary school officials.

The difficulty of defining acceptable boundaries for school dress regulations is readily apparent. Free spirits among youth are insisting on no restrictions of any kind. Many school officials still insist on maintaining a "responsible" dress code. Squabbling between activist youth and adult authorities has very likely had an impact on liberalizing dress and grooming standards, but perhaps it is that values have changed rather than standards. In this regard, the adult fashion world has been a most important ally of youth. Another change agent has been the courts—but only recently. Virtually all of the significant judicial decisions made prior to 1969 implied that the constitutional rights of youth were not an issue. The school's right to maintain order by imposing "reasonable" dress regulations was supported repeatedly as the courts affirmed a school's right to regulate student appearance.

The most cited precedent for this stance was the case of *Pugsley* v. *Sellmeyer,* Arkansas Supreme Court (1923), in which the court upheld the expulsion of a girl who used talcum powder on her face in violation of school grooming standards. Indeed the court showed little patience for troubling itself over the case, maintaining that "courts have other and more important functions to perform than that of hearing complaints of disaffected pupils of the public schools against rules and regulations promulgated by the school boards for the government of the schools."[1]

Prior to 1969 the courts insisted, with one inconsequential exception, that school regulations on student appearance have only to pass a test of "reasonableness," i.e., the regulations must be reasonably connected with educational goals. In the twenty-year period prior to 1969, only eight cases of note involved student appearance. According to Montfort Ray, in all eight cases the courts retained the test of reasonableness. By his analysis, in six of the eight the courts adhered to the historic tendency of using the test as an excuse for not examining the merits of particular cases.

As late as 1965, a Massachusetts court in *Leonard* v. *School Comm.* indicated its presumption that school regulations are almost inevitably reasonable, asserting that "findings made in good faith by a school committee, that a pupil's behavior so interferes with discipline and management of the school that his expulsion is necessary, are within its discretion and conclusive." The court agreed that the student's "unusual hair style" could disrupt and impede the maintenance of a proper classroom atmosphere and decorum. Several courts in various parts of the country have reached similar conclusions in similar cases. They have either reasoned, as in *Pugsley* and *Leonard,* that school systems must have had some reasonable justification for their regulations, or else have used as the test for reasonableness whether or not prior incidents were attributable to events a rule allegedly attempted to prevent.

There is an interesting contrast between the courts affirmation of the right of a student to control his personal appearance by wearing freedom buttons (*Burnside* v. *Byars,* 1966), and the denial of a similar freedom when long hair was at issue (*Davis* v. *Firment,* 1967). In the latter case the court did not agree that First Amendment liberties were at stake, since it found the issue of hair outside of the Amendment's protection for speech, writings and expression of views that could

[1] Montfort S. Ray, "Constitutional Law—A Student's Right to Govern His Personal Appearance," *Journal of Public Law,* 17 (1968): 151-174.

be legitimately and validly communicated. The important issue in these and other recent cases is that the focus of attention was turned to the constitutional rights of students.

Recent changes in school dress regulations, including a brief summation of court actions, is discussed by Frances K. Heussenstamm in "Public High School Dress Regulations: Some Sociological and Legal Implications." It is apparent from the historical facts which support her article that much is changing and will continue to change with respect to enforcing dress regulations. When student pressure, court mandates, and changing dress norms are all manifest at the same time, it is little wonder that all but the most traditional administrators feel comfortable making changes in their dress regulations. The article by Renato Mazzei, "Do We Need a Code of Dress and Grooming?" reflects the satisfaction of one vice-principal following abandonment of the dress code at his school and its replacement by a five-sentence guideline.

One need not accept the ideological argument favoring the abandonment or relaxation of dress codes to appreciate the wisdom of revising or removing them. The short "Wondering Out Loud" section which appeared originally in the *American School Board Journal* reflects the *Journal's* reservations about the wisdom—or lack thereof—in maintaining dress codes. A brief five-point code adopted by the school board of Evanston, Illinois, and also published by the *American School Board Journal* under the title, "Try This Dress Code on for Size," may be viewed as an attempt to broaden the concept of "reasonableness." So long as codes limit their concern to safety, health, and the rudiments of decency, a substantive issue over the constitutional rights of youth is not likely to develop. Nor is one likely to develop over the psychological implications of encouraging excessively normative behavior. On the other hand, it is now clear that activist students and the courts will no longer tolerate arbitrary dress and grooming standards.

TEACHER OPINION POLL

SHOULD A SCHOOL HAVE A DRESS CODE?*

Replies were close to unanimous in stating that schools should have a reasonable dress code. But many wanted it to be a cooperative venture by parents, teachers, and children.

* This Instructor Teacher Opinion Poll was conducted in the spring of 1969. A random sampling of 100 Instructor subscribers was asked to respond to the question. Returns given in the box below are certified by The Instructor Publications, Inc. All responses and names are on file in the Instructor offices, but respondents were given the option of having their names withheld.

Reprinted with the permission of the publisher from *Instructor* © October 1969, The Instructor Publications, Inc., Dansville, N.Y. 14437.

DRESS CODE IS NEEDED

"Schools should settle on some sort of dress code, and then stick to it."

Peggy Haemmerle

"A school's concern should be education, not dress. There should be a code, however, ruling on such things as see-through blouses. The code should be made by all concerned."

Jane E. Driscoll

"Without limits, wearing apparel will be too radical regardless of whether girls are wearing dresses and boys pants."

"If parents do not care how their children look, at least let's get the children to give a second look at themselves before they leave for school." Dolores B. Quinn

"Definite limits on clothing should be established."

Kenyon Cook

"Our society seems to be degenerating and anything we can do to prevent it will certainly be a credit to us."

One person stressed the need for self-determination.

"I feel students need to help make decisions on some policies that concern them. Without this valuable experience how can we expect them to suddenly emerge as mature thinking individuals?"

Another person felt the decision on a dress code was a community concern.

"I think a community poll of suggestions could be taken and then put these wishes into formal rules for all grades."

Mrs. James Swarts

WHAT IS REASONABLE DRESS?

Many replies expressed definite ideas about what is acceptable.

"A dress could be inappropriate because of extreme style, design, or flimsy material."

Ethel Aiello

"Many fads, although filling the requirements of pants for boys and skirts for girls, do not coincide with what might be considered good dress standards."

Susan Brown

"Skirts should be a reasonable length and pants should not be too tight."

Annette Courtney

"I think styles such as culottes should be permitted."   Gail A. Verner

Several replies emphasized that economics, weather, and type of activity should have some bearing on clothing.

"Much will depend on socioeconomic factors as to just what would be permitted as suitable dress."

Janet Freier

"I feel the town's economic status must be considered." Constance Forest

"Dress codes should depend on the season, location of the school, and financial means of the family."

```
┌─────────────────────────────────────┐
│              SCORE BOX              │
│                                     │
│ Should a school have a reasonable   │
│ dress code?          yes    90%     │
│                      no     10%     │
│                                     │
│ Who should make it?                 │
│               teachers       4%     │
│       parents and teachers  24%     │
│      children and teachers   4%     │
│   parents, children, teachers 58%   │
│                                     │
│ Is "any dress" OK as long as it's   │
│ pants for boys and skirts for girls?│
│                      yes    18%     │
│                      no     64%     │
└─────────────────────────────────────┘
```

"I think elementary girls should be permitted to wear pants during cold winter months."   Betty Collins

"There are times when girls should be wearing slacks for physical activities."
                                                              Nancy E. Stephens

Many responses discussed neatness and cleanliness as well as comfort.

"I think clothes can set mood. A child too dressed up is stiff and stilted, and cannot do work."   Margaret I. Brown

"I believe clothes should be cool and comfortable."

Several reminded that teachers should also dress reasonably.

"There must be an enforced code of dress for teachers." Gwendolyn Caldwell

A middle-of-the-road position.

"My idea of reasonable is whatever the children and their parents decide. I feel the decisions as to dress are between parent and child."

. . . AND A MAN WITH A PROBLEM

"I find some of the girls' dresses in 7th and 8th grades quite disconcerting while I'm trying to teach."

UNSHAVEN, UNSHORN, UNACCEPTABLE?

DANIEL ZWERDLING

Almost every high school administrator across the country has dealt in the past two years with students whose hair styles look subversively like Beethoven's— God forbid, even worse, like Jesus'—and whose faces generate un-Americanism like Lincoln's. The pattern is the same everywhere: A teacher apparently feeling threatened by a student's hidden ears or camouflaged chin marches him to the main office; here, the student awaits confrontation with the Vice-Principal in Charge of Discipline (perhaps even the principal), who insists that he denude his ears and chin enough to satisfy all Decent People, or face suspension or expulsion.

The student may or may not submit. If he has done too much outside reading for his own good, especially in the existentialists, he will probably refuse. And a school-wide and possibly community-wide controversy will explode.

I attended high school in a county which prides itself on having one of the best, most liberal public school systems in the nation. Yet during my three years there, the single most explosive, most recurrent issue was student dress, and especially hair styles. Hair excited more emotions than controversies over student-government participation in school affairs, religion in the school, even free expression of student opinion.

The administration fought long hair, the faculty fought it, the superintendent talked about it—and students left school because of it. Ironically, and somewhat sadly, the students who bore the brunt of the battles and withstood threats of suspension because their appearance "detracted from the educational process" (the phrase my school used) were often the very students who gave the educational process something to boast about.

One boy—doubly damned by long hair *and* blue jeans—won the coveted National Council of Teachers of English award, led the debate team, edited the yearbook, and starred in the annual senior class play. He emerged unbarbered largely because his suspension would have seriously hurt the play's success. (I was involved in one of these hassles when I grew a Lincolnesque beard. I finally shaved it off after numerous conferences with the administration, because my principal didn't want to be "embarrassed" when I received an award at a banquet to be attended by state newspaper and political figures. Subsequently, I grew another beard, which I still have.)

The tragedy is—and it *is* an educational tragedy—that schools poison and embitter student administration-faculty relations by shifting the focus from educa-

From *Today's Education*, 57 (November, 1968) 23-24. Reprinted with the permission of the author and the publisher.

Daniel Zwerdling is Senior Editor of The Michigan Daily.

tion, where it should be, to something as utterly inane as hair styles. Students justifiably lose all respect for educators who expend their energies fighting long hair and beards on the grounds that they detract from the educational process rather than actually talking about that educational process and trying to improve it.

Seriously discussing hair is as foolish (and boring) as debating the merits of brown versus black socks. But so many Americans are investing so much time, energy, and impassioned emotion in a ceaseless campaign to remove beards and long hair from the face of the nation that hair has become as volatile an issue as the war in Vietnam, the urban riots, or the dollar drain. And tragically the schools are both a chief protagonist and a casualty of the hair war.

Most of these men and women could probably relax if they knew the real reason why many kids stop shaving and going to the barber. The devilish truth of why I, for one, let my beard grow: I was sick with mononucleosis and had nothing better to do while I lay in bed for a month. And I wanted to see how it would look.

Most boys want to grow a beard simply to see if they can—perhaps to assert their masculinity. Like me, they want to see how they'd look. (Magazine ads tempt, "Add five sexy years to your face—buy a moustache.") Besides, it's less troublesome, less expensive, and fun. Even my bald-headed vice-principal admitted he tried growing a beard in his younger, more reckless days.

These explanations are disappointingly innocent for those who want headier, more political stuff. But very few boys ponder over Marxist-Leninist dialectics as they comb their hair or groom their beards; they are imagining what the pretty girl in class will say.

Psychologists, of course, can probe the hair-beard syndrome somewhat deeper (but if they do, let them give equal time to analyzing stay-pressed pants, wing-tip shoes, and $4,000 automobiles). They may find that the boy with unkempt long hair and grubby-looking beard often grows them because, not being handsome or self-confident to begin with, he feels insecure about his basic personal appearance.

By ignoring grooming habits like combing his hair and shaving, habits whose sole purpose is to make him "more attractive," he can ignore those confrontations with the mirror which remind him that no amount of normal grooming will make him look much better. So as an antidote to caring desperately how he looks, he doesn't care at all.

Of course, many boys pride themselves on keeping their long hair and beards beautifully trimmed and immaculate. Others, however, simply and genuinely don't care: They're repelled by the slick hair and smooth skin bombarding them from magazine, newspaper, and TV advertisements. These students feel deeply, and I agree, that we have more important issues than physical appearance to which we can devote our time and money.

To millions of deluded Americans, hair has become a hated symbol of the student generation's radical discontent with a society it did not create but now must inherit; a sure sign that the body underneath the hair takes drugs, doesn't aspire to law or business school, is unpatriotic, and opposes the war in Vietnam. Students are suddenly growing long hair and beards in an era of corporate executives and hair cream, and most people are at a loss to explain why.

Basically, long hair and beards have a simple gestalt, in my opinion: Boys want to let them grow. There is no political plot or mysterious motive or subtle ploy, no subversive undertone. A disbelieving neighbor approached me recently at a political coffee klatch, clinking ice cubes in his glass of Scotch, and sneered, "When you shave that damn hair off your face you'll look half human. What are you trying to prove?" I told him I was trying to prove nothing, I simply liked it. "Don't give me that," he shouted with veins puffing red in his neck. "What are you trying to *prove?*"

He refused to accept my beard as something entirely innocent and natural— in fact, biologically far more natural than a smooth face (I don't believe God gave men beards to support the razor industry). To him, my hair style had classed the rest of me as something less than human—and hostile.

People like my neighbor hate long hair and beards because they have convinced themselves that such styles represent certain political and social philosophies—which they hate. They have seen student activists challenge their traditional way of life and call for a change in institutions that may have suited our parents, but that now must respond to new needs (or so the argument goes)— and they have seen many of these students wearing beards.

Just as racists despise Negroes because of their black skin, so many adults hate boys because of their long hair. It is so much easier for a weak person to fabricate a group hate symbol than honestly and intelligently to confront individuals *as* individuals on the basis of personal merit. It is easier for a weak administrator to fight a student's hair than to try to understand his politics.

When a young man wears his hair or beard with defiance, it is only because he has first confronted irrational, vehement opposition—if adults do not care how I style my hair, what is there to defy? When a responsible educator—when any person—attaches more significance to fashions than to human values and threatens to punish those who don't conform to his tastes, the nonconformers are quick to assert their rights and to resist anyone who would deny them.

Hair? What valid reason could there possibly be for preventing a person from styling his hair in any way he chooses? How could any reasonably intelligent American "pledge allegiance to the flag . . . and to the Republic for which it stands"—and then deny to another a right so basic that needing even to defend it mocks it? How could any man denounce totalitarianism—and then scorn a boy because his hair does not conform to the traditional norm?

Hair? Instead of being angry, I'm incredulous and perhaps depressed. How ludicrous it is that schools erupt into bitter fights, that students are deprived of education, that people hate—because a boy arranges the hairs on his head in a particular manner.

I have enjoyed my beard and long hair, at first simply because I liked them, but later because I found they have enabled me to gain valuable insights about human prejudice. People scream hateful harangues at me from behind car windows, some men and women spit at me on the street, and restaurants have refused to serve me despite my coat, tie, and button-down collar. When I remove the hair from my face and from over my ears, these people will accept me. When other boys take the hair from their faces, their educators will let them return to school.

Hair?

DRESS CODES

A school is an institution of learning—not a place of institutionalism. The purpose of a school should be to instill in pupils the intense desire to grasp all knowledge possible in their realm. Many of today's schools sidetrack this unquestionable goal by "teaching" the outmoded *social acceptance code* of fading generations.

Art, music, and literature are various expressions of individualism. These three subjects are taught at schools. During a student's years in high school he is told to "think for himself." Is it right then, to squash his self-expression by dictating what he can and cannot wear?

A dress code has no place in schools of the seventies. It is a symbol of the generations that conformed without thought to elderly desires and demands. But the independence and knowledge of today's young won't allow them to conform. We DEMAND the right to freedom of expression in all phases of our lives. North Fulton STUDENTS it is time to demand your release from the prison of conformity!!!

DARIA

From *Internal Exchange* [North Fulton High School Underground Student Newspaper], II [n.d.].

PROBLEM: COACH SUSPENDS STAR OVER MOUSTACHE

The star of your high school football team has been suspended from the squad by the coach for refusing to shave a moustache he sprouted during the summer. Under the school's new dress code, there's no rule against moustaches, and the student insists the coach has no right to tell him to shave it off. The coach, on the other hand, says that the rules governing his team are up to him. "I've always insisted that my athletes maintain a neat, well-groomed appearance," he says. "I don't intend to start making exceptions now." Other students, proud of their championship football team, are incensed. One of them notifies the local newspaper, which plays up the story on page one, and the principal appeals to you for support.

What action do you take?

Reprinted from *School Management* magazine, 13 (December, 1969), 25-26.

CONSENSUS: THE STUDENT MUST SHAVE HIS MOUSTACHE

In the opinion of four panel members, the absence of a rule against moustaches is no defense for students who actually grow them. They back the coach's right to make the rules for his team members.

Says Elbert Fike: "The coach evidently has been consistent in his requirements for the appearance of his athletes. He is to be commended for his action because suspending the star of the team is no easy decision."

Fike resents the attempt of students to bring pressure on the coach by releasing the story to the newspapers. "Neither students nor newspapers are conducting the athletic program or determining what right a coach has to set standards for his boys," says the Linden administrator.

W. H. Bray qualifies his support for the coach by basing it on the assumption that, even though the dress code doesn't prohibit moustaches, it does forbid "unusual appearance" by students. With this in mind, he assumes that the student's moustache is exaggerated enough to qualify as "unusual."

Says Bray: "If these assumptions are correct, I support the coach, even if it means suspending the star player from the team." Bray's tack is to meet with the coach, the student and the principal and attempt to convince the student that his attitude is having an "undesirable" effect on the entire school.

"The player can grow the moustache later in life if he wants to," says Bray. "I think he'll understand that he could contribute to a winning year by getting behind the coach's rules and obeying them, rather than being persistent about his moustache. I would point out to him that his attitude is incendiary and not helping the school at all."

Another administrator who would appeal to the player's sense of "responsibility" is Kenneth Sheetz. But Sheetz attacks the issue from the angle of the effect of the student's recalcitrance on his own future plans: "Being dropped from the team can destroy any chances the student may have of getting a college scholarship—if this already hasn't happened by the information getting into the newspapers. No college coach wants a boy who thinks he is better than the coach. I would point out that the student body and the community, as well as the players and coach, have been proud of our teams in the past—their good appearance, their sportsmanship, their won-lost record. It is not the coach who is on the spot; it's the boy. Is he going to 'lose all' because of a silly moustache?"

Despite his firm stand on this incident, Sheetz thinks the coach should be more flexible in applying rules to the school's athletes. "Times are changing," he says, "and a neat, well-trimmed moustache is no longer as offensive as the coach might think. Perhaps we should agree that, in the future, the school dress code will be the rule for participation in all co-curricular activities."

Donald Skeahan bases his decision to support the coach on the principle that many restrictions apply to athletes that don't apply to the student body as a whole. A dress code that doesn't prohibit moustaches can't be construed as permitting them in any and all situations, says Skeahan, but the coach's position shouldn't be allowed to become so inflexible that a compromise is ruled out: "I would caution both the coach and the principal not to let the problem develop into a situation that would prohibit the boy's return to the squad if he ultimately chooses to comply with the regulations."

DISSENT: THE STUDENT HAS A RIGHT TO GROW THE MOUSTACHE

Raymond Spear sums up the reaction of the panel's dissenters on this question: "No coach, teacher or principal has the right to make his own rules and regulations unless they are within the scope of established school board policy. If my board has not established a policy prohibiting the wearing of a moustache and if the high school administration has not prohibited the wearing of a moustache during the regular school day, then I have no choice but to support the position of the student."

The only thing that could make Spear side with the coach would be evidence that the moustache "is detrimental to the health and well-being of the student, or injurious to the total effectiveness and discipline of the football team."

Joseph Porter agrees that it isn't the coach's job to decide matters of personal taste and good grooming. "What is and is not well-groomed is open to constant change," Porter says. "It cannot be the arbitrary whim of one person to decide. The qualifications for being on a varsity team have little, if anything, to do with appearance off the field."

Porter would like to work a compromise that would allow both sides to save face, yet settle the issue once and for all. "Hopefully, opinions won't polarize before something can be worked out," he says. "Perhaps the player will agree to shave off his moustache—he can always grow another one—and meet with the coach, the principal and myself after the season to discuss the problem as it affects all sports and school activities—not just football, and not just one coach. I think the principal would do well to solicit the assistance of the player's parents in arriving at a compromise for the welfare of the entire school."

The moustache problem is a familiar one to H. Francis Rosen, who thinks he's learned a lesson or two about handling it. "It would be better to allow the moustache than create a cause which could end up with a rash of moustaches in the school," Rosen says. "Speaking as a superintendent who has had staff members with beards and moustaches, I know it goes against the grain with me. But if I had made a big issue of it, I would have had more."

Every effort should be made to have the moustachioed team member conform to the guidelines set up by the coach, says Rosen. "But in the final analysis, the individual's rights must be protected. A school dress code cannot be made comprehensive enough to allow for every contingency. As disheartening as it might be for the coach and the principal—and probably the superintendent—it's better to allow the player to have the moustache."

PUBLIC HIGH SCHOOL DRESS REGULATIONS: SOME SOCIOLOGICAL AND LEGAL IMPLICATIONS

F. K. HEUSSENSTAMM

The percentage of American high schools experiencing "disruption" more than doubled from eighteen per cent in the 1968-1969 school year to forty per cent in 1969-1970. There is considerable discussion, not only by school administrators, but by the general public as well, of the factors to which this growing unrest can be attributed. A search for answers has led to a scrutiny of high school underground newspapers as expressive of militant student feeling. Analysis of the content of approximately one hundred diversified papers published between 1964 and 1970 reveals important areas of youthful concern which presumably could have led to confrontation. As might be expected, there is strong disagreement with government military policy in southeastern Asia. Unquestionably, the war in Vietnam has separated the generations. Divergence of opinion with the Establishment on solutions to such national problems as poverty, environmental pollution, drug law enforcement, abortion, and racism conceivably could have fomented campus disturbances. The most immediate personal cause of rage, however, in addition to complaints about "irrelevant" curricula, textbook censorship, and student body elections, would seem to be school codes regulating dress and grooming. Angry adolescent authors appear to find these codes the number-one irritant, devoting themselves to this subject more frequently than to any other topic.

Adult imposed restrictions on the length of hair, specifications regarding footwear, and regulation of skirt length have generated rebellion which shows no sign of abatement. Parents and school authorities have resisted the fads and experimental behavior, symbolic to teen-agers of their drive toward a more "organic" and less "plastic" life-style. This resistance has become associated in the minds of adolescents with the rigidity and stultification which they see in certain aspects of American high school operation. Finally, disciplinary administrative reactions to adolescent attitudes perceived as threatening have been, in many instances, directly responsible for turning high schools into hostile camps.

A MATTER OF FASHION

During the last five years, as longer hair for males has become identified with "youthfulness" and virility, reverse transmission of culture, characteristic of some aspects of intergenerational relationships today, has influenced many adult males

Reprinted with the permission of the author.

F. K. Heussenstamm is Research Associate, Center for the Study of Evaluation, Graduate School of Education, University of California, Los Angeles.

to experiment with sideburns, longer nape length, and "elegant" styling. Since January, 1970, newer hair styles, conflicting with the necessity of the business-man to maintain a conventional appearance, have led to the purchase of "estab-lishment" short wigs by fifty to seventy-five additional customers per week, according to one New York manufacturer. Other companies, responsive to con-sumer demand, are also supplying the same type of hairpiece. Longer hair, as well as the affectation of fake mustaches and sideburns, has called forth from the army a general order prohibiting all such appurtenances save those necessary to cover disfiguring scars. These developments reflect the general ambivalence of the society toward longer hair fashions which are obviously growing in popular-ity. Commenting on the centrality, social consequentiality, and rationality of the operation of fashion in collective behavior, Blumer takes issue with popular no-tions that fashion issues are superficial or trivial. He describes the conditions under which fashion is "entrenched" as a "basic and widespread process in modern life." Tides of fashion move in as a consequence of

> . . . pressure to change, to open the doors to innovation, the inadequacy or the unavailability of decisive tests of the merit of proposed models, the effort of prestigeful figures to gain or maintain standing in the face of developments to which they must respond, and the groping of people for a satisfactory expression of new and vague tastes . . .[1]

These forces lead Blumer to define the role of fashion in society as (1) the intro-duction of order in a "potentially anarchic and moving present," (2) the loosen-ing of traditional constraints to "free" behavior for innovative movements, and (3) "orderly presentation for the immediate future."[2] Fashion, thus, plays an im-portant part in shaping adult behavior in the society as a whole.

It seems likely that because the new hair fashions were adopted initially by young persons, rather than by adults, that they have come to be considered a threat to established societal order. This reverse of traditional practice is expli-cated by Mead.[3]

THE OPERATION OF ADULT CONSTRAINTS

Questionnaires returned by forty-three State Departments of Education indicate that regulation of pupil behavior and appearance is almost universally delegated to local school boards. In addition, three respondents volunteered copies of High School Students' Bills of Rights being considered for adoption. Local adminis-trators, who perceive a major part of their role as a mandate to prevent ado-lescent exuberance from offending public taste in the community, have tradi-

[1] Blumer, Herbert, "Fashion: From Class Differentiation to Collective Selection," *Sociology Quarterly,* 10, 3 (Summer, 1969) 275-291.
[2] *Ibid.* 289-290.
[3] Mead, Margaret, *Culture and Commitment: A Study of the Generation Gap* (1970).

tionally devised dress codes which allegedly reinforce community standards. Typical of the self-confidence with which schoolmen have pursued this task is an article from a 1961 issue of *School Management,* "How to Get Students to *Dress Right*" written by a superintendent of a large city school district.[4] The article presents a detailed list of "offensive" articles of apparel, labeling "unacceptable" such attire as dungarees and T-shirts.

Because adolescence is a period of experimentation with the "presentation of self in everyday life," feedback from peers assumes paramount importance in the lives of most youth.[5] This fact underlines the significance of the high school dress code controversies. A recent study of the personality correlates of dress conformity indicates that students who choose non-conforming attire are characterized by tendencies toward individualism and self-sufficiency. Conforming dress is adopted by students whose primary interest is maintaining harmonious relations with others, but who also place a low value on esthetics.[6] Educators should ponder the relation of these values to the objectives to the educational program.

Adolescent decisions about dress reflect youthful concepts of *authenticity* and the expression of personal *identity.*[7] When choices are challenged by adults, teen-agers are called upon to expand considerable psychic energy in self-defense. Resulting confrontation may transform a passing fad into a cause célèbre.[8] Thus, hair has become a symbol of the divisiveness of the generations. Given the choice between *conformity* to rules which are perceived as arbitrary regimentation (with attendant public humiliation that is implicit in admission of error in personal judgment) or *resistance,* some frustrated teen-agers and their equally frustrated, irate parents have turned to the courts for arbitration.[9]

COURT DECISIONS

The position of the courts on regulation of adolescent physical appearance, political advocacy, and other potentially "disruptive" behaviors is in a state of flux. In the first of a series of relevant cases which have come to trial since 1965, the

[4] Manch, Joseph, "How to Get Students to *Dress Right*," *School Management,* 5, 8 (October, 1961) 14-15.

[5] Roach, Mary Ellen, "Adolescent Dress: Understanding the Issues," *Journal of Home Economics,* 61, 9 (November 1, 1969) 693-697.

[6] Taylor, Lucy C. and Compton, Norma H., "Personality Correlates of Dress Conformity," *Journal of Home Economics,* 60, 8 (October, 1968).

[7] Mazrui, Ali A. "The Robes of Rebellion," *Encounter,* 34, 2 (February, 1970) 19-30.

[8] Weinberger, Morris J. "Dress Codes: We Forget Our Own Advice," *The Clearinghouse,* 44, 8 (April, 1970) 471-473.

[9] See for example, Van Til, William, "The Hair Decision of 1975," *Contemporary Education,* 41 (January, 1970) 146-7; Garber, Leo, "Black Armband Case Stirs Debate by Supreme Court," *Nation's Schools,* 83, 6 (June, 1969) 73-74; Garber, Leo, "Courts Cite Constitution to Uphold 'Long-hair' Rights," *Nation's Schools,* 85, 2 (February, 1970) 83-84; McCarter, William J., "Long Hair, Short Skirts . . . and the Courts," *Ohio Schools,* 47, 5 (March 14, 1969) 15-16; Joseph, Newton, "The Great Hair Hassle," *Today's Health,* 48, 3 (March, 1970) 30-33.

Supreme Judicial Court of Massachusetts upheld the right of a school board to suspend a pupil for "excessive" hair length. The defense argued against the dress code as being both unreasonable and arbitrary.[10] "Rock n' roll" musicians brought suit against Dallas Independent School District for preventing the young plaintiffs from pursuing their careers by depriving them of the long hair essential to their professional roles. The court upheld the principal's right to operate his school "as he saw fit," and the decision was subsequently supported by a U.S. Court of Appeals.[11]

In 1967, a student who was suspended for long hair was defended by an attorney who based his arguments on the Civil Rights Act. The First, Eighth, Ninth and Fourteenth Amendments to the Constitution were used in this major case,[12] but the court ruled for the prosecution.

With respect to the First Amendment, right of freedom of expression, it (the court) said that the student was not really trying to express anything; on the Eighth Amendment, it held that the requirement to cut his hair was not a "cruel and unusual punishment"; the Ninth Amendment was dismissed with the statement that while the right of privacy may not be fundamental, the same certainly cannot be said for the right of free choice of grooming. Finally, in light of the fact that the board held several conferences with the pupil and granted him a hearing with his own attorney, the court said there was no violation of his right to due process under the Fourteenth Amendment.[13]

By 1969, the picture changed markedly when four signal cases came to trial. In the first, a Wisconsin court found the invasion of privacy inherent in forced hair-cutting to be a violation of youthful rights guaranteed under the Fourteenth Amendment.[14] In the second, the U.S. Supreme Court ruled that the student right to wear black armbands to protest the Vietnam war was guaranteed under the First Amendment.[15] Bans originating from *fear* of possible disruption were no longer supportable under this ruling; consequently, in the third case, a federal district court insisted that the attempts at regulation of male hair length were unconstitutional.[16] Illinois jurists concurred.[17] Garber summarized legal developments of the year by suggesting that (1) hair length rules would be held to be reasonable "in the absence of any question of constitutionality," (2) the weight of opinion to date is not clear on the violations of the First Amendment, (3) vio-

[10] Leonard v. School Committee of Attleboro, 212 N.E. (2nd) 468 (Mass.).
[11] Ferrell v. Dallas Independent School District, 261 F. Supp. 545 (Texas).
[12] Davis v. Firment, 269 F. Supp. 524 (La.).
[13] Garber, L. O. . . . (1970) 83.
[14] Breen v. Kahl, 296 F. Supp. 702 (Wis.)
[15] Garber, L. O. . . . (1969) 73-74.
[16] Griffin v. Tatum, 300 F. Supp. 60 (Ala.)
[17] Miller v. Gillis, No. 69 C 1841.

lations of the Fourth, Fifth, Eighth, and Ninth Amendments are not relevant to these issues, (4) abridgement of the Fourteenth Amendment *is* involved if no evidence exists that long hair disrupts school activity and is *not* involved when such hair regulations are applied for reasons of physical well-being, i.e., in matters of health or to quell disturbances, and (5) there is a difference of legal opinion on whether these rules violate the "equal protection clause" or "due process clause."

EFFECTS OF CODE SUSPENSION

An assessment of the impact of removal of dress codes in a limited sample of California schools seems to indicate little subsequent change in student behavior. Typically, the announcement that almost all attire will be acceptable results in a temporary rash of aberrations, but norms tend to be re-established within three to four weeks. A correlation between relaxing of dress codes and high school disruption has yet to be established. Inspection of class photographs in a sample of yearbooks as an unobtrusive measure of changing styles[18] reveals steadily increasing male hair lengths in more than half of the schools represented, including some schools where strict codes are in force. A study of the effects of removal of constraints is critically needed.

PUBLIC POLICY IMPLICATIONS

Adolescent underground press editors have made dress regulation the number one target for attack on many high school campuses. Youthful experimentation represented by fashion is, as is suggested by the studies of Blumer and others, integral to individual and societal development. In addition, because the evidence indicates that the courts will no longer support rigid local parochial policing of the dress and grooming of adolescents, it is recommended that all such regulation, save for minimal safety precautions, be abandoned. Reasonable cleanliness, a matter of health and esthetics can be expected, and for safety, feet ought to be shod. The concept of "decent coverage," based on community expectations, is a matter for supportive counseling rather than punitive action.

[18] Suggested by David W. Martin, University of Texas at Houston.

DO WE NEED A CODE OF DRESS AND GROOMING?

RENATO MAZZEI

Until recently, Scranton Central High School's Handbook for Students carried a "Code of Dress and Grooming" which could have been a page taken directly from the mid-Victorian era.

From *Pennsylvania School Journal*, 118 (February, 1970), 195-96. Reprinted with the permission of the author and the publisher.

Renato Mazzei is Vice-principal of Central High School, Scranton, Pennsylvania.

To refer to it merely as a page is a gross understatement since the "Code" actually filled three pages of the Handbook and consisted of 35 separate statements, all of which were designed to control the dress and grooming habits of 1,300 high school boys and girls. In addition, a half-dozen items were appended to the list during the school year in order to keep abreast of the latest fad or fancy. These were announced in special bulletins to students after some serious discussions by principals and teachers. So as not to be found wanting, we concluded the peroration with a typical catch-all phrase condemning any "extreme hairstyle or article of clothing."

As vice-principal, I served, ex officio, as the chief enforcement officer of the cumbersome document.

Our Code was in the form of pointed suggestions and specific prohibitions. Many were unwieldy and difficult to enforce, e.g., "Perfume or hair oils should be kept to a minimum." Some were amusing, "Ties, if worn, should be tied at the neck," or "Belts must be worn where trouser loops are provided for this purpose." Others had outlived their usefulness, e.g., "Turtle necks may not be worn as substitutes for shirts."

Even though the specific content in these admonitions may have been indigenous to our school, the approach to the problem of student dress was probably not unlike that of thousands of other high schools across the country.

Needless to say, the Code caused much dissension, some embarrassment, and not a little unpleasantness among both students and faculty. There had been some indication, too, that the Code was being stretched almost to the breaking point, but in spite of this, there was no full-scale retreat from our basic position, namely, that school officials have the right to legislate a dress and grooming code and that they possess the commensurate authority to enforce it effectively.

In the enforcement, also, there was opportunity for some real "Daniels" to sit in judgment: How short must a skirt be in order to be acknowledged as "too short"? Where do you draw the line between what is acceptable in boys' hair length and what is not? Are culottes really skirts or are they pants? How long are "long" sideburns?

When teachers and administrators are expending time and energy debating topics like these, the cause of education must, of necessity, suffer in the process. Teachers are paid to teach; they want to teach; and that is precisely what they should be allowed to do, unhindered by petty considerations of this kind.

Moreover, when students strolling through corridors begin to duck out of sight at the approach of an administrator, then the academic climate is no longer a wholesome one.

Fortunately our school developed an active Student Council and it was at the urging of this group that we agreed to take a good hard look at the entire problem of student dress and grooming. Student representatives met with a committee of faculty and administrators in session after session at which the students aired their views freely.

The recommendations of this group then received approval of a majority of the teachers and became effective at the start of the new school year. The results were not insignificant.

The three pages and 35 statements formerly devoted to dress and grooming were replaced by five short sentences, which now represented an appeal to the students' personal pride and aesthetic sense rather than the imposition of an adult point of view frequently lacking logic to support it.

There were admittedly some misgivings among faculty members as to the outcome of such a reversal of a school's position, but just the first few weeks of the new term brought evidence that our anxieties could be set aside. Students were delighted and reacted in the spirit of cooperation which had initiated the joint effort. No outlandish effects were attempted.

Members of the faculty, too, were visibly pleased, relieved as they were of the pressure of enforcing a set of always unpopular and sometimes arbitrary standards. Gone was the tension generated by the constant vigilance required under the former conditions. The tug-of-war between students and faculty had dissipated.

There have been other benefits as well. Loss of class time has been reduced drastically. Last year 12 students lost class time in just the first four weeks of school because of improper grooming or attire; this year, only one.

An interesting by-product has been the lessening of effectiveness of the dissident fringe among the student population. This small group, ever ready to take up the cudgels for almost any cause in their rebellion against authority, found that their chief source of ammunition for spreading discontent had disappeared. That they will search for, and find another, is fairly certain; but for now, they have been decimated.

Although the long-range effects cannot be too accurately predicted, by and large, the experiment has had a most successful beginning.

WONDERING OUT LOUD

Oh, those silly "codes." Those outrageous, arbitrary, fruitless, presumptuous, smart alecky, meddling, haughty, holier than thou, capricious, suppressive, officious, self-defeating, dangerous sallies that attempt to dictate to U.S. citizens, of all people, what they may wear or how long their hair is to be, or where their skirts are to end or pants begin, or that what grows on their faces is to be removed. Those violations of constitutional rights that are scalding school boards in community after community.

And costing them money. When, last winter, the school board in Monson, Mass., fired a teacher (nontenured at that) for refusing to shave off a beard, the legality, if not the wisdom, of the move seemed questionable in view of a federal court decision a few weeks earlier that school boards have no right to prohibit male students from growing long hair, or wearing sideburns, mustaches or beards. Codes like that, the U.S. District Court in Wisconsin ruled, are unconstitutional.

Thus, it was murmured on this page, the Monson business seemed likely to give grief to the board.

It did. The U.S. District Court in Massachusetts ruled last month that the teacher gets his job back, keeps his beard, and receives both his back pay and compensatory damages as well.

And hear this: The court ordered the five members of the school board (who had resigned as a group, by the way, in reaction to harrassment they charged was coming from people who supported the teacher) and the superintendent to pay as *individuals* the more than $2,500 in damages and back pay, plus the cost of the action.

Just thinking out loud. Might school boards now want to consider getting out of the beauty business and on with the education business? It is likely, at any rate, to be cheaper that way.

TRY THIS DRESS CODE ON FOR SIZE

The best school "dress code," the courts* seem to be saying with increasing volume, is no code.

Or, at least, one that tries to govern best by governing least. The latter is what the high school board in Chicago's North Shore suburb of Evanston has tried to attain.

Six months in the making, the dress code actually is part of a broader policy on student behavior approved by the school board in late spring and instituted a few weeks before the end of the regular school year.

The district's Student Behavior and Dress Policy, to use its formal name, represents the work of a study committee of 14 parents, 14 students, 12 teachers, and one principal who paid particular attention, among other things, to recent court rulings that some school dress codes violate students' constitutional rights. Their conclusion: ". . . the careful regulation of student dress is no longer necessary or even desirable. Within broad limits, dress and appearance at school are considered a matter of individual taste."

* "This is a new day," said Federal Judge James B. Parsons in Chicago a few weeks ago when he ordered the Barrington (Ill.) high school board to admit a 17 year old male student whom the board had opted to ban from classes because of the student's shoulder length hair and mustache. "We cannot mold people who are going to run the world in 1980 in the shape of the people of the 1920s . . . it's bad education to suggest it," the judge said. Earlier, a federal court in Massachusetts ruled similarly in favor of a teacher (JOURNAL, October, page 6) ordering the members of the board, which had fired the bearded teacher, and the superintendent to reinstate the teacher and pay damages as individuals.

Those broad limits deal with cleanliness; possibility of disease; and distracting, inappropriate or indecent clothing.

Notice right off that no mention is made of prohibitions on facial hair or length of hair for boys. There simply are none. Even shorts and slacks for girls (boys, too), within the limits of good taste, are given official sanction.

Not to the superintendent's liking, by any means. Feeling shorts and slacks were inappropriate in the classroom, he presented the school board with an alternative code of his own that banned shorts and slacks.

But the board opted for the easier going code of the committee. School board president Daniel Phillips, who broke the 3-to-3 tie vote and killed the superintendent's recommendation, said he did it because "it was time for the board to forego the nit picking about how long is long and how short is short. It's up to the individual student and his parents to see that his dress is in good taste," emphasized Phillips. "Students shouldn't have to lean on the school administration to tell them to wear something conforming."

Need for a formal dress policy, the first Evanston has had, arose following increasing disputes between school staff and students over what was or was not permissible. Complicated by the fact that each of Evanston Township's four schools had only broad, general dress guidelines unevenly enforced.

"Although they were similar, the dress regulations, set by the administration of each school, not only were loose but varied from school to school as well," said Phillips, "One principal would strictly enforce a ban on facial hair or hair length while another would turn his head the other way over those same issues."

Principals' pet peeves (blue jeans, slacks, shorts, facial hair, hair length, you name it) soon gave way to this brief but formal five-point policy for the district:

1. "A reasonable cleanliness of person and of wearing apparel is expected as a matter of health and aesthetics."

2. To avoid injury to feet and the possibility of disease, "shoes, sandals, or boots must be worn in the building except in gym or theatre, as appropriate."

3. "For all students: Beach wear and active athletic wear are inappropriate except in gym or theatre. A decent coverage of the body is expected."

4. "For girls: Strapless dresses are inappropriate in the classroom. Skirts and culottes should be no shorter than mid-thigh."

5. "For boys: Cut-offs [because of their frayed edges] are inappropriate in the classroom."

Disciplinary action for violation of any of the five points includes individual counseling and use of referral report, a standard form referring a student usually to the principal or the school nurse or a guidance counselor; sending the student home to change and return to school, then possibly conferring with his parents; summary action (suspension or expulsion, with provision made for students under 16 to attend extension or night school) is reserved for repeated offenses.

SIX

FREE EXPRESSION AND THE STUDENT PRESS

Activist behavior on the part of students almost inevitably involves the scholastic press. Occasionally the problem is clear cut: a reactionary administrator censors the legitimate and responsible dissent of a student editor. When considered solely on the basis of frequency, such instances are rare. More often, a high school journalism advisor is forced to motivate an apathetic newspaper staff to probe, investigate, and then prepare adequate articles.

As with other issues, it has not been the apathetic majority who have forced school authorities to re-evaluate their policies; it has been the activist minority. In addition to sparking a number of underground newspapers, their efforts have helped produce something of a trend toward a more liberalized editorial policy in official student newspapers. Apart from the basic issue of censorship, challenges which outspoken activists pose for the schools are serious ones. For example, how can an official student newspaper teach responsible journalism if students are committed to ax-grinding?

Much of the controversy over the student press stems from disagreement between students and administrators over editorial policies. Not all of the issues are particularly complex; most may be resolved through concrete steps. One of the more obvious problems is that the high school newspaper generally operates without an adequate level of understanding between principals, advisors, and students. Policy is generally ill-defined, or else not defined at all. Indeed, a recent survey of 246 high schools revealed that more than 90 percent had no written policy or statement regarding the publishing of the school newspaper. Even when an "understanding" is arrived at between the principal, advisor, and student, the principal's disposition often remains the tenuous guide to what may be printed or not printed. When it is understood that most principals (75 percent in one study) stress the public relations or image-building function of the school paper, it is not surprising that they try to maintain tight control over what goes into the paper.[1]

Rather than see the student paper become the principal's house organ on the one hand, or the radical rag on the other, serious students of scholastic journalism would like to see the emphasis placed on the reader's need, desire, and

[1] Special Commission of the Journalism Education Association, *The High School Newspaper, Freedom of the High School Press, and Advisor-Administrator Relationship,* draft report, 1970. The editors are grateful to Miss Mary Benedict, chairman of the Commission for permitting them to study a draft copy of the report in advance of its publication.

right to know. Advocacy for a point of view has a legitimate place on the printed page. On the other hand, selective reporting and the deliberate slanting of truth in order to propagandize a point of view is something responsible journalists take a dim view of.

Censorship by administrators is a key problem as far as student editors are concerned. Galen Gritt's article, "Censorship Hinders Student Publications," represents this student view. Even now, few sanctioned student newspapers enjoy the freedom to report and comment upon issues as they see them, even when the reporting is consistent with conventional principles of good journalism. Tom Brueggemann's comments about freedom of the press at the upper-middle-class Evanston Township High School, in "Evanston Township High's 'Evanstonian' Achieves Complete Freedom of Press," would be looked upon with envy by most scholastic editors. Administrators who permit relative freedom to student editors do need to be prepared for some criticism—fair or unfair—of their policies; witness the editorial, "Education at Buena Needs Revamping," which appeared in the last issue for 1970 of Buena High School's *Buena Vista* (Ventura, California). Indeed, even some low assessments of the administration's competence may find their way into print; witness "The Peter Principle in Action: Or the Incompetent Shall Inherit Buena," which appeared in the same graduation issue.

For many students who intend to assert their rights through the medium of the printed word, the alternative to the sanctioned "above-ground" newspaper has been the "underground" press. Its backers almost inevitably explain the underground newspaper's origins in terms of alleged overrestrictiveness placed on free expression by administrators. Jon Grell's "Why the Underground Press?," represents such an opinion from the perspective of an activist student. The letter of a student journalist to Sam Feldman, appearing after the Grell article, demonstrates in some measure the frustration of a student at what he sees as undue repression by a principal. Perhaps the best balanced and most comprehensive review of the underground press issue to date was prepared by Frances K. Heussenstamm. As she points out in her article, "Activism in Adolescents: An Analysis of the High School Underground Press," the underground newspaper has established a radically critical attitude toward many established high school policies and practices and has become involved with many of the significant social and political issues facing the society at large. The impact of the movement does not seem to be diminished by the fact that most undergrounds die an early death, having run out of money, ideas, or readers.

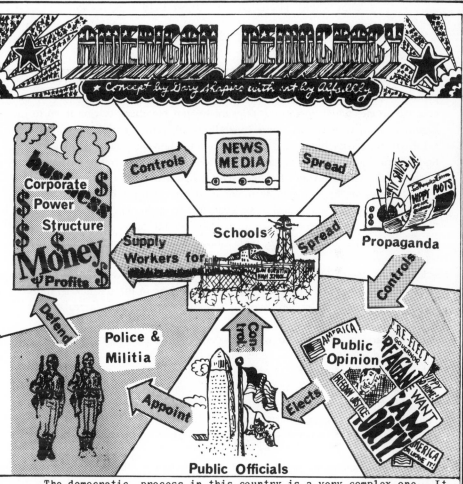

The democratic process in this country is a very complex one. It starts, not in the Constitution, not in the subversive Declaration of Independence, but in the hands of those who have the money, i.e., the power. They shall be referred to hereafter as the Bad Guys. The Bad Guys control the media, both through direct ownership, and through the influence of advertizing. Since the Bad Guys control the media, it spreads their own propaganda, and this propaganda generally controls public opinion. Next, public opinion, which is mostly Bad Guy oriented, elects our distinguished public officials. They are responsible for the police and the militia, who make sure that our great democratic process runs smoothly. Our public officials also control this nation's educational system. The educational system trains people to work, and to make money, for those who have the money, i.e., the power, in this country (the Bad Guys). The Bad Guys control the media, which controls public opinion, which elects public officials. . .   NIT

From *New Improved Tide* [John Marshall High School Underground Student Newspaper], III (June, 1970).

CENSORSHIP HINDERS STUDENT PUBLICATIONS

GALEN GRITTS, St. Louis, Mo.

The profusion of high school "undergrounds" today underlines the censorship problems of regular papers. School administrations and advisers reject or discourage articles which seem most relevant to staff members, driving them to the basement mimeo machines where frustrations are vented and often magnified.

Of course, censorship makes little difference when newspaper staffs are satisfied to print club and sports news. But students are asking more and more frequently, "Doesn't the role of a high school newspaper go beyond that?"

It is interesting to note two examples of uncensored publications among the official school press: *The Evanstonian* (Evanston Township High School, Evanston, Ill.) and *Silver Chips* (Montgomery Blair High School, Silver Springs, Md.). Both have combined good journalism with innovative, in-depth reporting on school issues or problems.

Last year, *Silver Chips* ran a series on the causes and prevention of vandalism and critically examined guidance counseling services in three articles.[1] The editorial page, often overlooked in other school papers, became a real forum of ideas for the staff and student body.

All this and more occurred with the cooperation, even respect, of the principal and adviser. Similar statements can be made about the *Evanstonian*.[2]

Not every school paper that enjoys freedom of the press can make claim to such high quality. But the point is that such publications do not become irresponsible mud-slingers or receptacles of four-letter words.

Just how are staffs restricted in what they can print? The most obvious method is outright censorship. The censored party knows who is behind the action and why. In this case, the staff can direct its frustration at a particular source, which seems to be, more and more frequently, the school administration.

However, there are more subtle ways in which free expression is repressed. A school policy may require that all news be strictly school-oriented. Accordingly, if an event is not school sponsored and not "representative of the school," coverage of it is "illegal."

Staff members feel ineffective and limited when told what to print. As a result, they begin to censor themselves, thinking that a topic is too risky even before the article is written. They may simply lose interest in the paper.

From *Revelation Now: A National Student Journalism Review*, 1 (January, 1970), 4. Reprinted with the permission of Barry Glassner, Coordinator-Publisher.

[1] "How Free Should the High School Press Be?" *Today's Education* (September, 1969), p. 53.
[2] See *Revelation Now*, October, 1969.

Established school papers, buried in policy restrictions, may be the real "underground press." They might grow up and become "viewspapers" as well as newspapers.

As one member of a censored newspaper put it, "if we could use all the energy it takes to fight the administration for constructive work on the newspaper, think of what we could accomplish!"

EVANSTON TOWNSHIP HIGH'S *EVANSTONIAN* ACHIEVES
COMPLETE FREEDOM OF PRESS

TOM BRUEGGEMANN, Evanston, Ill.

The term "freedom of the press" is often not a reality in many high school publications. Newspapers are usually controlled by outsiders—advisers, boards of education, administrations—with the result that free journalism, that is, the freedom to print what the students want, is often inhibited.

Such is not the case at Evanston, Ill., Township High School. The *Evanstonian* is allowed to print whatever stories the editors choose, with the adviser's approval based not on whether he approves the substance of the article, but only whether it is accurate and well-written.

With this situation, the *Evanstonian* has published stories on the convention disorders last summer in Chicago, fire hazards in the school, protests, both black

From *Revelation Now:* A National Student Journalism Review, 1 (October, 1969), 6. Reprinted with the permission of Barry Glassner, Coordinator-Publisher.

and white, against administration policies, and other controversial subjects.

This in itself is not very sensational. The reaction of school officials, however, is.

Allowing a student publication to freely report is, of course, hardly standard in high schools today. But by encouraging its publication, the Evanston administration has shown true interest in journalistic freedom.

The board of education this year increased the *Evanstonian's* budget to $12,000, $2,000 more than last year. This increase came after the first year the newspaper had criticized administrative actions and spoken as a voice of the students.

The Evanston superintendent has expressed a desire for the *Evanstonian* to provide a channel for student expression. He feels that the school, often rated as one of the best high schools in the U.S., can only be helped by allowing constructive criticism from students. And the newspaper, with a readership of over 5000 students and a faculty of nearly 400, can be an effective force in bringing about change.

To be most effective as a force, the paper this year will use more of a magazine style approach to reporting, with many in-depth and feature stories on various aspects of the school. If the editors feel that a school policy is wrong (the security in the school has become quite rigid this year, illustrating a definite need for change) the *Evanstonian* will run a front page analysis story bringing the situation into the open, pointing out the reasons for the policy and its faults. It will then follow up with an editorial on the subject.

A couple of examples on how this policy can be handled successfully: in the first issue the editors expect to run a quote by the superintendent in which he says that he expects little protest from students this year over school policies. This, in the staff's opinion, is rather naive, since staff members know many of the more active students (and even if they aren't protesting, the newspaper will be). So following that statement, the editors plan to juxtapose a comment from the superintendent last year in which he said that racial relations at Evanston were quite good. They were not.

In another story, the removal of tables from study areas and their subsequent replacement by individual desks to remove the questionable "problem" of talking among students will be reported, along with a picture of students still talking, except now standing up—creating a much worse problem.

These are only minor examples, of course, of what can be done within the realm of fairness and accuracy with journalistic freedom. However, this year the *Evanstonian* hopes to cover school policy in several areas in which the staff feels improvement could be made—security, curriculum, racial matters, and so on.

The administration, though, does not shudder at the thought of these articles. Rather, it welcomes them as responsible channels of student thought.

Whether or not they will be effective channels remains to be seen. The *Evanstonian* staff expects that it will exert an important influence, however. The *Evanstonian* can only expect to do so if its reporting remains fair in its criticism, and has articles which are read seriously by much of the school population. If the editors succeed in that, they will accomplish what so few high school news-papers have done—become an important voice in all school affairs.

And if the *Evanstonian* becomes a motivating force in bringing about change, ETHS will not suffer. It can only be helped.

'EDUCATION' AT BUENA NEEDS REVAMPING

Education is supposed to be what school is all about. But at Buena it is more than questionable if this is actually the case.

Except for a few inconsistent islands in the "school," Buena is preoccupied with things other than education.

The administration and "official" part of the school seems to spend most of its time on discipline. In order to do almost anything here, one has to perform in the officially sanctioned manner. No real deviation is allowed.

If discipline and forced conformity were dismissed from the top of the school's priority list, most of the administrators would be out of jobs, and many, many teachers would be bored.

The school should accentuate creativity, rather than conformity. Teachers should help the student to learn and learn how to learn; they shouldn't "teach," or dictate.

A high school should help a student along to "further learning" (college, etc.) or prepare him for some kind of an occupation after school. Increased vocational training programs are urgently needed.

The student should be helped to develop himself as an individual while also realizing his responsibility to others.

As we see it, the most important job of the teacher is to get the student inter-ested and to motivate him toward further learning in a subject.

The rigidity of class structure and curriculum must be relaxed to achieve this. And the teacher should not try to form the student into his definition of a "well rounded individual." Too many think this is their role: an idealogical Big Brother.

To implement any of these ideas would mean a radical change in the edu-cational system. This would take money, time, etc., that presently is not avail-able. Even if these were available, the change undoubtedly would not come about because so many in our society are afraid of change.

We think this is unfortunate—more than unfortunate. Education is related to prejudices, open-mindedness, and thinking. All are things that are needed for human interaction. Because of this, we feel that education is one of the most important, if not the most important, endeavors presently participated in by man.

From *Buena Vista* [Buena High School Student Newspaper], 9 (June 5, 1970).

THE PETER PRINCIPLE IN ACTION: OR
THE INCOMPETENT SHALL INHERIT BUENA

DAVID McMILLAN

At Buena, most of those who hold jobs of importance tend to be incompetent in these jobs.

This follows directly from "The Peter Principle" which states, "In a hierarchy, each employee tends to rise to his level of incompetence: Every post tends to be occupied by an employee incompetent to execute its duties.

In an article written by Dr. Laurence J. Peter, who originated the principle, he said, "The Principle applies to all levels in the educational hierarchy. Competent teachers become incompetent principals. . . . Frequently, the very characteristics that were responsible for the promotion were the source of incompetence at the new level."

An example might be Buzz F. Duckowsky, a coach at Buena. In the Midwest, as an assistant coach of several sports, he achieved a measure of success by instilling respect into his players and teaching them the traditional virtues in a manner that was also traditional. He moved to California, and again achieved success in the eastern part of the state. So, Buena hired him to come and be head coach of a sport, but his record hasn't been as good here as elsewhere. He cannot understand when some players question beliefs and practices he has held all his life and won't stand for it when the players won't accept these beliefs just because he is the coach. Thus disturbances arise that he can't handle as a head coach that he might have been able to in the past as an assistant coach. Presently, it is questionable whether he will remain as head coach of his sport next year because of the great number of complaints from parents.

Another example could be O. A. Softy, a high official at Buena. As a teacher, he taught a variety of topics and did his job without creating waves. He thus pleased his superiors who eventually promoted him to the job he holds now. He now tries to go on in his traditional waveless way, but this is all but impossible in his present position. When he is threatened with the least bit of controversy he gut reacts and gets carried away. Surprisingly enough, his waveless policy has not endeared him to his superiors in this district who realize he is doing this in hopes of even further promotion.

When someone becomes competent at one level he is drawn off to the next. The only way any work gets done in the educational system that causes the Peter Principle syndrome is by those who haven't yet been promoted or by those who are good enough to reach the top level of the existing hierarchy without reaching their level of incompetence.

Somehow, if the educational and whole system we live in is to remove itself from the ever thickening morass of bureaucracy, incompetence, etc. it is sink-

From *Buena Vista* [Buena High School Student Newspaper], 9 (June 5, 1970).

ing into, a way will have to be found to stop its workers from reaching their level of incompetence. But then again, maybe nobody's really worried about incompetence in this incompetent system.

WHY THE UNDERGROUND PRESS

JOHN GRELL, High School Independent Press Service, New York City

A great many people have written in to us inquiring about the why and wherefores of having an underground paper, and how to get one started.

To the latter, it can be said that there is no clear cut formula for starting a paper. You can only go about it through trial and error or by learning from the experiences of underground papers which have already established themselves. Also, it has to be remembered that you will definitely encounter resistance and hassling from the administration at your school or even from the local board of education. These measures, taken by the administrations, usually take the form of suspensions, expulsions, calls to your parents, "nasty" notes on the back of your permanent records card, etc., etc., etc. There is no real way to avoid these measures to stifle your freedom of speech and press. You will just have to contend with it as best you can, but expect them to happen. If things get too unbearable, a letter explaining the situation should be sent to the American Civil Liberties Union, 156 Fifth Avenue, New York, N.Y. 10010. They will either take action themselves, or give you the names and addresses of people in your area who will help you out. The ACLU has stated that it will defend any student whose "right to have access to varied points of view, to confront and study controversial issues, to be treated without prejudice or penalty for what he reads or writes" is denied. This does not mean that the ACLU will get you out of the hassles immediately, but it will defend you in a court of law if charges are to be brought against the administration of your school. Remember, though, if you are going to offer an alternative to the system's way of doing things, it will get a lot of people annoyed and hung-up. Expect it!

By now you're probably wondering if it's all worth it. I can only tell you the merits and accomplishments which have already taken place in the underground-press community.

We are a group of people who offer an alternative life style to that of the establishment. The word "alternative" is extremely important. We offer a completely viable way of living which concerns the socio-economic-political aspects of society; a new society, hopefully one which will be better than the present financially oriented society.

From *How Old Will You Be in 1984?: Expressions of Student Outrage from the High School Free Press*, edited by Diane Divoky, pp. 145-48. Copyright © 1969 by Avon Books. By permission of Avon Books, New York.

In order to bring about these changes, the media of communication is of the utmost importance. The more established papers (not high school papers) served as a link and pseudo-grapevine between people who felt the same way (East Village *Other,* Berkeley *Barb,* etc.). This was three and four years ago. They then began to offer an alternative to the established communications media in reporting news both within the movement and outside.

These papers accomplished the politicizing of the peope who were just turning on to the "New Politics." Today, when papers like *The New York Times* are able to control the minds and actions of its readers in the way that it deems necessary for the "good" of society, it can quiet the news in such a way that the people don't even know what's happening. Take for instance, the whole Vietnam war issue. It was played down in the press of this country prior to 1964 so that a vast majority of Americans didn't even know where Vietnam was. It was the underground press that made as many people as possible aware of what was going on. Take also the actions on the Columbia campus last spring. Who knew more about what truly happened: the readers of *The New York Times* or the readers of the *Rat*? The underground press deals in education, not in the stifling of issues.

This is also the case in high schools throughout the country. It is even more accentuated in the high schools because the ages of people attending high schools allows their minds to be more malleable, even though they may be totally apathetic or staunch "Wallace supporters." These people must be educated, and an underground paper is the only way of reaching an entire student body. An article about white racism in high schools will get more people talking and thinking than an article about the latest basketball game in the administration-sanctioned paper.

Those of you who are already part of an established press will know what I'm talking about. Those of you who are just starting will probably be able to understand and comprehend it. Your battle is half over once you get the masses of students talking about a certain issue (no matter what it is). Your goal is to get the people who have opposing points of view over to your side, to unapatheticize the apathetic, and to keep informed the people who already feel the same way as you. The only hard job that you will have is in distribution. You must get the papers to as many people as possible (even if they must be given away). If you are just starting out, you will find that at first you will sell only a minimal number of copies (very minimal!), but that as more people in the student body find out about it, your circulation will pick up.

Then there is HIPS. We are a news bureau which picks up items which we receive; it is up to the individual editor to print what he wants in any way he wants. We ourselves are having internal dissension on the minds of the staff because of the great distinction in issues which are important to high school students in different parts of the country. In New York, students are fighting for community control of schools and the setting up of a completely new alternative educational system, whereas in Kansas, let's say (no knock on those living in

Kansas), the students are still fighting over long hair hassles, of which there are none in New York. We try to print both types of things and, again, an editor may print the goings-on in New York or San Francisco, even if he is still fighting for the right to grow his hair long, simply as a means of showing students what to espouse to after they can grow their hair long. It is completely up to the discretion of the editor.

Things are happening all across the country in high schools, and students must all be made aware of the complete scene. This is HIPS.

TO SAM FELDMAN

"Dear Mr. Feldman,

I had the pleasure of attending your workshop, "The Student Journalist and Legal and Ethical Issues," at the JEA-NSPA meeting in Chicago. I was very impressed with your discussion of underground newspapers. My high school needs such a paper.

My high school is 38 per cent black. Until this year we have not had any racial problems. Recently, however, racists of both colors have caused many rumors of impending trouble to be started. So far the rumors have been just that, but without having them tracked down and spiked they could turn into realities. Every single article from our school newspaper related to race has been stopped an the principal's desk. "Sorry," he says, "censored."

Many of the students are extremely interested in politics. Every article on policies (ranging from reports on presidential candidates' speeches given to an attack on George Wallace) have been stopped on the principal's desk. Again, "Sorry, censored."

Our school newspaper had an editorial attacking the student council because it hadn't done anything all year. The article barely was printed and we received the suggestion (from a general) not to attack the do-nothing council again. So much for the principle of equal estates.

It was for these reasons that three of us (one other and myself attended the meeting) have decided to start an underground newspaper. To battle censorship and improve class, racial, and student relationships is our goal—to be expelled is our risk. We positively cannot allow our names to be discovered. The other two are presently on the regular newspaper staff and face a serious danger of being suspended from it. Normally I would be on the staff next year, I would face certain danger of being denied a position if our plans were discovered.

From *Communication: Journalism Education Today*, 2 (Spring, 1969), pp. 9-10. Reprinted with the permission of Sam Feldman and the publisher.

Sam Feldman is Assistant Professor of Journalism, San Fernando Valley State College.

We are taking you into our strictest confidence and ask if you receive any correspondence except from myself concerning our project not to reply. We stand in opposition to a conservative administration and without the knowledge of a conservative editor-in-chief.

We have written you to ask for help in our service. We would greatly appreciate it if you would answer the following questions:

What is the legal basis for expulsion?

Exactly at what point do we move outside the law?

Do you have any suggestions for secretly distributing the newspaper?

In general, we would like to have any suggestions or articles you think would help. Could you also please send us some sample newspapers?

We will reimburse you in money for any postage expenses, etc. The whole school will reimburse you in other ways if a race riot is avoided or freedom of the press restored.

Let us look forward to the day when we can dare, "Why not say school is for Kids?" Thank you for everything. We greatly appreciate any help you can give us."

Mr. Feldman Asks:

How would you answer this student?

There is no mention of an adviser in the letter. Why? Perhaps because the adviser in this case has refused to accept the responsibility of forming an editorial policy. Let us first try to answer the specific questions of the student.

Each state legislates the legal basis for expulsion, usually leaving this power to the local board of education. Only the board can expel in most states, not the administration, which can suspend.

ACTIVISM IN ADOLESCENTS: AN ANALYSIS OF THE HIGH SCHOOL UNDERGROUND PRESS

F. K. HEUSSENSTAMM

BACKGROUND

A prophetic minority of American adolescents identifiable in many respects with the counter-culture described by Roszak[1] were responsible for the appearance of a militant high school underground press in major American cities

From *Adolescence* (Libra Publishers, 1970). Reprinted with the permission of the author and the publisher.

F. K. Heussenstamm is Associate Professor of Education, Teachers College, Columbia University.

[1] Roszak, Theodore. *The Making of a Counter-Culture.* New York: Anchor, 1969.

during the 1960's. The "visionary imagination" which marks counter-cultural writing, with its emphasis on the affective aspects of human experience as opposed to "objective consciousness," characterizes much of the adolescent output. The extent of high school involvement in current movements of dissent is suggested by the development of an estimated 500[2] underground papers in the country as a whole. The Los Angeles area alone accounts for at least 100. A content analysis of one of these, *The Loudmouth*, adds dimension to the understanding of the movement, reflecting as it does both the content of the adult underground press, and the special preoccupations of the younger segment of the population. Further, an examination reveals some of the sources of the flood of "outrage" which dominates much of the writing. Studies of the underground press should yield additional data useful to counselors and psychologists, curriculum specialists, and teachers, and school administrators.

Spokesmen in a number of disciplines who have been commenting on the generation gap have come up with varying conclusions which provide a range of explanations for the insurgent and often highly threatening behavior of adolescents. Freudian-oriented Feuer[3] insists that because the generation gap is a fundamental fact of history with its roots in the traditional Oedipal struggles between fathers and their sons, youth are bent on dispossessing their elders. Kenniston has found in his studies that alienated[4] students, from the culture of affluence, showed disdain for their fathers and admiration for their mothers, whereas his radicals[5] were most often implementing ideas and ideals gained from their fathers; consequently, role dissonance in family relations, he has asserted, is in part responsible for conflict. Some observers attribute problems to twenty-five years of permissive child rearing by the World War II generation; also, this generation's vicarious living through their offspring may have irreversibly spoiled the children now coming to adulthood. McLuhan,[6] on the other hand, insists that youth instinctively understand the major fracturing changes in our society because of the impact of revolutionary technological, instant-simultaneous transmission of data to a population which was reared on "nose-counting" techniques. Margaret Mead agrees with McLuhan that because the older generations are unprepared, they may never be able to communicate in the new language.[7] She explains further that the new, international, inter-communicating network provides young people with the experience of living with multiple concurrent change, whereas the older generation knew only "se-

[2] Divoky, Diana, "Revolt in the High Schools: The Way It's Going to Be," *Saturday Review of Literature.* III (February 15, 1969), 83-102.

[3] Feuer, Lewis S. *Conflict of Generations.* New York: Basic Books, Inc., 1969.

[4] Keniston, Kenneth: *The Uncommitted: Alienated Youth in American Society.* New York: Harcourt, Brace, and World, 1965.

[5] Keniston, Kenneth. *Young Radicals.* New York: Harcourt, 1968.

[6] McLuhan, Marshall. *Understanding Media: The Extensions of Man.* New York: McGraw-Hill, 1965.

[7] Mead, Margaret. *Culture and Commitment: A Study of the Generation Gap.* Garden City: Doubleday & Co., 1970.

quentially emerging change." As a result, few adults have more valid insights than youth on the ramifications of this radical state of affairs. It is youth who must now teach their elders how to cope, she says.

Robert Merton,[8] who suggests that when an individual perceives both discrepancies between widely acceptable societal ends or goals and the means to attain those ends, an anomic condition exists in his culture. Anomie produces a variety of responses in given individuals—for example, *conformity,* which most American youth still exhibit, although Kenniston states that many youth from conservative backgrounds report they could be happy living in Canada, New Zealand, or Australia. If a youth doesn't conform to the dictates of society, he may *rebel* by way of delinquency; *retreat* into drug abuse or mental illness; develop the *ritualism* we have come to identify with cults and the hippie movement; or he may *innovate.* The invention of the underground press as a strategy to deal with profound *frustration* attributable to the paradoxes and complexities of mid-twentieth century life might well be considered an innovative strategy. Viewed in this perspective, the underground press assumes special significance to students of the adolescent society. Because this press is in the tradition of radical writings which often characterize rebellious periods of history, youth may not take sole credit for inventing the techniques of a literary assault on the status quo; moreover, there would also appear to be a contemporary pattern of adult influence exerted by the underground publications of which the New York *Village Voice* is a prototype. A pioneer of the underground press, the *Village Voice* for over a decade survived as a Bohemian echo of dissent. Sporadic publishing attempts of a similar type in San Francisco, Chicago, Boston, Philadelphia were short-lived until Art Kunkin began the *Los Angeles Free Press* in 1964. Since then there have been other underground ventures, at least forty such publications having achieved a modicum of success throughout the country. Others have flourished temporarily and then failed. The *Los Angeles Free Press,* ranking nationally as one of the major underground publications, is a genuine example of popularly oriented periodical; its circulation is now around 85,000 copies weekly. Nation-wide, an estimated third of a million Americans are reading the underground papers on a regular basis. It is reasonable to assume that a large proportion of these readers have been bright adolescents.

Recently, publishing staffs have confederated to form the underground press syndicate which facilitates interchange of advertising, news, and features recognized as "anti-Establishment, avant-garde, and New Left." The UPS, in general, serves "youth-oriented periodicals which share common aims and interests."[9] Mailing addresses and brief esoteric references to editorial focus are collected

---

[8] Merton, Robert. *Social Theory and Social Structure.* Revised. New York: The Free Press of Glencoe, 1957.
[9] Hopkins, Jerry. *The Hippie Papers: Notes From the Underground.* New York: New American Library, 1968.

in the *Underground Press Guide*,[10] which offers subscription service to all listees. According to statements made to the writer both types of services have been utilized by high school editors.

Following the 1964 advent of the *L.A. Free Press*, by *"Freep,"* as the title has been abbreviated by the youthful newsvenders along the Sunset Strip, the Los Angeles area high school underground press began its literary life. Two high school papers of the underground were printed within only a few weeks. The high school movement was also given some impetus by a young radio personality, Eliot Mintz, who, in late 1967 advertised new publications, read from selected issues, interviewed editors, and offered to give interested members of his radio audience an outline of suggestions for establishing new underground papers. He asserted that dozens of students responded with requests for assistance.

Even a superficial examination of individual copies reveals that the adult underground press has exerted a significant, if not a continuing, influence on the high school underground press in its emphasis on the so-called "pop" culture. Topics regularly treated by both the adult editors as well as their youthful imitators are the following: the rock and roll "industry"; psychedelic art; "mod" fashions; communal "happenings," such as "love-ins" and festivals; the underground cinema; and youth-oriented films of the "Easy Rider"—"Alice's Restaurant" genre. These areas of common interest bridge the gap between traditional adolescent and adult activities.

A more rigorous comparison of the content of adult and high school publications indicates overlapping interests in national and international problems. The editors are all vociferously opposed to American militarism in general, the Vietnam war, and the draft, and support "the resistance" movement. Stemming from this commonality of indignation over the expenditure of American resources for violent purposes, are other related and recurring issues. Thus, political articles tend to explore the "corrupting" effects of materialism, racism, and bigotry. Editors frequently question police practice in crowd control, in confrontation with minority groups, and in censorship.

There are many overlapping concerns of a more personal nature relevant to expansion and enhancement of states of consciousness through drug use, meditation, participation in rock concerts and light shows, and experimental sexual behavior. Attention is also focussed on problems of contraception and abortion. Adolescents use *their* papers explicitly to expose and protest against what they interpret as hypocrisy, irrelevance, boredom, and coercive practices in local public school administration, instruction, and organization.

High schoolers too have syndicated. A dynamic organization which has since 1968 provided a clearing house for their myriad activities, is the High School In-

[10] Korpsak, Joe. *Underground Press Guide: Showing Where It's Happening in Print.* Los Angeles: Other Press Pub. Co. [n.d.].

dependent Press Service (HIPS) in New York. HIPS has changed from a loosely operated student underground press association, a casual interchange established two years earlier, to an organized service providing weekly packaged mailouts of illustrations and news items. Subscribers pay four dollars per month. Underground Los Angeles papers almost immediately upon inception have announced their affiliation with the Student Underground Press Association also.

Diverse in format and style, the high school underground papers are now slicker than ever. Originally reproduced by hexagraph, ditto, or mimeograph, some of the most recent ones have gone to offset or Xerox type processes. A single issue may contain from one to nineteen pages, may appear weekly, semimonthly, or quite spontaneously and irregularly. The tenor of the writing is equally wide-ranging. When continuous series can be examined, the improvement of the quality of all aspects from the initial to subsequent editions is obvious and almost universal. Some papers have begun with polished faces, but this is not typical. A newspaper staff may number from one to a dozen members, but usually two or three students provide not only editorial leadership but also a nucleus around which other interested individuals revolve.

STUDIES

A preliminary attempt at systematic study of the high school underground press was conducted by Samuel Feldman, Coordinator of English and Journalism for the San Bernardino County Schools, in preparation for his book, *The Student Journalist and Legal and Ethical Issues.*[11] He reported 167 responses to 200 search questionnaires sent to high school journalism advisers in the fall of 1967. He uncovered twenty-one then defunct publications and seventeen currently active ones; in addition, he found that fifty-two schools had "rumblings of a precipitous nature," evidence that underground publication was imminent. Feldman estimated that one out of every ten Southern California high schools had an underground paper, with figures for the metropolitan area running as high as five out of ten schools. His profile of the underground press indicates that the papers were: (1) usually established in large public high schools (over 1500 enrollment), (2) generally found in urban middle class communities, (3) were staffed by students with no journalistic experience, (4) were destined to die with the graduation of the editor, (5) consisted largely of editorials, features, and poetry, with very little news or advertising, (6) expressed a liberal, anti-Establishment, antiwar, anti-administration position, and (7) were financed largely by means of sales with only 20 per cent receiving subsidies from parents or other sources.

R. Garry Shirts, of the Western Behavioral Sciences Institute at La Jolla, California, invited thirteen Southern California high school editors to a conference on the problems of education, as part of a predictive study on the attitudes and

[11] Feldman, Samuel. *The Student Journalist and Legal and Ethical Issues.* New York: Richards Rosen Press, Inc., 1968, 27-45.

values of future decision-makers. He found conferees both able to provide an in-process evaluation of their own education, and to propose solutions to problems which they thought had serious implications for the future. According to him, these youths did not fit the stereotype of the "rebellious teen-ager taking his fight for independence out on the schools."[12] His subjects freely acknowledged both the financial and intellectual support which they received from parents. This latter finding correlates well with Richard Flacks's observations of member-parent relations in his study of Students for a Democratic Society (SDS). Interestingly, at its beginning, most SDS members, too, were found to be attempting to put parental conviction into practice.[13]

When asked to describe or explain how they began their underground papers, Shirts's editors attributed their primary motivation to their attempts to validate judgments about issues:

> We are taught that opinions are important and that controversy can be useful in developing our minds. We are taught these things and, at the same time, provided with a school paper that stifles our opinions and avoids all controversy. A newspaper which is, in short, not the least bit conducive to intellectual growth or stimulation . . .[14]

Although they acknowledged the need for the conventional periodic bulletin reports about inter- and intra-school activities, they decried the absence of a forum for dissent and vigorous controversy.

In Shirts's workshop, which focussed on in-school problems as well as those in the larger society, student concern about the following topics directed most of the discussions: (1) stultifying protectionism, (2) insidious personal manipulation, (3) propagandizing or brainwashing, and (4) usurpation of individual dignity by the public schools.[15] As Cohen has pointed out, it would seem that being protected from unpleasant reality, controversy, and the natural consequences of their own actions is repugnant to perceptive adolescents. They wish to cope with genuine, rather than hypothetical, problems. This encapsulation of the developing young adult is one of the major dilemmas of our time; the lack of significant roles, the maintenance of dependancy, and the over-long pupa stage of American coming-of-age are precipitating alienation.[16]

The youthful critics of education participating in the La Jolla workshop agreed that their schools were trying to turn out ". . . unblemished red, white, and blue

[12] Shirts, R. Garry. "Underground High School Newspapers Editors Conference," *Pilot Policy Research Center Progress Report 3.* La Jolla: Western Behavioral Science Institute, November 15, 1967.
[13] Flacks, Richard. *Student Power and the New Left: The Role of SDS.* Paper presented at the Annual Meeting of the American Sociological Association, San Francisco, September, 1968.
[14] Shirts, *Pilot Policy. . . .,* 3, 1967, 4.
[15] Shirts, *Pilot Policy. . . . ,* 3, 1967, 7-8.
[16] Cohen, Albert K. *Delinquent Boys.* New York: Free Press, 1955.

students." Less well articulated was their feeling of helplessness in the face of administrative and faculty decision-making. Conference attendants strongly criticized student government for its lack of genuine autonomy ". . . of course, everyone knows right now it's a farce."

Further evidence of high school editors' disenchantment is to be found in two recent collections of high school underground press writings, *How Old Will You Be In 1984?* by Diana Divoky,[17] and *Our Time Is Now* by John Birmingham.[18] To be found here are powerful attacks on school practice, statements on the position of students as a minority in the larger society, analysis of contempt and social ills, and recommendations for amelioration of conditions.

Because the established high school papers consist largely of conventional reportage of sport, extra-curricular, and routine school events, the question which looms large is not difficult to phrase. Where can critical, committed, innovative adolescents express their feelings about issues? Certainly not in all classrooms. Buford Rhea's study, *Measures of Child Involvement and Alienation from the School*[19] and the researcher's own study, *Creativity and Alienation: An Exploration of Their Relationship in Adolescence*[20] indicate as yet no massive alienation attributable to constricting high school curricula, despite the criticisms made by numerous underground journalists. But the numbers of the alienated appear to be growing. Widespread disruption, violence, and dissention are reported on high school campuses daily. At the time he reported his study in 1966, Rhea concluded that the operation of "institutional paternalism," that is, belief in the omnipotence and benevolence of the system, was the effective countervening variable which prevented wider alienation from manifesting itself at the high school level. According to the underground high school spokesman, this countervening variable is steadily eroding.

ONE HIGH SCHOOL PERIODICAL: AN ANALYSIS

A complete set of seventeen issues of an underground paper, originating in a middle class urban Southern California high school was secured for content analysis. It was hypothesized that the papers would become (1) more conservative or institutionalized during the eighteen months of publication, (2) increasingly focussed on issues outside the school parameters, (3) responsive to discrepancies in the regularly published school paper, and (4) dominated by affective expression when compared with the regular paper, to compensate for the

[17] Divoky, Diana. *How Old Will You Be in 1984?: Expressions of Student Outrage From The High School Free Press.* New York: Avon, 1969.
[18] Birmingham, John. *Our Time Is Now: Notes From The High School Underground.* New York: Praeger, 1970.
[19] Rhea, Bufford, et al. *Measures of Child Involvement and Alienation from the School Program.* Chestnut Hill, Massachusetts: Boston College, 1966. Cooperative Research Project S-383.
[20] Heussenstamm, F. K. *Creativity and Alienation: An Exploration of Their Relationship in Adolescence.* Unpublished Ph.D. dissertation, University of Southern California, 1968.

absence of affect in the authorized school publication. *The Loudmouth,* a parody on the regular school paper *The Loudspeaker,* proved to be so provocative that by the end of its second phase of publication, a competing right-wing under-ground publication *The Truth* was being distributed to insure that "all sides of every issue" were being heard. This incident, in microcosm, is symbolic of the developing polarizing reaction to young radicals throughout the country.

The three major categories of articles derived from study of *The Loudmouth* were (1) off-campus societal concerns, (2) on-campus issues, and (3) miscellane-ous, which includes self-promotion, humor, creative writing, and advertising.

Hypotheses 1 and 2 were quickly disproved. The item of primary importance to staffers was their personal documentation of the Century Plaza Peace Demonstra-tions, which occurred during the Los Angeles visit of President Johnson. De-tailed stories, including maps, filled 18 per cent of all space during the initial period of publication. No mention of these violent confrontations, which re-ceived world-wide attention, appeared in the regular school paper. Combined with reportage of experiences at "love-ins," "be-ins," and other communal activ-ities in which the staff participated, almost one-fourth of the first publication phase, approximately six months, evolved from first-person experience.

The editors' perception of hypocrisy in American life, specifically that existing in the relationships between blacks and whites, and youths and adults, received student writers' attention, as did the problems of abortion (they were in favor of liberalized laws); capital punishment (they were opposed to it); loyalty oaths (they despised them); economic inequity (they felt guilty about it); and drug use (they ridiculed drug dependency while simultaneously seeking alterations in the law which mandated felony penalties for marijuana possession). They vigorously opposed the draft, favored an immediate end to the Vietnam war, and predicted the development of a movement which has become known as "the resistance." These controversial issues occupied slightly less than half of the first series of papers which began in March, 1967, and continued through the summer.

The on-campus issues which concerned the staff were the regulation and con-trol of student behavior, campus politics, dress codes, the students' serious in-volvement with problems of education in general, and friction on the campus be-tween rival groups. The high school dress regulations were considered a symbolic issue. Writers pointed up the irrationality of arbitrary, adult-imposed grooming standards by examining the changes in fashions which occurred from one school year to the next. That which was regarded as immodest or slovenly last year, styles or practices for which students were suspended then, were this year con-sidered acceptable.

Originally, educators' objections to long hair on males were based on their fears of possible effeminacy or even homosexuality. Others had previously had negative experiences with what they termed "shags"—pre-delinquent, long-haired youth. Because the wearing of longer hair was used by some Southern California male adolescents to identify participants in the marijuana subculture, the concern of adults was understandable. All long-haired males are not drug users, however, and the suppressive tactic of forced haircuts has done little to control drug use and abuse, and in many instances, has contributed to the advancement of the counter-culture.

About 14 per cent of the first year's column inches was dedicated to these problems. The promotion of the paper itself occupied 17 per cent of the total; humor and cartoons, all of which were editorializing or issue-related, took slightly less than 10 per cent of all editions; poetry and personal essays about 8 per cent. Advertisers included local bookstores, record stores, and eateries. And paid advertisements amounted to 6 per cent of column inches. In general, during the first year, off-campus controversies absorbed the staff's attention by better than a three-to-one ratio in terms of space allotment. In summary, 43 per cent of the publication was initially devoted to off-campus issues, 14 per cent to on-campus issues, and the rest to the miscellaneous items previously listed.

During the second phase of publication, approximately one year, some distinct changes were noted. Paid advertising doubled, and the amount of space devoted to promotion diminished as the paper established itself in the school community. At one point, the editors apologized for not printing all submitted material, although during the preceding period they had made repeated appeals for written contributions. Their ardor to espouse causes manifested itself in their dedication to the Eugene McCarthy campaign for the presidential nomination, and by their vigorous work in the community to support their political commitments. Politics per se thus occupied 10 per cent of the writing, but coupled with discussions of American morality and "hypocrisy," the treatment of political topics amounted to 25 per cent of the total output.

Writers continued to attack school dress regulations, censorship of textbooks, and student body elections. They also printed an exposé of faculty involvement and alleged coercion during the campus elections. They sarcastically raked the curriculum as "irrelevant" in many instances, particularly on controversial issues in the larger society. They scored other traditional school practices. During the second phase of the paper's existence, 30 per cent of editorial efforts went to off-campus issues, 33 per cent to on-campus problems, and the balance was divided among promotion, humor, advertising and creative writing.

Writers employed various tactics in criticizing traditional school practices as in the following example of irony:

> Homework assignments are becoming more and more stimulating. "Read the chapter and answer the questions at the end. Be ready for a test tomorrow. Current events are due next Monday" is a typical modern homework assignment. This displays great progress over what homework assignments were once like. Why forty years ago, a typical assignment might have been, "Read the chapter and answer the questions at the end. Be ready for a test tomorrow. Current events are due next Monday." It's wonderful to see how far we've come![21]

[21] Cott, Phil. Sir-Press. (October, 1967).

In general, the quality of the writing improved steadily after the initial publication, while a more esthetically designed paper emerged. Positions on issues were still dogmatically stated by Editor Mike Lukas, although there was an apparent feeling of confidence based on a minimum of conflict with the administration, certainly evidence of adult sensitivity at this particular school.

REACTIONS TO THE HIGH SCHOOL UNDERGROUND PRESS

Not all high school editors have been so fortunate as those of *The Loudmouth* because generally the reactions to the high school press on the part of the faculty, administrators, and school boards have varied greatly. It is impossible to assess the ultimate influence on students, faculty, administrators, and the communities in which the underground papers arise, for they are only a part of a national counter-cultural movement. Feldman reported great inconsistency in the attitudes of school newspaper advisers toward these "illegitimate," competing publications in their respective high schools. At one end of the continuum, his informants attributed the blame for student unrest to "communist influence" and on the other end to "youthful high spirits" and the "need for expression."[22]

Administrative responses to published criticism by students ranges along a conflict tolerance scale from liberal interest and dialogue to reactionary enactment of legal sanctions. The resolution of such conflict has been shown to be a function of an individual administrator's set to perceive his role in primarily *moral* terms —weighing his decisions in terms of the legitimacy of constituent expectations, or in primarily *expedient* terms—minimizing negative sanctions against himself and his system, or in some combination of their two modes of perception.[23] A few student editors have been expelled outright. Others, in the face of threat of expulsion, have been forced to transfer to neighboring schools. In some situations, editors have been recruited for the regular news staff; one adviser resolved his journalistic conflict by alternating weekly publication of school sponsored and underground issues.

Students have often been shocked by the harshness of repressive measures taken against them. The American Civil Liberties Union on at least one occasion interceded to protect the right of one California editor to distribute her papers. Here is the story exactly as it appeared in *Floyd,* an underground paper:

IN THE SUPERIOR COURT

LINDA C———, a minor, et al, Plaintiffs
versus

S——— City Unified School District, et al,
Defendants.

[22] Feldman, *The Student Journalist. . . . ,* 1968, 36.
[23] Gross, Neal, Mason, Ward S., and McEachern, Alexander, *Explorations in Role Analysis.* New York: John Wiley & Sons, Inc. 1958.

Last June, Floyd's *final issue for the school year was confiscated by the school officer and all of the distributing students were ordered into the vice-principal's office. The vice-principal informed us that FLOYD could not be distributed across the street or anywhere else around the area of M——— High. Since this time, many events have been occurring.*

During the summer a conference was held with my parents, a deputy county counsel, one of our lawyers, . . . representatives of the school district. No firm commitment could be obtained from the school representatives about the distribution of FLOYD. Mailing FLOYD was suggested, but because of the lack of money this is impossible.

Currently the American Civil Liberties Union is handling the case. There are two volunteer attorneys from . . . representing the involved students. A statement of facts has been worked out between the attorneys and is now in the hands of the county counsel's office, where hopefully they will be agreed upon. The current ACLU newsletter states that when the facts are agreed upon, a suit will be filed to determine the constitutionality of the school board's action.

This problem was eventually solved by several meetings between the attorneys, county counsel, and the school board, during which the board recanted its arbitrary decision and withdrew the distribution ban. No formal suit was ever filed. The editors then proceded to publish and distribute *Floyd* during the following school year. Legal action against papers has been taken in other parts of the country.[24]

PROSPECTS AND DIRECTIONS FOR DEVELOPMENT

In a 1966 high school version of the Students for a Democratic Society university manifesto, militants predicted the major issues that would be involved in subsequent high school disruptions.

Following are the resolutions, which form the body of the document:

I. Freedom of advocacy
   A. Press—a student controlled newspaper
   B. Speech
      1. An area where students may air their opinions to a student audience
      2. Outside speakers are allowed on campus
   C. Student political organizations be allowed on campus
   D. Students be allowed to distribute literature on campus
II. Student representation in administrative politics
   A. Student petitions and initiatives be legalized
   B. Local school policies be determined by students and faculty

[24] Divoky, Diana. *How Old . . .* , 1969. 10.

III. *Freedom of personal dignity*
   A. *Dress codes be eliminated*
   B. *Corporal, arbitrary, and unjust punishments be eliminated*
   C. *No forced self-incrimination*
   D. *No person or agency be given information about students without their consent*
   E. *Legal minimum wage for students working on campus*

Just as the college and university Students for a Democratic Society have clearly announced their intentions, so their high school counterparts have already pledged themselves to a program which has disturbed the superficial calm of many high schools. In its report on the underground press, the Western Behavioral Science Institute staff estimated that more than 80,000 members would be consolidated by 1973, if high school organization followed the pattern of SDS college organization. At the present time, at least one full time SDS staff member works on organizational problems of the high school population. An interesting shift in publications has come with the growing militancy of minority group adolescents. When more than 5,000 Mexican-American students walked out of the high schools in East Los Angeles during the spring of 1968 in their widely publicized "blowouts," the *Chicano Student News* and the *Garfield Striker* appeared simultaneously on high school campuses in the East Los Angeles, along with such adult publications as *Inside-Eastside* and *La Raza* to publicize the conflicts between community and school. The disruption of schools in both the black and Mexican-American communities is accelerating as the Black Student Union and United Mexican-American Students coalesce and, along with other groups, crystalize their objectives. These militants make their position clear in high school as well as adult underground press statements.

Although the high school underground papers emerged originally in largely middle class schools, they now blanket Los Angeles. Significantly, the period of time between the beginning of a protest, the collapse of communication, and the outbreak of violence has become compacted. High school students are adopting the patterns of violence we have been seeing on the college campuses. The desirable possibility of incorporating protestors into society as change agents may conceivably be realized in part through legitimizing their suggestions for structural alterations in power relationships as articulated in the Students for a Democratic Campus manifesto under the heading "student representation in administrative policies." The question is, can and should school administrators share power with constituents? To what extent can meaningful student representation be developed?

Ignoring high school protestors, denigrating their motives, and resorting to harsh suppressive or punitive measures to control their rage seem unlikely to restore a balance to the system. Simple solutions appear to be impossible.

SUMMARY

The high school underground press has not yet been studied in depth. Complete files of these ephemeral periodicals are rare. Moreover, the significance of these organs as both predictive and supportive of school disorders has been slow to receive recognition. There now exists a national network of high school underground communication paralleling that of adult publications. This press can be viewed as an important part of the dialogue between faculty, administrators, and students, as well as between the community in general and American youth. Through the medium of the underground press, certain students who are outspoken critics of adult society, who are innovative, who are committed to major social change, and who believe they are denied expression in authorized school publications, are articulating on-campus and societal problems but also proposing solutions.

Content analysis of a complete file of a high school underground paper *The Loudmouth,* extending over a period of eighteen months, indicates a radically critical attitude toward many long established high school policies and practices. It portrays the commitment of high school youth to the ideals of a more fully democratic and creative society. It also reveals a deep involvement with significant political and social movements in the culture as a whole.

The importance of the high school underground press as an indicator of present convictions and aspirations and especially of future political action, some of it violent, should not be underestimated.

SEVEN

RACIAL CONFLICT IN THE SCHOOLS

Trenton, N.J.—Fifty-nine persons arrested, sixty-one injured.

Providence, R.I.—Public and parochial schools closed from October 30 to November 4.

Akron, Ohio—Twenty-seven students arrested after a fight in the school cafeteria.

Denver, Colorado—Eight persons arrested and three guns confiscated by police who broke up fights at West High School.

Griffin, Ga.—Black youth shot to death as fighting broke out after a football game.

The above events occurred during 1969 and 1970. All were racially motivated and are representative of the more than 650 such disturbances reported in the nation's high schools in 1969-70. These were the serious disturbances, the ones which led, in several instances, to property damage, physical injuries, and even death. There were also quieter racially-inspired rebellions which occurred in an atmosphere free of physical violence. In these, minority students often demanded curriculum reforms within the schools themselves. Here is an example:

> *The Black Student Union of Berkeley High School in order to promote pride in being black, a knowledge of black heritage and culture, to rid ourselves of the results of centuries of racial oppression in America, and to make the school curriculum relevant to the needs of black people, do hereby make the following demands . . .*[1]

It is apparent that protests against racism in the schools take a variety of forms. Violent demonstrations and the petitioning of authorities for a redress of grievances have already been alluded to. It is highly likely that yet a third group of minority students, revolutionaries in their own right perhaps, are those who have quietly dropped out because the schools would not or could not give adequate attention to their culture and unique needs. Interestingly, certain data in the Kerner report,[2] the result of research by a high level commission on riots and civil disturbances appointed by President Johnson, reveal that a significant number of

[1] Los Angeles *Times*, November 25, 1970, Section C, p. 5.

[2] National Advisory Commission on Civil Disorders, *Report of the National Advisory Commission on Civil Disorders* (New York: Bantam Books, 1968), p. 425.

227

the participants in urban riots were public school dropouts. Whether and to what extent the participants had been involved in disturbances while in high schools was, unfortunately, not taken up in the report.

One familiar conclusion of the Kerner Commission was that racism is the nation's number one problem. Given the report's main focus on the extent and consequences of racism in American society, particularly as prejudice and discrimination have been related to riots and civil disturbances, it is not surprising that the schools are given some attention in the report. The commission wrote:

> *Education in a democratic society must equip the children of the nation to realize their potential and to participate fully in American life. For the community-at-large, the schools have discharged their responsibility well. But for many minorities, and particularly for the children of the racial ghetto, the schools have failed to provide the educational experience which could help overcome the effects of discrimination and deprivation. This failure is one of the persistent sources of grievance and resentment within the Negro community. The hostility of Negro parents and students toward the school system is generating increasing conflict and causing disruption within many school districts.*[3]

It would be a mistake to conclude that the Kerner report has sparked the call for an end to racism in the schools now being made by minority students. Far from it! The current militant activities in high schools by minority pupils would appear to be merely a reflection of the militancy of minorities in the nation as a whole. Such activity has been increasing in magnitude since the end of World War II.

The bases for the grievances of minority students are not hard to find—ability grouping which frequently places them in the lowest tracks, racist teachers and administrators (or those thought to be so), proportionately few minority teachers and administrators, a curriculum which fails to give attention to the history and culture of minority groups, a curriculum focused upon white, middle-class values based on the Protestant ethic, and the sheer isolation of minority students from the mainstream of high school activities.

Minority students frequently live in segregated residential communities. If they are residents of large urban centers, they are likely to witness high unemployment, high crime and excessive rents; they frequently see dropout behaviors among their peers, and they are more than privy to information about the domination, victimization and exploitation of parents, relatives and friends by whites. Add to this their observations of violent dissent and militancy in their own communities, successful strikes and walkouts by teachers, policemen, firemen and dis-

---

[3] *Report of the National Advisory Commission on Civil Disorders*, pp. 424-425.

enchanted students—all of which is dutifully reported by the nation's media—and the bases for racial disturbances are understandable.

The demands made by minority students for changes in school practices obviously cannot be considered outside the context of increased militancy among minorities as a whole and the racial dynamics of the communities in which the unrest occurs. There are a few instances in which student demands are unique to the local situation, but in the vast majority of instances there are great similarities among the demands made by both Black and Spanish-speaking minorities.

Some student demands for racial reforms in the schools were included in Chapter Two. Several articles in the present chapter take up where these earlier selections leave off and present a more penetrating perspective on the background, causes and likely consequences of the demands.

The first two articles are demands by Blacks and Mexican-Americans for educational changes in two school systems and include something of the context in which the disturbances occurred and of the efforts made for the resolution of conflicts. The first article, "A Place of Responsibility: Where It Worked Both Ways," describes a boycott by Black students enrolled in a suburban school system, while the second "L.A.'s Student Blowout," describes a boycott involving primarily Mexican-Americans in a large urban school district. In spite of differences in the racial composition of the participants, the size and location of the communities and the numbers of students involved, there are many similarities among the demands of the two groups. Indeed, their demands are hauntingly familiar: provide more minority teachers and administrators, offer more courses dealing with minority history and culture, give greater representation to minority students in school affairs and put an end to racism.

Two articles which follow place the demands of Black and Mexican-American students in a wider context. In the first, "Black Nationalism," J. Herman Blake looks at Black nationalism and Black protest in historical perspective, while Nancie L. Gonzalez, "Positive and Negative Effects of Chicano Militancy on the Education of the Mexican-American," examines the militancy of Chicanos (Mexican-Americans) in educational settings against a backdrop of Chicano militancy in other areas. Both pieces point strongly to the fact that current racial activism in the high schools has its roots in past and current historical and sociological phenomena.

A final article by Wittes and Wittes, "A Study of Interracial Conflict," examines the variety of forces operating in the resolution of racial conflict in one school district. Such an analysis highlights the need to look at racial confrontation in its appropriate historical, political, social and psychological perspectives, and, for purposes of intervention, to place the enterprise in some theoretical context: Wittes and Wittes's reference to systems theory as the basis for diagnosis and other intervention strategies, although sketchily presented in the present article, would seem to point the direction for future work in this area.

A PLACE OF RESPONSIBILITY:
WHERE IT WORKED BOTH WAYS

LLOYD E. PETERMAN

We often speak of the necessity for responsible protest but hardly ever say that reaction to protest must be responsible, also. This inconsistency may exist because the authority being bombarded by protest always finds it hard to submit to a higher authority. But being responsible means being able to answer, if need be, to a higher authority; being liable; being accountable. Oak Park High School is fortunate in having an administration that recognizes its responsibilities to education, and (this is the rare thing) is knowledgeable enough in the ways of human nature and individual natures to deal wisely with student dissidents. As a result, education at Oak Park High School was not disrupted.

They didn't teach us how to deal with student protest groups when we were taking school administration courses in graduate school. In fact, the textbooks did not even hint that we might face underground newspapers, student boycotts, or even student strikes—complete with picket lines and signs. Consequently, when student protest groups appeared at Oak Park High School, we had to develop our own techniques and call the shots as we saw them.

Student protest groups and talk of striking should not have been any surprise, however. Teacher militancy had already arrived, and a year before, the school district had witnessed a two-week teacher strike. It was not lost on the students that protesting and militancy worked. The civil rights movement along with the activities of the NAACP, the Black Power advocates, the ACLU, and other groups had aroused the hopes and expectations of our black students and had made them keenly aware of discrimination and economic differences. Their frustration with the almost imperceptible progress toward eliminating injustices was heightened. The growing militancy on the college and university campuses across the country, also, must have had a certain appeal to high school students and was bound to filter down. In addition, there were conditions inherent in the situation at Oak Park High School that no doubt made it a good candidate for the appearance of such protest groups.

Oak Park High School faced two separate protest groups during the 1968-69 school year—one black group and one white group.[1] It appears at this writing that they were dealt with effectively. What the protesters attempted to do, how

From *National Association of Secondary School Principals Bulletin,* 53 (September, 1969), 1-44. Reprinted with permission of the author and the publisher.

Lloyd E. Peterman, Ph.D., is Principal of Oak Park High School, Oak Park, Michigan.

[1] Only the protest of the black group is relevant to the present discussion, and hence is reprinted here (Eds.).

we dealt with them, and what happened will be of interest to those who may be faced with similar problems or who may want to know more about what is going on in the high schools.

THE SCHOOL AND COMMUNITY

Oak Park High School, located in suburban Detroit, is the only high school in the district and has an enrollment of about 1,550 students in grades 10, 11, and 12. About 100 students are black. The rest are white with only a sprinkling of Orientals. The white students come mostly from middle- and upper-income homes within walking distance of the school, while the black students are bussed from an adjacent but segregated community and have a lower socioeconomic background. Over 80 per cent of the graduates of Oak Park High School go on to higher education.

Given this situation, it is perhaps surprising that we have not had more racial problems and incidents. The black community is two miles from the school. This distance alone made involvement of the black students in extracurricular activities difficult. Cultural differences and differences in motivation and interests made it even more difficult. Efforts were being made to increase black students' participation in the clubs and organizations of the school, but their involvement was minimal.

The Detroit riots during the summer of 1967 had caused a great deal of anxiety in the community as to what would happen at the high school. During the following school year, there were tensions that erupted in a couple of rather serious fights during the month of February that involved several students of both races. Although the fighting was ended quickly and without any serious injury, the wild rumors and exaggerated fears that appeared in the community made it evident that we would have to do all we could to reduce tensions and improve race relations. Our efforts paid off and we survived the rest of the school year, including the death of Martin Luther King, without further incident.

Meanwhile, it was evident during the 1967-68 school year that our white students were also getting ideas about protesting. Complaints were heard that the Student Council did not represent the students; there was open questioning of discipline policies; charges were made that the school paper was "censored" and a "tool of the administration"; and an attempt was made to start an underground newspaper. Although there was nothing in the underground paper that was particularly offensive to the school, school policy did not allow it to be distributed on the campus. We warned the students of this prohibition, their efforts ceased, and the paper folded. Apparently it was unable to survive financially if it had to be sold off-campus.

THE SCHOOL RESPONDS TO CHANGE

It would not be correct at this point to picture the high school as a traditional institution that was resisting change and trying to weather the storms by just reacting to problems as they arose. On the contrary, the administration and staff were involved in several studies that were stimulating change. Planning for a new four-and-a-half-million-dollar addition to the high school had involved most of the staff. The Board of Education had employed consultants from Michigan State University to conduct a district-wide study of the curriculum. District-wide study committees were at work analyzing the Michigan State Report and recommending changes. The high school staff was carrying out a self-study using the *Evaluative Criteria* in preparation for a re-evaluation by the North Central Association, under which the school was accredited.

Several new programs had been started in the past three years. A humanities course was instituted as a team teaching venture involving teachers from art, English, music, science, and social studies. Experimental courses were set up, using paperback books and emphasizing student choice of reading materials and student involvement. Experiments in independent study were being conducted in foreign language and in English. Several of the new curricular programs had been adopted by various departments. For the most part, the staff was committed to a philosophy of change that sought to emphasize student involvement in decision-making, independent study, and individual initiative and creativity.

THE BLACK PROTEST GROUP—SCORE

As the 1968-69 school year got under way, word filtered back to us from the black community that a number of our black students had formed an organization called Student Congress on Racial Equality, or SCORE. Although they had some outside advisers who met with them from time to time, the group was organized and meeting regularly with almost no parent involvement at all.

The immediate aim of SCORE was to improve the lot of black students at Oak Park High School. To accomplish this, the group began to assemble a list of grievances and demands that could be presented to the high school administration. Comments were made from time to time by some of our black students that such a list was in the making. The concerns seemed to be largely directed against the staff and administration. Relationships between white and black students seemed to be better than in the past.

It was apparent Tuesday morning, October 29, that something unusual was afoot. Black students were congregating in the hallways before school began; the groups buzzed with excitement. At the end of second hour about 40 black students walked out of the building and began to march in front of it, carrying signs (delivered by someone in a car) which said, among other things:

WHITEY STARTED SEGREGATION, LET HIM END IT

WHITEY STARTED SEGREGATION, WE'LL PUT AN END TO IT

WE WANT RACIAL EQUALITY AT O.P.H.S.

STUDENTS BOYCOTT UNTIL WE GET EQUALITY

The time had come. As principal of the building, I could no longer think in abstract terms about student protestors. The situation was real. The students were out there marching. I had to make decisions.

As soon as the walkout began, I talked to some of the students and asked that the leaders of the group meet with me in my office. I was told that they had no leaders, but that a committee would come to see me. This committee didn't appear until eleven o'clock; everyone taking part in the strike was too busy getting their march organized and making a play for publicity. In this respect, they were successful: TV cameras and newsmen responded to their calls.

The six students who finally met with me were the generally-accepted leaders of the black students and, I was told, were officers of SCORE. They presented me with the following demands:

Demands of SCORE

1. More black representation
   a. Black student officers on Student Council and in class offices
   b. Black girls on homecoming court
   c. Better election procedures; fair elections
   d. Black teacher to support Afro-American Club
2. More black recognition
   a. Black page on school paper, also black staff members
   b. Black culture week
   c. Black club dances, black speakers on racism, assembly allowed
3. Black history course in January
4. Black qualified teachers
5. Incidents involving racism investigated, perhaps reprimanded
6. Temporary bussing for black students investigated further
7. Homage paid to Martin Luther King this year.

By the end of the hour we had discussed the demands only to the extend of clarifying their meanings. An additional demand was then made that all students who had walked out be permitted to return without penalty or reprisals. It was agreed that they would be allowed to return to classes without penalty beyond being counted absent for the periods missed, provided they returned to classes in the afternoon. In addition, I proposed that we set up a special committee of student leaders, faculty members, high school administrators, and central office administrators to meet with them at 8:00 a.m. the next day to begin discussing all demands and that the committee continue to meet until all issues were resolved. The representatives of the black students agreed to this and said that they would urge the marchers to return to class and await the outcome of the talks.

Our first lunch hour had begun at 11:00 a.m. We worried that tensions might erupt into fighting during the lunch hours, but such was not the case. Leaders in the march were making a real effort to keep it orderly and to prevent trouble. Black students took turns at coming in for lunch. White students reacted to the marchers in different ways: some were sympathetic, most were tolerant, a few were hostile. Any overt hostility was checked by the presence of staff members who volunteered their services during lunch hours. For example, taunting of blacks by whites was squelched before it could cause a fight. On the other hand, about 20 white students joined the marchers—some to show sympathy for the cause, a few just to have a lark.

Because we feared that tensions might result in fights within the building if the marchers were asked to return to classes in the afternoon, we decided to provide bus transportation and send them home for the day. By the time the bus arrived, about 2:00 p.m., the march had broken up and some of the black students had drifted off. The remaining black marchers left on the bus, while most of the white sympathsizers returned to their classes.

It should be noted that about 50 of our black students did not join the march and continued to attend their classes.

The school administration made no effort to contact all the parents of student marchers; however, a few of the black parents in leadership roles were called and told of the situation. By and large, they did not support the student walk-out and were anxious to cooperate with the school to see it ended. Since the black students were making a sincere effort to keep the march orderly and were attempting to be constructive, the parents were counselled to let the school handle it, which they did.

The next morning the committee referred to earlier met with five black students who represented the protesters. The committee, which I had picked, included two student representatives from the Student Council, the teacher-sponsor of the Student Council, the teacher-sponsor of the school paper, the teacher-sponsor of the Afro-American Club (a black teacher), the district Director of Public Information, the Deputy Superintendent, the Superintendent (who stayed for only the first hour of the first session), two assistant principals and myself, acting as chairman and moderator of the discussion.

The meeting was supposed to start at 8:00 a.m. but was almost a half hour late in getting started. The reason was, it seemed, that the black students had decided to continue their march until all their demands were met, and the leaders were busy seeing that the march got under way early in the morning.

In an opening statement to the committee and the representatives of the black students, I pointed out that because the students had not lived up to their promise to end the walkout, my promise to excuse the marchers' absence from classes was rescinded. Consequently, what was to be done with students who were striking was unresolved and would have to be determined. Without asking for a response to this statement from the black students, I then turned to their list of demands. As the discussion got under way, there was evidently a lot of hostility on the part of the black students, together with a considerable amount of misunderstanding about the position of the staff and administration in regard to the concerns they had expressed. Because of this, the general approach of the committee was to listen as sympathetically as possible to their explanations of their demands, to assure them of our sympathetic concern, to clear up misunderstandings, to give assurances that greater efforts would be made to improve conditions for black students at the high school, and to get them to see the limitations of what could be done.

An example of the misunderstandings on their part was the demand that the Afro-American Club be allowed to have a dance and an assembly when, in fact, both of these activities were already scheduled on the school calendar. Another example was their demand that instances of racism be investigated and "perhaps reprimanded." It was pointed out that not only were reported instances investigated and action taken where warranted, but also that a Board of Education policy existed which *required* such action.

The committee met until 11:00 a.m. that day (Wednesday) and again on Thursday. By Thursday noon nearly all issues had been resolved, and the students agreed that the walkout should be ended. The students asked for a caucus to talk over their next move. After their caucus, they asked to meet with me privately to resolve the one remaining issue—what was to happen to the students who were marching—and to put our agreements into writing.

When the black students' representatives met with me in my office along with the Student Council president and a white student who said she represented the white students who had joined the walkout, the contrast of their attitudes at that time to what they had been at the beginning of the committee discussions was almost unbelievable. You could not have found a more friendly and co-operative group of students. They were very anxious to work with me for settling things as quickly and peacefully as possible. They readily agreed to my suggestion that I write up an agreement and that we meet in two hours, after lunch, to go over it.

After a quick lunch, I sat down to write out an agreement. I tried to make it as positive as possible so that the students would feel assured that real efforts were being made to correct the injustices they saw. There was no point in being defensive or in stating that most of these things already were being done.

When the students returned after a couple of hours, they accepted and signed the agreement almost exactly as I had written it:

Agreement Reached on Student Concerns

Following is a list of the concerns presented to the administration and discussed by a committee of students, teachers and administrators along with a summary of the agreement reached on each of them.

1. More Black Representation in the Clubs and Organizations of Oak Park High School. Particularly the Council on Student Affairs.
    a. *Membership in the Student Council will be open to all students subject to attendance and participation requirements.*
    b. *The Executive Committee will review the appointment of chairmen of committees with the sponsor and administration to assure fair representation of all students.*

c. *Written election procedures will be developed by a committee of students and a sponsor to assure that elections are fair and impartial.*

2. More Black Recognition in the School Newspaper.

    a. *Greater efforts will be made to provide more information concerning black student activities. Such information is to be dispersed throughout the paper and not relegated to any specific page.*

3. More Support of the African Culture Club.

    a. *The sponsors will meet with the club in the evening at Carver School at such time as is mutually agreeable.*

    b. *Time for a suitable assembly for all students will be provided.*

    c. *A choice of dates for a dance or other suitable evening function will be provided.*

4. A Course in Black History to Be Started in January, 1969.

    a. *The faculty and administration of Oak Park High School will make every effort to obtain a teacher, provide a curriculum, and make the necessary schedule changes, subject to the approval by the Board of Education, to have a Black History course beginning in January, 1969.*

5. More Black Qualified Teachers.

    a. *Efforts to recruit black teachers will be made. Such efforts include notices to colleges and universities, notices to placement bureaus, recruiting through personal contacts and invitation by staff members.*

6. Incidents Involving Racism Investigated, Perhaps Reprimanded.

    a. *All incidents reported to the office which involve racism will be investigated.*

    b. *Guilty parties will be dealt with by reprimand, suspension, or dismissal as the case may warrant in accordance with the Board of Education Policy on Human Relations.*

7. Temporary Bussing of Black Students Investigated Further.

    a. *The temporary bussing of black students will continue.*

    b. *The possibility of a late bus will be explored.*

8. Homage to Be Paid to Dr. Martin Luther King Annually.

    a. *The Martin Luther King Scholarship will be continued.*

    b. *Special recognition to Dr. King will be given.*

In addition to the above agreement, the students agree to conduct themselves in an exemplary manner and to abide by all the rules, regulations, and policies of Oak Park High School.

Subject to the foregoing conditions, students who were absent from classes for the protest march will be allowed to return to classes Friday morning, November 1, 1968. They will be considered absent from school for classes missed and will be required to make up the work missed. When this work has been made up, their absences will be excused. No further punishment or conditions will be made.

Signed: Principal S   Signed: Student Committee (8) S

One decision remained: How to present to the entire student body the results of the student walkout and the agreement that had been reached. Upon request of the students, it was agreed that an assembly would be held at which I would make an address to the student body which would be followed by a presentation and explanation of the agreement by the committee of black students.

Attempts had been made during the walkout to keep staff and student body informed of developments. The faculty met Wednesday after school to discuss the issues. They agreed to urge all students to remain calm and avoid conduct that might erupt into violence. Since the news people were talking to students and taking pictures, I agreed to interviews for the TV stations. Two of the local stations carried the news story and gave the interview with me considerable coverage in their evening news programs. This seemed to help put things in their proper perspective.

At the assembly the next morning, I addressed the students as follows:

Today we are here to discuss with you the conclusion of the student walkout and the agreements reached on the concerns that were presented by a student committee.

While I certainly was not pleased to see students out of their classes, there were several aspects of what happened the last few days that were encouraging to me. I was gratified by the orderliness and good conduct of the students who marched. I was pleased by the conduct of the rest of the student body as they used patience and good judgment in their reaction to what happened.

But I think the thing that impressed me most was the committee of students present here on the stage who met with me and a committee of teachers and administrators to discuss the concerns.

It was evident from the beginning of our discussions that their concerns were real, that they wanted to do their best to prevent trouble and keep the situation orderly, and above all that they wanted to do what is best for all students at Oak Park High School.

I have such confidence in this group of students that I have asked them to appear before you this morning to express in their own words the concerns they presented and the agreements that were reached.

At this time I will introduce one of the spokesmen who will introduce the remainder of the group. . . .

The four students had agreed to divide the agreement into four parts, each presenting one. It was apparent that my confidence in them had not been misplaced. Each of the students attempted to be as objective as possible about the demands and the agreement. At times they seemed almost apologetic. There was no question that they were making a sincere effort to play down racial differences and to avoid hostilities. The student body responded very favorably.

After the students finished, I concluded my remarks:

> There is still an unanswered question that several students and teachers have been asking. That question is, "Is a student walkout or a strike the way to get things done and to make improvements at Oak Park High School?" My answer to that is no! The students who left school should not have been out of school. They missed their classes and they are going to have to make up their work. But even then, they have missed class time that cannot be made up.
>
> It is true that the strike and the protest march are considered legitimate means on the American scene today. But before a strike can be considered proper, these questions must be asked:
>
> 1. Are the demands legitimate?
> 2. Have all other means of settling the differences been exhausted?
> 3. Is it within the power of the parties against which the strike is called to make the changes demanded?
>
> Only if all these questions can be answered affirmatively should a strike be considered. And then it should be called only if the gains will be greater than the losses.
>
> We hear a lot about student power. I want to let you in on a little secret —I am for student power, too, and have been for a long time.
>
> I feel that way because it is part of my philosophy of education. I do not believe that education is some bunk that teachers pound into your heads. Education is not something somebody gives you, but something you get. It is something you get only when you are motivated, when you are involved, and when you want to learn. I also believe in student power because I believe in democracy—and this is the great heritage and tradition upon which this country is founded.
>
> It is because of my belief in student power that I want to see students involved in the student faculty committee. It is the reason I am pleased to see students involved in a committee to plan the noon activities program. It is the reason I am pleased to see the reorganization of the Student Council to involve more students and give them a more active voice in what goes on. It is also the reason I want to see our school paper speak for the students and to see that all students have the opportunity to be heard. It is the reason I feel that we should seek additional ways of getting students involved in the recommendations and decisions that are made.
>
> I would be the first to admit that everything is not perfect or as it should be at Oak Park High School, and that there are many things we could improve.

But I would also say that we have a great school that turns out great scholars and students who achieve and succeed in the colleges and universities and in the vocations of their choices to a greater degree than other schools. This is a tribute to a fine student body and to one of the finest staff of teachers I have ever worked with.

So, I would appeal to all students and teachers to seek every opportunity to get involved in this great concern of everybody—to make Oak Park High School a better school.

Thank you.

After the student walkout, things returned to normal rather quickly in the building. For the balance of the school year, race relations were better in the building than they had been for a number of years. No serious incidents of a negative nature occurred. In fact, several things of a positive nature happened.

We were fortunate to get a very fine teacher, Mrs. Francis Windham, who had secondary teaching experience in Afro-American history in the South, to transfer to the high school from an elementary school in the district. The Afro-American history course was started second semester with two sections of about 32 students each. About two-thirds of the students who signed up for the course were white.

Mrs. Windham also assisted in sponsoring the Afro-American Club and assisted the group in preparing an Afro-American assembly program during Negro-History Week. This assembly was one of the most enjoyed in the history of assemblies at Oak Park High School. Furthermore, the Club presented its program at three other high schools in neighboring districts where it was equally successful.

"L.A.'S STUDENT BLOWOUT"

JOHNS H. HARRINGTON

Thousands of students walked out of Los Angeles schools last spring to back demands for sweeping educational change. What are the lessons of such student "blowouts" for teachers and administrators?

A new kind of monster raised its head in Los Angeles last spring when the city school district faced its first student walkouts in a 113-year history. Whatever happens to the 13 grand jury indictments for conspiracy that are still pending as

From *Phi Delta Kappan*, 50 (October, 1968), 74-79. Reprinted with the permission of the author and the publisher.

Johns H. Harrington is Editor of School Publications, Division of Instructional Planning and Services, Los Angeles City Schools.

this is written, the repercussions of the events during the week of March 5 are likely to produce shock waves that will affect schools and minority groups in urban areas throughout the country. Certainly there are lessons to be learned from the "student blowout" that should be helpful to public school teachers and administrators elsewhere.

Five Mexican-American high schools on the east side were involved, but the primarily Negro Jefferson High School also closed its doors for three days. In two predominantly Negro junior high schools as well, pupils left classes for a time. Some set fires in trash cans and broke windows. As a side effect, 800 white students and nonstudents clashed with police in Venice some 18 miles across the city on the west side.

In addition to its large Negro population, Los Angeles is unique in that it has 800,000 citizens of Mexican descent—the greatest concentration outside Mexico itself. The city is also the most popular "port of entry" in the southwestern United States for immigrants from Mexico.

The extent of participation in the blowout is difficult, if not impossible, to measure accurately. Estimates vary with the point of view and knowledge of the observer. School spokesmen report that some 2,500 students joined in the walkouts, and another 1,000 stayed away from classes because of apparent fear of violence. In the main, however, demonstrations were nonviolent. Demands of demonstrators, agitators, and the few teachers who joined with them ranged from sweeping educational changes to abolishment of corporal punishment and permission to wear miniskirts.

Although the district staff said that newspapers exaggerated the extent and nature of the disorders, an indication of events during the week-long demonstrations can be gleaned from such reports as the following:

"Police and school authorities today are probing possible underground agitation as the cause of disorders Tuesday and Wednesday at four Los Angeles high schools. . . .

"One school official attributed the walkouts and rock-throwing, bottle-throwing demonstrations to editorials in an 'underground magazine' which urged students to 'rise up' and protest any conditions they did not like. Two policemen dispersing students at Roosevelt High were hit by flying bottles yesterday. One was hospitalized for treatment of an eye cut. . . . At Lincoln High about 400 young persons refused to attend classes. They were urged, a school official said, to attend a rally at a nearby park by a bearded youth who wore the uniform of the 'Brown Berets,' a militant Mexican-American group. . . ." (Los Angeles Herald-Examiner, March 7)

"Police Chief Tom Reddin warned today that 'professional agitators' are in for trouble for inciting school walkouts like the one at Belmont High School yesterday, where fires were set, police cars stoned, and six persons arrested." (Los Angeles Herald-Examiner, March 8)

"Two hundred young persons broke up a meeting of the City Board of Education and sent most board members fleeing out a rear door Thursday as a climax to a day of boycotts, arson, and the stoning of police cars at schools attended by minority groups.

"Mrs. Georgiana Hardy, board president, pounded her gavel and adjourned the meeting as a bearded member of the Brown Berets strode down the aisle and took over the guest speaker's microphone.

" 'If you walk out today, we will walk out tomorrow,' shouted the youth." (Los Angeles Times, March 8)

In a statement to the press issued March 8, Jack Crowther, city schools superintendent, declared:

"Every effort is being made to maintain an orderly and normal educational process in the Los Angeles city schools. Representatives of the Board of Education and Secondary Division staff are meeting today with student representatives of protest groups to discuss grievances which have been raised regarding some of the high schools.

"It is important to note that, despite the many disturbances at these schools in the last few days, the overwhelming majority of students have remained in class and continued their studies. . . ."

On the following Monday, Crowther addressed a letter to teachers in the schools concerned and asked that they read a message to students. It included:

"Let me emphasize that all of us agree with the desperate need to improve the educational program, buildings, and equipment in your schools. These are the very things which we are fighting for—and indeed on the very day that classes were being disrupted, I and members of the Board of Education were in Sacramento making a desperate plea to the State Legislature for more money to improve our schools.

"I think we can all agree that your viewpoint has been heard—and has been made known dramatically during the last four days of last week. Today your representatives will present their views to the Board of Education.

"Therefore, I am asking each one of you from this moment on to remain in school and continue your class work. Nothing further can be gained by leaving your classes, and the only result of such action will be further harm to your education. *Time lost from classes is gone forever and cannot be regained.* We know that your parents are anxious and eager for school to continue without further interruption."

Shortly after the first walkouts, the Board of Education took the following actions:

1. Agreed to hold a special meeting at Lincoln High School to discuss educational problems in the East Los Angeles area.

2. Granted amnesty to the students who boycotted classes since March 7.

3. Appointed a Negro principal, vice principal, and head counselor at Jefferson High School. (These assignments were already in process, however, when the demonstrations at Jefferson took place.)

But the board refused to order removal of police from the high school campuses or to ask for release of students who had been arrested during the demonstrations.

The demands and recommendations with which the board and staff were deluged both for and against the walkouts came from a wide variety of sources, including the Educational Issues Committee, a community group in East Los Angeles; the California Association of Educators of Mexican Descent; the East Los Angeles Coordinating Council; the Broadway-Central Coordinating Council; the Citizens' Compensatory Education Advisory Committee; the Los Angeles Teachers Association and the American Federation of Teachers; faculty and student groups, both official and unofficial; the community press; and "underground" newspapers.

The demands themselves covered almost the entire spectrum of the educational program, including:

- Free press
- Free speech
- Bilingual school personnel
- Bilingual instruction
- School buildings
- Cafeteria service
- Community relations
- Corporal punishment
- Counseling ratio
- Electives
- Fences around campuses
- Reading
- Reallocation of R.O.T.C. funds
- Suspension policies
- "Community parents" as teacher aides
- Dress and grooming
- Homogeneous grouping
- Mexican-American contributions to U.S. society
- Administrators of Mexican-American descent
- Teachers of Mexican-American descent
- Nonacademic assemblies
- I.Q. tests
- Library facilities
- Academic courses
- Prejudice of school personnel

- Open restrooms
- Eligibility for study body office
- Swimming pools
- Dismissal or transfer of teachers because of political or philosophical views

Ironically, some of the demands were direct quotations from statements by Crowther or Stuart Stengel, associate superintendent, Division of Secondary Education, regarding improvements in the educational program that they were seeking. Objectives that have been emphasized by Stengel as "imperative" include:

1. Development of practical testing instruments which will measure the disadvantaged pupil's true potential

2. More counseling services to provide continuous encouragement of pupils to fulfill their potential

3. Full elective programs available in all schools or within a reasonable geographic area, despite comparatively low enrollments in such electives

4. An expanded program for educable mentally retarded pupils

5. Improvement of vocational education programs which will train noncollege-bound pupils for gainful employment and the increased development of placement services

6. Improvement of textual and supplementary additional materials which are at both the pupil's ability level and the pupil's interest level

7. An expanded program of English as a second language

8. Provision for experimental classes taught in Spanish in various subject fields

9. Provision of sound human relations training for teachers and administrators

10. Provision for continuous follow-up studies to determine what's happening to the high school graduate

"It is my belief that the staffs of East Los Angeles secondary schools are doing an outstanding job, within the limitations of what is financially feasible," Stengel said. "I think that our program constantly improves, although not as rapidly, of course, as school personnel and community would like it to ideally."

Since the student blowout, the Board of Education and staff have been working on responses to the 36 major demands that were presented. As a barrage of scathing criticism from militant groups continued, Crowther told the board:

"It needs to be emphasized that, in the main, many of the items [demands] are essentially the same as projects which staff has, from time to time, presented to the board for its consideration. The list of demands has created two erroneous implications: 1) that little, if anything, has been attempted by the board and the district in trying to carry out educational improvements demanded by the students and community; and 2) that improvements have been carried out in other schools throughout the district, particularly in more affluent areas, at the expense of East Los Angeles schools.

"One other impression also needs to be clarified: that funds are available to carry out the list of demands. The fact is that no such funds are available without cutting elsewhere. The facts are that a major share of funds is already being allocated to minority area schools (an average of $53 more annually per student than in so-called advantaged areas). . . ."

When the Board of Education granted amnesty to students and appointed Negro administrators at Jefferson High School, the actions were criticized by demonstrators as not going far enough and also by some teacher and other groups for yielding to pressure.

A statement signed by 101 teachers from Roosevelt High School read in part:

"Let it be clearly understood that no teacher whose name appears on this petition wishes to leave Roosevelt. On the contrary, this petition is intended to reflect our loyalty to our school and our deep concern for our students.

"Under the present circumstances, however, we feel that, by submitting to the intimidation of a small militant faction, the Board of Education has acted in error.

"The Board's lack of firm action, its display of divided authority, and its non-support of local administrators and teachers in their efforts to uphold the provisions of the Education Code and the Administrative Guide of the State of California have made teaching virtually impossible.

"Because of the board's vacillation, teacher morale is depressed, student attitude is confused, and administrative authority is undermined."

Despite the crisis and conflicts of views, however, within a week after the boycott school programs were resumed as Superintendent Crowther and his staff continued to seek additional funds to strengthen the educational program and made both immediate and long-range plans to heal the wounds.

Observers within and without the school system attributed the walkouts to a wide range of causes. Obviously, some were related to recent incidents, such as dissatisfaction with local policies, cancellation of a local high school play, and unrest on college campuses. Others, however, concerned problems that have been growing in intensity for years. Although all agreed that additional help is needed for pupils in East Los Angeles—as in many other urban areas throughout the nation where students should have better educational opportunities and there has been an influx of new residents—some have claimed that the blowout was spontaneous while others have contended that the "rabble-rousers always present" somehow had managed to gain enough momentum to enlist widespread student and community support. Another version was that political opportunists saw a power vacuum and seized the opportunity to cut a niche for themselves. In referring to the blowout in the *Los Angeles Times* for March 17, 1968, Dial Torgerson wrote, "It was, some say, the beginning of a revolution—the Mexican-American revolution of 1968."

Whatever the cause, or combination of causes, there were many advance indications that storm clouds were reaching threatening proportions. In its February 11 issue—nearly a month before the crisis—the *East Los Angeles Gazette* carried a banner on page one which read, "Walkout by Students Threatened at Garfield, Five Other Schools." The story began as follows:

"The threat of a student walkout, dramatizing overcrowded conditions and alleged disregard of cultural heritage in Eastside high schools, which may be staged May 3 (or sooner), is presently hanging over the heads of school administrators.

"The original area of concentration was considered to be Garfield, Roosevelt, Lincoln, and Wilson high schools, but it was learned this week that planners are now trying to encompass both Huntington Park and Bell high schools in the proposed mass absence. . . ."

Julian Nava, Mexican-American member of the Board of Education and a history professor at San Fernando Valley State College, was quoted in the February 25 issue of the *East Los Angeles Gazette* as saying, "It is 'a healthy sign that [East Los Angeles] students are finally speaking up' in regard to educational demands and threats of a walkout if the student's voice goes unheeded." The story added:

"The Board of Education member made it clear he did not favor any form of student violence but, rather, regarded the complaints of local students as a major step for the Mexican-American people."

In contrast with Nava's position, "underground newspapers" published many inflammatory articles for months prior to the walkout. For example, in the December 25, 1967, issue of *La Raza,* one of the militant community publications that have recently been established, a columnist said:

"I almost vomited in the Belvedere auditorium recently. The place was jammed with people when some guy . . . leader of some Daddy Club spouted nonsense. He gave a talk about the group and then fell apart saying that his group are good guys. WE ARE NOT AGITATORS, he said over and over.

"All he had to say was something like this: 'I'm a good Mexican. I keep my mouth shut. I don't make waves. I keep my blind followers doing the same. Please don't criticize this school or any other or I won't get a chance to speak at things like this. I'm in with all the Gringos here and they all like me so don't ruin anything. I like this even though the strings on my back itch and the top of my head aches from getting patted so much by my blue-eyed friends. Please join us but only if you don't bring up anything important like changing the school so they do a better job. Just come to the meetings, keep your mouth shut, and come to our dances. Oh Goodie!' . . ."

This item appeared in *Eastside Inside* on December 8, 1967:

"The boys' vice principal would make an excellent night watchman and the registrar could always tag along and help with the flashlight or keys or something.

"The principal should remain at home. I mean, really, he doesn't do anything. He could always telephone or write a letter once every two or three weeks and

I'm sure he could accomplish as little as he has by being present. Why be only ninety percent ignorant of the school's problems when you could be completely ignorant. . . ."

The *Free Student*, another underground newspaper, carried an attack labeled "Student Gov't a Farce," which read in part:

"There are basically two ways of ending the administrative control of student government. Different schools may find one or the other more effective. . . . By acting and not talking, we can end the farce of student government."

These excerpts are mild compared with other items in the underground press, many of which ridiculed individual members of school staffs. In spending a few hours scanning a sampling of the papers, a reader gets the impression that the writers consider nothing right with the educational program—including personnel, facilities, and governing policies.

Since the educational blowout, many steps have been taken to help meet the needs it dramatized. Most of the measures, however, were already on the drawing boards before the shrill voice of dissent shattered the educational calm. Among innovations have been:

1. Appointment of James Taylor, a Negro, to the newly created post of assistant deputy superintendent of instruction (with the rank of an assistant superintendent).

2. Assignment of John Leon, a Mexican-American, as head of a new instructional planning center in East Los Angeles.

3. Authorization by the Board of Education of two highly "innovative" educational "complexes," to be located in East Los Angeles and the Watts area. (Plans for the complexes were initiated long before the blowout.)

"This project is an approach to provide a real breakthrough in the education of minority-group young people by doing an all-out job of providing a variety of services and programs in a concentrated area and by using the newest ideas to put them into effect," Crowther commented. "A flexible, specific program for each school in the complexes will be developed. Our plan is to have ideas come from the school community—by involving parents, other community members, teachers, and administrators."

4. Appointment of Edward Moreno as supervisor of bilingual education in the Instructional Planning Branch and issuance of a study report on what has been done, is being done, and is planned in the Elementary Curriculum Bilingual-Bicultural Program.

5. Conduct of the largest summer school in the history of the Los Angeles city schools, involving 149,000 pupils at 259 locations.

Both elementary and secondary schools offered special classes of various types. One program included five educational enrichment centers for elementary school pupils of varying socioeconomic backgrounds.

6. Teaching of conversational Spanish to 210 teachers in summer workshops.

7. Establishment of the Eastside Bilingual Study Center for approximately 1,800 adults at Salesian High School.

8. Employment of 88 bilingual clerks.

9. Provision of workshops for school personnel to develop greater understanding of the Mexican-American culture and community.

10. Establishment of a classified personnel office for the school system on the east side.

Although instructional materials had already been designed especially to help minority group students, more have been developed and others are on the way. An instructional guide on Mexico was published in 1959, and *Angelenos—Then and Now, Californians—Then and Now,* and *Americans—Then and Now* were issued in 1966. The latter series consists of pupil materials for elementary schools which describe the contributions and achievements of members of minority groups. Spanish editions of various pupil materials have been printed or are now being translated. A leaflet called "Blending of Two Cultures" focused on services for Mexican-American pupils.

Reference lists for teachers and pupils include "A Selected List of Books on American Ethnic Groups for Secondary School Libraries," "Recommended Books on American Cultural Minority Groups for Elementary School Libraries," and "Bibliography of Books in Spanish Compiled from Recommended Titles for Secondary Libraries."

Although it is too early to say whether L.A.'s student blowout has been properly patched up or what organizers may think of next, it must be evident to most observers that a heavy thrust is being made by the Los Angeles city schools to provide the kind of education that all pupils need. Many would agree with John Leon, director of the new instructional planning center in Los Angeles, when he recently said:

> It seems to me that in American education we have three major phases. In the first, the schools blame the homes for the failures of children. In the second, the parents and other citizens blame the schools. Now we must enter the third phase, in which schools and homes share the blame for educational problems and work together toward their solution.

Unlike a Grade B movie, however, the story does not necessarily have a happy ending. In fact, for the time being, at least, there seems to be no ending at all. An article in the *Los Angeles Times* for August 4 reported that the Educational Issues Coordinating Committee of East Los Angeles had "rejected" the Board of Education's handling of the 36 "student" demands for educational reforms. The coordinating committee also has requested status independent of the board and asks that the committee and the district staff choose an independent group of educators to investigate East Los Angeles problems.

"We are not going to be put off," the *Times* quoted the Rev. Vahac Mardirosian, chairman of the committee, as saying. "We are not going to go away."

The student blowout and its aftermath in Los Angeles have dramatically illustrated the need for better communications between schools and community, more financial help, and greater emphasis on minority group culture. Perhaps the most important lesson, however, is the urgency of decentralization in urban areas to encourage local participation and to assure provision of an educational program that meets local needs. In the future, community influences undoubtedly will have a greater impact on curricular offerings and other aspects of individual school programs.

BLACK NATIONALISM

J. HERMAN BLAKE

Abstract: Black nationalism has been one of the most militant and strident protest movements in the Afro-American community since the early nineteenth century. In its earliest manifestations, political nationalism sought to separate black people from the United States; economic nationalism sought to break down racial barriers through developing economic strength in the black community; while cultural nationalism sought the same goal through the development of racial solidarity and black consciousness. The various strands were brought together into an integral form of nationalism by Marcus Garvey after World War I. The Nation of Islam continued the emphasis on integral nationalism under the leadership of Elijah Muhammad but added a significant religious component. Contemporary trends in black nationalism reflect the profound influence of the late El-Hajj Malik El-Shabazz. Political nationalism has been expanded to include a new and unique emphasis upon land, as well as emphasis upon self-determination for black communities and accountability of black leaders. The growing strength of cultural nationalism is seen in the new manifestations of black consciousness. The nature of the current trends indicate that black people see themselves as part of the American society even though they feel very much separated from it. Future trends in black nationalism may be significantly affected by the most persistent racial barrier in America —the color line.

The price the immigrants paid to get into America was that they had to become Americans. The black man cannot become an American (unless we get a different set of rules) because he is black.

LeRoi Jones

From *The Annals of the American Academy of Political and Social Science,* No. 382 (March, 1969), 15-25. Reprinted with permission of the author and publisher.

J. Herman Blake is Acting Associate Professor of Sociology at the University of California, Santa Cruz.

It is one of the bitter ironies of American history that the seeds of the contradiction which created black nationalism were sown in the colony of James-town in 1619. When the settlers accepted twenty captured Africans as servants—an act which eventually led to slavery—the reality of black inequality in America was established at the same time that the rhetoric of democracy was articu-lated.[1] Black nationalism has been a major form of protest against this contradic-tion since the early nineteenth century. Early nationalist protest followed several different emphases, but in the twentieth century these different strands were in-corporated into a unified form of protest. The most recent trends in black na-tionalism reveal some unique features which have significant implications for future developments.

Black nationalist thought is a consequence of the duality of the experience of Afro-Americans, a people who are identified by racial characteristics as different from the "typical" American and denied full participation in this society for that reason, while, at the same time, they are expected to meet all the responsibilities of citizenship. It reflects the negative self-image which many black people have unconsciously developed, and the sense of hopelessness that has persisted in the Afro-American community as a consequence of being treated as inferiors.

EARLY TRENDS

The first distinctive form of black nationalism was the desire to separate from America expressed by some free blacks in the early part of the nineteenth cen-tury.[2] The proponents of this form of *political nationalism* argued for the estab-lishment of a black nation in Africa or some other territory. Their views were based on a conviction that Afro-Americans would never receive justice in Amer-ica and that the only hope was to leave the country and establish a political entity for black people. The apex of this development came at the Emigration Con-vention of 1854, when three men were commissioned to investigate the possibil-ities of emigration of blacks to Central America, the Black Republic of Haiti, or the Niger Valley in West Africa.

The apparent permanence of American slavery and the racial barriers set up against freed blacks led these men to the conviction that true justice and equality for black people would never be reached in this country, and there were other territories to which they might emigrate. Thus, those in favor of emi-gration argued that the only hope for the black man was to leave this country and establish a black nation in which the emigrants could live free from fear, racial prejudice, and discrimination. The Civil War and emancipation of the

[1] Vincent Harding, "The Uses of the Afro-American Past," *Negro Digest*, Vol. 17 (February 1968), p. 5.

[2] E. U. Essien-Udom, *Black Nationalism: A Search for an Identity in America* (Chicago: University of Chicago Press, 1962), chap. ii; and August Meier, "The Emergence of Negro Nationalism," *The Midwest Journal*, Vol. 4 (Winter 1951), pp. 96-104, and *ibid.* (Summer 1952), pp. 95-111.

slaves brought black agitation for emigration to a halt, and black people devoted themselves to the task of becoming a part of the American society.

Though emancipation increased the hopes of blacks that full participation in the society was forthcoming, post-Reconstruction developments made it increasingly clear that such was not to be the case. The depressing conditions which followed the Hayes compromise led to the development of philosophies of self-help, particularly as expressed in *economic nationalism*. This emphasis called for racial solidarity and economic co-operation as the solution to the problems of the Afro-American. The growing influx of Europeans into Northern cities and factories increased the pessimism of some influential Afro-Americans and led them to look for salvation within the race. Booker T. Washington, a major proponent of economic nationalism, felt that industrial education and the perfection of agricultural skills in the rural South would lead whites to the realization that black people were worthy of equal treatment. In his famous Atlanta Exposition Address of 1895, Washington revealed that he was aware of the impact of European immigration upon American industry, and evidently felt that this trend closed the doors of opportunity in the North to blacks. Therefore, he pursued a policy of racial solidarity and economic self-sufficiency, establishing the National Negro Business League in 1900 for the purpose of stimulating business enterprise. At the 1904 convention of the League, Washington viewed the developments of black businesses through the support of black people as crucial to the removal of racial prejudice in America.[3] Unlike political nationalism, economic nationalism revealed a desire for participation in the society, but in the face of rejection by Americans, the economic emphasis worked on strengthening the internal community as part of an attack upon the racial barriers.

Cultural nationalism was another response to the denial of equality to Afro-Americans. Like economic nationalism, the emphasis was upon racial solidarity, with added attraction given to the development of racial pride and dignity. These goals were sought through the study of the history of the black man and his contribution to mankind. The essential belief of the cultural nationalists was that a scholarly analysis and study of the history of black people throughout the world, particularly in America, would show blacks and whites that Afro-Americans are descended from a proud heritage and have made outstanding contributions to human progress. It was thought that such an understanding would have two consequences: (1) It would give blacks a positive self-image and further the development of racial pride and solidarity; and (2) it would show whites that blacks were no better nor worse than any other race and that because of their contributions, they should be fully accepted into the society.

Although there were attempts to develop the study of Afro-American history before the Civil War, cultural nationalism received its greatest impetus during the latter part of the nineteenth century. The desire to give scholarly attention to the historical past of the black man resulted in the organization of the Asso-

[3] Meier, *op. cit.*

ciation for the Study of Negro Life and History in 1915, and to the establishment of the *Journal of Negro History*.[4]

Political, economic, and cultural forms of black nationalism all had their roots in the social conditions confronting Afro-Americans. During the days of slavery, the desire for emigration and separation increased with the growing conviction that slavery would never be eliminated. It is noteworthy that the emigration movement among blacks reached its most significant point during the 1850's and that such interest declined with the onset of the Civil War. In the latter part of the nineteenth century, economic and cultural nationalism developed as a consequence of continued hostility and repression. The end of Reconstruction, the rise of Jim Crow, the lack of economic opportunity, and similar conditions led to the development of economic and cultural attempts to foster individual and collective strength within the black community while pursuing an attack upon the prejudiced and discriminatory behavior of the larger society. The major proponents of these various emphases came from the upper levels of the Afro-American community. Martin R. Delany, a supporter of emigration, was a physician and Harvard graduate; Booker T. Washington was the undisputed leader of black people from 1895 until his death in 1915; and Arthur A. Schomburg, Carter G. Woodson, and W. E. B. DuBois were all highly educated and literate men. Black nationalist movements did not develop a foundation among the masses until after World War I.

TWENTIETH-CENTURY PATTERNS

Black nationalism as a mass movement followed the creation of a ready audience and the combination of the various strands of nationalistc thought into an integral whole. When Marcus Garvey, a native of Jamaica, established the Universal Negro Improvement Association and African Communities League (UNIA) in New York City in 1917, he brought *integral nationalism* to a people who were looking for hope in what appeared to be a hopeless situation.[5]

Garvey made his strongest appeal to the many blacks who had migrated out of the South shortly before his arrival in the country, seeking employment in the industrial centers of the North. Agricultural depression and the appearance of the boll weevil in Southern cotton had made living conditions extremely difficult. At the same time, the European war had placed heavy demands on Northern industry, and the supply of European immigrant labor had been cut off. Therefore, Northern industrialists began a campaign to induce blacks to leave the South and work in Northern factories. It is estimated that in one two-year period a half-million black people moved to the North.[6]

[4] *Ibid.*
[5] Edmund David Cronon, *Black Moses: The Story of Marcus Garvey and the Universal Negro Improvement Association* (Madison: University of Wisconsin Press, 1955). The UNIA was actually organized in Jamaica in 1914 by Garvey, but he experienced his greatest success in the United States.
[6] Cronon, *op. cit.*, pp. 22-27.

The many blacks who made this journey found that though they were often openly recruited, they were seldom welcomed, for they were crowded into urban slums and faced a continual round of unemployment, depression, and indigence. Furthermore, they met the massive hostility of whites—many of them newly arrived in this country—who saw the black immigrants as threats to their economic security and reacted against them with devastating riots. The continued hardships of the blacks and the intense hostility of the whites created a situation in which Garvey's appeal seemed eminently rational. They were the same conditions which led to earlier forms of nationalism, except that the blacks perceived them in a much more intensified manner than previously. Garvey's integral form of black nationalism flourished in this situation, and its significance was not only that it was the first major social movement among the black masses; it also indicated the extent to which they "entertained doubts concerning the hope for first-class citizenship in the only fatherland of which they knew."[7]

The UNIA program combined previous emphases in black nationalism. Drawing upon the Booker T. Washington philosophy of economic independence, Garvey established various commercial enterprises, among them the Black Star Line, a steamship company designed to link the black peoples of the world through trade, and the Negro Factories Corporation, designed to build and operate factories in the industrial centers of the United States, Central America, the West Indies, and Africa. In the tradition of the political nationalists, Garvey sought to have all whites expelled from Africa so that it could become a territory for black people only. He told Afro-Americans that race prejudice was such an inherent part of white civilization that it was futile to appeal to the white man's sense of justice. The only hope was to leave America and return to Africa. His vigorous promotion of racial solidarity and black consciousness was one of his most lasting successes. Exalting everything black, he renewed the assertions that Africa had a noble history and urged Afro-Americans to be proud of their ancestry. Coming when it did, his program had a profound impact upon the black masses, and even his severest critics admit that in the early 1920's, his followers numbered perhaps half a million.[8]

The Garvey movement did not show the dualism found in earlier nationalist sentiment. It was a philosophy that fully embraced blackness and vigorously rejected white America. Although the movement declined after his imprisonment in 1925, the integral form of black nationalism was to continue. In the early 1930's the Lost Found Nation of Islam in the Wilderness of North America was established in Detroit, and began to grow under the leadership of Elijah Muhammad.

After two decades of relative obscurity, the Nation of Islam experienced rapid growth during the 1950's, particularly when the brilliant and articulate ex-convict, Malcolm X, began speaking around the country in the name of the organi-

---

[7] John Hope Franklin, *From Slavery to Freedom* (New York: Alfred A. Knopf, 1963), p. 483.
[8] Cronon, *op. cit.*, chap. iii; Franklin, *op. cit.*, pp. 481-483.

zation. Like the UNIA, the Nation of Islam is an unequivocal rejection of white America and a turn inward to the black man and the black community as the only source of hope for resolving racial problems. Unlike the UNIA, the Nation of Islam contains a strong religious component which is a major binding force in the organization. There is the Holy Koran which provides scriptural guidance, Elijah Muhammad (The Messenger) who provides everyday leadership, an eschatology, and a set of rituals which give the members a valuable shared experience.[9] The rejection of white America involves a rejection of Christianity as the religion of the black man, English as the mother tongue of the black man, and the Stars and Stripes as the flag of the black man. Muslims also refuse to use the term "Negro," their family names, and traditional Southern foods, which are all taken as remnants of the slave condition and a reaffirmation of that condition so long as they are used.

The Nation of Islam places great emphasis upon black consciousness and racial pride, claiming that a man cannot know another man until he knows himself. This search for black identity is conducted through the study of the religious teachings of Islam, as interpreted by Elijah Muhammad, and through the study of Afro-American and African history.

Muslims also follow a strong program of economic nationalism, with their emphasis upon independent black businesses. Muslim enterprises, mostly of the service variety, have been established across the country and have been quite successful. They are now opening supermarkets and supplying them with produce from Muslim-owned farms. There is also some movement now into light manufacturing.

The Muslim emphasis upon a separate territory for black people gave new emphasis to political nationalism. They have never specified whether that land should be on this continent or another, but they have consistently argued that since blacks and whites cannot live together in peace in this country, it would be better if the blacks were to leave the country and set up an independent nation. In the Muslim view, such a nation would be an Islamic theocracy. This new element of political nationalism, emphasizing land rather than Africa, emigration, or colonization, has become a significant element of contemporary black nationalist protest.

The Nation of Islam had a profound effect upon the development of contemporary trends in black nationalism. There are very few ardent black nationalists today who have not had some close contact with the Nation of Islam either through membership or through having come under the influence of one of its eloquent ministers. Even though the Nation of Islam grew rapidly there were many black people who were deeply influenced but were not persuaded by the doctrine of total separation from America or by the religious emphasis. This was particularly true of college-educated blacks. The break between Mal-

[9] Essien-Udom, op. cit.; and C. Eric Lincoln, The Black Muslims in America (Boston: Beacon Press, 1961).

colm X and the Nation of Islam in early 1964 had a profound impact on current trends by spurring the development of black nationalism among countless numbers of blacks who supported the Muslim emphasis upon black consciousness and racial solidarity.

The Universal Negro Improvement Association and African Communities League under Marcus Garvey and the Lost Found Nation of Islam in the Wilderness of North America under Elijah Muhammad have been very successful and influential forms of integral nationalism. Both the leaders and the followers came primarily from among the black masses of the urban North, whose lives had not seen the steady progress toward perfection which characterizes the myth of the American dream of success. These two movements brought the various threads of nineteenth-century black nationalism together, and wove them into a matrix out of which the more recent trends in black nationalist thought have developed. Contemporary trends, however, add some distinctive elements of their own which are shaping black nationalism and the current pattern of race relations in America.

CONTEMPORARY DEVELOPMENTS

The development of black-nationalist-protest thought in recent years is related to the same conditions which produced such sentiment in earlier periods, as well as to some new and unique conditions. In recent years, the urbanization of the black man has proceeded at a very rapid pace. In 1960, a higher proportion of the black population (73 per cent) were residents of the cities than ever before, and this proportion exceeded that of the white population (70 per cent). Not only are blacks moving into the cities; whites are moving out, so that more of the central cities are becoming all-black enclaves. Between 1960 and 1965, the proportion of blacks in central cities increased by 23 per cent while the proportion of whites declined by 9 per cent.[10]

It is not simply that black people are now predominantly urban; in recent years, black urban residents have become new urbanites for two major reasons. Not a small proportion of the immigrants to central cities are younger blacks who are generally better educated than those whites who remain in the cities.[11] Furthermore, a new generation of black people is coming to maturity, young people who were born and raised in the urban black communities. They do not use a previous Southern pattern of living as the framework through which they assess their current situation, but use an urban, mainstream-America framework, usually learned from the mass media rather than experienced. These youth comprise a very large proportion of the urban residents and are less enchanted

[10] U.S. Department of Commerce, Bureau of the Census, *Current Population Reports,* Series P-20, No. 157, December 16, 1966.
[11] Karl E. Taeuber and Alma F. Taeuber, "The Changing Character of Negro Migration," *American Journal of Sociology,* Vol. 70 (January 1965), pp. 429-441.

by the view that, although things are bad, they are better than they used to be.[12] As such they are very critical of attitudes of those blacks who see the situation of the black man as improving. A small but significant proportion of the new urbanites are young people who have graduated from first-rate colleges and hold white-collar positions in integrated firms. The subtle prejudices which they have encountered, along with the empty lives of the many middle-class whites whom they have met, have increased their awareness that there is a style and tone of life in the black community which gives much more satisfaction than that of the white middle class.[13] The heightened interaction of black youth as a result of urban living, the coming-of-age of a generation of post-World War II youth, and the rejection of some white middle-class values in the attempt to articulate values which grow out of the black experience[14] are some of the internal dynamics of black communities in the 1960's which are producing a new upsurge in nationalism.

The postwar independence movements around the world have also affected the thinking of black people. Earlier generations of black nationalists predicted the rise of Africa as part of the world community. They had preached about the day when "princes would come out of Ethiopia," but the present generation has witnessed that rise. Black urbanites, seeing African diplomats welcomed by American presidents and taking leading roles in the United Nations, became increasingly bitter about the limited freedom and opportunity of Afro-Americans.

While Africans and Asians were gaining independence and taking seats in the halls of world council, the gap between black and white Americans was not changing perceptibly. Since 1960, black males have not made appreciable gains on white males in income and occupation, black communities are more separated from white communities than ever before, and the education of black youth is still woefully inadequate. Even for those middle-class blacks who appear to have made many strides during the 1960's, the evidence indicates that they have made large relative gains over lower-class blacks, but have not reduced the gap between themselves and middle-class whites.[15]

There is one major positive change that has taken place in the past few years, however; a higher proportion of black youth are completing high school and college. Such youth are not following past patterns of individualistic escape from the black community—with their heightened awareness and knowledge,

---

[12] Claude Brown states this issue well by raising the question: "Where does one run to when he's already in the promised land?"—*Manchild in the Promised Land* (New York: The Macmillan Company, 1965), p. 8.

[13] This fact has been discovered by white middle-class youth as well, and they now seek to experience the authentic feeling-tone of Afro-American existence. Among black people, this new form of rejection of white America is authenticated by one's possession of that ethereal quality "soul," and is expressed in the "funky" music of black artists.

[14] For a particularly profound and moving articulation of such issues, see Vincent Harding, "The Gift of Blackness," *Kattallagete* (Summer 1967), pp. 17-22.

[15] J. Herman Blake, "The Black University and Its Community: Social Change in the Sixties," *Negro Digest*, Vol. 17 (March 1968), pp. 87-90.

they are becoming more involved in black communities as residents and as activists. An important and new element in black nationalism is this union of black intellectuals and the black masses. While nationalism in the nineteenth century was notable for its lack of mass support, and for its lack of intellectual backing, in the mass movements of the twentieth century in recent years, intellectuals and the masses have combined their skills to give new impetus to nationalist movements. An excellent example is the development of the Mississippi Freedom Democratic Party.[16]

The key figure in the development of the recent trends was the late El-Hajj Malik El-Shabazz. After his break with the Nation of Islam, he began to link the struggle of Afro-Americans with the struggle of oppressed peoples throughout the world, and particularly in Africa. He also emphasized *human rights* rather than *civil rights*, thereby increasing the hope that the Afro-American struggle might come before the United Nations. In this way, he internationalized the conditions of Afro-Americans and increased their awareness of the value of links with the non-Western world.[17]

Malik El-Shabazz gave new emphasis to the possibility of reform in America, an idea which was not contained in the view of either Marcus Garvey or Elijah Muhammad. In his "The Ballot or the Bullet" speech, he expressed the view that it was possible to produce a bloodless revolution in this country. His views were close to those of earlier nationalists who saw the development of the inner strengths of the black community as a first step in attacking racial barriers.

Another key contribution was his ability to appeal to both intellectuals and the masses and bring them together. El-Shabazz was very widely read, and a brilliant and articulate spokesman. His knowledge and logic impressed black intellectuals deeply. He was also an ex-convict and a man of the streets. Consequently, those who were the most deprived could identify as strongly with him as could the intellectual. His dual appeal to intellectuals and the masses, along with his emphasis upon racial solidarity, helped to bring these two elements of the black community into greater harmony.

In addition, Malik El-Shabazz spurred the development of black consciousness and black dignity. He was a living example of the positive effect of black consciousness, and there were few black people who met him who were not profoundly moved by what he was. Said one writer: "The concept of Blackness, the concept of National Consciousness, the proposal of a political (and diplomatic) form for this aggregate of Black Spirit, these are the things given to us by Garvey, through Elijah Muhammad, and finally given motion into still another

---

[16] Stokely Carmichael and Charles V. Hamilton, *Black Power: The Politics of Liberation in America* (New York: Random House, 1967).
[17] Malcolm X, *Autobiography* (New York: Grove Press, 1966); also, the brief movie *Malcolm X: Struggle for Freedom* gives important insights into his post-Nation of Islam ideas, including his expansion of the concept "Afro-American."

area of Black Response by Malcolm X."[18] Another captures the nature of the appeal of El-Shabazz:

> It was not the Black Muslim movement itself that was so irresistibly appealing to the true believers. It was the awakening into self-consciousness of twenty million Negroes which was so compelling. Malcolm X articulated their aspirations better than any other man of our time. When he spoke under the banner of Elijah Muhammad, he was irresistible. When he spoke under his own banner, he was still irresistible. If he had become a Quaker, . . . and if he had continued to give voice to the mute ambitions in the black man's soul, his message would still have been triumphant: because what was great was not Malcolm X but the truth he uttered.[19]

In the minds of present-day nationalists, El-Hajj Malik El-Shabazz was the greatest prince to come out of Ethiopia, and he is now the martyred saint of the movement.[20]

The articulation and development of the concept of Black Power continues the emphasis on an integral form of black nationalism,[21] yet with new elements. The political emphasis of Black Power renews the hope for reform in America, but with attention given to a reform of *values* as well as *behavior*. As such, it strikes more deeply at the basis of the problems separating blacks and whites. Black Power advocates also add a strong community orientation to black nationalism. They have not sought to build a unified mass movement around the country, but rather to develop programs and policies relating to the particular needs, conditions, and expressed desires of specific communities. The articulation of Black Power by a student-based organization, along with its community orientation, continued the unified approach of the intellectuals and the masses.

The development of black nationalist thought since the rise of El-Hajj Malik El-Shabazz has brought new emphasis to old issues, particularly the political and cultural forms of nationalism. The political emphasis is developing around the issues of colonization of black people, land, independence, self-determination for black communities, and the accountability of black leaders. When Malik El-Shabazz began to link black people with the Third World—a trend continued by Black Power advocates—black people became more aware that their situation in this country was very similar to that of colonized peoples throughout the world.

[18] LeRoi Jones, *Home* (New York: Morrow, 1966), p. 243.
[19] Eldridge Cleaver, *Soul on Ice* (New York: McGraw-Hill, 1968), p. 59.
[20] See the moving eulogy of El-Hajj Malik El-Shabazz by Ossie Davis in *Liberator*, Vol. 5 (April 1965), p. 7.
[21] Stokely Carmichael, "What We Want," *New York Review of Books*, Vol. 7, September 22, 1965, p. 5.

The large numbers of blacks in central cities, along with the presence of agencies of social control directed by forces outside of the black communities, bears a strong resemblance to a colonial situation.[22] This awareness has brought many blacks to the realization that such aggregations are similar to nations in the same way that Indian tribes saw themselves as nations, and they now occupy a territory which can be viewed as their own. LeRoi Jones puts it thus:

> What the Black Man must do now is to look down at the ground upon which he stands, and claim it as his own. It is not abstract. Look down! Pick up the earth, or jab your fingernails into the concrete. It is real and it is yours, if you want it.
>
> All the large concentrations of Black People in the West are already nations. All that is missing is the consciousness of this state of affairs.[23]

This awareness and consciousness is growing rapidly, and the emphasis upon self-determination for black communities is evidence of this fact. Indeed, if one understands this intense desire of black people to control their own communities and to determine their destinies, the urban insurrections of recent years take on another facet. If the community is seen as a colony and the social control agencies as colonial agents, then spontaneous outbursts may also be interpreted as attempts to reaffirm local rather than foreign control of the community. An altercation between a police officer and a black man is an assertion of colonial control, and the ensuing outburst, however destructive, is a reaffirmation of the view that such control does not lie exclusively with the colonial agencies.[24] Related to self-determination is the emphasis upon accountability being developed by nationalists. This view holds that those who hold positions of power which affect the black community must answer exclusively to the black community.

Colonization, land, self-determination, and accountability are the basic elements in recent developments in black nationalism, particularly the expansion of its political emphasis. Such views led one group of black militants, the Federation for Self-Determination in Detroit, to reject a grant of $100,000 from the New Detroit Committee in early 1968 on the grounds that there were too many controls attached to the grant. Such views led the militant Black Panther party, based in Oakland, California, to begin to develop a political program on the grounds that black men who represent either of the major political parties cannot be held wholly accountable by the black community. Similar examples can be found in black communities across the nation, for these views are crucial aspects of the present framework of action of black nationalists today.

[22] For two excellent articulations of this view, see: Carmichael and Hamilton, *op. cit.*, chap. i; and Cleaver, *op. cit.*, pp. 112-137.

[23] Jones, *op. cit.*, pp. 244 and 249.

[24] See Anthony Oberschall, "The Los Angeles Riot of August 1965," *Social Problems*, Vol. 15 (Winter 1968), pp. 322-341.

In recent years, black consciousness has received added impetus in terms of racial solidarity and a positive self-image. Thus, there is the new emphasis upon black as beautiful, and black youth are adopting African-style clothing and wearing African or natural hair styles.[25] They are seeking to establish black studies and black curricula on college campuses. These courses of study, however, are to have a strong community and service orientation, rather than to become wholly intellectual pursuits. It is unquestionably the development of black consciousness and racial solidarity, along with the attitude of self-determination and black accountability, which has spurred the revolt of black athletes in many colleges and the attempt to obtain a black boycott of the 1968 Olympic Games. This is a new and revolutionary black consciousness, exemplified by El-Hajj Malik El-Shabazz and activated among black communities across the land.

SUMMARY AND CONCLUSION

Black nationalism has been one of the most militant and strident forms of Afro-American protest. It has grown out of the social conditions which have repeatedly indicated to black people that, though they are in this country, they are not a part of this country. The most recent emphases in nationalist thought are clearly developing the inner strengths of the black community through cultural nationalism, and expanding the concept of political nationalism. It may well be that black people will find that after all other barriers between the races have been eliminated, the barrier of color will prove to be ineradicable. Such a realization will give new and revolutionary impetus to black nationalism.

> Some of us have been, and some still are, interested in learning whether it is ultimately possible to live in the same territory with people who seem so disagreeable to live with; still others want to get as far away from ofays as possible.
>
> Eldridge Cleaver

---

[25] I received an excellent personal view of the impact of the new black consciousness on youth while teaching Afro-American history to junior high school youth each summer in a black community near San Francisco. In 1966, I showed the youths a picture of Crispus Attucks, and some of them exclaimed, "He's sure got a nappy head." In 1967 this same picture was greeted with the comment, "He's got a boss natural." This was the same community and some of the same youth. The only thing that had changed was their consciousness of themselves.

POSITIVE AND NEGATIVE EFFECTS OF CHICANO MILITANCY ON THE EDUCATION OF THE MEXICAN-AMERICAN[1]

NANCIE L. GONZALEZ

STATEMENT OF THE PROBLEM

During the school year of 1968-69 there were more than a dozen riots, sit-ins, walkouts, and other militant protest gestures staged in various high schools and colleges throughout the Southwestern part of the United States and elsewhere by a new and extremely vociferous type of Mexican-American. Suddenly, the non-Spanish-speaking community in many areas was made to realize that the apathetic, resigned, and humble Mexican (if he ever did exist) has been replaced, transformed, or at least joined by his brothers of a more bellicose stance. The new Chicano, like the older Mexican-American, wants change in the relationship between him and his society, but he has new means for making his wants known to the public. It is ironic that researchers for at least 40 years have detailed most of the problems to which the young Chicano today is addressing his attention. We have known the effects of the present educational system upon this minority for a very long time, but as Armando Rodriguez has said repeatedly in speeches throughout the nation, "There comes a time when we must simply hit people over the head in order to have any effect."

It is not difficult to outline the demands of the Chicano voices today, and it is also possible to perceive various currents of interest which, although not united in terms of their overall philosophy, have nevertheless coalesced in a focus upon the problem of education for the Mexican-American today.This paper will attempt to name and describe the various types of activist Chicano movements operating primarily in the five Southwestern states of California, Texas, Arizona, New Mexico, and Colorado, but also in Chicago, Kansas City, and other areas where large numbers of Mexican-Americans live. A classification will be offered as an aid to analysis. This will point up some of the basic elements involved, including age, economic, and probably philosophical differences among the members of the different organizations. Some of these groups are unique, one of a kind, being focused primarily upon a single problem or endeavor. The majority, however, have multiple purposes, and differ from each other only in emphasis or in some of the factors noted above. The actual demands being made by these groups will

Nancie L. Gonzalez is Professor and Chairman of the Department of Anthropology at the University of Iowa, Iowa City, Iowa.

[1] This paper has been prepared for the Southwestern Cooperative Educational Laboratory, Albuquerque, New Mexico. Grateful acknowledgement is made to Terry Alliband, who ably assisted in the review of the literature.

be outlined, and suggestions made as to the social context with which they are associated. Finally, I will suggest some of the probable effects on education of the different types of militancy, and suggest areas for further research to help us better understand the situation as it develops.

THE MOVEMENTS

To this writer's knowledge there has been no research focused specifically upon modern Chicano militancy except for that dealing with Cesar Chavez's United Farm Workers Organizing Committee, and the Alianza de los Pueblos Libres headed by Reies Tijerina in New Mexico. The information included here, in addition to the few scholarly sources available, comes from a perusal of Chicano newspapers and from an occasional story in an Anglo paper or magazine such as the ALBUQUERQUE NEWS, THE NATION, and NEWSWEEK, as well as from reports on conferences and congresses of Chicanos and others dealing with Chicano affairs.

It should be stressed that from a social scientific point of view we really don't know much about the new Chicano activists, other than that they are young. We know little about the kinds of socioeconomic backgrounds from which the most vociferous come, their total goals, world views, etc. Hopefully, this situation will be remedied in the near future. A few journalistic accounts have appeared, and various scholars have referred to militancy in essays (Bongartz 1969; Ericksen 1968; Gonzalez 1969; Guzman and Moore 1966; Heller 1970; Love 1969; Romano 1969; Swadesh 1968). In preparing for this paper, the writer sent letters to all members of the Chicano Press Association asking for copies of their publications and any other information they might have concerning the role of Chicano organizations in pressing for educational change. Two of the communications were returned unopened, with notices to the effect that the organizations were no longer at this address, and had not left any forwarding instructions. In another case, a letter was received stating that the newspaper was no longer in existence. The writer is a regular subscriber of still another paper, and materials were received from two others. The remainder failed to reply, nor was this researcher able to obtain copies of their newspapers. Therefore, most of the information concerning organizations is derived from news reports in EL CHICANO (San Bernardino, California; EL GALLO (Denver, Colorado); and EL GRITO DEL NORTE (Española, ñola, New Mexico). Nevertheless, a surprising number of organizations *was* mentioned in these three papers, and the writer believes that most of those with a broader national scope have been included. It is also clear that numerous regional and even local groups are beginning to appear. Although not all of these have been identified in this paper, the fact of their probable existence can be stated, and a few of them can be described.

It is difficult to classify the organizations because many of them have overlapping interests and memberships.* On the other hand, there do seem to be some

* In the original article the author included in an appendix a listing of forty-one organizations.

criteria by means of which we can group them. For example, there are some which have been in existence for some time, and which are composed mostly of middle-class Mexican-Americans interested in furthering the general welfare of their ethnic group and in providing a mutual-aid environment for their members. These function for the most part as social clubs, but may also be active as political pressure groups. Here are included the GI Forum, the League of United Latin American Citizens (LULAC), the Alianza Hispano-Americana (probably the oldest of all groups to be mentioned here), the Community Service Organization (CSO), the Mexican-American Anti-Defamation Committee, the Mexican-American Political Association (MAPA), and the Political Association of Spanish-Speaking Organizations (PASO).[2] Actually, the last four are much younger than the first three as organizations, but operate in a similar relatively conservative fashion. Members of these groups, most of whom are Hispanos who have "made it," are activist in the sense that they work together to try to get Mexican-Americans elected to public office, appointed to positions of responsibility at various levels of government, and to combat some of the worst features of discrimination and derogation. Nevertheless, these groups have never engaged in what might be called militant action, preferring to use the quieter mechanisms of distributing pamphlets, making radio and newspaper announcements, and seeking victory at the polls.

These groups also serve to further their internal solidarity by giving fiestas, dances, and other social functions for members and their families. The Alianza Hispano-Americana has for years published a magazine carrying news of members, and especially of those who have been successful in the Anglo world.

Other organizations, also relatively new and also largely conservative in overall philosophy, include the Southwest Council of La Raza, the Colorado Federation of Latin American Organizations, and the Council for Civic Unity (located in the Bay Area, and actually a coalition of minority organizations). The Southwest Council of La Raza is largely supported by the Ford Foundation, which also sponsored the Mexican-American Study Project conducted at the Graduate School of Business Research at UCLA. These organizations differ from the above in that they are umbrella structures with a more complex internal organization. They are also likely to have a broader, program-oriented schedule of activities, and operate less as a mutual-aid society or social club. The Chicano Press Association is also an umbrella type structure in that it includes a variety of newspapers, and in this capacity, must be considered an integral part of the total movement. The papers themselves vary in emphasis, quality, format, and political stance, but significantly, do not include all those Spanish language newspapers published. EL HISPANO of Albuquerque, is not, for example, a member. Sometimes a newspaper seems to be especially related to a particular organization. EL CHICANO, for example, has found it necessary to deny that it is a mouthpiece for MAPA. EL GRITO DEL NORTE quite openly serves as a means of furthering the cause of

---

[2] It is not known to this writer whether this is the same as the organization sometimes listed as PASSO, Political Action for Spanish-Speaking Organizations.

Tijerina's Alianza. EL GALLO regularly carries news items and advertisements concerning the activities of Corky Gonzales and the Crusade for Justice.

There are a few organizations which cater especially to the poor and extremely disadvantaged. These are largely composed of poor people, although the leadership is frequently drawn, at least in part, from outside that group. Here we would include the Alianza Federal de los Pueblos Libres (formerly the Alianza Federal de Mercedes) in New Mexico, the League of United Citizens to Help Addicts (LUCHA), the Chicano Welfare Rights Organization, which like Life with Pride in Albuquerque, is composed largely of women on welfare, the Dependency Prevention Commission, Community Action Groups, the Mexican-American Legal Defense and Educational Fund, and the United Farm Workers Organizing Committee. Most of these have one particular issue with which they are most concerned, ranging from the recovery of lost Spanish land grants in the case of the first, to the effort to improve the condition of migrant laborers in California. They stress education of the poor to know their rights, and to band together in order to secure them. Although some of these have also taken a stand on education of Mexican-Americans, this has not been their primary concern. We shall also include here the Crusade for Justice and the National Chicano Congress of Aztlan, which are also aimed at the less advantaged Mexican-Americans, but which have multiple purpose programs.

This is a rather large number of groups which are specifically concerned with improvement of formal education for Mexican-Americans. Some of these are made up of educators themselves—the Association of Mexican-American Educators (AMAE), the Congress of Hispanic Educators, and the Mexican-American Parent Advisory Organization (MAPAO) in San Bernardino, California. As might be expected, these particular groups behave in a fashion not designed to create riots. However, their demands are accented by the activities of a number of very active, in some cases, militant youth groups. These include the following: UMAS (United Mexican-American Students), by far the most important, widespread, and active of all the student organizations; MAFS (Mexican-American Federation of Students); MASC (Mexican-American Student Confederation), MAS (Mexican-American Students), MECHA (Movimiento Estudientil [sic] Chicano de Aztlan); MAYA (Mexican-American Youth Association); MAYO (Mexican-American Youth Organization); MASA (Mexican-American Student Association); CLO (Chicano Leadership Organization); the Brown Berets, and a number of what appear to be local youth groups. Interestingly, the names of the latter tend to reflect only ethnicity, thus differing from most of the others, which describe their interests and frequently form acronyms which are themselves symbolic of their cause. Thus, for example, there are found, among others, La Causa, Los Carnales, Los Boleros, and Los Caballeros de Nueva Spain. At first this list, which I am sure is only partial, appears to include a bewildering array of organizations—especially for an ethnic group the members of which have been characterized as non-joiners. Certainly this is a myth which should long ago have been exploded, but which now must certainly be abandoned.

Let us see what sense we can make of it all. It is noteworthy that the newer organizations function in a variety of institutional situations. These include schools, prisons, churches, sub-communities such as barrios of the larger urban conglomerations, among drug addicts, and among persons bound together by the fact that they are all on welfare. Even the older organizations were based upon feelings of unity which stemmed from a commonality of experience or interest—members might all be veterans of World War II, businessmen, members of the same community, etc. It is important to note that Chicanos seem to prefer organizing their own interest groups rather than joining those of Anglos, even when their goals are identical. For example, last fall there was a Chicano moratorium committee established in East Los Angeles, which demonstrated against the Vietnam war as a separate pressure unit. Similarly, in some communities a Mexican Chamber of Commerce working side by side with, but separately from, the Anglo Chamber of Commerce can be found. From evidence gleaned from news accounts in the various media mentioned, it seems that the youth groups sometimes behave similarly to Anglo youth groups in their efforts to get things done and to organize. Thus, they elect queens, serve dinners in order to raise money, sponsor talent shows, etc.

The youth groups have been organized mostly through the high schools and in the colleges of the Southwest. The Brown Berets is an example of a youth organization with a base in the community rather than in the schools. It is possible that the functioning of this organization might be better understood if compared with the small gang (Palomilla) activities of Mexican-Americans in South Texas as described by Rubel (1966). The descriptions of Pachuco gang philosophy and solidarity during the 1940's suggest an historical basis for the community-based youth protest groups (Griffith 1948).

However, one of the most outstanding elements of most of the youth organizations and the factor which distinguishes them from all the more conservative organizations of their elders as well as from earlier movements such as that of the Pachucos, is the influence of the Black civil rights movements. The Chicanos have adopted a number of slogans and other symbols of their cause, some of which are directly taken from the Blacks, such as the brown berets worn by members of that organization, and clearly modeled after the berets worn by the Young Lords and the Black Panthers.

In an attempt to define the word "Chicano" one young man noted that it was as difficult to define as "soul." Similarly, the phrases "Brown Power," and "Brown is beautiful," appear from time to time even in the press, and clearly denote the influence of the Black Power movement. A direct translation of "We shall overcome" is the slogan "Venceremos."

Other symbols which have been utilized by the young Chicanos include the shout of "Huelga!" This word, meaning "strike," derives not only from the grape pickers' strike in California, but reflects the Latin American aspect of the culture. Latin American students shout "Huelga!" whenever they wish to protest the establishment. Similarly, "el grito" refers to "el grito de dolores," the rallying cry which set off hostilities in the Mexican Revolution. In addition, one finds the phrases "La Causa," "La Raza," "Carnalismo" (brotherhood), and most recently, "Aztlan," an Aztec word used here to signify peace, brotherhood, and the desire for a separate Chicano homeland in the Southwest. It literally means "land to the north," which is logical if one's referent point is Mexico. Even the term "Chicano" has become symbolic of the new radical youth. Again quoting from EL CHICANO, "A Chicano is a Mexican-American with a non-Anglo self image," and further, "Yesterday's Pachuco—today's Chicano" (January 12, 1970).

However, the Chicanos strongly assert their independence from other civil rights groups, and have even been known to be hostile to the demands of other minority groups. In this regard, one statement taken from EL CHICANO went as follows: "La Raza is not white, is not black; La Raza is La Raza, a separate, unique people who have much to contribute."

Another interesting element of the young Chicano movements is their use of drama as a mechanism for teaching their still uncommitted brethren and the larger society. Thus there are in the California region alone El Teatro Chicano, El Teatro Popular de la Vida y Muerte, El Teatro Campesino, and El Teatro Urbano. In explaining this it is tempting to recall the successful use of dramatic effects by the Catholic Church in the original conquest of Indian minds and souls in the Southwest and Mexico. However, it is also noteworthy that this technique has been used with some success by both black and white radical youth movements in our nation. I suggest that the latter is the most direct source of inspiration.

It is clear in the case of some of these groups that their interests are closely bound up with the problems of other oppressed segments of the population both in the United States and in the world at large. Thus, in one issue of one of the more militant newspapers, stories were carried on the following subjects: The Alianza Federal de Mercedes, Women Guerrillas in Vietnam, the Chicago Eight Conspiracy Trial, The Indians of Alcatraz, SNCC, Jose Martí (the Revolutionary Hero of the 19th Century Hispanic Caribbean), Che Guevara, a quote from Camilo Torres (the martyred Columbian revolutionary priest), the Young Lords in New York City, the massacre of students in Mexico City last year, the evil effects of drug addiction, the pollution of our environment, and an announcement of a conference to be sponsored by the Crusade for Justice in Denver.

MILITANCY AND MEXICAN-AMERICAN EDUCATION

Let us briefly review the demands of the new Chicano voices. There seems to be general agreement on measures needed to improve the education of their young. There is an overwhelming demand to strengthen instruction in the Spanish language and the culture which it symbolizes—a demand which reflects their fear of cultural deprivation and eventual annihilation as a distinct ethnic group. Furthermore, it is recognized that the Chicano child, when entering the first grade with little knowledge of English, is unable to compete with his Anglo peers and tends to fall a little farther behind each year until the gap is too wide to be made up. There is a felt need, indeed a firm demand, that bi-lingual education be offered to Chicanos. By this is meant instruction in Spanish, with English being taught as a foreign language until the child has sufficient grasp of both so that instruction may be given in either one. Some Chicanos (and some Anglos) feel that in order to avoid the deleterious effects of inevitable segregation, this kind of bi-lingual education should be applied to *all* children in those areas of high Mexican-American settlement. Other Chicanos urge such measures only for Chicano youngsters. In the latter case, the problem may be exacerbated by the difficulty of distinguishing between Chicano and non-Chicano, since to an increasing extent the Spanish language has already been largely abandoned for home use. Some children of Spanish heritage would fall into the same category as Anglos who learn Spanish as a foreign language. In any case, the ultimate goal is the ability to communicate with equal facility in both English and Spanish by the fourth or fifth grade. It would seem that this goal should hold attraction for both Mexican-Americans and Anglos, since there are obvious advantages to being bi-lingual in today's world. Furthermore, studies show that the truly bi-lingual child performs better than the monolingual child (Kosinski 1963; Peal and Lambert 1962).

Other demands relating to change in the educational system include a revised testing procedure for Mexican-American children to indicate more accurately their achievement and potential success. Numerous studies have shown that when tested in the English language, the Spanish speaking child tends to do poorly, and is thereby often relegated to "retarded" status, from which he is rarely elevated. Thirdly, there is a demand that the teachers and school administrators know more about both the heritage and the current condition of the Mexican-American child outside the school. It has been repeatedly suggested that all teachers and administrators presently employed be required to take courses to update them in this knowledge, and to teach them at least the rudiments of the Spanish language. At the same time there are demands for the hiring of more Spanish speaking teachers and administrators across the board.

A fourth demand is that the curriculum be adjusted so that the Mexican-American child learns of the role of his Spanish and Indian forebears in the discovery, colonization, and development of the New World and especially of the United States. It is expected that such emphasis will lead to greater pride in their ethnic group, and concomitantly to a greater sense of personal worth and dignity. The U.S. Commission on Civil Rights (1968:31) noted in comparing Mexican-American and Mexican born children in schools in the United States that the former tended to be less secure and generally timid and ashamed. Clearly, the self-image of these children is the result of social experiences which tend to denigrate the Mexican-American culture and its bearers. For Anglos, such education may help to destroy commonly held derogatory stereotypes. Similarly, and as a logical extension of this demand, there is the idea that teachers should emphasize the present role of the Mexican-American in the United States as a whole. Although it is primarily at the college level that one hears the cry for a program of Chicano Studies, there is generally the feeling that greater attention should be placed upon dignifying the Mexican-American culture in *all* its aspects.

There is also a need for the development of teaching materials which reflect the already extant pluralism in the Southwest. Thus, stories should include some Spanish surnamed children as playmates of "Dick and Jane." The drawings in textbooks should also be revised so as to reflect Mexican-American phenotypes.

Finally, it is being urged that the Mexican-American community as a whole should be drawn into the school decision-making process. It has been pointed out that the Mexican-American child is not school-oriented because his family as a whole is not (Rodriguez: n.d. *Counseling and Guidance for the Mexican-American Student*). It is felt that the school authorities should not simply sit back and cluck about the fact that Mexican-American parents do not come to the PTA meetings. Rather, there should be positive efforts to seek out the parents and to find meaningful ways of including them so as to engage their interests in the problems of their children and of the school system as a whole.

At the college level there is a demand for compensatory education in the sense that policies should vigorously favor members of minority groups rather than simply giving them equality. Thus, at a minimum, there should be larger numbers of scholarships for Mexican-Americans in existing institutions; and preferably there should be developed tuition-free high quality colleges in order to further remedy the fact that so few Mexican-Americans go on to the universities. Finally there are demands which are more symbolic in nature but which may be equally important in terms of assuaging student ire. These include demands that Mexican food be served in the school cafeterias, that cafeteria prices be lowered, that permission to speak Spanish on the school property be granted, that Mexican music be played at school dances, and that Mexican-Americans be included among class officers and on Student Senates.

These demands illustrate that the education designed for the Anglo middle-class American has never actually reached groups with different histories and social characteristics. Even in comparison with other deprived segments of the population, the Chicanos come out poorly. The drop-out rate in some high schools in the Southwest has at times been over 60% for Chicanos—higher than for any other group (Rodriguez 1968:3). In California, where the Mexican-American population is twice that of Blacks (Rodriguez 1968:2), the latter nevertheless outnumber Chicanos nine to one in the Berkeley Opportunity Program. The average Chicano in California reaches only 8th grade, while the Black achieves 10.5 years of education, and the Anglo 12.1 years (Bongartz 1969:272). The Chicano believes, perhaps with reason, that the louder voices of the Black minority group have been instrumental in achieving some progress for them in the schools. Whether this is true or not, it is clear that Chicano silence has been broken forever. The push from now on will be to convince school authorities that it is wrong and useless to try to change the children who fail; that it is rather a necessity to change the system which failed them.

This leads us to a consideration of still another matter—one which is recognized by the most militant, and perhaps explains their alliance with interest groups beyond the narrow Mexican-American range itself. The question must always be asked—education for what? It is clear to many that the broader parameters of the American system limit the kinds of jobs and way of life open to the Mexican-American youth, regardless of what education he may receive. As Rodriquez has said, "The education they are receiving, even with a high school diploma, will not prepare them for much more than what they can obtain without that diploma." This means that the drop-out rate is perhaps a response to the realization that school for the Mexican-Americans does not bring the same rewards that it brings for the WASP. This point has been made by Lyle Shannon (1968:52) who says, "Not all Mexican-Americans . . . have the same definitions of success as do Anglos. Those who do find that the larger society is not organized in such a manner that the payoff comes to them in the same way that it comes to Anglos."

PROBABLE EFFECTS OF MILITANCY ON THE EDUCATION OF MEXICAN-AMERICANS

a. SHORT RUN EFFECTS

It seems likely that the kinds of militant philosophy and action now being presented to the Mexican-American student may temporarily increase the drop-out rate by providing dissatisfied, unhappy, isolated Chicano students with a new focus for identification. It may make more students aware of their condition, and thus increase dissatisfaction. It is likely that the youth groups will more and more infiltrate the high schools where the problems are worst. College students have, by definition, "made it"—they have struggled through the maze of WASP education and gained admission to elite status. These college students themselves may very likely reach out to organize high schools and communities in order to help those brothers and sisters not as lucky as they are.[3]

High school students are especially good targets for this type of awareness education because by this time in their lives many have fallen so far behind through their poor beginnings that there are obvious and painful differences in performance between them and their Anglo peers. They are now also fully aware of even the most subtle prejudice and discrimination. Unlike Blacks, the Mexican-American is not often outstanding in athletics, and therefore does not even have this kind of activity within which to bury his frustrations.[4]

On the other hand, the increase in organized Chicano clubs within the high

---

[3] A good example of this is the recent action of UMAS on the campus of the University of New Mexico. This group discovered a long-standing case of discrimination against Mexican-American employees in the physical plant. They called this to the attention of the administration, faculty, state legislature, and community at large. The situation has not been completely resolved, but UMAS has made a good beginning at increasing the awareness of the local Spanish-speaking community as well as that of the Anglo population.

[4] However, Griffith (1948:54) has noted that in Los Angeles in the early 1940's Mexican-American youngsters were granted a favorable reputation in athletics, music, and woodcrafting.

schools may also have the effect of decreasing the drop-out rate by giving the students a cause for which they can work within the school system itself. If these clubs are encouraged, rather than ridiculed or repressed, they may serve to absorb the energies of the students, and in the long run detract from the more revolutionary demands which would seem to be inevitable otherwise. That is, these clubs may dissipate their energies in striking for Mexican foods, Mexican queens, Mexican class officers and the like, rather than making any real changes in the system as a whole.

There is also the possibility that, if the demands are not quickly answered in one way or another, there will be increased violence in the schools, resulting in the destruction of property and possibly of lives. There is good reason to believe some elements of the new Chicano youth movement are fully capable of taking really violent action. Such groups will not be satisfied with token improvements such as those outlined in the preceding paragraph. To the extent that the community and school boards fail to make basic changes as demanded, they may expect increasingly violent action. This in turn may force communities to respond to their demands by reorganizing the school systems along the lines described. In those areas with a heavy Mexican-American representation, it is likely that the process of drawing the community into the schools may succeed in forcing some of the issues related to preparation and hiring of teachers. In areas where Anglos are still able to dominate the school boards and set school policy, it may require a long-drawn-out series of small but violent incidents to have any effect.

Certainly, the issue of bi-lingual education is one which may create polarization, not only between the Anglos on the one hand and the Mexican-American group on the other, but even within the Mexican-American group itself. Since many of the older generation feel that they were able to succeed in an economic sense only when they substituted English for Spanish as their native tongue, many of them feel strongly about this particular issue. They and their parents suffered so much because of the stigma of speaking English imperfectly and with a "foreign" accent that their reaction is frequently to repress Spanish altogether. It will require considerable education of this group before they are likely to devote time, effort, and money to bring Spanish back into the system in such a fundamental way as that suggested by the proponents of bi-lingual education.

It is likely that considerable discussion and procrastination will occur before this issue is resolved. On the other hand, there is also some evidence that even the most conservative are finding it unfashionable today to deny their Spanish cultural background, especially if they are in the public eye. Even those who believe most firmly in the "melting pot" philosophy would be wise to reconsider this position if they wish to continue garnering votes among their brethren.

b. LONG RUN EFFECTS

If the demands outlined above are met, and if the present education of Mexican-Americans is improved, it will eventually result in a pool of more skilled and professional Mexican-American workers, who will in turn demand open opportunities in the world to which they graduate. Education does not change the value system simply by teaching new values. Rather, it tends to reinforce and support current ones. But it seems clear from recent events involving today's under-30 generation, that it *can* force change by producing a sophisticated, aware graduate, who understands finally why his group, or any other disadvantaged group, is in the fix it is in. Such graduates yearn for change, and are susceptible to revolutionary philosophy when they feel powerless to bring it about in any other way.

Perhaps it is for such reasons that the established elements have put aside action on problems such as those dealt with in this paper. Evidence has been steadily accumulating for over 40 years that has never been taken into account in the actual school programs. Perhaps there has been a fear that improved education will make the Chicano "forget his place." If it is meant by this that he will recognize that he has been poorly treated, it is a correct assumption, of course, and today's climate confirms it. But it is now too late—the cat is out of the bag, and failure to provide it with catnip and tasty food may bring total disaster for the system as we now know it.

Many of those clamoring for change say that they do not want to destroy the system, they want only to improve it. But they must recognize that improvement of the educational system will point up defects in the larger social system. This then, may lead to efforts to improve that as well. I would predict that increased awareness of the world through improved education will radicalize more Mexican-Americans—make them more dissatisfied with the way things are put together. As part of this change there is likely to be a change in the personality structure and role of Chicano females. Even today the younger Chicanas are less cloistered, less reticent than the ideal taught by their culture. They are attending rallies, speaking out, writing in newspapers, and joining the activist males in demanding their rights.

In spite of some attempts to suggest otherwise (Romano 1969), the new militancy *is* different from Mexican-American protests in the past. It is a product of the new youth and the New Left, from which it has drawn inspiration and sustenance. There is a kind of pan-minority philosophy here in which ethnicity becomes subordinated to socio-economic considerations. The *rhetoric* of the Chicano movement stresses ethnicity, but at the same time it is clear that their major goal is the same as that of United States Blacks and American Indians—namely a place in the decision-making apparatus and process, and through this, a better way of life for the disadvantaged of their group.

Let us briefly consider the relationship between the kinds of demands made by the older Spanish-speaking activists and those of the Chicanos. Groups such as the G.I. Forum, LULAC, etc. were concerned about the acceptance of Mexican-Americans on all social occasions. They wished to improve the status of their group through desegregation of schools, equal acceptance of Mexican-Americans in politics and employment, and in society as a whole. Their means for achieving these goals lay primarily in internal education. By this they often meant "self-improvement," or acculturation to some of the Anglo patterns. Primarily, they were concerned with learning English and with the outward symbols of the Anglo world. In a sense they were following the philosophy of "beating the Anglos at their own game," in order to achieve some success in the Anglo world. As a whole they were quiet as individuals, lobbying through their organizational fronts, but rarely causing any ripples in the smooth waters of their communities. As such, they were relatively successful. In New Mexico especially, the position of Spanish-speaking persons has improved steadily since World War II (Gonzalez 1969). Yet, they did not necessarily become Anglicized in this process. They lived double lives, perhaps, but overwhelmingly tended to retain much of whatever it is that makes this group distinguishable from all others. The important point here, and one which many militants will reject, is that they *remained* basically Mexican-American (or Spanish-American). At the same time, there was too often an unhealthy lack of ethnic pride, except in New Mexico where the social fabric was woven a bit differently.[5]

The modern Chicano, on the other hand, is also interested in the goals described above. However, *in addition,* he stresses retention of the Spanish language and culture as well as a recognition of the value of his heritage by both Mexican-Americans and Anglos. And finally, he is concerned with forcing Anglos to recognize the fallacy of the notion of "cultural deprivation" in that it is the middle-class American system and not the Chicano that is deprived!

The means used by the youths are also quite different from those of a generation ago. The Chicano youth has focused upon the school system and the lower-income community as the primary targets for change. Mexican-American internal education focuses upon the plight of the poor modern Chicano, and the formation of new organizations and mechanisms to carry forth the new philosophy and to force the kinds of changes here outlined. In a nutshell, the new Chicano wants the Anglo and his society to change in order to accommodate him, rather than vice-versa, as seems to have been the case in the older activist organizations.

Finally, some of the most militant also want

1. a revamping of the whole society,

2. liaisons with other minority civil rights groups and with Third World liberation efforts, and

3. a revolution within the Chicano society itself.

The means by which they hope to achieve these include the items mentioned above, but also any violent action necessary in order to make themselves heard, and to destroy the existing system should that appear necessary.

It is not clear to this writer whether the leaders of the most militant branches of Chicano activism fully understand the implications of their philosophy for the future of Chicano culture itself. That is, it seems that many of the values and characteristics most frequently touted as being typical of the Spanish world view and sociocultural system will soon be forced to disappear in the effort to conform

[5] See Gonzalez 1969 for elaboration of this point.

to supra-ethnic civil rights trends. The newspapers referred to above, particularly EL GRITO DEL NORTE indicate that this process is already underway. For example, the latter paper exhorts its readers to examine the role of the Catholic Church vis-à-vis minorities everywhere, and severely criticizes the Church for its elitist position. Similarly, the young people today frequently find themselves in opposition to their elders, even within their own families. This is likely to place stresses upon the traditional unity of that group, as well as upon the authority of the older over the younger. Finally, as mentioned above, the position of the woman is very likely to undergo drastic change. As the young Chicanos increasingly confront the outer world, the new women's liberation movements will to an increasing extent affect the young Chicana. Similarly, her role as the protected, silent, and obedient wife and mother will soon be considered inadequate by the girls who are encouraged to take part in the protest marches.

It has been noted by Ericksen (1968) that the most activist among Mexican-Americans are those already most Anglo in their attitudes—more aware of their rights and of the "machinery of democracy." Also, Heller (1970:454) has recently done a study showing a new trend toward upward mobility among Mexican-American youth. Both of these observations indicate that acculturation is already indeed underway. It is ironic that the very movements which most stress the retention of the Spanish language and culture should be those which step irretrievably past the boundaries of ethnicity in their cooperative efforts. Social scientists have documented the behavior of many immigrant groups who first reject and then stress the retention of the symbols of their ancestry—the latter occurring only when they have already nearly disappeared into the melting pot, and as Heller has noted, the Mexican-Americans, unlike the Blacks, *do* have the social characteristics of immigrants.

Before World War I there was in the United States a generally favorable climate toward cultural pluralism. Germans and other nationality sub-groups in the Midwest used their language as one means of warding off Americanization. World War I, with its Americanization movement, brutally forced these groups to conform. This, in spite of the previously open attitude exemplified by John Dewey who said in 1915 ". . . Our public schools shall teach every factor to respect every other, and shall take pains to enlighten all as to the great past contributions of every strain in our composite make up" (quoted by Gordon 1964:139). It is possible, of course, that had World War I not intervened, the plural society might have become the American Way. Today, admittedly there seems to be a resurgence of enthusiasm for the recognition of the worth of different ethnic heritages within the nation. Let us hope that no reactionary movements step in to interfere with the fulfillment of the potential these seem to hold. However, should the society be faced with further internal or external crises, there is always the danger that real or imagined national insecurity will lead to greater intolerance of difference, and that the philosophy of the plural society will be crushed.

Should this happen, there is likely to be increased polarization within La Raza. Some will continue to assimilate towards the Anglo middle-class way of life, where they have already found that it is possible to succeed. On the other hand, even those who think they are not assimilating are likely to be drawn increasingly into the radical orbit of the New Left, where cultural differences are also likely to disappear.

SUGGESTIONS FOR RESEARCH

A final note lest the readers think these remarks have come to a pessimistic conclusion. Much of the foregoing is of necessity conjectural. Research is sorely needed, both on the Chicano middle class, and on the new Chicano militants themselves. But more than this, I would stress the need for a greater understanding of the United States society as a whole. I suggest that we will never understand Chicano militancy without understanding the causes of the pressures placed upon this and other minority groups. There are suggestions recently within the field of anthropology that what is most lacking is an understanding of the power structure and of the roles of various segments of our population in determining the life pattern of others. It is clear that there are certain components which have virtually no control over their own fate, much less that of others. As in reference to life in the Black ghettos, it is not enough to study the ghetto, but we must understand how it fits into the total city, region, nation, and analytic social structures of which it forms a part.

My specific recommendations for further research include the following:

1. Studies of the various kinds of Chicano organizations described herein. A determination of their composition, means of recruitment, goals, methods of operation, etc. A model for this kind of study might be that illustrated by Sargis (1966).

However, it should be noted that there are problems involved in trying to secure information concerning these movements. Ideally, the investigator should not only be trained in social science, but be a member of La Raza as well. Many of the activist youth are understandably suspicious and even hostile toward outsiders. On the other hand, some sympathetic Anglos may be better received than a Mexican-American who is perceived to be a Tio Tomás. The National Science Foundation has received at least one proposal for such a study to be done next year. There also exists a Master's thesis written at San Francisco State College in 1966 (Sargis) which deals with the goals, aims and operation of various Mexican-American organizations in the Bay Area of California.

2. Research on the interrelationship between Chicano militancy and other protest movements of the past and present. It is clear that these movements are not unique, but share characteristics with many others occurring through history, as well as with contemporary civil rights movements throughout our own nation and in other parts of the world (Gonzalez 1969; Love 1969).

3. A study of the implications of improved education along the lines demanded by the Chicano activist today. Is the society as a whole ready to admit the Chicano to full participation? Studies such as that of Shannon (1966) are important models for this.

4. Studies of the ways in which the Anglo power structure is likely to respond to the efforts of activist minority organizations. For example, will the prejudiced Anglo listen to a Mexican-American telling him how to behave towards his people, or is he more likely to listen to another Anglo telling him the same thing? It might be hypothesized that as Mexican-Americans and Blacks now want to be taught by others like themselves, so do Anglos prefer being "told off" by other Anglos. In relation to this point, it is frequently true that the activist minority groups reject *all* Anglos. We need to have research on the effect of this upon the likelihood that their demands will actually be met.

I am sure that other readers may find other kinds of studies suggested to them both by the data and the thoughts presented in this paper, as well as by other observations of militant movements. I hope that this will at least form a starting base, and serve as a stimulus to further thought and research.

References

Bongartz, Roy
    1969 "The Chicano Rebellion." *The Nation,* March 3, 271-74.

El Chicano Inc.
    El Chicano, 1669 Vine Street, San Bernardino, Calif. (an independent newspaper: editor—Marta Macias McQueen)

Ericksen, Charles A.
    1968 "Uprising in the Barrios." *American Education* 4 (10):29-31 (Nov.)

Gonzalez, Nancie L.
    1969 *The Spanish-Americans of New Mexico.* University of New Mexico Press: Albuquerque, New Mexico.

Gordon, Milton M.
    1964 *Assimilation in American Life.* Oxford U[niversity Press], N.Y.

Griffith, Beatrice Winston
    1948 *American Me.* Houghton Mifflin Co., Boston.

Guzman, Ralph and Joan Moore
    1966 "The Mexican Americans: New Wind from the Southwest." *The Nation,* May 30, 645-48.

Heller, Celia S.
    1970 "Chicano is Beautiful." *Commonweal* XCI (16), Jan. 23, 1970, 454-58.

Kosinski, L. V.
    1963 "Bi-lingualism and Reading Development," Ph.D. thesis, Univ. of Wisconsin.

Love, Joseph
    1969 "La Raza: Mexican Americans in Rebellion." *Trans-action* 6(4):35-41, February 1969.

Peal, Elizabeth and Wallace Lambert
  1962   "The Relation of Bi-lingualism to Intelligence." Psychological Mono-
        graphs, No. 546, 76, November, 1962.

Rodriguez, Armando
  1968   Mexican-American Education, An Overview. Paper presented before
        Resources Among Mexican-American Teachers in the Denver Metro-
        politan Area. Mimeo.
   n.d.   "Counseling and Guidance for the Mexican-American Student." Unpub-
        lished manuscript.

Romano, Octavio I.
  1969   "The Historical and Intellectual Presence of Mexican Americans." *El
        Grito* 2 (2):32-46.

Rubel, Arthur J.
  1966   *Across the Tracks: Mexican-Americans in a Texas City.* [University of
        Texas Press] Austin, Texas.

Sargis, Albert Louis
  1966   Networks of Discord: A Study of the Communications System Between
        Spanish-Speaking Organizations and Their Community. Master of Arts
        thesis (unpublished). San Francisco State College, San Francisco, Cali-
        fornia.

Shannon, Lyle
  1966   The Economic Absorption and Cultural Integration of Immigrant Workers.
        Department of Anthropology and Sociology. University of Iowa, Iowa
        City, Iowa.
  1968   "The Study of Migrants as Members of Social Systems." In *Spanish-
        Speaking People in the United States,* June Helm (ed.). American Ethno-
        logical Society, University of Washington Press: Seattle and London,
        34-64.

Swadesh, Frances L.
  1968   "The Alianza Movement: Catalyst for Social Change in New Mexico."
        In *Spanish-Speaking People in the United States,* June Helm (ed.).,
        American Ethnological Society, University of Washington Press: Seattle
        and London, 162-77.

U. S. Commission Civil Rights
  1968   *The Mexican American.* Washington, D.C.

A STUDY OF INTERRACIAL CONFLICT

GLORIANNE AND SIMON WITTES

Terror flicked through the eyes of the white, female teacher as the black youth she had been scolding raised an iron pipe to strike her. Fear was also evident on the faces of the boy's classmates.

The pipe struck—and a chain of events began which soon led to a crisis situation in this high school. The youth, a school board member's son, was suspended. Rumors about the incident spread quickly through the school district; tension mounted. Black and white students began to accost each other, individually or in groups, and parents—black and white—were enraged. In desperation, the superintendent closed down the school after a black-white melee in the building, and reopened it two days later with community members policing the halls.

This incident and its aftermath took place early last fall in a suburban high school on the outskirts of a large midwestern city. The school, which we'll call Riverview High, although that's not its name, draws its population from communities that are divided along racial and socioeconomic lines: One part is almost entirely white with a lower and an upper middle class background predominating; the other is almost entirely black with somewhat lower socioeconomic levels. Recently integrated, Riverview had approximately 1,500 students, 60 percent white and 40 percent black, when its disruptions began.

The current high rate of secondary school disruptions and the commonality of the issues behind them suggest that there is an interaction between the forces in society at large and those within the school. When the outside forces are as powerful as interracial divisiveness, tension, and conflict, the result is highly combustible for the school. This was the case at Riverview. The school had become a microcosm of the conflicts in the larger society around it. As such, it was a model for case analysis of the ways in which serious community-wide racial strife and power relationships affect the functioning of various role groups within a school system.

Shortly after the incident occurred between the black student and white teacher, we at the Center for Research in the Utilization of Scientific Knowledge selected Riverview High as a site for "action research." Our center, located at the University of Michigan, sent teams to a number of troubled high schools this year, not only to study their problems but to help them find solutions.

Systems theory served as the basic framework for the intervention model we designed for Riverview High, on the premise that all parts of the school-com-

From *American Education*, 6 (June, 1970), 7-10. Reprinted with the permission of the senior author.

Dr. Simon Wittes is director of several high school intervention projects sponsored by the Center for Research in the Utilization of Scientific Knowledge. Glorianne Wittes, a former social worker, is a program associate at the Center.

munity system affect one another and must, therefore, be included in any intervention plan. Our project has a twofold objective: to diagnose the interaction within and between role groups in the system and to train role group members within the system in problem-solving, communication, and organizational skills so that they might deal constructively with the crisis. Our long-range goal was to help the system utilize its conflict to stimulate needed educational reform.

Initial diagnosis of the system was done through a series of workshops for members of all role groups which perform specific functions in the school-community system: the communities themselves, the 1,500-member student body, the 45-member faculty, the acting principal, the superintendent, the seven-member board of education. Our diagnosis revealed that the incident that precipitated Riverview's crisis was merely symptomatic of underlying issues and conflicts between these role groups which had not been put to use constructively. Interracial conflict and power issues were manifesting themselves within these groups to impede, rather than assist, educational reform.

THE COMMUNITY

Conflict between the races in the school district was increasing in intensity, because geographical redistricting had brought together two suburbs that previously were totally segregated. Many whites wished to flee the neighborhood in the face of the redistricting, but did not have the income to do so. White militancy was high with an active Ku Klux Klan.

In the black community, the spectrum of political persuasions ranged from those who might be designated "Toms" to the few considered to be radical militants. The latter were feared by the majority of both the blacks and whites, but the mythology that surrounded them was much fiercer than the reality. In fact, the leading black militant figure of the community struck us as "the man in the grey flannel dashiki."

The conflict between vested interest groups in these communities was played out in the school. Two rival parent groups were formed, each competing for the right to monitor and police the halls, each lobbying for special privileges from its "own" representatives on the board. Ostensibly these parent groups were supposed to maintain order in the school so as to create a better educational environment, but it became increasingly clear that they were, in fact, focusing on power issues instead. The rival groups worked actively to elect board representatives who would support their interests, and they attempted to manipulate board members at public meetings.

THE BOARD

Our diagnostic sessions with the board soon made it clear that most members were utilizing their positions to further personal and political aspirations. They were building political constituencies and support among school personnel at the expense of the system's overall health. While the district was on the verge of financial bankruptcy the board agreed to an extremely generous salary contract with teachers. Further, a salary contract that had been negotiated with administrators was reopened and sizable increases were granted. Board members also became involved in administrative matters not within their province, for example, by supporting custodians and other nonacademic personnel in their battles with the administration.

The building of individual political power bases combined with interracial tension to impair the board's effectiveness in making policy decisions that fostered quality education. At the time of the crisis, the board was composed of four white and three black members. The unsurfaced, unresolved racial tensions between these individuals, reinforced by the demands of their own community groups, contributed to their ineffectiveness. For example, when a white member withdrew her children from the school, much of the black community perceived her action as a further indication that the board itself did not totally support an integrated school system. The board also continued to back a personnel manager who discriminated against blacks. This seemed to heighten the friction between black and white board members and resulted in the continued lack of black personnel in the district.

ADMINISTRATION

The new superintendent, hired shortly after the event that precipitated the school disruptions, was determined to bring about some badly needed educational reforms. However, he also had high ego needs for power and status. Immediately upon his appointment he demanded policy decisions that resulted in moves that distressed all role groups in the district. His immediate dismissal of a new, white high school principal caused much anxiety among other faculty and administrative personnel. Although this principal was regarded as highly ineffective by both the white and black communities and by school personnel, his dismissal was, nonetheless, cited by whites as an instance of the superintendent's preference for blacks.

The superintendent's rapid moves to take over and make decisions brought him hostility from board members who believed he was usurping their powers. He was not able to get student support either. He had alienated them by turning down their requests to work actively in one of the school's financial campaigns, fearing the community would believe the school system was manipulating students for its own ends. Without support from the board, faculty, students, or community, the superintendent was in a vulnerable position, despite his grasp of the educational issues and needed reforms.

FACULTY

Caught in a near-bankrupt system which for years had not been able to supply adequate services, materials, or inservice training, the faculty had grown apathetic, was alienated from students, distant from the community, and resentful of the administration and board. Their own ranks were split between two rival teachers' organizations. Although little interracial conflict existed within the faculty—there were few black teachers—tension was manifested in the attitudes of some white teachers toward black students and black community people. Educational issues were often lost in the face of prejudicial attitudes toward students and a cold war between rival teacher groups.

Teachers also felt incompetent in the face of the increasing number of black students with their different life styles, speech patterns, and educational needs that the existing curriculum did not satisfy. A few teachers recommended new programs to meet the needs of these students, but were turned down by the board on the basis of insufficient funds. No inservice training was provided to help the faculty deal with their sense of incompetence and frustration.

This situation had two outcomes: First, many teachers retreated behind the doors of their classrooms, distant from students and each other, with the feeling of "the heck with it. I can't teach these kids or change anything anyhow, so I'll just put in my time here." Secondly, teachers adopted a more militant posture, hoping for economic gains to replace the psychological satisfactions they craved.

STUDENTS

The models for interracial interaction afforded students by the adult community had devastating repercussions for Riverview High. The students reflected all the bickering, tension, and prejudice around them in their attitudes toward one another. Although blacks were a minority in the school, they held most school offices. White students claimed that blacks had used coercive tactics in the elections; black students said whites had been apathetic and did not organize behind their candidates. Physical abuse between gangs and individuals increased until all after-school activities, extramural sports and dances were cancelled. To add to their frustrations, the seniors feared they would not be able to graduate, because a financial deficit threatened to eliminate programs needed for graduation credit.

Students turned all their frustration about irrelevant curriculum and mediocre teaching on one another instead of focusing it upon the board, administration, faculty, and community. They had no organizing skills or models for organizing to achieve change. As a result they were either apathetic or violent in the face of intolerable conditions. The presence of parents in the school as hall monitors added to their consternation, bringing community tensions into their domain and raising intergenerational conflicts.

CURATIVE STRATEGIES

This short case study highlights how different role groups in a school-community system defended their vested interests but did not always address themselves to educational issues and needed reforms. Studies of other school crises lead us to conclude that the vested interests noted in this study are typical of school systems. In addition to the conflict between role groups, however, there is often conflict within role groups. At Riverview High the latter variety of conflict was interracial in nature and had developed to an extremely high degree. Because various vested interests were not publicly acknowledged, the ensuing conflict led to ineffective learning and administrative processes that resulted in violence, disruption, and crisis.

Consequently, we initiated a program designed to reduce interracial tension at Riverview High. We chose students as the target of our intervention program: They were available on a daily basis, had indicated interest, and possessed the necessary energy and commitment. These criteria seemed to be minimal if the program was to have some chance of success.

Our goal was to start a program with educational significance that would be an integral part of the school. Therefore, we chose a human relations class format carrying three hours of credit. Its content includes discussion of institutional racism, black and white consciousness, prejudice, community and school structures, and the functions of organizational power. Teachers of the class helped design it and had inservice training to prepare them for their task. Project staff consulted with parents and with the principal as well as with teachers on curriculum design, applied behavioral science, human relations training, and effective school-community communications as part of the program. Although the program has started with a small core of committed students and teachers, we hope eventually to broaden it to include other students, parents, community members, and police officers.

While the situation at Riverview High dictated the choice of a human relations class as an intervention format, the nature of the problems there also allowed for other strategies. The highly politicized nature of the school board suggests that training in school system analysis and policy-making skills might be appropriate for board members. Such training would encourage them to make policies designed to improve education. A second strategy might concentrate on changing the school's government. Its goal would be to provide students with decision-making power in relevant areas of school life—curriculum, teacher evaluation, accountability, and hiring practices. Students would be trained in analysis of systematic power structures and problem-solving and decision-making skills in order that their developing abilities to solve problems might be complemented by the power to implement their solutions.

Still another strategy might be the establishment of an ombudsman responsible directly to the board of education, with power to investigate and resolve student grievances. Such an ombudsman would take a stance of neutrality and work vigorously to correct students' complaints about a system in which they presently have no legitimate way of seeking redress.

PREVENTIVE MEASURES

To this point, we have suggested strategies to be utilized in the face of crisis. But there are also a number of strategies to which school systems could turn as preventive measures. In the case of Riverview High, black and white students came, for the most part, from segregated elementary schools. Their communities were characterized by racial tension, and family norms mitigated against productive interracial contact. A strategy to ensure minimal interracial disruption would involve, at the very least, desegregation at the elementary level and inservice training for all school personnel involved to modify interracial attitudes and behavior.

A second preventive strategy grows out of the fact that nearly all school systems tend to deny the problem of conflict, whether it be within or among role groups. We therefore believe there should be an ongoing analysis of school-community systems to collect data about behaviors and attitudes among all role groups involved. Problems should be brought out into the open and legitimately faced. Collection of such data, however, is only a first step in this preventive strategy. The second is to implement programs and processes that respond to the problems discovered in the data.

In Riverview High, as in many other high schools in crisis, a major source of the disruption is the community itself. It is unavoidable that societal conflicts across generations, races, and classes will be manifested in similar conflicts within a school. It is, therefore, the responsibility of the school to give recognition to the existence of these conflicts and to utilize them strategically for meaningful educational reform. Some sort of conflict is probably inevitable, but it need not develop into disruption and violence; in fact, conflict can be acknowledged, analyzed, and legitimatized so that it becomes a force for constructive educational change.

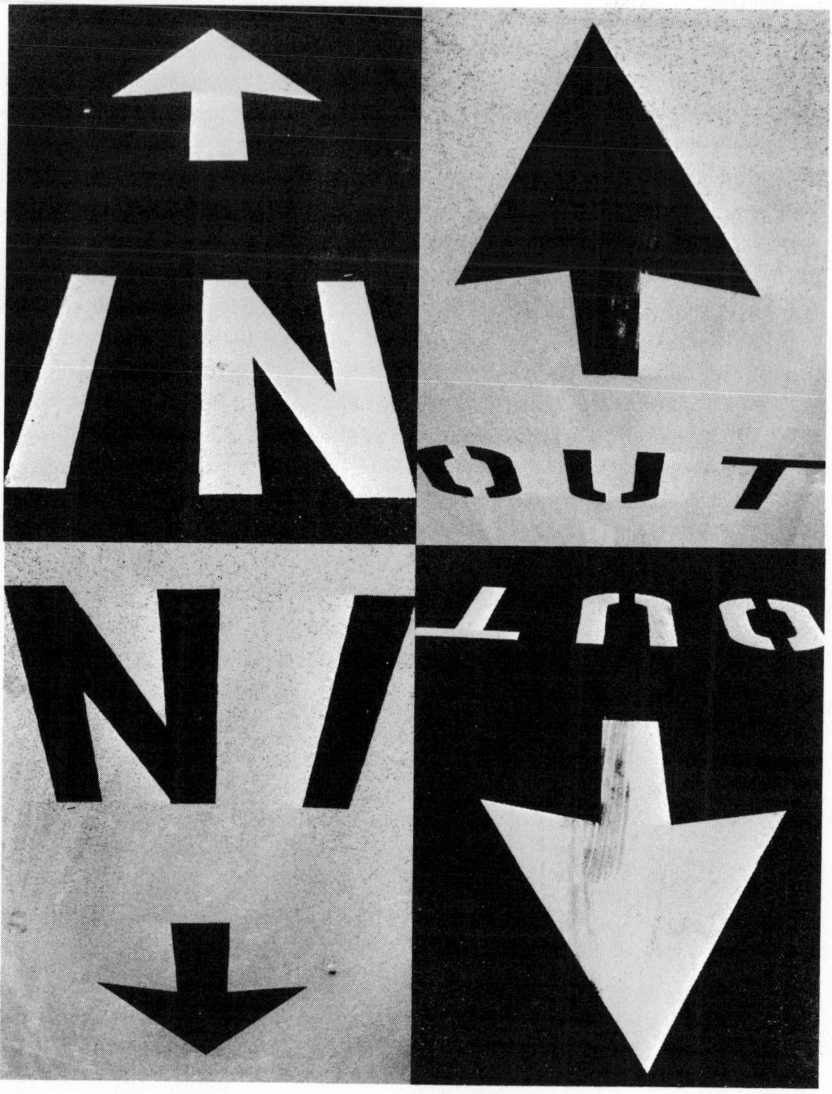
IN
OUT

PART THREE

DIRECTIONS FOR THE FUTURE

EIGHT

ALTERNATIVES: MANNING THE BARRICADES

In spite of reports of student disruption and even damage to school property, parents and the public at large have remained quite supportive of schools. Indeed, according to an opinion sample conducted by the Gallup organization in the fall of 1969, the public's only serious complaint about schools was the lack of discipline allegedly found in them. Of those interviewed, 49 per cent thought the schools were not strict enough; 44 per cent thought discipline was about right. Parents with children in school were slightly more supportive: 52 per cent felt that discipline was about right, while 45 per cent thought it wasn't strict enough. Happily, the concern for discipline was not serious enough to reflect adversely on teachers. Three out of four adults indicated they would like to have a child pursue public school teaching as a career, and 57 per cent indicated they would send their child to a public school even if they could afford to pay for private education or if tuition was free at non-public schools.[1] A similar study conducted by Louis Harris a few months earlier revealed essentially the same findings. Of the parents interviewed, 62 per cent felt that maintaining discipline was a more important function of the schools than encouraging intellectual inquiry; nevertheless, 78 per cent rated teachers as good to excellent.[2]

Given the attitudes reflected in these public opinion samples, schoolmen have good reason for seeking the most effective strategies for maintaining discipline in the schools. Basically two clear-cut strategies are available for the resolution of conflict: (1) repression, i.e., the use of various legal and non-legal means to preserve order in the existing system; and (2) the exploration of alternatives which seek either to identify and modify root causes of dissent and activism, or to modify various aspects of the school program and structure. Often the situation itself dictates which approach will be employed. In cases where rocks are already coming through the windows, the reasonableness of alternative one is clear. For longer-range solutions, alternative two should have considerable appeal.

The present chapter deals with approaches which are designed to preserve order and, often by implication, to maintain the school in its present form. Approaches which explore alternatives to one or more aspects of the school curriculum, or to the organization of schools themselves, are presented in Chapter nine. The extent to which the two broad philosophies are used in individual

[1] "How the Public Views the Schools," *Scholastic Teacher*, 95 (December 8, 1969): 1-2.
[2] Louis Harris, "What People Think About Their High Schools," *Life*, 66 (May 16, 1969): 22-23.

school districts is unknown, albeit there is some reason to suspect that the first enjoys relatively greater popularity. If the data reported by Lesley Browder, "Bergen County Battle Plans; What to Do *Before* Students Demonstrate" are representative, they suggest that harsh, non-conciliatory practices may be predominant. In this study of administrative plans for dealing with student disruption in thirty-two New Jersey school districts, only about one-third of the respondents included seeking out causes of a disturbance by meeting with disaffected students as part of their "battle plans." On the other hand, some 65 percent indicated that their "plans" included punitive action for those involved in disruptive events.

One may infer—as indeed the editors of this book have inferred—that school boards, administrators and teachers can do much to head off disruptive student behavior by taking an enlightened approach to solving school problems well in advance of confrontation. With a total 1968 high school enrollment in the United States of 12,721,000 (grades 9-12), it is hardly suprising that a small number would be persuaded by revolutionary rhetoric. Two selections in the present chapter, one by the House Committee on Internal Security, *SDS Plans for America's High Schools,* and the other by F.B.I. Director, J. Edgar Hoover, "The SDS and the High Schools," serve the function of pointing out an apparent need for "manning the barricades" where revolutionaries are active. While only the most naive can deny the existence of a small revolutionary band of students and non-students, overestimating their influence and attributing the main thrust of student activism to direct communist revolutionary influence would be folly. To the extent that this activity distracts school authorities and the public at large from the need for educational reform, it can be counterproductive.

Administrators have been urged repeatedly to take the initiative in seeking the causes of growing student militancy and to determine appropriate alternatives for achieving changes in school policies and practices. This notwithstanding, there is good reason to believe that students will not easily win the right to help determine school policy. A poll involving 5 percent of the nation's school administrators conducted in the summer of 1969 found that 51 percent did not believe that students should have a greater voice in decision-making. On the other hand, 74 percent agreed with some of the student complaints but not with their more direct-action methods of forcing change.[3]

Thomas A. Shannon's "Legal Aspects of Confrontation" describes legal tools for use by the school principal in dealing with student disorders, including (1) enforcement of school regulations relating to student conduct, (2) arranging for the enforcement of criminal law, and (3) resorting to the civil law through the sanction of contempt of court charges for violation of a court order. The objective of such actions is to repress those who would become involved in confrontation since, according to Shannon, high school confrontations "attempt to replace reasonable discussion with raw power in an open and infamous manner

[3] "Schoolmen Split Over Student Involvement," *Nations Schools,* 84 (September, 1969): 47.

. . ." for purposes of winning "blind and uncritical acceptance of the demands made by those who resort to it."

Detailed plans for countering disruptions have been prepared in numerous states and local communities. California's "Proposed Plan to Cope with Student Unrest and Disturbance," is only one illustration. This and similar plans specify duties and responsibilities of the clerical staff, custodial staff, parent corps, students, faculty, principal and other administrators in the event of a disturbance. The proposed California plans are so complete as to include a prepared statement which presumably can be used in almost all situations. It reads:

Your present actions indicate the existence of a problem. The solution of this problem cannot be reached without a careful examination of the facts . . . The faculty and administration share your concerns . . . We pledge our sincerity in meaningful dialogue.

It is entirely likely that such a prepared statement, particularly if read without attention to the dynamics of the local situation, could serve to further inflame the students. One might reasonably presume that in many situations a history of failure at "meaningful dialogue" is at least partially responsible for the confrontation in the first place. Although the California document is intended only to provide guidelines for action, it is deficient in that it ignores the need to adopt strategies based upon the dynamics of the local situations and does not appear to give sufficient attention to the actual causes of disruption.

The editors of *School Management,* in their article "Strategies for Coping with Student Disruption," have shown some recognition of the need to take account of student and community dynamics in developing battle plans to deal with confrontations. Various strategies actually used by school districts in coping with student sit-ins, boycotts and violence are examined.

While the present chapter includes some strategies for dealing with the immediate problems of disruption and confrontation, it need hardly be said that such procedures can be perceived, at best, as only stopgaps or dike-plugging. No actions by school administrators are as good as those which forestall disruptions, confrontations and other forms of dissent by showing sensitivity to student needs and desires, the changing times and social conditions. Such concerns are taken up in the next and final chapter—"Alternatives: New Directions."

BERGEN COUNTY BATTLE PLANS; WHAT TO DO *BEFORE* STUDENTS DEMONSTRATE

LESLEY H. BROWDER, JR.

Precautions, procedures and punishments for student disorders cannot be defined under an across-the-board set of regulations. But an analysis of administrative battle plans in one of the country's heavily populated counties can provide insights into how a majority of superintendents feel such disruptions should be handled.

Recently, the New Jersey State Board of Education issued a mandate that each school district submit "a specific plan for coping with potential student disorders." Bergen County, one of the state's largest and fastest-growing areas, is representative. Of 72 school districts, 42 are operating secondary schools. Ten secondary districts did not supply enough information. The remaining 32 serve as a valid example of administrative plans for student disruptions.

In a few districts, action would appear swift and harsh, as judged by written statements like this one: "Any outbreak . . . shall be considered lawless behavior, and shall be subject to proceedings and penalties as provided by existing laws." Most administrators, however, approach the situation with more extensive planning.

Who Is Notified? Early warning and preparation procedures, where only the possibility of a disorder exists, are found at 25 percent of the districts. These plans include notifying the building principal as a first step. Four districts (12.5%) mention early notification of the superintendent and placing the police on standby alert.

When action really starts, the number of plans for notification increases to 68.8 per cent of districts, with 56.2 per cent calling for immediate notification of the building principal and the school superintendent. Where staff members are formally notified (21.9%), a few districts have rather elaborate code signals to inform staff personnel, without alarming the students.

Five districts intend to notify student leaders and ask them to "be on hand" to speak with disorderly students. Four others feel it necessary to state that staff members are obligated to notify the administrator in charge when an outbreak occurs.

Lesley H. Browder, Jr. is Associate Professor and Chairman of the Department of Education Administration at Hofstra University.

Police Involvement: All but one of the 32 districts have plans that include law officers. The majority favor placing the police on alert as soon as the situation actually starts (62.5%), but calling them in only as a last resort (71.9%).

Exactly who makes the final judgment to call police to the scene is difficult to determine. Usually the plans imply that the administrator-on-the-spot should make that decision. More than half the time (56.2%) this person is expected to be the building principal; 12.5 per cent of the plans place this responsibility on the superintendent.

No plan attempts to provide instructions to the police on the handling of disorderly students.

General Approaches: The most prevalent ideas for actual handling of student disruptions are:

1. Use the threat of police as a lever to disband students (43.5%).

2. Request the students to disband (40.6%).

3. Request parents of identified disorderly students to come and remove their children (40.6%).

4. Set some form of time limit for disbanding, "or else" (37.5%).

5. Request spokesmen from the ranks of disorderly students (37.5%).

6. Attempt to seek out causes by meeting with disaffected students (34.4%).

7. Inform students officially that they are in violation of school policy or regulations and they must comply (31.3%).

Some of the less frequently mentioned items for controlling student disorders are: ask nonparticipating persons to leave the disorder area immediately (21.9%); request staff members to assist in containing the disorder (21.9%); dismiss classes at the discretion of the superintendent (15.6%); insist that students disband before any issues are discussed (15.6%); consult with the board president (15.6%); and isolate and contain the disorder (9.4%).

Two plans freely state they will allow a demonstration to continue—if it doesn't interfere with the operation of a school.

Protective Actions: Exactly one-half of the plans include a variety of procedures to protect persons and/or property during a disorder. These show efforts to retain nonparticipating students in their classes if the disturbance occurs during school hours (28.1%); to direct the staff to take an attendance check for later identification and explanations from missing students (28.1%); to exclude unauthorized persons from the school grounds (25%); to secure the buildings as well as possible, locking file cabinets and unused facilities (15.6%); and to ban outside telephone calls by unauthorized personnel (12.5%).

Single plans favor requesting the staff to be nonviolent, except in matters of pure self-defense and student safety, and asking unassigned personnel to report to the principal's office for deployment.

The criterion of success for any plan is presumably whether it will work. In the long run, however, the means used and the attitudes reflected by administrators to quell a disorder may have a greater lasting effect on the school and community than the rather limited end of "putting it down."

SDS PLANS FOR AMERICA'S HIGH SCHOOLS

REPORT BY THE COMMITTEE ON INTERNAL SECURITY, HOUSE OF REPRESENTATIVES, NINETY-FIRST CONGRESS, FIRST SESSION

FOREWORD

The Committee on Internal Security in the course of its current investigation and hearings into the involvement of the Students for a Democratic Society (SDS) in revolutionary violence has received evidence that this organization has greatly intensified its efforts to establish a foothold in the high schools of our Nation.

What is the basic SDS philosophy? What are its aims and purposes? Why does the SDS want to recruit high school students? What is the SDS blueprint for the radicalization of high school students? What success has SDS had in organizing high school students? What is the nature of the SDS threat to our high schools? What positive action can be taken to thwart the SDS threat to our high schools? Some answers to these and other questions regarding the high school operations of the SDS are reviewed in this committee report.

There is a parallel to be drawn between the attitudes of SDS activists and the well-known attitudes of Fascists and Communists. Each believes the end justifies the means. They are militant, arrogant, and intolerant toward those who do not believe entirely as they do. They have little or no faith in the democratic process, and their views on legitimate authority and the rule of law are uniformly negative.

Those who now rally to the support of the SDS can be under no illusions. The issues are clear. The aims of the SDS were spelled out in an SDS position paper printed in June 1969: "The goal is the destruction of US imperialism and the achievement of a classless world: world communism." Those are the views of the leadership of SDS. They are not necessarily the views or objectives of many of the thousands of SDS members. But if such goals can be advocated by those who are leading some of our college and university students, certainly we cannot afford to ignore or underestimate the potential of SDS efforts directed at our high schools. This committee report offers a basis for understanding the philosophy of SDS and its manifested determination to develop a revolutionary consciousness in the youth of our Nation.

December 12, 1969.   Richard H. Ichord, *Chairman*

Reprinted from the original document. Prepared and released by the Committee on Internal Security, Washington, D.C., 1969.

Students for a Democratic Society (SDS) is an organization of militants known for its revolutionary activities. It has established its identity with growing violence and lawlessness. Members of the SDS take great delight in desecrating the American flag and disparaging American institutions. By its own declarations it adheres to Marxist-Leninist concepts, and a portion of SDS members now pays homage to the "thoughts" of Mao Tse-tung. Many Americans find SDS statements, stances, and deeds bewildering. For that reason, it is important that all citizens, particularly educators, be made fully aware of the insidious nature of the SDS and its current plans to win over high school students.

BASIC CONCEPTS

Basic to SDS is the idea that contemporary American society is corrupt, evil, and oppressive—and must be destroyed. To reform it, they insist, to change it for the better, is impossible. SDS says our Nation's system of government and traditional values must be destroyed.

As for certain minority struggles against the U.S., the 1969 convention of SDS in Chicago declared:

> We support the struggles of the black and Latin colonies within the U.S. for national liberation, and we recognize those nations' rights to self-determination (including the right to political secession, if they desire it).[1]

With respect to international relationships, the same convention declared:

> We support the struggle for national liberation of the people of South Vietnam, led by the National Liberation Front and the South Vietnamese Provisional Revolutionary Government. We also support the Democratic Republic of Vietnam, led by President Ho Chi Minh, as well as the Democratic Republic of China, the People's Republics of Korea and Albania, and the Republic of Cuba, all waging fierce struggles against U.S. imperialism. We support the right of all peoples to pick up the gun to free themselves from the brutal rule of U.S. imperialism.[2]

The full impact of the threat which this movement poses to our national stability and security becomes more evident when viewed in the light of what SDS has wrought in the last 5 years in terms of property damage totaling millions of dollars; in requiring the calling out of Federal troops, National Guard units, and police forces across the Nation to meet SDS planned and sponsored student disorders, and the massive way in which SDS has given the world the impression that young America hates everything in our free society.

[1] New Left Notes, vol. 4, No. 23, June 25, 1969, p. 1 (published by SDS National Office, 1608 West Madison St., Chicago, Ill.)
[2] Ibid.

Many of the SDS leaders have publicly declared themselves to be revolutionaries dedicated to the Marxist-Leninist ideology. For example, Mark Rudd, William Ayers, and Jeffrey Carl (Jeff) Jones, leading national officers of the SDS, publicly identified themselves as revolutionary communists during a televised interview over station WJW-TV in Cleveland, Ohio, on August 30, 1969. The transcript of this televised interview was made an exhibit in the SDS hearings held before the House Committee on Internal Security on October 30, 1969.

The June 18, 1969, issue of the official SDS publication, New Left Notes, sets out, in a position paper, the goals of Rudd, Jones, and Ayers:

The goal is the destruction of US imperialism and the achievement of a classless world: world communism.

AIMS AND PURPOSES

Never before in this country has there been such a determined effort by young people to destroy established authority. SDS has made it emphatically clear that mere change and revision are not its objectives. Armed with a long list of "nonnegotiable" demands, it has as its immediate goal to wreck our educational system. On June 18, SDS said in New Left Notes—

it is crucial not to build consciousness only around specific issues . . . but to use these issues to build toward the general consciousness that the schools should be shut down . . .

The long-range objective of SDS, as reported in New Left Notes, is, in effect, to serve as an initiator and nucleus of a revolutionary youth movement which would grow and build support among other elements of the population for an eventual violent revolution with Communist goals.

In this connection, new directions were charted for SDS at the December 1968 SDS National Council meeting. A regional SDS publication entitled Notes from MAGGIE'S FARM described the new strategy this way:

That strategy has been called "Toward a Revolutionary Youth Movement." It has correctly identified SDS primarily as a student organization, isolated from the masses of American people on elite university campuses. And, it has called for SDS to become more than it is: to transform itself, in the only organic way open to it, from a student movement into a working class youth movement.[3]

The same publication announced:

[3] "Investigation of Students for a Democratic Society, Part 2 (Kent State University)," hearings before Committee on Internal Security, U.S. House of Representatives, June 24-25, 1969, p. 628—Committee Exhibit No. 22.

This summer, the Ohio Region of SDS is calling for summer programs in three cities: Akron, Cleveland, and Columbus. . . .

Jeff Jones, SDS national interorganizational secretary, asserted in *New Left Notes* on July 8, 1969, that part of the SDS strategy and program for the months ahead would involve working to expand into "working class high schools, community colleges, neighborhoods, and shops."

Thus, SDS leaders feel they have found a new outlet in high schools for SDS militancy. In nearly a score of States since the fall semester began, high schools have become the staging area for the spread of SDS revolutionary philosophy.

SDS leaders have boasted that, starting out from almost zero some 7 years ago, the group currently has some 40,000 adherents. However, *New Left Notes* has commented that the members of SDS who are in high schools are the most underrepresented group in the organization. The publication suggested that a high school organizer would be able to make high school members much more than just peripherally involved in the affairs of the SDS and in this manner could begin to help build a more nearly solid high school movement.

BLUEPRINT FOR RADICALIZATION

The SDS has a blueprint for radicalization of high school students. Distributed in high schools throughout the country in 1968 under the title "HIGH SCHOOL RE-FORM: toward a student movement," the publication states:

> *Even acts like the starting of trash can fires and the pulling of fire alarms are actually forms of protest directed at the school as it is now constituted. Not only the militant defense of hair and clothing styles against administrative attack, but the adoption of such styles themselves, as a part of the hippy culture on the high school campus, indicates a general disgust with the values and attitudes that our generation has been force-fed.*
>
> .   .   .   .
>
> *Our first task, then, is to show the students that we are on their side, and have many of the same concerns they do. One method is to begin agitation around issues students are already concerned about. We should be in the forefront of any student protest against administrative action. . . . [Emphasis in original.]*

A national SDS high school policy was promulgated in late 1968, at an SDS National Council meeting in Boulder, Colo., where a special "high school resolution" was passed. The resolution declared that high schools only prepare students for life in a "sick" society. It pointed out that—

> *the school cannot change to the extent we want unless we change the system which uses it [therefore], we will organize in the high schools to move students to overthrow that system. . . .*

The resolution called for: (1) the hiring of a national high school coordinator, (2) regional organizations and local chapters of the SDS to make high school organizing a large part of their program, and (3) the national circulation of an underground paper currently being published by the Los Angeles High School chapter of the SDS.

An SDS "Organizers' Manual for the Spring Offensive" in 1969 contains the following information:

> It has become clear within the last year or so that high school organizing —particularly in working class high schools—is of vital importance to the development of our movement. High schools are almost uniformly like prisons: they teach nothing but the crudest versions of bourgeois ideology, impose offensive disciplinary rules, spending most of their energy keeping kids off the streets while waiting to enter the job market or the army. Further, high school students are rebelling with greater and greater frequency, and make the possibility of cross-city and working class youth movements much more possible.[4]

The manual cites specific examples of alleged militarization in high schools —the draft and recruiter assemblies and the tracking system.

Another source provides a little publicized account which helps explain SDS concentration on "working-class" high school students. In July of 1969 a delegation of SDS leaders, including Bernardine Rae Dohrn, member of the national interim committee of SDS; Kathie Boudin of the SDS national action staff; and Dianne Maria Donghi, Theodore (Ted) Gold, Eleanor Stein Raskin, and Howard Jefferson (Jeff) Melish of New York's SDS organization, were part of a larger delegation of Americans who went to Cuba to meet with Viet Cong and North Vietnamese representatives.

In a special "Vietnam Supplement" to New Left Notes published after that visit, Vietnamese advice on the best type of recruit for the SDS was qouted:

> At the meeting in Cuba with the PRG [Provisional Revolutionary Government of South Vietnam, basically consisting of elements of the Viet Cong], Van Ba (head of the PRG delegation) told us: "When you go into a city, look for the person who fights hardest against the cops. THAT's the one you talk all night with. Don't look for the one who says the best thing. Look for the one who fights."

SDS CLAIMS TO SUCCESS

In hearings held October 20-22, 1969, testimony brought out that the SDS, following a planned program to build a fighting cadre among high school youths, established three communes in Columbus, Ohio, during the summer of 1969.

[4] Ibid., p. 609—Committee Exhibit No. 15.

SDS pursued a program of attempting to talk to and recruit high school students engaged in summer sessions and to incite and inflame teenagers on the street. The SDS activities in the high schools, essentially consisting of passing out SDS literature and talking with students, were conducted before classes in the morning, during lunch breaks, and after classes in the afternoon. On July 15, 1969, obscenities were painted on the walls of five Columbus high schools.

New Left Notes of August 1, 1969, printed the text of the leaflet passed out by SDS'ers following the outbreak of rioting in Columbus. The violence in Columbus was described in the leaflet as "part of a world-wide revolution against big businessmen and the government (U.S.) they own" and as "a PEOPLE'S WAR OF LIBERATION." "And we must aid them and others who are rebelling, in any way we can," the leaflet declared.

Testimony before the committee, October 20, 1969, also summed up SDS activity with teenagers at a playground.

Two teenagers from Columbus confirmed for the committee that SDS activists had advocated theft, arson, and bombings, as well as the killing of policemen. The SDS members had initiated such discussions with youths of high school age in July 1969 at a school recreation area popular with teenagers. Lured by an offer of free beer and a gun display, the youngsters even brought along their friends for a second meeting and another dose of SDS propaganda. The teenagers were told that if they would organize with SDS, the SDS would provide them with guns and teach them to kill "pigs" (police officers).[5]

Further testimony from a Columbus policeman provided added details:

Mr. Romines.[6]   Mr. Hilton,[7] as a juvenile officer in this particular area, did you have occasion to talk with any of the juveniles who were contacted by the SDS members?

Mr. Hilton.   I did.

Mr. Romines.   What did the juveniles tell you?

Mr. Hilton.   The juveniles advised me that the SDS members were talking to them about the big businessmen in Columbus, namely, Lazarus and the Wolfes.

Mr. Romines.   What is Lazarus?

Mr. Hilton.   Lazarus is a large department store in downtown Columbus.

Mr. Romines. And Wolfes?

Mr. Hilton.   Are the owners of the Columbus Dispatch. They stated that these were the kind of people who were making it tough on the teenagers, that they had all the money and were cheating the teenagers from the money and the jobs they should have, and they also contemplated the burning down of Lazarus Department Store.

[5] Testimony of Roy Sims and James Yantis, Oct. 20, 1969, before House Committee on Internal Security.

[6] Stephen H. Romines, assistant counsel, Committee on Internal Security.

[7] Roger Hilton, Columbus, Ohio, juvenile bureau, Columbus Police Dept.

Mr. Romines.   *Who is "they"?*

Mr. Hilton.   *SDS members.*

Mr. Romines.   *Did they actually advocate to the teenagers burning down the store?*

Mr. Hilton.   *They did.*

Mr. Romines.   *Did they advocate anything else?*

Mr. Hilton.   *Advocated going into Upper Arlington.*

Mr. Romines.   *What is that?*

Mr. Hilton.   *This is a suburb of Columbus of the high income bracket. And stealing from these residences, and from the people there, to gain money to support their movement.*

Mr. Romines.   *Let me ask you this question, Mr. Hilton: What was their expressed attitude toward the police department?*

Mr. Hilton.   *The attitude toward the police department was commonly referred to as pigs. They did advocate violence toward the police department, the mayor, and the safety director. They did advocate killing police officers. They did state that they would get the teenagers weapons and these weapons were to be used to kill pigs, or the police.*

Stephen Wosary, assistant principal of the Garfield High School in Akron, Ohio, testified before the committee on October 28, 1969, regarding an incident to show just how SDS operated on the high school level during the summer school session:

Mr. Wosary.   *At approximately 11:40 a.m. (July 22, 1969) the school and classrooms were entered by outsiders who disrupted the normal school day's proceedings.*

Mr. Romines.   *Approximately how many outsiders were there, Mr. Wosary?*

Mr. Wosary.   *Approximately 10.*

Mr. Romines.   *Did they all enter one room or did they enter different rooms?*

Mr. Wosary.   *They entered different classrooms.*

Mr. Romines.   *Did each one enter a different classroom?*

Mr. Wosary.   *It appears that they did, yes.*

Mr. Romines.   *What did they do when they entered the classrooms?*

Mr. Wosary.   *Generally upon entering the classrooms they began to inform the students or invite the students out of the classroom out into the streets and in most instances began going up and down the aisles, distributing literature to the students.*

Mr. Romines.   *Did these outsiders have permission to be in the classrooms?*

Mr. Wosary.   *No, they did not.*

.   .   .   .

Mr. Romines.   *As a result of these SDS'ers' coming into your high school, what action did you take?*

Mr. Wosary.   *Upon being notified that they were in the classroom, I proceeded to the nearest classroom to my office where I found the young man delivering what amounted to a speech and distributing the literature that I mentioned.*

I asked him to leave the classroom and told him he was trespassing. I indicated that his presence would only be tolerated if he had a visitor's permit.

Mr. Romines.   *Did he leave?*

Mr. Wosary.   *No.*

Mr. Romines.   *Did any of them leave when they were requested?*

Mr. Wosary.   *No.*

Mr. Romines.   *Under what circumstances did they eventually leave?*

Mr. Wosary.   *At approximately 11:50 I began to dismiss the various classes. I went from room to room dismissing classes.*

Mr. Romines.   *After you dismissed classes, did the students then leave?*

Mr. Wosary.   *Yes, the students enrolled in the summer school left in a very orderly fashion and they were immediately followed and joined by the people who identified themselves as SDS members.*

SDS held a summer orientation program in Detroit on May 30–June 1, 1969. Of seven females who were identified in committee hearings as being present, four were identified as participants in a subsequent summer disturbance at a school in a suburb of Detroit (Macomb County Community College) and two in a disturbance at South Hills High School in Pittsburgh.

Gerald Joseph Hankus, associate professor of sociology at Macomb County Community College in Warren, Mich., in the suburbs of Detroit, related to the committee on October 28 that on July 31, 1969, he was giving an exam to about 30 students, including adults, who were taking a special summer course in sociology.

Mr. Hankus recounted how he was sitting at the back of the class grading papers, but the front door to the classroom was open to allow fresh air to circulate through the room. At approximately 11 o'clock, about 10 girls—not students at Macomb—marched into the room suddenly, chanting "study, hate, kill, work" and some SDS slogans. They moved in a circular fashion at the head of the class and then halted to allow each of their number to deliver a brief harangue about the alleged oppression of women and black people. Mr. Hankus said they seemed particularly concerned about the supposed denial of women's rights and one of the older adult students taking the course—a Mr. Michael Nuss, who had been employed for over 30 years at the Chrysler plant—took exception to these remarks, contending: "I have seen your type before in the factory. You people are troublemakers."

He was standing at his desk, and the militants pushed him roughly back into his seat. Mr. Hankus sought to go out the front door to enlist help, but the girls pushed his desk to block his exit, and the demonstrators jumped on top of the desk to prevent his climbing over it. Mr. Hankus then managed to slip out the rear door to call the campus police.

Another witness before the committee, Eric B. Latos, described the scene from the point of view of one of the students taking the exam:

Mr. Latos.   . . . We were taking a final examination in the classroom and we were working away, and all of a sudden these girls came in and started marching around with the flag and started passing out the different pamphlets.

At first I paid absolutely no attention to them at all because my mind was on the final examination and I didn't care less about these girls coming in.

But after, I would say, a couple minutes, I did have to look up since they were making so much noise and I paid attention to what they were saying and the obscenities that they were shouting.

Then they got in front of the classroom and they had little speeches that they all had prepared. Mr. Nuss is the one that got pushed down at first when this one young lady said that there was inequality of women and the like, and he got rather upset about this, and I really can't blame him.

He got up and voiced his own opinion. After he was pushed down I said, "Don't you have any respect for your elders?" since he had to be at least three times as old as these young ladies were. They told me to shut up.

I said, "I am taking a final examination, and everyone else is in this room, and I feel that this final examination is more important than what you have to say. If you want to come back later, fine, but we all want to take this final examination right now and would you please leave?"

They said, "School does not mean anything, you don't learn anything here." They used a few other obscenities. At this moment I got up and tried to go out the front door of the classroom.

Well, as Mr. Hankus already told you, they had a table there, but I tried to get out and that is when a whole bunch of these girls jumped on top of me and everything and a little commotion occurred at this time, but I finally got away and got out the back.

I didn't know that Mr. Hankus had gotten out, and while I was going to get help he was coming back with help.

That sort of sums up what happened in a few words.

Mr. Sanders.[8]   Did you receive any injury in this scuffle?

Mr. Latos.   Well, as was previously stated, I got bitten and kicked and hit and the like, but it was not anything really to get excited about except for the bite.

Mr. Sanders.   Did you receive medical treatment?

Mr. Latos.   Yes, I did.

[8] Donald G. Sanders, chief counsel, Committee on Internal Security.

Mr. Sanders. *What was that?*

Mr. Latos. *I got a tetanus shot for it. I probably should have gotten a rabies shot, but at the time I really didn't think of it. But since I didn't flinch or anything or the like later, I just sort of forgot about it.*

Another example of outside influence was noted in a recent high school disturbance at Pittsburgh, Pa. On September 8, 1969, 26 out-of-town females of college age were arrested in a melee at South Hills High School. It is noteworthy that two of the individuals arrested had been at the previously mentioned Detroit summer orientation, and three of them had been participants in the Macomb County Community College disruption. It is interesting to note that one of the 26 arrested has also been identified as the SDS member who opened the gas company account for one of the communes in Columbus during the summer.

The South Hills High School disorder was mapped by a group of attendees at the SDS Midwest National Action Conference and National Interim Committee meeting held in East Cleveland, Ohio, August 29 through September 1, 1969. One person in attendance gave the others a description of the disruption at the Macomb County Community College.

Dr. James R. Johnston, principal of South Hills High School in Pittsburgh, told the committee that on the first regular school day, September 4, 1969, a number of slogans were written across the doors of the school such as "The VC Will Win," "Ho Lives," "October 8-11," "SDS," etc. The slogans had been sprayed on the sandstone of the school building in red paint, making it nearly impossible to remove them.

During the committee's hearing of October 30, 1969, committee counsel asked if anything else happened that day:

Mr. Johnston. *At approximately noon a teacher came into my office and said that there was some sort of a demonstration going on out in the street, that a group was marching down the street distributing pamphlets of some sort. I left my office and went immediately to the outside of the building——*

.   .   .   .

Mr. Johnston. *I moved to the street and I saw out on the street, on the sidewalks, the remnants of pamphlets that evidently had been distributed by this group of which the teacher spoke. . . .*

.   .   .   .

Mr. Johnston. *I saw the literature all over the place, and as I started back into the office to see if I could notify some authorities, a group of approximately 10 or 12 girls came marching down.*

Mr. Romines. *Were these all females?*

Mr. Johnston. *They were all females, all dressed in similar attire.*

Mr. Romines. *What was the attire?*

Mr. Johnston. *They had sweatshirts and slacks with the exception of one girl, and I took particular notice of her. She had an army shirt on that was unbuttoned, and she had nothing under it.*

I saw these girls walking arm in arm down the middle of the street. They had red rags tied on their left or their right arm. I can't recall. They crossed over in front of me. I asked them what they were doing, and they refused to answer.

Mr. Romines. *As they walked down the street were they chanting at all, Doctor?*

Mr. Johnston. *No, not this group. The preceding group that the teacher had seen were chanting, she had reported to me.*

Mr. Romines. *Do you know what the preceding group had been chanting?*

Mr. Johnston. *Out in the street something about "Ho Lives," and "Join us." Let's see. "Let's Break Jail."*

Mr. Romines. *There were two groups of girls, is that correct?*

Mr. Johnston. *That is correct.*

. . . .

Mr. Romines. *What happened next, Dr. Johnston?*

Mr. Johnston. *I went on upstairs to inform the local police. No. 8 station. When I called them he said to me, "You're about number 14 to report this incident." So I said, "All right, let's get the police down here and have these people removed." Then I went back onto the street and at this moment I ran into my vice principal, Al Fascetti, who had just chased this first contingent of girls out of one of our lower hallways.*

Mr. Romines. *So the first group had actually entered your school?*

Mr. Johnston. *The first group had entered the school, they had burst their way through a door which was guarded by a teacher who, I am sorry to say, was teaching his first day of school—burst through the door, went running through the hallway yelling, "Jail break, let's close down the school," and in running through lifted up their blouses or their T-shirts exposing bare breasts.*

Mr. Romines. *Do you know the approximate size of that group?*

Mr. Johnston. *I would imagine that in that first contingent there must have been 20 or 25.*

Mr. Romines. *All female?*

Mr. Johnston. *All females.*

One of our men coaches stepped in front of one of the girls in an effort to stop her, and she hauled off and socked him right in the jaw. With the help of a few other coaches, the vice principal, and several teachers, they were shoved outside the building onto another street that parallels the first street that they marched down. This is Harwood Street.

Mr. Romines. *Did the two groups then perhaps converge?*

Mr. Johnston. *The two groups then converged on Harwood Street, and Mr.*

Fascetti and I and a few other teachers went out of the building and onto Harwood Street, and there we saw one of the girls standing on top of a car, ranting and raving at our students.

Mr. Romines.   Do you remember what she was ranting and raving about, what she said?

Mr. Johnston.   Just briefly I caught snatches of her conversation, because I felt that my job was more as a buffer between our several hundred students who were outside at that time and the SDS membership. I did hear "Power to the People," something about women's liberation. Also references to the People's Republic, references also to "Join us October 8 to 11 in Chicago."

At that time a police car—actually, it was a police ambulance—had pulled up alongside the car on which this girl was standing. The SDS membership, all the girls, were surrounding this car. The police ambulance had pulled up alongside the car and there were two policemen. They were stationed between the ambulance and the automobile. One of our students said, "They have a Viet Cong flag, let's get it."

.   .   .   .

Mr. Johnston.   . . . So two boys grabbed the flag from the girls who were carrying it.

The girls then attempted to get the flag back. By that time it was a little late, it was ripped to shreds.

The policeman who was closest steeped in between my two boys and the SDS girls, and with this the entire membership of SDS descended upon the policeman.

Mr. Romines.   Now approximately how many? These would still be all females?

Mr. Johnston.   They were all females.

Mr. Romines.   Approximately how many descended on the policeman?

Mr. Johnston.   There must have been very close to 50 all surrounding this car, and when they descended upon the policeman of course they came from both sides of the car and they wedged the policeman between their own vehicle and this automobile.

.   .   .   .

Mr. Johnston.   . . . They were clawing, scratching, kicking, screaming, aiming for the eyes. I know that I have read things about how well they are trained in karate. I saw no karate; I saw a typical female fighting, biting, scratching, kicking.

UNDERGROUND PRESS

A number of underground newspapers have appeared at many high schools across the Nation. For the most part, the central theme which pervades these papers is a criticism of the "establishment," government, school administration, law enforcement, the draft, and the Vietnam war. Also featured are obscene photographs and stories, as well as announcements of interest to hallucinatory drug-users. Believing newspapers to be effective vehicles for agitation, the SDS encourages the establishment of underground papers at the high school level.

NATURE OF SDS THREAT

The high schools in the United States are clearly targeted by the radical left, and particularly SDS, for "activism." High schools are recognized as the recruiting grounds for future college radical activists. In the examples brought to the attention of the committee, it was indicated that, in terms of recruiting new members among high school age youth, SDS so far has been unsuccessful. But in its attempts at temporary disruption of classroom and schoolyard activity, SDS has been most successful. For this reason, educators must be alert to the potential of SDS in fomenting trouble.

For the immature young high school students the advent of the SDS activists in their school may provide a new and different outlet for excitement. SDS does not hesitate to take advantage of these teenagers, for they are enthusiastic workers and a source of needed "bodies" to join in SDS-sponsored demonstrations. Interviews with some of those young people hint they are not fully aware of why they are demonstrating and do not realize the deeper, more serious implications of what they are doing. The ability of the SDS activists to seize upon items of discontent and to fan the sparks of discontent into actual violence presents a clear and present danger.

WHAT POSITIVE ACTION CAN BE TAKEN TO THWART SDS THREAT?

The militancy of the SDS student movement makes it incumbent on educators to understand the exploitation of student power. If a very small percentage of students mobilize that power, they can bring the operation of any educational institution to a grinding halt. Moreover, there exists in many communities a nonstudent minority which may align itself with students if the situation reaches crisis proportions.

The frequent success which SDS has achieved in exploiting discontent on college campuses makes it imperative that high school authorities be prepared to meet varying degrees of disruptive dissension, protest, demonstrations, and even violent disorder. School authorities should consider formulating a program in advance to serve as a guide for handling techniques of leafleting, sit-ins, rallies, marching, chanting, disruption of assemblies, invasion of classrooms, and painting of slogans. Officials should resolve in advance such problems as the identities of teachers or administrators who will have authority to assess the severity of the incident, who will be authorized to issue an order or instruction to the dissidents, what must be said under various circumstances, what measures will be effected in the event of noncompliance, initiation of disciplinary procedures, and at what stage the assistance of law enforcement authorities will be sought and by whom. It is most advantageous to work out local solutions to these matters by consultations between school officials and police, prosecutors and judicial authorities on the municipal, county, or State level.

Teachers and administrators must develop a closer rapport with the student body and endeavor to be more responsive to legitimate complaints and grievances. But, equally important, school officials must be prepared to wield firm and effective authority in dealing with young activists who seek to create chaos in our educational system.

Long ago the protest methods of SDS exceeded the bounds of legitimate and orderly dissent. SDS has now developed to the point where it is a virulent force which threatens the traditional values and institutions of our democratic society. Because of the dedicated commitment of SDS activists to the use of direct action and violence in attaining their objectives, it can be expected that efforts will be intensified to win recruits of high school age, and increasingly hostile efforts will be exerted to "shut down" the high schools of our Nation.

APPENDIX: FACTIONALISM WITHIN SDS

To recognize and comprehend SDS activities fully, it is important to understand the factional groupings within the organization. At present, it manifests itself frequently as three organizations.

On June 22, 1969, SDS broke into two factions near the conclusion of its national convention at Chicago. One group, the Maoist-oriented Progressive Labor Party (PLP) faction headed by John Pennington, established its headquarters in Boston, Mass. The second group, the Revolutionary Youth Movement (RYM), remained in Chicago and took over the SDS national office. The RYM itself divided into two factions, RYM I or Weatherman faction headed by National Secretary Mark Rudd, and RYM II headed by former National Secretary Michael Klonsky. RYM II claimed that the Weatherman's street-fighting tactics would alienate rather than attract the masses of supporters needed for the success of any revolutionary movement. RYM II advocated recruiting working youth and eventually even older workers by a strategy in which SDS showed an interest in the day-to-day grievances of black and white workers and joined with them in "united front" demonstrations and strikes to improve their conditions. The PLP faction of SDS also advocated patient efforts to recruit worker support, but proposed that SDS remain basically a student organization having an "alliance" with workers beginning with those employed on college campuses.

Some of the recent high school disorders have been engineered by the Weatherman faction of the SDS.[1] Weatherman gets its name from a line in a Bob Dylan song called "Subterranean Homesick Blues"— "You don't need a weatherman to know which way the wind blows." Its members are among the most

[1] Hearings Oct. 20-22, 28-30, 1969, Committee on Internal Security.

militant of the SDS factions. The SDS Weatherman faction argues that a world-wide revolution is already in progress among colonized people and among blacks in this country. In order to support such a revolution, the Weatherman faction contends, a revolution must be waged at home and a potential revolutionary class lies in alienated property-less high school youths, most affected by the draft and "jail-like" schools. Industrial workers are dismissed by the Weatherman faction as hopelessly bigoted and college students as inherently middle class. To win high school students to their cause, the Weatherman faction indicates it believes it is vital to prove it is not composed of timid intellectuals.

In this connection, the SDS Weatherman faction planned a massive demonstration for the Chicago area during the period of October 8-11, 1969, designed to "bring the war home." Among the plans made for this period was a "jailbreak" theme to be used on October 10 to gain support for the demonstrations from high school students.[2] However, this planned high school "jailbreak" theme never materialized because on the first day of the demonstrations, October 8, the Chicago police arrested a substantial number of the SDS Weatherman faction for their participation in violent activity in downtown Chicago.

[2] From *New Left Notes* reference for Oct. 8-11 demonstrations: as an "offensive against the schools. The action will be something around the idea of a 'Jailbreak' . . ." Committee Exhibit No. 43, Oct. 29, 1969, Hearings, Committee on Internal Security.

THE SDS AND THE HIGH SCHOOLS
A STUDY IN STUDENT EXTREMISM

J. EDGAR HOOVER

Three shocking incidents happened recently in different cities of the United States. The episodes, though separate in themselves, are part of a national pattern.

Incident Number 1. Jake, a high school student, age eighteen, knocks on the door of a small house. Another student, David, age seventeen, answers.

"I've come for the class," Jake says.

"Yes, come right in," says David.

David escorts Jake into the front room. Some fifteen to twenty young people are present. They have started the class. Jake takes a seat.

What is the class?

David, as leader, defines the purpose: to discuss how high school students can disrupt their schools, organize trouble, harass the administrative staff, and

From *The PTA Magazine*, 64 (January, February, 1970), 2-5, 8-9. Reprinted with the permission of the author and the publisher.

J. Edgar Hoover is Director of the Federal Bureau of Investigation.

even, as David emphasizes, "take over the school" if the opportunity should present itself.

It is a group of student extremists from various local schools learning the techniques of disruption!

Incident Number 2.   Three young men stand on the sidewalk at the entrance of the grounds of a high school. It is morning and pupils are arriving.

Who are these young men?

They are members of the Students for a Democratic Society (SDS), a militant New Left group.

The young men offer the approaching students a leaflet. Some accept; others don't.

What does the SDS leaflet state?

In essence, that the high school is a prison and the students are being exploited.

It asserts that there are a "lack of student power," "rudeness from teachers," "ridiculous dress codes," "no say in course content," "too many irrelevant tests," "unfair grades," "no opportunity to evaluate teachers."

Do students want to do something about "these deplorable conditions"? If so, the leaflet urges them to come to a certain center sponsored by a local college SDS chapter. There they can have discussions, read books, view films, and receive help in mimeographing papers and leaflets.

You, the student, are welcome to attend!

Incident Number 3.   A student walks into his high school library. There on the table he finds an odd-looking paper with a provocative or unusual name such as *The Rat, The Radish, The Spark, The Free Press.*

He's never seen a paper like this before. It's poorly printed. The editing is sloppy. Obscene words and cartoons are frequent. There are articles attacking the high school, the government, the military.

Schools, he reads in one article, are a "twelve-year course in how to be slaves." There is an announcement of some student workshops: "Classroom 'Guerrilla Tactics'—how students can effectively teach in the classroom"; "Radical Teachers and Radical Students—how they can work together." Another item talks about student actions: "Others tore up bathrooms and desks and broke windows to tell them how we see the schools." In still another article, he sees the cartoon of a guerrilla fighter and these words:

"In the final analysis, Revolutionary Culture is only a step towards R-E-V-O-L-U-T-I-O-N!!! It analyzes, seeks, and deals with the enemy. It points to the enemy as not being only an obviously discernible person, but possibly YOUR OWN MOTHER!! AND REVOLUTIONARY CULTURE TEACHES YOU TO DEAL WITH THE ENEMY!!"

What is this publication? It is a high school "free press," or "underground," paper, one of many in the nation.

How did it get into the school library?

It was smuggled in by a sympathetic student or faculty member and left there purposely.

A class in how to foment disruption in high schools, the leafleting of a high school by a radical group for the purpose of encouraging student discontent, the smuggling into high schools of obscene, filthy papers advocating revolution—a few years ago these episodes would have been almost unthinkable.

But no longer.

High schools are today being specifically targeted for New Left attack, the downward thrust from the college level of student turbulence.

Not that high schools are currently being disrupted like colleges. But every indication points to increased student extremism on the secondary school level in 1970.

What is at stake here could well be nothing less than the integrity of our whole educational process as well as the institutions and values of our society.

For that reason, let's take a closer look at SDS's strategy toward high schools.

What is SDS? Why is it trying to disrupt high schools? What is it trying to inculcate into youthful minds? And most important, what can we, as parents and teachers and responsible citizens, do about the problem?

(Let's remember, when we talk about student extremism, that it exists in many forms. In addition to SDS extremism, we have black extremism—a growing problem—as well as extremism from Old Left groups. Perhaps never before have our schools on all levels been so subjected to extremist pressures of all types, white and black, left and right.)

SDS AND ITS MENTALITY OF EXTREMISM

Just a short time ago SDS was virtually unknown to Americans. Today it is almost a household expression, meaning revolutionary and extremist students bent on destruction and riots both on and off campus.

The key emphasis of SDS is extremism, violence, and revolution.

Founded in 1962 by a small group of students at Port Huron, Michigan, what we call SDS moved quickly from a rather mild protest group into a grotesque, destructive genie that last October staged a violent "bust" in Chicago, proudly hailed by its own press as a "war" against the nation:

"Five hundred of us moved through the richest sections of Chicago, with VC flags in front, smashing luxury apartment windows and store fronts, ripping apart the Loop, and injuring scores of pigs [extremist term for police]. It was war—we knew it and the pigs knew it."

Though small in numbers (a claimed membership of some 40,000 in 200 to 250 chapters) and beset by factionalism, SDS has been a key instigator in numerous campus riots. With the group increasingly under Marxist influence, SDS hatred is directed against all facets of our society (called the Establishment). It seeks not reform but blind destruction, with little if any thought of what is to take the place of the system that is to be destroyed.

In carrying out its aims, SDS has developed the activist tactics of the guerrilla fighter. Who are SDS's heroes? Fidel Castro, Mao Tse-tung, Che Guevara, Ho Chi Minh. Why? Because in SDS eyes these men are rebels, guerrilla fighters who have attacked the Establishment in their own countries.

This is what SDS leaders believe they are doing: attacking a society whose democratic principles, morality, and values they not only detest but seek to eradicate. They possess, in their minds, a duty, an impelling destiny or mission to destroy the society in which they live—not tomorrow or next year, but now.

THE COLLEGE SDS AND HIGH SCHOOLS

This guerrilla approach of SDS is directed against high schools. In SDS eyes, they are part of the hated Establishment. In SDS's opinion, the entire educational system (college, secondary, and elementary) is a vast factory and prison where students are molded into robots to staff, operate, and perpetuate the Establishment.

"The function of the schools under capitalism," says one SDS document, "is the preparation of an ideological army for imperialism."

Therefore, SDS-ers feel that it is their job as "guerrillas" to subvert the high schools. Here are thousands of young people, impressionable and at a point in life where they are making critical judgments about the values of life and society. ("Activity in the high schools is probably the most significant new tactic on the left today," writes one New Leftist.) These students should be influenced, or, to use a favorite SDS term, "liberated." Still another SDS term is "jailbreak."

"JAILBREAK," says an SDS paper. "We move on the high schools of Chicago. The schools are prisons and the prisoners must be liberated." (In some isolated instances, SDS-ers have physically stormed high schools.)

Now let's examine just how SDS, primarily a college group and small in numbers, is able to reach into high schools.

Experience shows that SDS attacks are largely (though not exclusively) instigated by college SDS members (or chapters), especially if the school is near an institution of higher learning where SDS is active.

Actually only in rare instances has SDS been able to organize a chapter inside a high school. The very nature of high schools, with their scheduling of classes, absence of dormitories, close supervision, makes the establishment of a chapter most difficult. SDS, therefore, operates in high schools primarily by creating a nucleus of a few SDS-motivated students (usually not members but sympathizers) to work inside the school as catalysts for radical action. If a student's older brother or sister is a college SDS member, or a faculty member is sympathetic, the infiltration process is accelerated.

Just how do college SDS-ers reach high school students and attract their interest?

1. *By leafleting high schools.* This is a fairly common occurrence, with college SDS-ers standing near a high school and handing out literature about the SDS or inviting students to support them in some project.

2. *By holding seminars, conferences, and workshops.* In an eastern state, high school students participated in SDS-sponsored anti-Establishment classes during the summer. In a western city, some eighty high school students attended an SDS conference, where the SDS line on imperialism, capitalism, and the "power structure" was set forth. SDS and communist literature (writings of Marx, Lenin, and Che Guevara) was available.

3. *By assisting in the publication of an underground paper.* College SDS-ers can aid in the publication of a high school underground paper (which may be in the form of a leaflet or brochure) by furnishing editorial direction, printing equipment, and money. Often these high school papers are so obscene, vitriolic, and intellectually shallow that they soon disappear. If there is no high school underground paper, the college SDS may invite high school students to write an article for the SDS college underground paper.

4. *By encouraging high school students to observe and/or participate in college SDS-sponsored demonstrations.* The key objective here is not so much the physical presence of these students to support an SDS project (though this can help), but their exposure to the rough-and-tumble tactics of on-the-street confrontations. In one instance, some fifty high school students participated with SDS students in seizing a college building.

5. *By trying to secure speaking invitations in high schools.* In one instance an SDS-er spoke to a school assembly at the invitation of an international relations club; in another case, under the auspices of the student government. Nothing pleases SDS better than to have official (or unofficial) invitations to address students.

6. *By working through faculty members who previously were either members of or sympathizers with SDS (usually as students in college).*

SDS AGITATION INSIDE THE HIGH SCHOOL

The college SDS has attracted and developed some student sympathizers in high school. How is agitation carried on in these schools?

SDS's approach here is to stir up as much dissatisfaction as possible in the student body on *within-the-school issues.* SDS, though a revolutionary Marxist group, realizes that these young people are not yet proper revolutionary material. The vast majority couldn't care less for slogans about fighting "imperialism" and "warmongers." Many, it is true, are concerned about national issues such as the war in Vietnam and the draft, but in reality it is the immediate, at-hand student issues inside the school that, as one young lady told me, really "turn the kids on"—issues such as dress regulations (how short a skirt a girl is allowed to wear or how long a boy's hair should be), cafeteria service and/or food, disciplinary rules.

These are the issues that SDS seeks to exploit.

If a student is suspended, let's say, for wearing his hair too long or using drugs or abusing a teacher, how is this handled by SDS?

It simply shows, says SDS, that *you*, the student, really mean nothing in this high school. The school is part of a wicked, corrupt Establishment that is trying to turn you into a robot. You have no freedom, no rights, no opportunity for creative expression. These rules are simply designed to make you part of the "system."

"Both student and teacher are tool *and* product of administrative totalitarianism."

The school administrator (usually the principal) is what might be called, in SDS eyes, *the resident dictator*. That is, he is the on-the-spot symbol of the hated Establishment:

"The administrator, whose real function is nothing greater than the maintenance of the campus (a task which could be easily performed by a simple-minded computer), has become the lord and master of our schools, commanding unbounded fealty."

Before an incident is staged, SDS (in its printed literature) makes clear that careful advance preparations must be made:

1. *Is this the best possible issue on which to harass the administration?* Unless a highly volatile issue is chosen, about which many students are concerned, the incident can backfire.

2. *Gain support by talking about the issue with other students.* "Show the students that we *are* on their side and have many of the same concerns they do." A good time to talk about these issues, says an SDS pamphlet on high schools, is during physical education classes.

3. *Contact minority groups in the school to solicit their support.*

4. *Consider the possibility of an underground paper.* When the first issue is printed, mail a copy to as many student cliques as possible ("so that the paper is IN"). Why mail it? "Mailing is emphasized because any attempt to distribute such a paper on campus would result in those responsible for it being crushed by the administration."

5. *Try to secure as much nonstudent support as possible: teachers, parents, religious groups, unions.* This includes PTA's. "We should get our parents active in PTA *and* make a concerted effort to get PTA support. In all our dealings with these groups, our position should be polite but firm. We are asking them for support because we feel that in many areas our interests are mutual, but [we impress on them] that this is a student movement and we have no intention whatsoever of giving up any of our power to adults."

The SDS has no illusions about its ability, even with careful preparation, to carry off permanently effective protests. But it cites what can be done:

• At one school, thirty students destroyed their student activity cards and "sat in" for the first ten minutes of the fifth period in protest against an assembly's being called off for the third time.

• At another school there was "a storm of protest over the suspension of a student for wearing his hair too long. . . ."

• Actually, SDS says, "even such seemingly destructive actions as starting trash can fires and pulling fire alarms are forms of protest directed at the school as it is now constituted."

SDS GOALS

SDS goals in high school agitation are both immediate and long range.

The immediate goal, of course, is to foment student unrest and turbulence for the specific purpose of harassment. The SDS is an activist group, more interested in confrontation and conflict than in study and ideology.

The long-range goals are several:

• *To radicalize, as much as possible, selected students* who might, upon entering college, be recruited into SDS and extremist activism. SDS realizes that only a small minority will either agree or be sympathetic. "The job of radicals is not to lead the youth," says one New Left writer. "It is to find young leaders and help make them radical."

• To build, if possible, a *radical consciousness* among the students as a whole; that is, to inculcate in even unsympathetic students a feeling that there is an "evil" Establishment, that their education is "irrelevant," and that society is corrupt; to undermine respect for the law; to try to tear down our national heroes and look for everything bad in our country; to urge students to be cynical about our values; and to discourage genuine cooperation between adults and young people.

• To develop a *link with the future working class.* Many high school students will not go to college but will obtain jobs instead. If, while in high school, they can be radicalized to a certain extent, they may be catalysts of future radical action; for instance, in labor unions. "If they can be socialized into a new ideology, the making of a radical industrial working class is both theoretically and practically possible."

• The ultimate long-range goal, of course, is "liberation" or "jailbreak"—that is, *the complete disruption of the educational process.*

WHAT OF THE FUTURE?

SDS is badly split, and its organizational future is uncertain. The present factions are *Weatherman* (the most militant group, so called from the words of Bob Dylan, "You don't need a weatherman to know which way the wind blows"); *Revolutionary Youth Movement II* (which recently declared itself a separate "anti-imperialist" youth group); and the *Worker-Student Alliance* (controlled by the Old Left pro-Red Chinese Progressive Labor Party).

But regardless of what happens to SDS as an organization, the extremist mentality remains. In America today we have a minority of young people, many of them well trained academically, who have become disaffected from the fundamental values of the nation. These radicals, regardless of how they may quarrel among themselves, agree in their critical analysis of our society: that it is rotten and should not be reformed but destroyed. Speaking more and more in Marxist terms, this minority works for a revolution.

WHAT CAN WE DO?

1. Be appreciative of the majority of our current generation of poised and intelligent young people. The extremist minority, though influential, represents only a numerical few of our young people. Let's not condemn a whole generation for the extremist tactics of a few.

2. Recognize that student dissent is not necessarily identified with extremism. Legitimate dissent is part of our tradition. We want young people to think for themselves; this is the very heart of our educational process. On our campuses we have students with a vast variety of viewpoints—sincere idealists, with deep and honest convictions of protest, as well as extremists. We must be careful of our facts. Let's not sweepingly categorize all dissent under the label of extremism.

3. Distinguish between peaceful change through democratic processes on the one hand and destructive violence on the other. Our system is based on the inevitability and desirability of change. But this change must be within the law, not carried out by violence.

4. Remember that any educational or school decision made under the threat or actuality of violence, blackmail, and coercion sets a dangerous precedent.

The growing infauation with violence is one of our nation's most pressing problems. Education can function only in an atmosphere of mutual trust, a desire to search for the truth, and a willingness both to speak and to listen. Schools simply cannot function under the fury of the mob, the shadow of the barricade, or the fist of the disrupter.

5. As adults we need continuous and sincere communication with our young people. All too often adults "tune out" the young. Yet many of them have important messages. Let's talk to them—and maybe they in turn will listen to us. I'm sure the most effective school administrators, teachers, and parents are those who communicate with young people, are responsive to their legitimate needs and aspirations, and provide meaningful counsel.

6. Adults, especially teachers and parents, should set good personal examples for young people. Here is one of youth's major complaints—that adults talk in one way and act in another. The power of personal example, reinforced by personal conviction and courage, can be contagious for the good.

Let's admit that we have weaknesses in our society. Let's also assert that our society is working through legitimate processes of government to correct those weaknesses. We want young people to know what good will, hard work, and commitment to the positive can accomplish in a democratic society.

7. Keep faith with America. This means that in our pluralistic society we may have disagreements and conflicts, separate groups and interests, but that we all work for the best interests of our country. America needs a reaffirmation by its people of the heritage of freedom which gave it birth.

The very presence of an extremist minority of young people—as in SDS, which rejects our democratic values—should give all Americans concern. . . .

LEGAL ASPECTS OF CONFRONTATION

THOMAS A. SHANNON

"Confrontation" in a high school setting is an attempt to replace reasonable discussion with raw power in an open and infamous manner. It is an effort carefully calculated to push the high school principal, as the primary administrative representative of the Peoples' legally constituted governing board of a high school, into a totally untenable position to exercise his delegated administrative authority over faculty and students in a reasonable, prudent and constructive manner. The main guideline for confrontation is: "If you cannot bend the high school principal through blatant intimidation, then befuddle him to such an extent that he will act during and after the confrontation in a heavy-handed and grossly inappropriate manner, which will alienate him from the majority of faculty and students in the high school, as well as a populous, articulate segment of the community served by the high school, thus reducing the principal's capacity to respond in an effective way to the crisis created by the confrontation."

Confrontation has only one goal: To win total, blind and uncritical acceptance of the demands made by those who resort to it. The extent to which the demands of high school students participating in confrontation are "negotiable" or may be modified is a function either of the lack of crucial student, faculty or community support which the confrontation leaders sense is a fatal disability to their cause or of an *innocent* use by a relatively unsophisticated group of students of an unusual technique of dealing with a school administration which the nonsense of extensive national or regional publicity has shown to be successful elsewhere.

The conditions in which confrontation occurs in a high school are characterized by *either*

1. an autocratic, perhaps even despotic, administration which opposes or discourages any significant, independent and important student involvement in operating the school, or

From *Journal of Secondary Education*, 54 (May, 1970), 195-201. Reprinted with the permission of the author and publisher.

Thomas A. Shannon is Schools Attorney, San Diego Unified and Community College Districts, San Diego, California.

2. a core group of activist students who absolutely insist upon having the ultimate or final say in the management of the school (in the case of young persons who aspire to something like constructive leadership) or whose most fervent desire is to destroy the school (in the case of the young persons whose despair over their own role in society has transformed them into anarchists or nihilists).

When either of these sets of conditions, or some combination thereof, exists in a high school, the high school principal has a potential confrontation problem on his hands. And the high school student body changes so profoundly on a regular basis each year that the assurances a high school principal may give himself *this* year that no confrontation will occur may not be valid for *next* year.

Confrontation in no way changes the basic duty of the high school principal to insure that classes operate without disruption and that good order and discipline prevail on the campus. The law is very specific in this regard. As the United States Supreme Court said in *Tinker vs. Des Moines Independent Community School District,* which was decided February 24, 1969 and has become known as the "armband" case:

> . . . *conduct by the student, in class or out of it, which for any reason— whether it stems from time, place, or type of behavior—materially disrupts classwork or involves substantial disorder or invasion of the rights of others . . . not immunized by the constitutional guaranty of free speech.*

In order to prevent material disruption of classwork, conduct involving substantial disorder or an invasion of the rights of others, the high school principal has three basic legal tools to use:

1. enforcing school regulations which delineate standards of acceptable student conduct necessary to preserve the educational decorum.

2. arranging for the enforcement of the criminal law by law enforcement authorities; and

3. resorting to the civil law to control conduct through the sanction of contempt of court for violations of court orders, such as injunctions or wardship orders.

The use of any of these three legal tools is the application of lawfully constituted power. And the effective application of power is a delicate matter, as anyone who knows power appreciates. There is a plethora of school regulations and laws which may be invoked in an attempt to maintain a satisfactory level of civil order on a campus during and after a confrontation. The problem is selecting the *right* school regulation or law, under *all* the circumstances, which will best handle the behavior problems always generated by confrontation. And it is here that the professional judgment factor of the high school principal comes into play. In an earthy analogy, you do not use a 10-gauge shotgun to kill a pesky mosquito; on the other hand, you do not take on a snarling, enraged bear with a flyswatter.

Before the high school principal can make his selection of sanction, he must have answers to several crucial questions. Some of these questions are:

1. Who are the students confronting you?

2. What are their demands?

3. Are they organized?

4. Do they deliberately plan to throw the campus into disorder or is the disorder an unintended or negligent by-product of their confrontation?

5. Are "outsiders" involved in the confrontation?

6. If "outsiders" are involved, do they appear to occupy positions of leadership in the confronting group?

7. Does the confronting group have any real leadership or merely big-mouths who are always standing in *front* of the group?

8. If the confronting group does have leadership, to what extent can this leadership influence the actions of the group? Who are the leaders? Are they "over-articulating" the demands of the confronting group? (That is, if the majority of the confronting group is demanding better food in the cafeteria, are the apparent leaders attempting to verbally expand this issue into a phony issue of who controls the curriculum of the school?)

9. Can the group or its leaders be dealt with in a rational or reasonable manner? Or are they intractable in their demands?

10. Will negotiating with the confronting group give them more power (or credibility) than they now have? (That is, do you "legitimize" the confronting group's leadership by negotiating with it?)

11. What will be the precedent ramifications of negotiating with the confronting group on future problems in the school?

12. What kind of support does the confronting group have in the community?

13. What are the community expectations of the high school?

14. What is the posture of the high school teachers in the situation? This is an important consideration in this era of "professional negotiations." What are the expectations of the teaching staff? What impact upon their morale will certain courses of action selected by you have?

15. What is the posture of the majority of students?

16. What is the posture of the Governing Board? This is a *crucial* question in the high school situation because Governing Board members are elective officials who are close to the people of the local community, as contrasted with the appointive University Regents or State College Trustees whose "community" is the whole State. The political pressure on high school Governing Board members to "restore order" will be terrific. As a high school principal, you must be aware of this reality and be sensitive to it, or you will be caught in a vise, with the people and the Governing Board on one side and the students on the other side.

This is only a partial listing of questions the high school principal must resolve before he can make an intelligent selection of the law or school regulations which he will invoke to control the problem.

If, in the best exercise of a high school principal's judgment, he has decided that the confrontation has not and will not result in any criminal conduct, and that the conduct problems created by the confrontation can be handled by student conduct regulations in effect at the school, he then has isolated his remedies down to short or long-term suspension and possible initiation of action looking toward expulsion of the errant students[1] and, for school staff members who confound his efforts at restoring peace on the campus, the filing of charges seeking their dismissal from school district employment.[2] Under the law, the high school principal has total responsibility over his staff and students.[3] While the principal may share his authority with teachers and students in virtually any way he decides helps him to govern his school, he cannot share his fundamental responsibility for the results which accrue because of the exercise of that authority. Regardless of how "collegial" or "democratic" a principal's school administration may be, he will be held strictly accountable for the conduct of his students at school as the high school principal. So the principal must be ready at all times to make the tough decisions because the law designated him as the one responsible for supervision and control of his school.[4] And he should accept this as an important challenge! Where anarchy exists, repressive measures are always forthcoming and repression always wins because society will not permit itself to be destroyed. Where repressive measures are too great, the repression becomes as evil as the anarchy. The principal knows his school better than anyone else and knows how much *school* repression is sufficient to control the situation.

If the principal expects any kind of violence to occur as a result of the confrontation or believes that persons other than students or school staff may become caught up in the confrontation, then I believe he has simply no choice but to call in the law enforcement authorities. This does not necessarily mean that the police will immediately take action once police leadership arrives on the campus. But, being present, they will be in a position to determine when and what kind of police action, if any, is indicated by all the circumstances of the developing situation.

Because confrontation is an attenuation of mob politics, violence is always possible. Also, today young people in high school are being recruited and enlisted as activists in political and social causes by adults ruthlessly intent upon broadening their own bases of political power; therefore, the chances that "outsiders" will be involved in a confrontation generally are high. In view of these facts, you will want some kind of understanding with the police. Accordingly, it is absolutely crucial that you develop, as quietly and unobtrusively as possible, a plan of action with local law enforcement officers and prosecuting attorneys. If

[1] For suspension and expulsion, see Sections 10601-10609, 9012-9014, 9021 and 9301, Education Code and Sections 300-307, Title 5, California Administrative Code.
[2] For dismissal of certificated employees, see Sections 13403-13446, Education Code.
[3] Section 5800(m), Title 5, California Administrative Code.
[4] *Ibid.*

order cannot be maintained, if the normal functions of the high school are interrupted and cannot be restored, and if educational objectives cannot be attained, I do not see any other acceptable alternative than to call for assistance. And the kind of assistance needed, only the police can give.

The primary aims of the police are to protect life, safeguard property, and restore order. These factors are delicately balanced by the police in deciding how to handle a particular decision—and that decision depends on the facts of the immediate situation. Once the police are present on campus, the choice of "many" officers/"fewer" officers; armed/unarmed; uniform/mufti; charge/retreat; become matters of *police tactics*. However, the police should cooperate fully with the high school principal in attempting to resolve the conflict. The kind of cooperation between the principal and the police to handle the problem in the best manner possible will not be as readily developed in the heat and passion of an actual school disturbance generated by a confrontation. However, if the principal and the police have a confidential "emergency plan," and it is reviewed from time to time with the police, the joint, overall competency of the principal "under fire" will be greatly enhanced. In the development of his advance confidential "emergency plan," the principal should include the school district's legal counsel, and prosecuting attorneys from the City Attorney's office and/or the District Attorney's office. It is important to emphasize that the "emergency plan" be as specific and detailed as possible; if it is merely a philosophical declaration of generalities pledging "cooperation" and "mutual assistance" it will be vacuous as a practical matter and of no real value if or when a campus emergency occurs. Moreover, the "emergency plan" should be reviewed regularly in a most discreet manner by the agencies which will implement it. Once an "emergency plan" is formulated, it is easy to become somewhat complacent—but personnel change and memories fade, so it is crucial that reviews of the "emergency plan" be conducted on a regular basis.

The police will enforce the criminal statutes on and near the school site if they determine that police action is necessary during or after a confrontation. The high school principal should be familiar with these statutes. There is available through the office of the California Attorney General an excellent compendium of the laws relating to the maintenance of good order and discipline on public school grounds in our State. It was written by Robert T. Granucci, Deputy Attorney General, and is entitled *Protecting the Schools—Legal Remedies for Disruptive Conduct*. It is available at no charge to high school principals either directly through the Attorney General's office or through the State Department of Education. It is required reading for every high school principal.

Some of the statutes which he will want to know about are:

1. *Penal Code Section 602(m)*—Makes refusal to leave a public building after close of normal business hours a misdemeanor. Staying in a building over night is an old trick of school confrontations.

2. *Penal Code Section 647(b) and 653(g)*—Makes loitering about schools a crime.

3. *Penal Code Section 626.8*—Makes remaining upon or near school premises

after having been requested to leave when such presence results in interference with peaceful conduct of the activities of the school a crime. For this statute to be fully operative, the governing board of a school district should adopt a definition of what is *not* "lawful business" on school grounds. The San Diego Board of Education has adopted the following activities as being *not* "lawful business":

(a) Selling or giving pupils magazines, newspapers, or circulars which are not approved for distribution by the chief administrative official of the school or his designated representative prior to distribution.

(b) Encouraging pupils to disobey or otherwise disregard the regulations or orders of the Board of Education, the chief administrative official of the school, or members of the certificated staff of the school or the ordinances of the City of San Diego or the laws of the State of California.

(c) Participating in any activity on the school grounds which is determined by the chief administrative official of the school or his designated agent, to be an interference with the peaceful conduct of the activities of the school or disruption of the school or its pupils or as reasonably probable to lead to such interference or disruption.

4. *Education Code Section 13558.5*—Makes it a misdemeanor for nonstudents over 16 years of age to come upon school grounds and willfully interfere with the discipline, good order, lawful conduct or administration of any school class or activity of the school with the intent to disrupt, obstruct or inflict damage to property or bodily injury.

5. *Penal Code Section 409*—Permits declaration of an "unlawful assembly."

There are merely a few of the many statutes which can be invoked to maintain law and order on school grounds. A full listing would include conspiracy statutes, laws prohibiting the contributing to the delinquency of a minor and statutes governing the declaration of juvenile delinquency.

From the viewpoint of the high school principal, the main immediate advantage of arrests is the summary removal of leaders and "outsiders" participating in unlawful disruption during or after confrontation which gives the principal a chance to fill the leadership vacuum in a positive and constructive way looking toward reestablishment of educational decorum on the campus.

Finally, the high school principal may wish to consider obtaining a protective court order from the civil side of the local Superior Court. An injunction is especially appropriate where "outsiders" come near the school site for purposes of agitating students. These persons are very well informed about the criminal law and are so wily in going about their task of spreading disruption and discontent that it is sometimes exceedingly difficult to pin them with a criminal conviction. Violation of an injunction is punishable by contempt and the judicial determination of whether or not an injunction has been violated is easier and more speedily attained than is a criminal conviction.

Generally, in order to obtain an injunction, the school district legal counsel must show that there is an imminent danger of violence or damage to property, a significant disruption of the educational program, or an impending violation of law, any or all of which will produce irrevocable harm to the schools and which cannot be protected against through any other suitable legal remedy. The main advantage of an injunction is the clearing of the area of leaders and "outsiders" participating in the disruption. In this sense, it serves the same function as an arrest. Other collateral benefits of an injunction as far as the schools are concerned are that by its issuance of the injunction, the local Superior Court has made a public judicial finding that the results of the confrontation are absolutely unlawful and the injunction tends to develop support for the difficult position of the schools.

In conclusion, a high school principal and his staff should not become unduly concerned about the many threats they will hear during and after the confrontation that they are going to be sued for having the temerity to interfere with the dissenters' self-styled "constitutional right" to disrupt and close down a school. If he acts in a *non-malicious* manner, he will have nothing about which to be concerned. Even if he is sued, his school district will provide him with a legal defense and pay any general damages that would be assessed against him. But the chances of such a suit being successful are remote indeed if he acted in a reasonable and non-malicious manner during and after the confrontation.

PROPOSED PLAN TO COPE WITH STUDENT UNREST AND DISTURBANCE (CALIFORNIA)

INTRODUCTION:

This plan has been provided by the Special Committee To Develop an Emergency Plan for Student Unrest and Disturbance on Campus for the purpose of providing guidelines to the principal and his staff in case of impending disturbances or riots.

Students in our present society who have become involved in action that will lead to ways of confrontation with adults, leaders, or the "system" have caused difficult incidents in many schools. It is important that demonstrations be detected early. The earlier a demonstration is detected, the less of a chance it has of influencing the health, welfare, and safety of those people involved or those people who are spectators.

PROPOSED PLAN:

Upon becoming aware of the first signs of general student unrest (gatherings of large groups of students, large numbers of students tardy or refusing to go to class, pattern of general refusal to obey or defiance to teachers, outbreaks of

From *High School Student Unrest,* Education U.S.A. Special Report (National School Public Relations Association, 1969), 41-48. Reprinted with permission of the publisher.

student fighting or unprovoked assaults), the principal should take the following steps:

1. Meet with his administrative staff to determine whether or not a student disturbance is probable or imminent either on or outside the school grounds.

2. If a disturbance is probable or imminent, telephone the superintendent (or in event of his absence, his designated representative) immediately and inform him that there is an emergency and that you are proceeding with the emergency unrest plan.

3. Assuming approval of your action will be given, in order to prevent harmful delay, immediately place the emergency plan into effect.

The emergency plan is as follows:

THE PRINCIPAL OR ADMINISTRATIVE STAFF SHOULD:

1. Arrange to have movie and still pictures taken.

2. Arrange to have tape recordings made, if possible.

3. Arrange to control or have all phone calls monitored.

4. Be ready for false (fire) alarms that may require P.A. announcements.

5. Inform the District Office of the situation and action being taken.

6. Notify Public Safety or local police or sheriff's office and request they stand by *off* campus to keep outsiders from joining the student group.

7. Request both uniform and plain clothes personnel.

8. Arrange to have portable P.A. system in principal's office.

9. Announce or name the situation—"Inciting a riot," "Disturbing the peace," "Unlawful assembly," "Disrupting normal school activities," or "Refusal of loiterers to leave."

10. Ask students to either join the "hard core" demonstrators or "go to class."

11. Release no information to news media.

FACULTY SHOULD:

1. Continue to hold classes according to schedule.

2. Those teachers with preparation periods should assist in getting cooperative students to attend their classes.

3. Support the actions of other staff members.

4. Assist cooperative student leaders' actions.

5. Contribute to the efforts of leaders, be they officers, teachers, administration, police, or parents, in their efforts to control the situation.

6. Take roll and record tardies, if necessary, for later verification.

7. Do not release students without direction from the principal.

8. Lock classroom doors and close windows.

9. All staff members and teachers on prep are to report to the principal's office for directions.

10. No bodily contact between staff members and/or students. Let the police handle the individuals who refuse to leave campus.

11. Disregard fire alarms unless so directed by an administrative P.A. announcement.

12. Physical education classes are to return to locker room, dress, and remain there.

13. Team-up when possible in case later verification of events is necessary.

CUSTODIAL STAFF:

1. Lock all restrooms.

2. Secure work area, lock laundry, kitchen, desks, cabinets. Secure trash cans if possible to prevent fires and potential vandalism.

3. Stand by for further assignment.

CLERICAL STAFF:

1. Stay at work stations to monitor telephone calls and relay instructions.

2. Lock the safe and all files.

PARENT "CORPS":

1. Wear normal dress.

2. Act only as "observer."

3. Remain apart from dissident students.

4. Move around and be seen by students.

5. No bodily contact with students.

6. If students wish to confer with you, please listen.

PRIOR ARRANGEMENTS:

1. Have a prearranged plan as to assignments for pictures being taken, tape recorders available, phones being monitored.

2. Know how you are going to use personnel: faculty, students, parents, and custodians.

3. Establish prior contact with local public safety or sheriff's department as to whom to contact in the event of an emergency.

4. Be prepared to communicate with the demonstrating students. Use a bull horn if public address system is out.
   a. Read prepared statement (1) below.
   b. Provide opportunity for them to comply.
   c. Urge dispersal and return to class.
   d. If verbal statements not possible, prepared statements (1) should be handed out.
   e. If deemed necessary, warn students they could be subjected to disciplining measures or suspensions.

PREPARED STATEMENT

Your present actions indicate the existence of a problem. The solution of this problem cannot be reached without a careful examination of the facts. You are requested to return to class. Failure to return to class will be in defiance of one or more of the following laws: E.C. 13557, E.C. 10609, E.C. 9021, P.C. 415, P.C. 407, P.C. 409, P.C. 416, and may result in suspension from school.

The administration and faculty share your concerns. Therefore, we solicit your cooperation in complying with our request. An open meeting to discuss these matters with your indicated spokesman will be held within 24 hours. We pledge our sincerity in meaningful dialogue.

5. All information to news media will be handled through district office.

6. Have a law enforcement official witness and hear the school official make the announcement for the demonstrators to leave.

7. The law official should also make the same announcement.

8. If necessary make arrests.

9. Hope you never have to use this material.

PROCEDURES RELATED TO MAJOR STUDENT DISORDERS (CALIFORNIA)

BEFORE THE INCIDENT OCCURS

1. As soon as the principal becomes aware that a disorder might occur, he shall inform the assistant superintendent in charge of his attendance area. If the assistant superintendent is not immediately available and time is of the essence, the principal shall notify the deputy superintendent. In the absence of the deputy superintendent, the principal shall notify the superintendent.

2. If it becomes quite apparent that real trouble is imminent, it would be appropriate to notify the watch commander's office at the police station.

WHEN AN INCIDENT OCCURS

1. Notify police watch commander.

2. Notify the assistant superintendent.

3. Implement action per procedures outlined below for special types of disturbances.

NONSTUDENT INVOLVEMENT

When the disturbance involves nonstudents, treat the case in accordance with instruction from the police representative. Whether it is advisable to consider "loitering" as "unlawful assembly" is best determined by the law enforcement agency. Under no circumstances should an administrator attempt to remove outsiders without the assistance of the police representative.

If the number of nonstudents is sufficiently small for the administrator to manage a formal refusal to leave campus, he may proceed with the following steps:

1. Make sure that the person or persons have no "lawful business" at the school, with at least one (1) adult witness.

2. Obtain all possible evidence on the individuals—names, addresses, photographs inside building if possible.

    (a) Reduce to writing the names of all eyewitnesses; the District Attorney will take statements.

    (b) If possible, observe the individuals yourself.

2. Direct them to leave, with at least one (1) adult witness.

4. If they refuse, indicate that their remaining is in violation of Penal Code Section 602.9 and, if possible, hand them a copy of the Code Section or read it aloud.

5. If they still refuse to leave, call the police. Talk to the desk officer and tell him of violations of 602.9 of the Penal Code.

6. Police will take charge of the individuals and remove them from the campus.

7. Throughout this procedure, be sure that you are observing every possible detail and write it down as soon as possible. A full description of an incident will many times result in the District Attorney charging a person with other violations (e.g., disturbing the peace, threats of violence, use of obscene language, assault). It is suggested that one (1) staff member be assigned to record all details.

The administrator is cautioned that each step is extremely important to follow to insure eventual prosecution by the District Attorney's office.

Special Note: If students are in class at the time nonstudents arrive on campus, it is important that all students remain in class until the nonstudents leave or are removed. If students are out of class at the time nonstudents arrive on campus, it is important that students be required to report to their next assigned class and stay there until the emergency is over; unless personal safety of students would be better served by dismissal with orders to vacate school premises.

STUDENT INVOLVEMENT

At any time when an emergency arises involving participation of any part of the student body, it is important and required that all teachers maintain an accurate record of students absent from class. During such emergencies, it is necessary for each teacher to maintain a written record of all events when so requested by the principal. Records shall include time, names, locations, and any other pertinent information. A record may look like this:

1:15 P.M.—State of emergency called.
1:16 P.M.—Roll call shows following students absent from class: (list)
1:17 P.M.—Students ordered to remain in room until dismissed by teacher.
1:20 P.M.—Classroom disturbed by four (4) nonstudents. (describe)
1:20 P.M.—John Jones and Mary Smith left class contrary to orders of teacher.
1:30 P.M.—Observed _____#_____ students physically molesting a student in the patio. Witnesses: Jay Malone and Marian Pitt.
1:31 P.M.—Locked classroom door unless or until personal safety of students dictate dismissal with orders to vacate school premises.
2:00 P.M.—Dismissed class on signal from principal.

> Signed, dated, and submitted to principal
> before leaving campus.

Penal Code Section 602.9

Any person who comes into any school building or upon any school ground or street, or sidewalk, or public way adjacent thereto, without lawful business thereon and whose presence or acts interferes with the peaceful conduct of such schools and disrupts the school or its pupils or school activities, and who remains there, after being asked to leave by the chief administrative official of that school or any designated agent of the chief administrative official who possesses a standard supervision credential or a standard administration credential, or who carries out the same functions as a person who possesses such a credential in the absence of the chief administrative official, the person is guilty of a misdemeanor. The term "school" as used in this section means any elementary school, junior high school, senior high school, or junior college.

The term "lawful business" as used in this section means a reason for being present upon school property which is not otherwise prohibited by a statute, by ordinance, or by any regulation adopted pursuant to statute or ordinance.

PROCEDURES FOR HANDLING STUDENTS WHO REFUSE TO ATTEND CLASS:

1. Disconnect automatic bell systems.

2. If students are not in class, sound emergency alarm system which will get them into the classroom.

3. Disconnect automatic fire alarm system, but maintain a standby watch to reconnect in case of fire emergency.

4. Terminate use of all telephones immediately except as directed by the principal.

5. Lock all appropriate doors and protect files.

6. Notify authorities.

7. Identify leaders where possible.

8. Direct students to return to class, making certain your instructions are clear and understandable.

Students who respond to instructions shall be treated as tardy to class. Students who fail to respond to instructions shall be required to leave campus under provisions of Penal Code Section 602.9

The safest place for students is in the assigned classroom under the supervision of their teacher. The last thing to do is dismiss students.

Only when the building is threatened by fire or bombing shall the principal evacuate the plant. However, any student wishing to leave the school should be dismissed if there is genuine danger of his injury if he remains.

Special Note: If a parent calls for a student at the office, a release will be effected, provided such release can be made without danger to school personnel. The protection of the school plant and personal equipment of staff is the proper function of the police department, not the custodial staff.

In the interest of consistency and sound procedures, whenever a superior assumes command of a situation, he should not relinquish the command until the emergency is declared over. The subordinate shall serve in an advisory capacity.

When an incident involves both students and nonstudents, the principal will attempt to return students to class first and then proceed with the procedures of Section 602.9.

FOLLOW-UP PROCEDURES

When, in the opinion of the administrator-in-charge, it becomes necessary to remove participating students or teachers from the classroom, the following procedures are to be followed:

Students (High School and Junior High):   Immediate suspension pending a hearing. The parents will be notified immediately by telephone, where possible, followed by a written communication at the earliest possible date. The written communication shall set forth the reasons for the suspension and the date and time of the hearing. The hearing will be under the direction of the principal in the presence of the assistant principal, student management; the student's counselor; and the area assistant superintendent. When the facts are ascertained, the Committee will make a finding. Parents shall receive written notice of the findings. Before the parents are notified, the superintendent shall be notified by the area assistant superintendent.

Parents who wish to appeal the findings of the Hearing Committee may notify the Board in writing via the office of the superintendent.

Students (Elementary Only):   The hearing will be held by the principal in the presence of one of the student's teachers and one or both of the parents. Until such time that the facts prove otherwise, it is felt that a hearing at this level will be more characteristic of a parent conference than of a formal hearing used in the upper grades.

Teachers: Teachers, whether permanent or probationary, will be proceeded against "for cause" pursuant to Educational Code Section 13403-13441.

NEWS MEDIA—RELEASE OF INFORMATION

The office of coordinator of publication and communication is publishing a suggested outline of procedures for news releases. Until such time that a formal plan is published, principals will notify that office in the initial phase. The coordinator of publication and communication, or his representative, will direct all releases from a designated space at the school. Principals should plan to make themselves available for a press conference as soon as such a conference can be held without encumbering the procedures outlined above, unless they are material witnesses. If so, "no comment."

EMERGENCY PLANS

Each principal will prepare three (3) copies of the attached Emergency Plan forms at the earliest possible date. One (1) copy remains in the office; two (2) copies are to be sent to the area assistant superintendent's office for further distribution.

CLOSING OF SCHOOL

Responsibility lies with the superintendent and the board of education.

Emergency Plan for Campus Disturbances

Each principal shall complete three copies: (1) area assistant superintendent, (2) police department, (3) office file.

Name of School: ———————————————————————————

Address: ————————————————————————————————

School Telephone: ——————————————————————————

Emergency Telephone: ————————————————————————

Location of Command Post: ————————————————————

Asst. Supt. in Charge: ————————————————————————

Emergency Telephone: ————————————————————————

Describe briefly the method to be used to declare a state of emergency. (Be sure to include all auditory or visual signals, if any.)

Describe briefly the "All Clear" signal and how it will be communicated to all personnel:

Describe below the emergency methods and procedures used to bus students.

Emergency Plan for Campus Disturbances (Form 2)

Indicate below who will perform the following duties:

Name

——————————————————— Disconnect bell system

——————————————————— Disconnect fire alarm system

——————————————————— Sound all auditory alarms

——————————————————— Telephone switchboard

——————————————————— Emergency telephone station

——————————————————— Public address system

——————————————————— Notify proper superior

——————————————————— Lock permanent record files

——————————————————— Notify police

——————————————————— Notify fire department

——————————————————— Notify coordinator of publication and communication office

——————————————————— Lock exterior doors

STRATEGIES FOR COPING WITH STUDENT DISRUPTION

An urgent call from your high school principal: Several hundred students have congregated in front of the school and refuse to go to their classes. A half-dozen youngsters are outside the principal's office, clamoring to confront him with a list of "ultimatums." Another group of students is in the P.A. studio, broadcasting appeals for a general boycott of classes. At least one brief fistfight has broken out and several dozen students are roaming the hallways. "What," the principal wants to know, "do we do now?"

What indeed?

Do you tell the principal to "sit tight" while you personally rush over to the school? Do you call the school board president? The board attorney? The police? How do you handle the students outside the school? What about the others—those in the principal's office, in the P.A. studio, and the nondemonstrating youngsters? And what about the staff? How do you respond to the flood of phone calls coming in from parents? What are your immediate objectives—to restore order as quickly as possible, or to find out what's bugging the students?

The time to consider these questions is not when you're tight up against the wall. The time is now.

School year 1969-70 promises to be a year of widespread confrontation between students and the "power structure" of public school systems. It seems inevitable that more and more administrators throughout the nation will be faced with the kind of disruption that is currently exacerbating college campuses and urban high schools.

If you take the view that "it can't happen here," you may be right—but you may also be one of the first, and worst, hit.

This special report—a follow-up to an early SCHOOL MANAGEMENT report on student unrest*—is designed to help you anticipate the possibility of student disruption in your district. If nothing else, it will force you to do some careful "what-if" thinking about the options open to you in different types of disruptive situations.

The administration that "blows its cool" during a student confrontation flubs an opportunity to convincingly demonstrate its capacity for leadership. As one of the college presidents quoted later in this report so aptly notes: "Students are testing the clarity of adults' response." The clarity of your response will be determined largely by the amount of realistic planning and thinking that precedes it.

Reprinted from *School Management* magazine, 13 (June, 1969), 54-58.

* See "Special report on student unrest in the public schools," *School Management*, November, 1968.

WHAT SCHOOLMEN HAVE LEARNED ABOUT HANDLING THE SIT-IN

Sometimes spontaneous, sometimes carefully planned, the sit-in—pioneered decades ago by Mahatma Gandhi and his followers—is the disruptive tactic most widely used by students.

GREENVILLE, MINN.: GIVE A LITTLE*

Twenty-three high school students sat down in the corridor ouside a classroom where military recruiters were conducting interviews. Protesters said they were opposed to the war in Vietnam and, if recruiters were going to be allowed in the school, then anti-war spokesmen should also be allowed. Earlier that day, students had distributed anti-war leaflets.

Reaction: Principal John Brooks met with demonstrators in the hall and told them recruiters were guests and "wouldn't be treated otherwise." However, he agreed with the demonstrators' right to invite anti-war speakers to school.

When recruiters moved to a larger room—to accommodate the unexpectedly large turnout of *friendly* students—Brooks invited the demonstrators to come along and talk to the recruiters themselves. Or, Brooks said, they could remain in the corridor. The demonstrators accepted the invitation to talk to the recruiters.

Result: The incident was over 15 minutes after it began.

Aftermath: Handling of the confrontation was criticized by many, including a town councilman, who thought that the demonstrators should be punished. But Brooks stood by the original action. Since there were no school rules governing such a situation, he said, the demonstrators had violated no rules, and the incident hadn't lasted long enough to disrupt regular school business. Most participants had missed no classes, and therefore wouldn't be penalized, Brooks said. Critics are adamant, however, and still insist that the students should have been suspended.

TEANECK, N.J.: BE READY TO PLAY GAMES

About 35 high school students, led by a faculty member, occupied Principal William Hendry's office. They were demanding, among other things, a black history course, more student voice in teacher evaluation, more guidance counselors and more attention to non-college bound students.

Reaction: At first, Teaneck administrators played a waiting game. They let students keep the office, while they gathered personnel to deal with the situation

* Greenville, Minn., is a pseudonym. The incident described is completely accurate but, at the request of district administrators, all names have been changed.

In addition to the superintendent, Hendry called in his guidance director, parents of participating students, student leaders who were not participating in the sit-in, and members of the city's community task force, which had been created a few weeks earlier to investigate and make recommendations about student needs in the community. The police were also called, but in small numbers. They were dressed in plain clothes and kept hidden.

Although the sit-in had begun in the early morning, it was late afternoon before attempts were made to establish close contact with the occupying students. Aim: to "get to the heart" of demands.

Administrators had free access to Hendry's office, although the occupying students wouldn't relinquish it. Students presented their list of demands to the administrators, and, one by one, the demands were discussed and machinery was set up to handle them. That night, Teaneck administrators: *agreed,* in principle, that students should have more voice in teacher evaluation; *set up* procedures for establishing a student advisory committee for Superintendent Joseph Killorey; *agreed* to make a place for student representatives at Hendry's monthly "cabinet" meetings with key administrators and teachers.

After all student demands had been discussed, Hendry suggested to the students that there was no further need for them to be in his office. They could continue their demonstration, he said, but would have to leave the school building. He said that those who refused to leave might be arrested—but no other disciplinary action was threatened.

Result: At 4:30 a.m., 19 hours after the occupation began, the demonstrators abandoned Hendry's office. Two students remained behind to clean and vacuum the room. Others moved outside, where—with several parents—they picketed for most of the next day.

Aftermath: Hendry's decision not to discipline the sit-in participants led to minor backlash from some students, in the form of a 237-signature petition calling for penalties for the demonstrators. Hendry agreed to meet with petition leaders, but refused to alter his original decision to limit penalties to zeroes for missed classwork.

The faculty member who led the sit-in, however, was suspended without pay, pending civil and school board hearings.

In addition to the steps taken on the day of the sit-in, Teaneck has since established these committees to alleviate further grievances:

A student-teacher-administrator board, to deal *specifically* with the issues brought up by the sit-in.

A township student advisory board, comprising four students each from grades 6-12, to meet with the superintendent on a regular basis.

A student advisory board to the town council, comprising two students from each of the city's two junior high schools, four students from the parochial school, four non-student youths and eight students from the high school, to meet regularly with the town council to discuss community problems concerning youth.

XENIA, OHIO: DON'T BYPASS STAFF

Angered by the expulsion of a Negro girl from the high school cheerleading squad, about 100 black students sat down in the lobby of the school at the beginning of morning classes. Their beef: the cheerleader's expulsion was "too severe" for the offense. (Out of uniform, she had cheered for Xenia's all-black wrestling opponents during a match. She said her action was prompted by "derogatory comments" she heard about blacks from Xenia fans.)

Reaction: Superintendent Frank Mayer told the students that, if they would clear the lobby, he would immediately meet with their representatives in the school's music room. The students agreed. Mayer promised them that he would review the matter with the school's principal and the cheerleader coach—who had ordered the cheerleader dismissed from the squad—and would report back to the students that afternoon. In return, he said, the students should return to class. The students were not penalized for participating in the sit-down.

Result: Half an hour after the sit-in began, the students were back in class. Mayer met with the principal and the cheerleader coach—and he modified their ruling to a one-game suspension and probation for the rest of the season for the offending cheerleader.

Aftermath: Protesting black students were satisfied, but Mayer's actions set off a chain of events that included:

Resignation of the cheerleader coach as coach.

An angry meeting of the teacher's association, at which Mayer was criticized for failing to support the coach's decision and for bypassing a recently adopted grievance procedure for appealing such decisions.

A threatened boycott of classes by white students, who said that the blacks were "getting away with too much."

Analysis

The administrative reactions described here are remarkably similar. In each case, the immediate concern of schoolmen was *not* "getting the school back to normal"—it was finding out why the demonstrators were unhappy. In each case, the administrative procedure for dealing with the demonstrators could be interpreted as "negotiating." And in each case, demonstrators were lightly punished—if at all—for taking part in the disruptions.

Despite these similarities, when the incidents were over, each district was confronted with a wholly *different* situation:

Xenia was on the verge of a struggle that would encompass issues only vaguely connected with the original dispute over the black cheerleader's suspension.

Teaneck still faced picketing by erstwhile sit-in participants—and some parents —and had to deal with a student petition criticizing the administration's failure to discipline those participants more harshly.

Greenville, where the smallest and shortest demonstration took place, remained embroiled in a dispute over the failure to discipline participants.

Why the disparities?

For his part, Xenia Superintendent Frank Mayer admits that he committed a tactical error by handling the original incident almost entirely by himself. He kept in close contact with the students and staff members who were involved, but his unilateral decision to modify the cheerleader's expulsion was a clear violation of an established district procedure for reviewing such matters. Under the standard operating procedure, parents of a student involved in a contested disciplinary ruling must complain, in writing, to the schools' principal, asking that the ruling be changed. If that fails, the appeal must go to the superintendent, then to the board.

When the teachers interpreted Mayer's action as a threat to them, he was forced to backtrack and to implement the standard procedure—*after* his decision had been announced. Thus, he incurred the wrath of teachers and students!

The cheerleader's parents subsequently filed a written complaint with the principal, who stood by his original decision to expel the girl from the squad. When the complaint reached Mayer, he stood by his reversal of the principal's decision. Then, the issue was referred to the school board, which amended the ruling slightly by suspending the cheerleader for two games, instead of one. Predictably, the publicity surrounding the incident attracted a large throng to the school board meeting at which the ruling was made.

Thus, Mayer's strategy was successful to the point that it got the sit-in participants back into class in short order. But it backfired by opening up a new area of conflict with his teachers. During the week that followed the sit-in, Mayer found himself enmeshed in a struggle to placate an angry staff, and to compromise feuding factions of black and white students, who grabbed the opportunity to bring long-standing complaints into the open.

Mayer's lesson? "When you have a written policy for dealing with student complaints, *stick* to it," he says. "If you don't have such a policy, develop one. And in any event, never act so quickly that you don't have time to consider all of your options."

Ironically, although Mayer drew criticism from white students for failing to discipline the black demonstrators, he does believe that a firm, no-nonsense policy regarding disruptions can help head them off.

"We had no set penalty for students who engaged in disruptive tactics, so I used my own judgment," he explains. "Later, we established an automatic three-day suspension policy for any student who participates in a demonstration that disrupts classes. If we'd had that policy at the time, and *enforced* it, I think we would have had considerably fewer problems."

NEEDED: A POLICY

Teaneck Principal William Hendry agrees that lack of a district policy, with guidelines for individual schools, puts the local administrator on the spot.

"Your actions are based on spur-of-the-moment decisions," he says. "It's tough not to be irritated by the situation, and tougher to keep that irritation from influencing your actions."

The solution, in Teaneck, was to delay overt action and to find out, by talking to the students, what their grievances were.

Surprisingly, says Hendry, most of the students' demands were already in the process of being met—by programs in the planning stages that the students didn't know about. "When we explained this, some of the steam went out of their demands," he says. "But they still wouldn't leave my office."

The premium that the demonstrators placed on maintaining "control" of Henry's office was underscored when he suggested that they move to the auditorium to discuss their demands. Says Hendry: "When we made that suggestion, they agreed to it only on condition that they send *representatives* to a meeting in the auditorium while others stayed behind to continue the sit-in. It was a kind of game-playing; we always had an open-door policy, but it was very important to the demonstrators to feel that they had *control* of that room."

Granted the luxury of hindsight, Hendry thinks that he would change only one ingredient of Teaneck's strategy for handling the sit-in. "Students occupied the office early in the morning," he says. "We spent a lot of time deciding what to do and gathering the people to do it, so that it was late afternoon before we began serious discussions with the demonstrators. If I had it to do over, I'd get that dialogue going *much* sooner."

His advice to other administrators who might someday be confronted with the same tactic: "Don't do anything until you've calmed down. Then, get *person-to-person* communications established and start thinking about your options for handling the grievances."

STUDENT COUNTER-PRESSURE

In Greenville, peer group counter-pressure apparently played an important part in breaking up the demonstration quickly. Says a staff member involved in handling the incident: "The crowd of students waiting to talk to the recruiters tended to put the demonstrators down. I think that had something to do with why the sit-in ended as soon as it did."

He believes that the administration's acknowledgement of the demonstrators' right to make their point, and a calm, reasoned response to their demands, were also keys to ending the incident.

The dispute over penalties, although still a touchy issue in Greenville, is slowly subsiding.

"We didn't punish the demonstrators because, frankly, they had violated no school rules," the staff member says. "If we had set some arbitrary penalty, I think we would have bought ourselves a bigger bundle of trouble."

WHAT SCHOOLMEN HAVE LEARNED ABOUT HANDLING THE BOYCOTT

The quickest, surest way for students to get reams of publicity for their grievances is to stay out of school.

PATERSON, N.J.: GET HELP FROM ADULTS

Black students staged five days of protests, capped by a two-day boycott of classes at Eastside high school by about 700 students. Demands ranged from relatively minor money matters (new uniforms for athletic teams) to major shifts in curriculum (abandonment of the "track" system). On the first day of the demonstrations, 175 blacks staged a four-hour sit-in at the school cafeteria, but left at the end of the regular school day at the request of the police. On the second day, the sit-in resumed in the auditorium. Most students again left when ordered out at the end of the day, but 56 who refused to leave were arrested, and 15 of them had to be carried from the building. On the third day, sit-in participants were persuaded to leave by a local black minister and a student protest leader, but they vowed to march on a school board meeting that night. On the fourth and fifth days of the demonstrations, hundreds of students boycotted classes entirely.

Reaction: As soon as the demonstrations began, Eastside principal Jacob Weber established direct contact with representatives of the dissident students. Alternating between his office, where he discussed demands with sit-in leaders, and the site of the demonstration itself, where he spoke often with the entire group, Weber relied on face-to-face communication. Also called in to deal with the students were local black ministers, priests and rabbis, along with community leaders and parents of the students involved.

The Paterson school board met directly with sit-in leaders. The board immediately granted several of their demands. It agreed to hang pictures of black heroes in the school corridors and the pictures are hanging there now. The students, however were not satisfied.

Police, ordered into the school by Paterson Mayor Lawrence F. Kramer, were, according to Weber, "restrained." Arrests on the second day resulted in brick and bottle throwing incidents outside the school.

On the third day, after demonstrators left the school, intending to march on the school board meeting that night, they discovered that the board had cancelled its meeting. Sit-in leaders said this action, along with the continued presence of police in the school, was why they shifted their tactic to an all-out boycott. They claimed they had been led to believe the police would not be in the school that day.

After a special assembly on the fourth day—granted by Weber to allow demonstrators to present their demands to the entire school—the boycott began. During the two days that it lasted, Weber and other administrators attempted to maintain contact with the demonstrators through parents and black community leaders. Administrators urged students to return to classes, but threatened no reprisals for the boycott. When school closed on Friday afternoon, boycotters were still out.

Over the weekend, parents and community leaders expressed sympathy for the students' demands, but strongly urged them to return to class. Some students responded by establishing a "liberation school"—but lack of adult support for the boycott forced them to abandon the school after one day of operation.

Result: On Monday—a week after the disruptions began—most students returned to school and resumed classes peacefully.

Aftermath: In the week following the demonstrations, the school board hired a black assistant principal—one of the students' demands—for Eastside high school. It turned over administration of other student demands, including improvement of toilet and gymnasium facilities, to Weber.

Students arrested during the disruptions stood civil trial, one at a time, on charges of juvenile delinquency (most received suspended sentences), but no reprisals were taken against other participants. Students demanded amnesty for those arrested, but, police pointed out, charges were filed by the mayor, so only the judges could dismiss them.

Student demands for changes in the school's guidance department and elimination of the "track" system (Weber prefers to call it "ability grouping"), have been turned over for study to a citizens' advisory committee comprising parents from both the black and the white communities, faculty members and school board members—but no students. Recommendations of the committee will be considered by the school board and acted upon in the near future.

There have been no further demonstrations and Weber feels that attitudes at the school are "much better" than before the boycott.

MALVERNE, N.Y.: WAIT THEM OUT

Angered by the school board's refusal, at a public meeting, to rule on a list of demands submitted by students a month earlier, hundreds of Negro students engaged in a week of disruption, which included:

An eight-hour sit-in at the school by some 400 black students.

Four days of carefully organized boycotts and demonstrations outside the high school by hundreds of blacks, their parents, and sympathetic whites.

An attempt by protest leaders to seize the school's public address system to broadcast its demands to students who remained in school.

Demonstrators were demanding substantial curriculum changes, more black school personnel and a student advisory committee to the board.

Reaction: At the board meeting which, protesters said, provoked the demonstrations, board members declared that they would take no "immediate" action on any of the student demands until a study was completed into their practicality. The meeting was repeatedly interrupted by shouts from the floor, until board members walked out and conducted the rest of the meeting in private session.

The next morning, when students began the sit-in in the high school lobby, administrators continued meeting with their leaders. No attempt was made to clear the demonstrators until 4 p.m., when all students were normally required to leave the building.

When students refused to leave, police were called in and warned participants that, if they did not leave, they would be arrested for loitering. After the warning, students cleared the building. That night, after meeting in closed session, the board said it was ready to meet "anyone at any time" to discuss the students' demands. But it would not tolerate further disruptions at the school. Furthermore, it said, police would be stationed at the school to make sure that only students and faculty entered the building.

The following day, Friday, protesters staged a brief march through the school building, then left to begin the boycott. Police were ordered to guard the school over the weekend. Protesters vowed to resume their disruptions on Monday, but administrators said that the school would stay open. The board refused to issue an official response to the students' demands, but met informally with boycott leaders on Sunday.

On Monday, demonstrators entered the school in the morning and briefly took over the building's three cafeterias to begin "freedom classes." Shortly thereafter, Superintendent James S. Carnrite entered and told the students that they were suspended and would be arrested if they didn't leave the building. Students left, but met outside in the school's athletic bleachers. They decided that those who wished should reenter the school and voluntarily be arrested. Subsequently, 137 students—and parents—were peacefully arrested. They vowed to resume the boycott the following day, but indicated that they didn't wish to be arrested again.

On Tuesday, about 200 students massed peacefully in front of the school. Board president John W. Lewis, Jr. told the group that all suspended students were free to return to class that day and he said he was urging the school's administration to expedite their demands. Students dispersed peacefully after chanting slogans against Carnrite for ordering the arrests.

By Wednesday, the number of boycotters had dwindled to about 125. They again marched peacefully in front of the school, handing out mimeographed lists of their demands. Boycotters also issued a call for dismissal of all charges against students arrested on Monday.

Result: Protesters, despite failure of the administration to satisfy their demands, returned to classes on Thursday. Demonstration leaders said that they would give the board "time to think" about their demands, and vowed to resume the boycott if they weren't eventually satisfied.

Aftermath: Although students returned to classes, they continued to stage daily demonstrations in front of the school. On the first day back, meetings with school officials broke off when 100 students walked out of school, claiming negotiations were fruitless. Administration officials agreed to draw up a written reply to the demands by the end of the following day.

When the reply was made public, student protest leaders indicated that they were "not entirely satisfied," but were pleased with the response to their key demands. Among the demands granted by the board:

A black history course would be started the following month.

Black personnel would be hired in all areas of the school's operations, including teachers, guidance counselors and clerical positions.

A Swahili course would be implemented, if enrollment were sufficient to justify it.

The word "black" would be substituted for "Negro" in references in the school's newspaper.

A student advisory committee to the board would be formed (three board members had agreed to act as liaisons between the group and the board).

The board submitted its reply on official stationery—but they left it unsigned. Positions of board members had been determined by a telephone poll, and the board never did meet as a group to decide which demands to accept, one member said. In all, school officials acceded to eight of the students' 14 demands.

Despite their original endorsement of the board's action, protest leaders subsequently indicated that they were not satisfied. They continued noisy demonstrations in front of the school each morning, until threatened with suspension. Students then said they would "wait and see," what further action the board took before deciding whether to resume demonstrations. There have been no significant disruptions since the board's official reply.

Analysis

Lesson: When a boycott erupts, be ready to wait it out. Apparently, this willingness to wait—until "negotiations" with students are completed, or until the demonstration simply peters out—can be an important element in keeping the lid on potential violence and in avoiding "physical force" situations that martyr demonstrators.

The rewards of patience as part of the "strategy" for dealing with the boycott are amply established by experiences in Malverne and Patterson. At the end of the fifth day of demonstrations in Malverne, active participants had dwindled from some 300 to about 125. In Paterson, patience on the part of administrators gave demonstrators' parents a chance to exert influence that played an important role in ending the boycott.

Sometimes, an administrator has no choice but to bide time while students demonstrate. Says Malverne Superintendent James Carnrite: "I'm convinced that you reach a point where students are determined to go ahead and do their thing, and no amount of reasoning, threatening or anything else can stop them."

Also, Carnrite points out, administrators in Malverne had been meeting with students for months before the disruptions, but they staged the boycott anyway.

Another point: It may not take long before students discover for themselves what a protest leader in Malverne admits about the boycotts there. As a tactic for securing student demands, he says, the boycotts "accomplished nothing."

Thus, simply waiting for a demonstration to play itself out can be an effective part of the strategy for ending it. But, in the meantime, administrators face the problem of maintaining some degree of order, and, when necessary, clearing a building of demonstrators so that disturbances to other students are kept at a minimum. There are several critical considerations:

Calling the police. A district that calls in the police has not *necessarily* lost its cool. Between them, Malverne and Paterson logged a total of 197 arrests of students and parents—yet the lid never blew off in either district. Why?

"Parents and community leaders helped keep things calm," says Paterson principal Jacob Weber. "We used police, but only as a last resort. Students had plenty of warning, so they could clear out if they didn't want to get arrested. Police, for their part, were carefully restrained, and didn't exacerbate the situation."

Students, Weber is quick to point out, were also quite restrained and "respectful of property."

In Malverne, students made a conscious decision to be arrested after meeting with lawyers and boycott leaders. They marched proudly into the police station and reveled in the publicity.

In two respects, ordering arrests of demonstrators worked against schoolmen in Paterson and Malverne: 1) in both cases, most publicity about the arrests was favorable to the students, who didn't miss the chance to accuse police of "irregularities" in the way the arrests were handled, and 2) in both cases, dismissal of charges against the arrested students immediately became one of the demonstrators' demands.

But the arrests did score one big plus for schoolmen seeking to control the demonstrators: after being arrested once, students almost universally expressed the desire to avoid being arrested again. Thus, they stayed away from situations that might lead to arrest—making it easier for administrators to keep demonstrations outside of the school building.

Leveling with the press. One of the motivating forces behind student disruption is that the youngsters know they can "get in the papers" while they put the pressure on the administration to act on their demands.

Throughout the five days that active demonstrations were being staged in Malverne, protesters—who were quick to admit that publicity was one of their primary aims—met nightly to plan the next day's actions. They dispatched fliers to the community to publicize their demands. They actively sought the press, and carefully explained their position to reporters.

Malverne schoolmen—who had a list of the student demands a month before demonstrations broke out—reacted with only vague statements for publication. Often, board members simply refused to comment. Press coverage of the incident was, therefore, remarkably one-sided, and the protesting students managed to monopolize the headlines.

Avoiding rigid positions. After meeting on the night of the first demonstrations, Malverne school officials announced that all student demands would be carefully considered and decisions would be made according to their "merit." But no action could be taken until recommendations of administrators were received, they said, emphasizing that those recommendations would almost certainly take several weeks to complete. Only one week later, however, students had an official, written reply to their demands from the board.

Included in the board's reply were concessions that it had rejected only a week earlier (putting its reply in writing was one of them). Among those concessions were approval of a black history course to begin in May (previously the board had insisted that the course would have to wait until September, because no teachers could be found) and approval of a course in Swahili, if enrollment were high enough to justify it (previously, the board flatly rejected demands for the course).

Thus, although the board's response to the student demands was flexible, its initial statements gave the impression that it was adopting a rigid stance. Before the incident was over, Malverne schoolmen were in the uncomfortable position of having to back down on some of their earlier public statements.

Involving the community. Conspicuously absent in negotiating the settlement in Malverne were parents, clergymen and leaders of the black community—people who did play an important part in ending the Paterson boycott. Reason: In Malverne, members of the adult community were rather awed at the organization and determination of their youngsters in staging the demonstrations. "The students," says Carnrite, "were beyond the control of their parents." Thus, parents left them alone, and, in fact, sometimes *joined* them in demonstrations.

In Paterson, on the other hand, parents supported the goals of their youngsters, but repeatedly urged them to return to classes once their demands had been presented and administrators began to respond to them. Paterson students, who later charged that they had been "betrayed" by the adult community, could not continue the boycott without adult support.

Significantly, then, calling in parents and other adults is no guarantee that the administration will get help.

Doling out discipline. In Malverne and Paterson, the end of the boycott came about in different ways. But both districts disciplined boycotters the *same* way.

Whether participating in the boycott a day or a week, students suffered no more than the normal penalty for unexcused absences. They were, in effect, "playing hookey," and to deal with them in any other way is to invite administrative headaches.

"You can't deal with several hundred kids the same way you could with just a few who disrupt classes," says Paterson's Weber. "It's administratively impossible."

Inevitably, failure to take stronger punitive measures can lead to "backlash" from the community, especially when the boycott involves racial issues. In Malverne, for example, a committee of whites promised a 1,000-signature petition, demanding that the board enforce charges against students who were arrested.

"Mail was heavy on both sides of the question," says Carnrite. "But we had to stand behind the actions already taken. Students were free to walk away from arrest at any time, and several of them did."

WHAT SCHOOLMEN HAVE LEARNED ABOUT HANDLING VIOLENCE

When violence breaks out in a school, your first priority is to stop it. But how? And what then?

MIAMI, FLA.: BEWARE OF POLARIZATION

An apparently unprovoked attack by about 20 black students against whites took place in the cafeteria of Central high school. Instigated by a group of students who reentered the school after participating in a sit-in and walkout earlier in the day, the melee resulted in hospitalization of seven white students. The attack was brief, but tables were overturned, chairs thrown, and an atmosphere of fear pervaded the school.

Reaction: After a hurried meeting with his staff, Principal Daniel Wagner ordered the school closed for the rest of the day and all of the next, to give things a chance to "cool off." Twenty-five of the students identified as participants in the fight were suspended from school for 10 days.

The incident took place on Thursday. The next day, Wagner met with black students, then with a group of black parents and white parents. In response to expressions of fear for the safety of their youngsters, Wagner told parents that extra teachers and a full staff of school "security officers" would be on hand when the high school reopened Monday.

School officials did not consider calling in regular, uniformed policemen, Wagner said, because they did not feel they would be needed. Administrators were, however, in contact with the police, and intended to call them in if necessary.

On Sunday, 110 angry white parents met with school administrators and demanded that some "fight prevention" measures be taken in the school. Administrators repeated their assurances that extra teachers and security officers would be on hand, but some parents said they wouldn't allow their youngsters to attend school until they felt it was safe. White students, charging that the administration "coddled" blacks, threatened to boycott schools. At the meeting, whites formed a committee of eight parents and three students to take a list of complaints about the administration's handling of black demands to a board meeting scheduled for Wednesday.

Result: When schools reopened on Monday, more than half of Central's 1,900 students stayed away. (Blacks comprise about 35% of the school population.)

On Tuesday, more than 900 students were still out.

On Wednesday, attendance was equally bad. At the board meeting that night, the board indicated that it would appoint a biracial committee of parents, administrators, teachers and students to study the school's race problems.

On Thursday, about 25% of the school's students still had not returned to classes.

On Friday, attendance was down about 23%. School officials announced that a black assistant principal would be appointed the next week. A black administrator was one of the demands presented to the board by black students and parents.

By the following Monday, attendance at Central high school was near normal, and an uneasy calm ensued.

Aftermath: As a result of the incident, and of the subsequent expulsion from school of eight black students identified as leaders of the violence, attitudes at the school and in the community have polarized, says Wagner. The biracial committee appointed to look into the school's problems has collapsed, and "vocal militants" of both races are vying for the spotlight. The expulsion of the eight black students prompted a brief sit-in by about 100 Negroes at the school, but they dispersed peacefully after being threatened with suspension.

After a lengthy battle, the board adopted a new policy on expulsions, which permits a student expelled from one Dade County school to be immediately accepted into another school. The new policy has been hotly condemned by Miami teachers.

GLEN COVE, N.Y.: MOVE QUICKLY AND STRONGLY

About 35 black and white youths brawled at the high school, wielding chains, sticks and other weapons. One white youth was hospitalized with head injuries. Less than 10% of the school's 1,600 students are Negroes.

Reaction: The school was immediately closed for the rest of the day (Friday) and remained closed Monday. Monday night, the board announced, at a crowded public meeting, that more than 35 Glen Cove policemen would be stationed in the district's junior and senior high schools the following day to enforce a rigid set of "emergency measures," including:

1. Barring students from loitering in the halls, lavatories or at their lockers before and during homeroom periods.

2. Barring students from leaving a class, study hall or lunch period without a pass.

3. Suspension of students for leaving school grounds, congregating in racial or ethnic groups or wearing any type of arm band.

4. Suspension of students caught fighting or "hustling" others for money.

5. Temporarily barring all outsiders from all schools.

The police would remain, the board said, until the schools were safe for all pupils at all times.

In addition, the administration—as one of its first acts—had quickly compiled a "fact sheet" on the incident. Copies were distributed to all priests and ministers in time for discussion in their churches on Sunday morning, just two days after the brawl. The purpose of the fact sheet, says Superintendent Robert Finley, was to "kill rumors before they started."

The board also set up a committee of five faculty members to recommend changes needed in the school, and a citizens' commission to study the incident. Fourteen students, named as participants in the fight, were suspended.

Result: The school was reopened on Tuesday, with no further incidents. With police patrolling the halls, the school remained peaceful. About 325 students were absent, compared to a normal absentee figure of about 100.

Aftermath: Despite charges by some residents and students—white as well as black—that the board had "overreacted" to the incident, most Glen Cove residents enthusiastically applauded the board's response.

During the nine school days following the reopening of the high school, police were gradually withdrawn. In the meantime, six black and six white youths —all of whom admitted taking part in the fights—began staging "peace talks" at a YMCA across the street from the school, with administrators taking part. The students issued a statement, calling for withdrawal of police from the building as soon as possible and condemning the use of physical force except when necessary "to defend oneself from attack." The students also requested permission to hold an all-school assembly to present their recommendations and answer questions from other students. School officials granted the request for the assembly, but delayed it a few days to give the situation an opportunity to "cool off" more.

Initially, the administration set up a panel of six white and six black adults to hear the cases of the 14 suspended students and recommend action. The panel, however, came under fire from local civil rights groups because it had no "legal status," and it was disbanded. Subsequent review of the suspended students by the board resulted in charges against 11 of them being dropped immediately for lack of evidence or misidentification. The remaining three remained under suspension pending further investigation into the incident.

Analysis

Did Glen Cove overreact?

Did Miami vacillate?

In Glen Cove, administrators moved with lightning speed, bearing two priorities in mind. First, put an end to the violence. Second, get the facts about the incident out to the community.

In Miami, administrators were equally concerned with ending the violence, and they also moved quickly. But the steps they took weren't nearly as drastic as the restrictions imposed on students in Glen Cove. And, despite constant meetings with students and parents of both races, rumors about the incident grew, and stories of beatings, shakedowns and other alleged actions of black students against white were swapped by parents and students alike. The result, in Miami, was polarization of the races even *before* the school was reopened.

One of the immediate effects of the incidents, in both districts, was a growing fear among black and white parents that their youngsters weren't safe in the schools. Students, too, were fearful. Following the outbreak in Glen Cove, several youths indicated that, if they returned to school at all, they would be armed with knives and chains for self-protection. In Miami, the fear was manifested by the white student boycott and charges that the administration was letting blacks "run the school."

Each district used a different approach for dealing with this fear—and with the problem of violence itself. Glen Cove administrators announced, *specifically*, that 35 policemen—fully two-thirds of the community's police force—would be on duty in the schools until it was safe to remove them. They would enforce a stringent set of regulations designed *specifically* to eliminate situations which might foment trouble. Ways to alleviate the conditions which led to the fight would be earnestly sought. But in the meantime, parents were told, there would be no more fights at the school.

NO DRASTIC MEASURES

In Miami, administrators did not outline specific plans for coping with the immediate problem. Instead, parents and students were assured that "extra" teachers and security officers (ex-policemen hired by the school for prevention of vandalism, assaults, etc.) would be on duty. No other emergency measures were indicated and the actual number of "extra" officers on duty was not revealed, so parents and students never knew *specifically* what fight prevention measures were being taken.

In Glen Cove, then, despite cries of "overreaction" from some parents and students—and despite a belief among some blacks that the police were in school for protection of whites—there was little doubt, among the majority of the community, that the school was *safe*. When the high school reopened, attendance was down, but not nearly to the degree that it was at Miami Central.

Moral: The onus is on the administration to present, first, a "short-range" plan for preventing future outbreaks and insuring the safety of its students and, secondly, a "long-range" plan for dealing with the implications of the incident: causes, effects, and changes necessary to cope with them.

A COMMUNITY PROBLEM

"The school became the battleground for what is actually a community problem," says Glen Cove Superintendent Robert Finley. "We relied on a strong show of force to clamp down on trouble, but we also made it clear that we couldn't handle the situation alone."

Glen Cove's attempts to involve the community in the problem were characterized by the establishment of the panel of six white and six black parents to review the cases of the 14 students suspended for taking part in the fight. Although the panel was disbanded, its existence did indicate that school officials were moving to let community residents have a hand in solving the problems which led to the incident.

Ostensibly, the Glen Cove fight grew out of a previous altercation at the local YMCA, where black youths and white youths engaged in a fistfight over an alleged attempt of one group to extort a quarter from a member of the other group. Officials speculate that, on the day of the fight at the school, both groups were seeking revenge.

The cause of the cafeteria brawl in Miami is even less precisely known. It began as a sit-in by about 90 Negro students, who gathered on the school's patio shortly before lunch to present a list of demands to Principal Daniel Wagner.

"When the students began to gather and refused to return to classes," says Wagner, "some teachers tried to prevent others from joining them. The Negroes presented their demands, but apparently regarded the teachers as 'police,' and refused to talk about their grievances. Regular police had been called, and when a squad car pulled up outside the school, the group began to leave. Its leaders said they wouldn't talk with the police there, but would meet with me later in the gymnasium. Then they left to go to lunch."

Later—for a group of about 20 dissident blacks—was only a matter of about 10 minutes. They entered the cafeteria and blocked the serving line. When a teacher asked them what they wanted, a witness says, they began running out of the cafeteria. Overturned chairs and tables, and attacks on white students occurred on the way out. The incident, says Wagner, lasted no more than one or two minutes.

The brevity of the fight, and the fact that so few students were involved, were considerations in the administration's decision to avoid calling in regular police when the school reopened the following week.

POLICY WAS INADEQUATE

If confronted with the same situation again, though, Wagner thinks he would react more strongly, and more quickly.

"Ironically," he says, "we had a policy for dealing with situations like the walkout. We were to isolate the demonstrators and keep them talking, which we tried to do. But there was nothing in the procedure about what to do if they *refused* to talk. If it happened again, I would move, as soon as possible after the talking stopped, to suspend the demonstrators, tell them to disperse, and turn the matter over to our security force."

By acting more quickly, Wagner believes, the administration can remove the *threat* of violence from the school.

NINE

ALTERNATIVES: NEW DIRECTIONS

Although hard-line strategies are being used to repress student dissent and activism, many thoughtful and positive programs are now being instituted. The present chapter summarizes some of the more important and interesting of these. For the most part, the programs stem from considerations concerning the nature of the revolution facing the schools and the direction such activities are likely to take in the future. These directions have been well articulated by Maurice Gibbons who asserts in his article, "Changing Secondary Education Now," that the trend in educational practice will be far greater freedom of choice for students, increased personal and individualized instruction, greater participation by teachers and students at all levels of decision-making, a diminished emphasis on rules, schedules and programs, and increasing interaction between the school and the community. Gibbons goes on to spell out a variety of proposals for change in the schools which can be implemented *now*. In contrast to the many relatively abstract principles and suggestions which abound in the activism and dissent literature, here are a set of well-grounded ideas for change immediately available to school officials.

Following an examination of social and psychological conditions leading to confrontation and rebellion, Dr. Berlin in "From Confrontation to Collaboration," describes the results of group role playing and discussion sessions (and individual consultation) conducted by a psychiatric team with school administrators and teachers. The techniques used require skilled professionals who understand the personality dynamics and motivations of those involved in confrontation and rebellion. Understanding the dynamics of administrators and teachers as well as students is required, although attention is frequently limited to students alone.

Earlier writings in this volume have pointed to areas of student grievances and the supporting sociological, psychological, political and individual factors in youth themselves leading to activism and dissent. The work of the Philips team (Chapter One) occurred after confrontations had actually taken place. Similarly, a number of techniques for coping with activist behavior and disruption were presented in Chapter Eight. Certain dimensions to be considered in approaching problems of dissent and activism have thus been marked out, e.g., adopt a hard line after confrontations have occurred or engage in dialogue after confrontations have occurred. But what of prevention? The vast middle ground—the area where attempts are made at understanding and prevention—would appear to be the arena which will prove most productive in the long run. The articles which follow describe a variety of techniques which can be (and have been) used by school personnel in mollifying the effects of dissent and activism.

Mark Chesler, in a speech delivered at the Annual Meeting of the Metropolitan Detroit Bureau of School Studies, Inc., presented a number of "Promising Directions for School Change" stemming from his experiences in consultation with a variety of school districts on problems of student dissent. Among the key suggestions and critical needs identified by Chesler are the participation of a third-party negotiator, the need to generate and test new models of organizing schools "along lines that do a more effective job of discovering and processing grievances and injustices," the development of accountability, the need to recruit sympathetic, effective teachers, and the need to "develop better models for the transmission of intellectual content and experience."

In a companion piece Chesler has also included a description of role playing, a potentially very useful device in ventilating feelings and sensitizing various protagonists to the feelings and attitudes of others. The use of role playing in dealing with dissent and disruption is described in a general way in the article by Berlin. Chesler and his associates at the Center for Research on Utilization of Scientific Knowledge go on to describe specific "Role Playing Exercises that Highlight Student School Conflict in Secondary Schools."

Throughout this volume the voices of students have been emphasized. What is the problem from the student's point of view? What are their concerns, recommendations and proposed solutions? One of the more interesting findings of a Harris poll conducted in 1969 was that far more students complained about rules being too lenient and sloppily enforced than complained about arbitrary structures, and a clear majority appeared generally satisfied with things as they were.[1] Abolishing the grading system was rejected two-to-one by students. On the other hand, curriculum innovations were favored by an overwhelming majority. More field work outside the schools was favored by 76 percent of the students, and 65 percent wanted more of a chance to work directly with the community. More student say in the area of policy making was favored by 58 percent of the students (as compared to 35 percent of the teachers and 20 percent of the parents). A majority (54 percent) saw student participation in policy making as "very important," compared to 30 percent of the teachers, and 25 percent of the parents. Practically two thirds of the students thought they should have more to say about making rules and determining the content of the curriculum. In both cases their feelings were not shared by nearly as many parents or teachers.

Several very thoughtful educational documents which make recommendations (and demands!) for changes in school policies and practices have been prepared by students. One such document appearing in the present chapter, "Recom-

[1] Louis Harris, "What People Think About Their High Schools," *Life*, 66 (May 16, 1969): 22-23.

mendations to Superintendents, Principals, Assistant Principals, and Deans of Students in the Area of High School Unrest" prepared by a group of North Carolina students, includes a variety of specific suggestions for mollifying high school student dissent and confrontation.

Most suggestions for answering dissent and correcting the school's ills concern initiating changes in existing school programs, e.g., providing for greater involvement of students, strengthening human relations training, exercising greater care in the selection of students, etc. Doubtlessly many of these proposals have proved useful in a number of instances. Formidable obstacles make understandable the reluctance of educators to propose radical restructuring of the schools. Such obstacles make programs such as that at Parkway of Philadelphia all the more remarkable (Resnik, "High School With No Walls—It's Happening in Philadelphia"). Here in a "school without walls," using urban Philadelphia as a laboratory, many suggestions with respect to school programming are being implemented. The plan is designed to lead students toward greater involvement and meaningful learning on the one hand, and to decrease alienation, confrontation and other forms of silent and vocalized dissent on the other. Though differing in operational structure and format from the Philadelphia experiment, Portland's Adams High provides another example of an unconventional high school. Its program is described by John Guernsey in "Portland's Unconventional Adams High."

While the bulk of student activism and dissent has been centered in institutions of higher learning, with a somewhat lesser amount also present in secondary schools, there is some reason to believe that even the elementary schools may become involved. LaMar Miller, in his article "Pupil Activism Can be a Positive Force," suggests activities at the elementary school level that make use of and forestall dissent and confrontation. Activism at the elementary school level may well be a direction of the future and a most provocative challenge for educators.

CHANGING SECONDARY EDUCATION NOW

MAURICE GIBBONS

These are tough times to be a principal, particularly of a secondary school. The pressures for change are increasing in intensity—the revolution is upon us—yet the pressures to maintain the institution much as it is must seem insuperable.

From *National Association of Secondary School Principals Bulletin*, 54 (January, 1970), 30-40. Reprinted with the permission of the author and the publisher.

Maurice Gibbons is Associate Professor at Simon Fraser University, Burnaby 2, British Columbia.

The principal is caught in this two-way stretch with no possibility of relieving the pressure that does not involve considerable risk. In his unique and lonely position of responsibility for the school and responsibility to community and superiors, resolving the dilemma is unavoidably his problem. While increasing activism among students, teachers, and parents, as well as rapid social, intellectual, and technological developments comprise an irresistible force, the school as we have known it is not an immovable object. It will change, and continue to change, or be abandoned, or circumvented or destroyed. Despite the problems—the difficulty of changing complex school organizations and operations, the demands of many masters, the weight of old traditions and their trappings, the failure of research that should guide but is ambivalent and inconclusive, financial limitations and the masses of time-diverting trivia—despite these difficulties, the thrust is toward dramatic change, and the administrator must find his own way.

While the tendency among schoolmen—as I have observed it—is to resist this pressure, it can be a benevolent challenge to chip away anachronistic accretions and launch the school into the mainstream of our time. Principals individually have the power to act in their schools, and collectively can be the educational decision-making power in their districts if they have the support of teachers and students. That support is more readily available now than ever before to leaders committed to the reform of traditional schooling. The most salient feature of activism among teachers and students is that only extremists are presently convinced schools must be destroyed. The main body of the "vanguard" are seeking a means of making learning more meaningful, more personal, more humanistic. They are challenging the sincerity and the humanity of institutions of public education: the relation between espoused values and performance. The wise administrator will respond to these concerns and mobilize them while rationality is still possible. The question to be answered here is what are some of the alternatives he can consider for changing secondary education now?

The suggestions that follow are based on the assumption that education is now moving, and will continue to move, toward greater freedom of choice for students, more personal and individual instruction, greater participation by teachers and students at all levels of decision-making, diminishing emphasis on rules, schedules, and programs (displaced by personal regulation, general flexibility of activity and self-direction in study), and increasing interpenetration between the school and the community.

I recommend one operating principle for changes in this direction: innovation should involve change in the relationship between the student and his teachers concerning the act of learning, change in the opportunities for learning (range of situations, facilities, personnel), and changes in the distribution of authority. Modifications of content or organization alone tend to be superficial.

And one comment about the relationship between idealism and hard-nosed practicality. The advocates of "realistic" approaches to education often seem preoccupied with details, immediate situations, and lurching changes, if any.

Innovation tends to be a paint-job rather than reconstruction, the pursuit of fashion rather than a rethinking of the schooling process. An ideal, the shape of the best ideas one can conceive of, is the magnetic north for direction in day-to-day activity, and as such is its necessary partner. Forging that ideal is the continuing business of every administrator, teacher, and student.

I. COMMUNICATE, CONSULT, COOPERATE

1. One-way communication from the top levels of authority down is inefficient and now dangerous. It is important to communicate by *interaction* with faculty and students. Meetings with representative groups of teachers (especially those who are concerned), students (especially the concerned and outspoken), and parents (especially those who are prepared to contribute) for open discussion on policy and practice are essential. Faculty-student interaction is equally important. Authority should learn what is happening and should seriously consider delegating much of its long-cherished power.

2. *Involve* faculty and students in decisions concerning the classroom and the school. Responsibility can only develop where responsibility is given. The quality of decisions and output will likely increase. Also, there may come a time when you need to look behind you and find a solid phalanx of support. Makers of arbitrary decisions arbitrarily suffer the consequences of them. Those who share power gain power.

3. Discussion and decision-making by faculty and students must be authoritative. Just as rational discussion is only possible when participants can express their opinions freely, so it only makes sense when conclusions lead to action, to *implementation*. Student governments and many faculty meetings are travesties of involvement. Several ways of interacting, involving, and implementing are suggested below.

   a. Some schools are being run by faculty teams with regular change of chairman.
   b. Some schools are including students on all committees. A few grant them equality with faculty in voting.
   c. In some schools students cooperate with faculty in informal "senates" to initiate changes.
   d. A few experimental schools are being run by students in cooperation with resource faculty.

Many schools are changing already, some dramatically and apparently successfully. Visits to these schools and discussions with administration, teachers, and students are rich sources of ideas.

II. EXTEND THE RANGE OF CHOICES

Relief from the terrible sameness of much schooling can be achieved by encouraging teachers to vary learning opportunities for students within each course.

Another way is to extend the alternatives among courses. The desirability of any particular suggestion will depend on the framework developed by the faculty and the students.

1. Allow alternatives within the present structure. For instance, why can't each tenth grade English teacher offer a different English course so that students can choose among them (perhaps one language and one literature course to make up one course credit)? Courses could run for only half the year enabling students to build a varied year's program.

2. Create new courses, particularly in areas of high student interest: Developing a Personal Philosophy, Protest in the Modern World, The Art of Primitive Peoples, Pop Culture, The Science of Things Around You, Survival on Land and Sea. Collect suggestions from students; then survey the entire student body. Clear at least one slot for such courses.

3. Offer mini-courses students must combine into a year's work during high school to receive one course credit. They can be two to six weeks long on such subjects as photography, yoga, pot-throwing, girls carpentry, astrology, and telescopes. Students can participate in planning them and perhaps in teaching them.

4. Permit students to present proposals for independent work-study, projects, activities, pursuits of any kind, in school or out. Offer full credit and make advisors available.

5. Arrange pursuits of all kinds outside the school (either in conference with students, or advertised as opportunities for choice): a month's apprenticeship with a sculptor, architect, computer analyst or hair stylist. Why not allow private music lessons with approved masters for credit? Other possibilities: Studying French in Quebec, rock climbing in Colorado, politics in Victoria, wood carving on an Indian Reserve and acting in a theatre company. Circulate a list of people willing to come to the school and work with individuals or groups in their area of special competence.

6. Concentrate on required subjects during part of school time and set aside an afternoon (every afternoon?) in the week or a month in the year for students to organize or request courses and activities or to plan for themselves individually.

7. Offer courses in the evening and during summer. This makes it possible to loosen the daily schedule, to offer more alternatives to slower and swifter students, to provide more opportunities to include outside specialists and sites for instruction, and to utilize the school plant more fully.

8. Make attendance to all or certain classes optional. Permit sitting in on other classes where there is space.

9. Provide course alternatives (programed courses; series of tapes, films, experiences, and activities; reading lists; faculty-prepared course packages; a sequence of assignments; "correspondence courses"; a project or projects; "challenge"

units and courses) with sponsoring teachers to advise and grade assignments or terminal examinations. These can be very challenging or adapted in different ways to particular students.

10. Dwight Allen (*Nation's Schools,* April 1968) suggests, among other means of individualizing instruction: permitting differential times for assignments, due dates, course completion and examinations; permitting slow students to collaborate in meeting course requirements; allowing exceptional loads (double courses in a given period, or fewer required subjects); allowing variable credit for courses (extra credit for exceptionally thorough work, half year credit rather than failure for poor work, etc.); permitting students to tackle courses at any level they think they can handle; and allowing students to suggest substitute assignments and activities in courses.

III. INDIVIDUALIZE AND COMMUNIZE

The individual at work on his own and the individual working within a community of associates are involved in complementary modes of education. By *individualization* I mean the move toward self-direction, not toward more precise prescription or the freedom to do the old work at one's own pace. By *community* I mean interaction with other students and adults in the school and beyond it, not just group activities dominated by tasks and instructions teachers impose.

1. Programs and instruction throughout our schools would be put in more practical perspective if grade twelve were considered a completely individualized, independent, self-directed year of study and activity, and if all preceding years of schooling were considered preparation for it. Irrevocably students are independent learners after June of their twelfth school year.

2. To be independent in education, students must learn to perform many of the functions presently practiced by teachers and administrators—examine alternatives; formulate personal curricula; pursue study, experience, and productive activity on their own; evaluate their performance; determine the next sequence and so on. How can these be taught? What resources will be necessary? What new roles must the teacher learn? How could the resulting diversity among the students' work be organized and assessed? What implications would there be for administrators in a situation that reversed the process of decision making?

3. In addition to self-directed individual education, students need the give and take of groups for feed-back about the quality of their learning, for personal development, for mastering the skills of discussion, and for socialization by interaction rather than instruction. Such groups should be varied in the kind of membership and should be initiated as often by the student as by the teacher.

   a. In classes the teacher should often set the stage for group discussion and activity, formal and informal.

b. Students should study the management and dynamics of groups, and would benefit from some forms of sensitivity training.

c. Opportunities for discussions and seminars between students and parents or other adults in the community will help to close the generation gap by reducing their isolation from each other, and will balance group delibera- tions by confronting adults with student idealism and students with harsher realities of adult life.

The question remains, how can we actually reestablish a sense of community in education? Perhaps as Herbert Thelen *(Education and the Human Quest, 1960)* suggests, this can only be done if we conceive of education as a function of the whole community, with school as only one of several recognized contexts for learning. Newmann and Oliver *(Harvard Educational Review,* Winter, 1967) de- scribe three contexts: the school, the laboratory-studio-work setting, and the community seminar. The focus of the community seminar is on issues of central public concern and it may involve field trips, briefing sessions by specialists, dis- cussion among adults, students and resource people in the group, and perhaps public action.

IV. INTRODUCE DRAMA, SERVICE, AND SOLITUDE

1. These three elements, of great importance in personal development, are too often displaced by our fetish for measurable academic achievement. By *drama* I mean the experience of meeting a challenge to the courage, imagination, stamina and determination. One way of providing drama would be to offer a program patterned on the Outward Bound model (surely the forest and the sea—the out- of-doors—are the great unused resources of schools). Students combine aca- demic work (astronomy, geology, ecology, etc.) with the skills of outdoor life (woodcraft, seamanship, mountaineering, life saving, conservation, fire fighting, mountain rescue, and so on). The four-week school concludes with a three day solo during which the student must survive alone in the woods with little equip- ment and no supplies. This could be a particularly important experience for boys, especially in early adolescence.

2. By *service* I mean the dedication and donation of time and effort to assisting the ill, old, handicapped, and housebound; to helping younger or slower students with their studies; or to working on some community project. Each year students, individually or in groups, should be permitted, expected, or required to perform some such service in school time or on their own.

3. By *solitude* I mean experience in a situation conducive to meditation and contemplation, a sustained experience remote from the mass media, the pres- sures of school and community, and command performances under the scrutiny of peers; a confrontation in which students face themselves. I do not know how this can be done, only that some way must be found to encourage students to explore and develop the inner life. School is a crowd experience usually. The solo

in the woods or at sea, the service experience may provide solitude. The situation, the atmosphere, is important. Some instruction in contemplation, the inward dialogue, may be necessary. The wide interest in Zen may provide a vehicle for this purpose. A meditation-room may not be too far-fetched. Perhaps students can be free to leave the school to walk the beach or sit under a tree. Otherwise, how?

V. EXPERIMENT: PLAN, DEVELOP, EVALUATE

A school that is not experimenting is educationally dead. A school that experiments without careful planning that involves all faculty (and students?) associated with the project is wasteful of time and effort. Experimentation that does not involve day-to-day and week-to-week assessment and change is constipated. Experimentation that does not involve evaluation of the program's success is mute.

By experiments in schooling I do not mean basic test-tube analyses of learning and development or one-shot classroom research by academic specialists, but the continuing invention and development of educational ideas by schoolmen: staffs examining the situation in their schools, gathering information about teaching and learning, and launching a sustained cycle of formulation, development, evaluation, and reformulation of imaginative proposals for schooling. Joint *planning* is important. Expressing ideas, hearing others, sharing in the formulation of a solution is the stimulus to conversion too often limited to small curriculum committees that may communicate their product to others, but not the experience of the planning process that made the course clear and desirable.

Ideas—whether for reorganizing the staff, changing the school program, or creating a new method of teaching a course—will not emerge ideally formed from a committee. New-born, they are only beginning their *development*. Teachers implementing ideas require time and assistance during the term, to assess what is happening and to decide what changes should be made. For instance, many students plunged into a free classroom may be stunned into inactivity by the change. The teacher must decide whether to give them time to acclimatize, instruction in managing free time, formalized subject courses, or some other alternative.

For this intermediate (formative) assessment and for final (summative) assessment of the idea refined through development, an independent evaluator would be of great assistance to a staff. His job would not be to *evaluate* teachers or students but to evaluate programs, to provide teachers with information about their approach and the responses of students that would assist them in making decisions about the course development should take. It is an interesting comment on our attitudes to schooling that we systematically evaluate students but not the school program—at least, in any school I know of. Do we really mean that students can fail, but the school is always successful? In schooling as experimentation—planned, developed, and evaluated by the staff—the fallibility of the program is recognized and attacked. Some steps in this direction are outlined below.

1. Many administrators claim they encourage teachers to experiment, yet their teachers often say that experimentation is frowned upon and conditions (a unilateral program, prescribed texts and curricula, exams, and so on) make it impossible. Tell your teachers that thoughtful experimentation is desirable, help clear obstacles from their path, and tolerate their mistakes during the period of development. Ask for or maintain a fund to support enterprising proposals.

2. Identify imaginative teachers, seek out their ideas, put them in touch with others of like mind. Permit groups of teachers to embark on their own programs within the school. More formally, it is possible to establish schools within a school. Dividing the students and faculty into teams or houses, let them plan their own programs, share facilities. Another approach is to work with a faculty (and student? and parent?) team to design and implement the academic program.

3. As the administrative team for a school district, why not design a master plan for experimentation of a different kind in each school, pooling your findings, sharing solutions to problems, and planning a development sequence for your community of schools. What would happen if each school in a district developed a unique philosophy that it practiced in a unique program, and students with their parents were permitted to choose the kind of education, the school, they preferred? Teachers would also be able to choose schools of their preference.

4. The literature of research has begun to emphasize the importance of local investigation into educational problems, yet most principals find their schools are too large and unwieldy to launch programs sharply contrasting with presently established ones. Few feel they can afford to chance failure. But many questions could be asked, many techniques could be attempted and polished, and many roles could be developed (e.g. program developer, program evaluator) in a local experimental unit with a small volunteer population. Teachers drawn from the district and supported by trainees and research personnel from the universities could work in close cooperation with the district for their mutual benefit. Such cooperation would provide quality experimentation, trial runs of proposed school changes, a spur to educational development, a means of up-grading faculty, an alternate site for teacher training and a greater possibility of funding the project. We know little about nurturing individual rigor in free situations. How about attacking such a problem together—school district, university, and the community?

CONCLUSION

This paper is not the outline of a program but a menu of changes that seem in keeping with emerging trends in education. The items in the menu are topics for consideration, discussion, and hopefully some implementation by administrators and faculties interested in reconstructing the programs in their schools. Three themes underlie each item: ventilation, diversification, and cooperation. A stifling educational program can be ventilated by an explosion (and likely will be at the present rate of revolution), but how much more profitable to do now what should have been done long ago—open up alternatives, giving students choice, greater control over their schooling, and a greater measure of freedom. But it would likely be a mistake to substitute one fixed program for another. Is there any reason why several routes and rates through any course or program cannot be tolerated within the same structure (except that it is administratively easier not to)? Try substituting diversity for singularity. Still it would be a mistake, I think, to hand down to heads of departments a memo demanding ventilation and diversification. The value of ideas is not absolute (unless they are our own). I suggest initiating discussions with faculty and students and in a cooperative effort permitting everyone to contribute to the new program, thereby enhancing it and establishing personal investments in it.

I have listed some ideas but said little about implementing them. Variation among features of the local situation and personnel makes the task unique in each school. But two things seem axiomatic. Students presently on fairly traditional programs require transitional experiences and instruction to move easily into a new program, particularly if it involves new routines, responsibilities, instructional procedures, and relationships with faculty. That is, before students used to traditional schooling are launched on such an enterprise as self-directed study, they should be trained in the required skills, supervised in practice runs, and gradually given their heads. Also, no one should expect to devise a new program in committee that will not need many changes and improvements in class. By planning both time and personnel for regular assessment and development, you can make disasters as well as successes merely data for the continuing growth of better schooling. And that is the name of the game.

Involvement in secondary education today is often a harrowing experience, particularly for administrators. The pressures to change are great, the alternatives are many, but the system is ponderous and the consequences are all too unpredictable. Still, the secondary school administrator has the power and the contact—with teachers, students and parents—to initiate assessment and redirection of the school program. With that power, the responsibility for change rests with him.

FROM CONFRONTATION TO COLLABORATION*

IRVING N. BERLIN, M.D.

Of what help can mental health professionals be to teachers and administrators who find themselves directly on the firing line with rebelling students? This paper describes group role-playing and discussion sessions with school personnel that eased their tautness and actual fear by giving them a framework for understanding confrontations.

Confrontation of authority, in all avenues of life, is with us today. Youth confront their teachers, school, and college authorities; blacks confront the white community and its agencies. Confrontation and its usual result—counterconfrontation—leads to riots, chaos, disorganization, and to backlash and revengeful calls for law and order. The role of mental health professionals in this process is unclear; but an analysis of some of the problems already examined by sociologists and social psychologists, plus some understanding of the individual dynamics in these situations, provide a dynamic framework within which both individual and group confrontations can be examined and illustrated. Such a framework can help mental health professionals to help others more effectively assess the problems.

It is clear from the writings of Cohn-Bendit,[1] Deutsch,[2] Shoben,[10, 11] and others that there are some prerequisite conditions for student confrontation and rebellion. They appear to have validity for many individual confrontations as well. These conditions are—

1. Legitimate complaints about an institution's failure to meet its students' needs.

2. Arbitrary and authoritarian reactions of administrators and others in power toward the demands.

3. Refusal to listen to and understand the students' anger about existing problems and lack of readiness to negotiate with the students.

4. A moral rather than a task-oriented approach; that is, the right of students to make demands indicates they are ungrateful for the schooling made available versus having a common problem, i.e., "How do we get the best education possible in our institution?"

* Presented at the 1969 annual meeting of the American Orthopsychiatric Association, New York, N.Y.

Irving N. Berlin, M.D., is Professor of Psychiatry and Pediatrics, and Head, Division of Child Psychiatry at the University of Washington, Seattle, Washington.

5. Retaliatory feelings and behavior on the part of challenged administrations and faculty when they feel incompetent either in the work they are doing or in the face of the challenges and when they have no techniques for managing them.

6. Fear of democratic participation in decision-making, especially about potential loss of power and authority.

7. Most institutions have become rigidified and do not change to meet the challenges of technology, population mobility, and the new curricular and teaching alterations required for relevance.

Thus, many administrators and faculty members find a need to defend the status quo because dynamically radical change provokes anxiety and is frightening. Confrontation about these issues therefore often results in irrational responses.[6, 13, 14]

Our experiences with individual confrontation were brought to our consultation seminars by mental health workers from ghetto junior and senior high schools. Their experiences confirmed our previous work in another ghetto area. The complaints of teachers and administrators and their pressure on guidance personnel and others to solve the problems did more than reflect the chaos in the schools and the poor learning atmosphere due to defiance by minority students; it also said a great deal about the people involved. Most teachers and administrators involved were anxious about open challenge to their authority, reluctant to examine the relevance of their teaching methods, and in contrast to effective teachers in the same schools, they could not ignore testing behavior such as keeping coats on and swearing in class and they attended only to the problem of increasing the learning possible in the classroom.[5, 7] In addition, some teachers avoided confrontation by ignoring events that seemed to be leading to a crescendo of defiance and breakdown of the learning situation. In desperation they would then finally demand prompt punitive action by administrators to restore order in the classroom.[9, 12]

Authoritative and secure administrators were able, by example, to be helpful to their teachers. They not only could recognize very early signs of trouble among the students and talk about school problems, but they would look with their faculty at the need for bringing about curricular change, etc. Though these efforts were difficult and painful, they did not result in authoritarian, repressive measures which escalate school confrontation and conflict. The school guidance worker, who had, with consultation, been able to work with the faculty, began to share some of our previous experiences. We discussed some possible methods of working with these overwhelming teachers. We had in mind two tasks: (1) helping these teachers find some alternatives to their almost invariable response to challenge; and (2) helping them reassess their educational tasks as teachers with these children.

I will illustrate efforts with groups of teachers and with a group of administrators who met with several of our guidance staff around the problems of individual confrontations and challenges posed by what were always described as "irrational and hostile demands" of militant students. We combined two methods —the use of group demonstrations and discussion augmented by frequent individual consultation.

GROUP SESSIONS WITH TEACHERS

First we did a series of demonstration group workshops, two each week for three to four weeks, in the target schools with 20 teachers at a time. A very forthright social worker who could enact the violent, angry, abusive adolescent confronted another worker as teacher. In this setting we had the worker, as a teacher, do two things: First, his observing ego described his feelings on confrontation—his anxieties, fear, anger, frustration, desperation, and violent desire to hit back. Second, we had the worker demonstrate the way in which one could try to listen to the angry fury of the student and reduce its intensity by concerned interest in the adolescent and by attitudes and words which used a theme and variations of, "Okay, you're mad as hell at me, but I'm not sure I understand what you want of me and how I can be a better teacher for you." The student then replied with specific accusations and examples of the teachers' not caring about the student as a human being, his retaliatory—often radically biased—behavior, his lousy and indifferent teaching, the poor and often inappropriate curriculum planning, etc. The concerned teacher responded with, "Okay, maybe some of these complaints are justified but where do we start to change them?"

The first reactions from the groups were always shock at the accuracy of the hostile, vituperative nature of the portrayal of the minority adolescent. There was usually clear agreement about the accuracy of the description of the teachers' feelings while under attack. However, usually there were very mixed reactions about the methods demonstrated in dealing with the confrontation. We then asked some fairly secure teachers to play the adolescent, which they did with scathing effectiveness. On subsequent occasions we asked the less secure teacher to play that role as a more secure teacher tried to deal with the confrontation. We stopped the role-play at critical moments to evoke comments and suggestions for behavior on both sides. The discussion was always lively and heated. Finally, we involved the least secure teachers in the role of the confronted teacher.

During this period of three to four weeks, two sessions per week, the workers talked individually with the teachers most in trouble to inquire about how the group sessions could be more useful. During consultation we got the teachers involved in discussing their own reactions to difficult students. The consultants' understanding comments about how threatening these confrontations were would occasionally help some teacher to consider with the worker how he might try to consistently use one of the attitudes suggested in the group meeting when dealing with a very difficult youngster. Subsequent consultations were used for discussion of what did or did not work and what modifications seemed in order.

This on-the-spot followup and encouragement seemed to work very well. More teachers were able to be more flexible with their students—more open and less repressive. Often consultation continued much beyond the period of demonstration.

One of the outcomes of the group sessions was the learning of alternative methods of handling confrontation. Some desensitization took place as teachers identified with the actors and later were able to participate. A beginning consideration of the previously unalterable and unsuitable curriculum and a hard look at some of their teaching methods also resulted as the teachers tried to meet these youngsters' needs. Sometimes the worker acted as a catalyst to get administrators to join the group in discussing how the curriculum could be altered to be more interesting and useful. In this setting the more flexible and creative teachers had their long-awaited hearing as they described those techniques in their subject that seemed to work and interest their students.

Again, individual consultation was helpful to some very rigid teachers. Persistent encouragement in their efforts to change their teaching style and to find new curriculum aids was enhanced as the consultant clearly acknowledged how difficult such change was and how much guts it took to make such efforts. After a time, some of the teachers discovered that they could teach differently without loss of classroom control. Several teachers voiced satisfaction about beginning to again feel competent and effective as teachers as their efforts began to pay off.

One of the most dramatic moments in the demonstrations usually occurred when we tried to illustrate that attacks and confrontations were not just aimed agains teachers as individuals. The worker who demonstrated the teacher role asked in bewilderment, "Why me? I'm trying to be understanding and helpful. What's so terrible about me?" The worker playing the student replied that he hated any smug, sweet, superior, aloof authority. He wanted some sign of individual concern and understanding of his needs and problems. No matter how "nice" the teacher was, he felt usually rejected and actually experienced some retaliation because of racial and cultural differences, expressed attitudinally, which unless explicitly pointed out with examples were not in the awareness of educators.

GROUP SESSIONS WITH ADMINISTRATORS

We did a similar series with administrators where I played teacher, since it was evident that the administrators would enjoy having someone with greater status on the hot spot. The prompt followup with individual consultation was equally important and sometimes helpful with rigid, retaliatory administrators who were in real trouble.

We moved from discussions of individual confrontations to discussions with administrators of their problems around group confrontations, especially their dealing with the angry and sometimes irrational demands *en masse*. We used case histories of successful and unsuccessful meetings and confrontations to demonstrate what seemed to work and to analyze the data together. For example, one rather mild, elderly high school principal's office was invaded at 4:30 in the afternoon by 15 minority activists who demanded that three-fourths of the teachers be fired, a new curriculum be instituted, and that they be given authority to interview and hire all new teachers and approve all the curriculum. They threatened to burn down the school that night if their demands were not met. The principal, alone with a custodian and a few scattered teachers in the school, felt helpless and very frightened. Under the circumstances, however, he asked the group into the conference room to discuss the problems with them. During an hour of discussion, the principal agreed with the students' criticism of the curriculum and the unhelpful attitudes of some of the teachers. He asked the students to name a committee of students and teachers to meet with him to plan a more relevant curriculum. At the end of an hour the principal asked the students if they wanted to wait and present their problems to the superintendent that same day so they could together secure his support of the needed changes. The students agreed that the next day would be fine.

In another instance a very secure and flexible administrator in a similar confrontation became rather angry with the irrational aspects of the demands and made a counterdemand of the students after he had listened carefully for a time. It was *their* education and he wanted *them* to come up with some ideas and plans for implementation of their valid demands. He understood the problems but felt helpless about obtaining the needed official support to institute change. In the furious debate he maintained his concerned interest, and no matter what the provocation he demanded the students' thoughtful participation in solving the problems raised. He asked them to get some parents, teachers, and community representatives involved. One of the minority student leaders said later, "I didn't know the old man really cared. He seemed kind of out of it before. We really dug his demands, especially because he believed we had ideas about what and how we could be taught better and who could do the job." This is an excellent example of the authoritative versus the authoritarian approach.

We were also able to use an example known to all that was disastrous. A junior high school principal, a former physical education teacher who ruled by brawn and threat, called the police in the face of a mass confrontation. This led to a riot and the closing of the school. Since some of us had worked with this administrator, we were able to describe where we had failed. First, in case discussions around individual confrontations, he could not be helped to consider the distinction between confrontation as a challenge to his authority—which was in part always there—and confrontation as a statement about the problems and the troubles of the ghetto youngster. He could not recognize a confrontation as a student's comments regarding his hopeless world and the school's failure to help him find any way out. No matter how much data about the family problems, previous schooling, or neighborhood history, etc. that we presented, this principal still saw any angry, threatening kid as a personal affront. It meant not being liked or respected, a very personal threat that could only be met with force. Thus, we could not help him to talk to students about how change could be brought about to meet their needs. His way had to be the only way, and his decisions were final. In contrast was our success in demonstrating to this administrator how to interview paranoid, angry parents. He could understand the parents' pathology and did not feel as personally involved. Thus, he learned to listen and to be helpful and flexible in working things out with them. It was clear to all the administrators, some who were not unlike the principal under discussion, that the sense of insecurity and urgent need to use force to maintain order posed a very severe problem. As we examined case studies together in terms of the impact of counterforce and retaliation on the learning process and the school atmosphere, they could agree that it only increased the need for violent rebellion, reinforced the conviction that administrators were the enemy, and that under these conditions no learning could take place.

After four months of weekly meetings and many individual consultations, one of the administrators in our group, the junior college dean of men, helped us to recognize that we had not correctly understood several aspects of the problem underlying mass student confrontation. He described in detail the events of the previous week which had been a failure in handling a confrontation. Police were called to handle the riot, and massive destruction of the school property had occurred. He described how for some weeks minority students and student activists had made repeated efforts to meet with the administration. Some faculty had also supported the students' position; yet after several meetings with administrators, the massive confrontation nevertheless occurred with bitter results. He first described his own sense of bewilderment and helplessness that reason, efforts at conciliation, and dialogue had not been enough. Only as the details unfolded did we gain some understanding of what had been missing.

The several minority groups of students and other activists had presented the administration with demands for a greater say in the curriculum and greater involvement in its teaching. They protested that as a vocational college it ill-prepared them for jobs; its equipment was ancient and in no way similar to that they would use on a job. The black, Mexican-American, and Indian students demanded that their history and literature be properly presented in the curriculum. Most of all they resented the attitudes of their instructors and the administrators —that they were still children who didn't know what was good for them and should have no voice in what was taught, how it was taught, and who taught it. They demanded change *now*. They had waited long enough in their ghettos for others to recognize and respond to their needs. They intended to force change *now*. The urgency, anger, and impatience with endless dialogue and administrative delays were not correctly assessed, nor was there clear student involvement in problem-solving. The administration's repeated pleas for patience and their use of a chart to illustrate the chain of command they had to go through only gave the students a sense of the impotence of the faculty and administration to effect change. They were, therefore, determined to force it in any way possible.[3,4,8,9] One of our consultants, a black social worker who had been consulting with that particular administrative staff, sharply pointed out that his warnings and predictions had been ignored.

We began to see how unprepared a school or college system was for rapid response and integrative action. There was little evidence of creative anticipation of problems and almost no community involvement of school people. The estrangement between the school and the community made responsiveness, communication, and mutual engagement in problem-solving impossible. Several of the administrators voiced their troubled beliefs that one could not find integrative solutions to such situations. It was almost as if they were hoping that if one lived through one or two of these difficult experiences that the troubles would then go away. The dean of men spelled out the realities—the schools were not out of the woods and he at least wanted some help with planning for the troubled future. Again we turned to our black social worker consultant who restated his perceptions of the development of the problems and offered some tentative solutions that had emerged from previous meetings.

We had data now from several schools whose continued involvement of concerned school personnel with the community kept the schools in tune with community needs. School people learned especially how the schools might become more responsive in their curriculum and their teaching methods and how school mental health workers might be more responsive to the particular needs of some students and parents.

We used this data from school-community efforts to discuss with administrators how they might help some of their teachers become more alert to the possible meanings of difficult student behaviors, as well as to the educational needs of their students. More flexible and more imaginative teaching was a must. The administrators then began to talk about their own difficulty in shifting from set curriculum standards which are prescribed by the system to a curriculum that would educate more of their students. Some of them were especially concerned with their own tendency to take the easy way out and expel difficult students rather than to learn what it takes to help the students learn more and stay in school. Adapting more rapidly to changing student needs, involving students more in the assessment of these needs, and evaluating the effectiveness of the schools' efforts, raised the spectre of loss of authority and status. These issues were repeatedly considered and examined most effectively in the context of the schools' role to educate students to become responsible participants in their society.

SUMMARY AND CONCLUSIONS

After these discussions and the crises that had occurred, it became evident that schools needed to use their mental health personnel to work with teachers and administrators to keep the students in school rather than to get rid of them. This also required new roles of mental health workers, and only a few of them had learned to work in this way.

The threat of crises and violence forced the most adaptable of the administrators to begin to plan ahead to avoid trouble by inviting student and community involvement in planning for a more meaningful education. Other administrators, although they could see the effectiveness of these methods, were unable to participate in such involvement or to use consultation to improve their capacity to deal with confrontation more flexibly and to reexamine their function in the schools. Under the great and repeated stress, many of them left these schools.

We were able through demonstrations and discussion followed by individual consultation to give some administrators and teachers a framework within which to understand confrontations. As they could acknowledge the legitimate complaints, distinguish between authoritative and authoritarian responses, and recognize from our role-playing and discussions how one could understand anger and respond to it positively, they seemed more at ease in their schools. The efforts to help educators distinguish between moralistic attitudes which turned kids off and task-oriented ones which involved them in mutual problem-solving was more difficult to get across. In our role-playing we were able to indicate the universality of retaliatory feelings on being confronted and to demonstrate techniques of becoming aware of such feelings and not acting on them. The need for participation of students and community members in planning and evolving better education was both threatening to some and appealing to others because it meant getting community help to mount needed programs. Many educators expressed greater willingness to try new methods and approaches after these sessions.

For mental health personnel it required some role changes as well. They often had to be the ones who could interpret both student and community needs as well as be able to help educators find a more flexible and integrative way to meet these needs. Some school guidance personnel found themselves unable to function in these roles. Others found these roles compatible with their understanding of interpersonal and organizational dynamics and their capacity to function flexibly in a variety of new roles with students, educators, and the community.

In conclusion, our experiences in this school system very greatly paralleled the necessary and requisite factors for confrontation described by some of the authors quoted. It was our experience that our efforts—successful and unsuccessful—could be understood as part of a dynamic process.

References

[1] Cohn-Bendit, D., et al. 1968. "The Student Rebellion." *This Magazine Is About Schools,* Summer, 1st section.

[2] Deutsch, M. 1968. "Conflicts: Productive and Constructive." *In* Kurt Lewin Memorial Address. Amer. Psychol. Assn., Washington.

[3] Fanon, F. 1963. *The Wretched of the Earth.* Grove Press, New York.

[4] Feuer, L. 1968. *The Conflict of Generations*. Basic Books, New York.

[5] Friedenberg, E. 1963. *Coming of Age in America*. Random House, New York.

[6] Gans, H. 1968. "Toward the 'Equality Revolution'." *New York Times Magazine*, Nov. 1968.

[7] Goodman, P. 1962. *Compulsory Mis-Education*. Vintage Books, New York.

[8] Malcolm X. 1965. *Autobiography*. Grove Press, New York.

[9] Rosenberg, M. 1965. *Society and the Adolescent Self-Image*. Princeton Univ. Press, Princeton, N.J.

[10] Shoben, E. 1968. "Means, Ends and the Liberties of Education." *J. Higher Educ.*, Feb. 1968:61-68.

[11] Shoben, E. 1969. "The New Student: Implications for Personnel Work." *CAPS Capsule*, Spring:1-7.

[12] Solnit, A., et al. 1969. "Youth Unrest: A Symposium." *Amer. J. Psychiat.*, March 1969: 39-53.

[13] Trimberger, E. 1968. "Why a Rebellion at Columbia Was Inevitable." *Transaction*, Sept. 1968:28-38.

[14] Widmer, K. 1969. "Why the Colleges Blew Up." *Nation*, Feb. 1969:237-240.

From DISSENT AND DISRUPTION IN SECONDARY SCHOOLS

MARK A. CHESLER

.   .   .   .

PROMISING DIRECTIONS FOR SCHOOL CHANGE

In a number of cases it is clear that students and educators need help in learning when and how to use each others' resources. The traditional role obligations of educators, which invests them with the care of their charges, makes it difficult for professionals to see students as being able to contribute to the educative process.

Similarly, students are expected to conform to and accept the judgments, decisions and behaviors of professionally trained personnel. When this orientation is coupled with the social distance inherent in the organized status differences of the school situation, we can see why faculties are not easily involved or prepared for the peer intercourse required for compromise or attention to grievances. Another reason it is difficult to engage students and educators in these processes is that so many people are unskilled in any kind of negotiation. Many students and faculties do not know what it means to compromise, they are

From *Dissent and Disruption in Secondary Schools*, ERIC Document (July, 1969), pp. 4-7. Reprinted with permission of the author.

Mark A. Chesler is Project Director of the Educational Change Team, The University of Michigan.

dreadfully concerned that in a negotiating situation they are going to lose control over their entire career and organization. When one is in a position of historic power, of course, negotiations do imply new power arrangements and, therefore, some loss of absolute control. These historic and structural barriers to peer exchange may require the presence of a third party referee, consultant or mediator in negotiations. A person trained in school issues could, if he were truly concerned with educational improvement and trusted by competing parties, help move past rhetoric, fear and misunderstanding to redress and change.

We also need to generate and test new models of organizing high schools along lines that do a more effective job of discovering and processing grievances and injustices. Throughout the school year, throughout all of the crises and noncrises, educational and social issues must be discovered and treated before they create disruptive levels of concern. I do not mean we should cool off or repress conflict, or engage in subtle forms of tokenism; nor do I mean that educators should learn how to manipulate or use students as tools to do what faculties originally wanted to do. I do mean that we must try and create social systems where people can pay attention to conflict and dissent long before it gets to open warfare. I also mean we must build new forms of legitimate power in the school that better mirror the current realities of community and student power. It's not just altruism or good intentions that may motivate educators' consideration of these possibilities; often it's only the threat that youngsters will use power for disruptive purposes that actually promotes their inclusion in legitimate decision-making roles. And it is this reality that will prevent or punish tokenism or deceit in the long run; once aroused and conscious, students are not likely to be duped or manipulated for long.

An example of the concept of shared power could involve the creation of student-faculty committees to establish local curricula, conduct judicial proceedings, and actually help make school policy. This does not mean simply revamping the old, worn out kinds of student governments or the inclusion of a couple of "good" students as advisory members once in a while in faculty meetings. Such programs will not satisfy students who know their governments and councils have not been meaningful political systems in the past. The distance between students and teachers or administrators in this regard is often quite discouraging. For instance, in one school we have been studying the President of the Student Council resigned because none of the faculty would listen to her. She felt the teachers and administrators maintained tight control over the student council and did not permit it to do meaningful things. Although students voted for student council members, the principal and faculty advisor seemed to make most of the important decisions. When youngsters confronted their faculty advisor and the principal with their feelings, they were told "well this is the way it is at school board meetings too, this is the powerlessness and futility that we face. So you might as well learn how it feels right now." The youngsters weren't satisfied with that answer, and began to organize new forms of self-government and expression outside of the impotent council.

In order to develop student energy and commitment in the process of school management, more responsive and meaningful political systems will have to be built. One procedure might involve handing major decisions over to a student-faculty government system wherein the principal would operate as an executive secretary responsible to this plural status group. Great care would have to be taken to insure effective use of a feedback system where information and policy preferences were communicated back and forth between representatives and their various constituencies. Together we could stretch our imaginations and no doubt develop many ways in which students can have real power in saying how schools are run. We're certainly not doing so well without students that we can afford to be smug or superior about their talents and potential contributions. It's probably true that many students want no part of this responsibility, but that's not a relevant argument; I believe meaningful participation has such important educative value that we should unilaterally attempt to secure its implementation. Students as well as faculty might gain important experience and have new learning opportunities in the test of representative internal politics. Teachers and administrators, in particular, would have to begin to deal with the school in a representative political, as well as a professionally responsible, manner. If there is to be a chance for anything but brief test sequences and ultimate failure we will have to train all parties for the skillful performance of their new political roles. New structures will not run themselves; they will need to be staffed by participants who are well trained to do their job.

Another innovation which could help adjudicate various interests would be the establishment of an apparatus to handle grievances. Such a mechanism, and the occupants thereof, would have to be more than passive recipients of complaints. Their charge would be to find conflict where it is, create it where it ought to be, and help it get dealt with quickly. They would have the mission to discover, receive, perhaps escalate, and publicize facts and feelings about injustice so it can be dealt with before it explodes into warfare. In order to perform this job, the role occupants would have to be seen as invulnerable and universal presenters and resolvers of school injustices. Persons who wished to report grievances should be granted enough protection from retaliation to facilitate their use of the system. There is no question a grievance system would have to be concerned with the full range of school issues, as much with student or principal injustices to teachers as well as vice versa. Through the operation of this procedure smoldering anxieties, tensions, disagreements and conflicts may not have to stay so hidden or repressed that they burst forth in drastic and uncontrollable forms. It is, of course, yet another question as to how, and how effectively, any appeal body actually may deal with the issues raised. As with other alternatives, special training will have to be given to role occupants and to students and faculties in experimental schools, so that all parties may be prepared for new rules and procedures. Moreover, faculties and students will have to keep a watchful eye over this process to guard against its use as an administrative control device or a student Kangaroo Court.

Another range of possibilities lie in the general effort to make schools and faculties publicly accountable to the clients whom they serve. Educators are, rather typically of professionals, not accountable to the consumers of their roles, but to their own professional guardians. This protects educators from consumer pressures in important ways, but it also robs their clients of the effectiveness of appeals of arbitrary behavior. Public scrutiny of the average reading scores in comparable classes or schools is one way a community can begin to assess staff performance. Such evaluation makes schools and schoolmen more accountable to parents and citizens for what they do with their youngsters. Another, more intimate, form of feedback could involve students in evaluating the professional behavior and performance their faculty members exhibit in the classroom.

Another important step in the development of public accountability would be to create new linkages between schools and the communities they serve. This emphasis would require schools extending themselves into communities as well as reaching out to enlist communities in educational policies and affairs. In practice this probably would mean the utilization of store front classrooms, of freedom schools, of course credit for varied experiences both inside and outside the school. It also would mean the use of parents as full teaching colleagues, the inclusion of a group of community agency people advising principals in the management of the school, and the preparation of parents to manage the schools.

We also will need to develop new course content and better models for the transmission of intellectual content and experience. One possibility is to provide students with course credit for analyses and treatments of issues confronting the schools. Perhaps a dozen students can meet regularly with the principal of the high school; their job may be to learn about schools, to learn about the politics of education in the community, to create special courses in race relations or black studies, to design a new way of running the high school the next year, or to actually run it. When students get course credit for such planning it is not seen as an extra-curricular activity, but rather as fundamental to the educational process. This planning activity for a small group could be broadened into a course for large numbers in the legitimate curriculum.

Perhaps it is not necessary to note that the recruitment of sympathetic and effective teachers is absolutely necessary. In the absence of such skillful legions many educators hoped that counselors would be directly helpful to students with complaints. Counselors have failed almost completely at this job, and their function is being taken over by young black faculty members and occasionally by exciting whites. Counselors themselves are almost never mentioned as people who can be depended upon to raise real problems, who can keep confidences, or who will stand up for students' concerns. The exorcising of these counselor functions, and the training and development of teachers who can teach well and demonstrate their concern for students seems to be an important, albeit traditional, priority.

Unless we are really prepared to do more than *talk about* change there is no point in entering into cross-racial or cross-generational dialogue. And if we are prepared, we have to demonstrate very quickly that we are. There have been so many false starts, unkept promises and unworthy trusts, that I wouldn't blame anyone for not investing heavily in another false start. Some youngsters are saying, for instance, "I'm tired of talking. I am not coming to another damn meeting unless the principal does something to demonstrate his good faith. I have stopped messing around." Many students are still prepared to talk and make new starts; but it is not clear how long they will stay this way. It seems worthwhile, in terms of the stakes that are abound, to invest in some dialogue; but it is necessary to caution educators to invest in dialogue only if they are willing to commit themselves to taking some action on the just grievances presented. Otherwise, we may as well be prepared for continuing and increasing confrontation and disruption in our schools.

ROLE PLAYING EXERCISES THAT HIGHLIGHT STUDENT-SCHOOL CONFLICT IN SECONDARY SCHOOLS*

MARK A. CHESLER

Intergenerational Focus

SCENE I

GENERAL SITUATION

School protests occurred in some neighboring high schools this past week; there were also some rumblings in your school. The school principal has been quoted in the local newspaper as believing that most disruption is caused by a few troublemakers, some of whom aren't even students. Moreover, he has said he doesn't expect serious trouble in this school because: (1) there are a few problems; (2) he is always ready to listen to students; and (3) students know he will deal firmly with any disruptive behavior.

This is a large high school drawing most students from middle-class and upper middle-class backgrounds. About 90% of the students are white and 10% are black.

Several students are talking together to prepare to ask the principal for a meeting to discuss some concerns.

* Designed by the staff at the Center for Research on the Utilization of Scientific Knowledge, The University of Michigan, Mark A. Chesler, director.

From *Dissent and Disruption in Secondary Schools*, ERIC Document (July, 1969), pp. 1-4. Reprinted with permission of the author.

ROLES

B/Student #1: You helped organize volunteers for the Kennedy campaign last summer. Now you're becoming involved in anti-war activity. School rules prohibit wearing buttons or passing out literature.

B/Student #2: You helped write the first issue of an underground newspaper critical of administrative paternalism. It reviewed modern entertainment and used some profanity. School personnel do not know who wrote it.

B/Student #3: You've just inherited six beautiful skirts from your sister at college. School officials threatened to send you home if you wore skirts that were too short.

B/Student #4: Last year you led a small demonstration protesting the school's remaining open during the funeral of Martin Luther King. You don't trust the newspaper, and want to know exactly what the principal said.

B/Student #5: You're a junior—one of the "brains." You've just received traditional English, History, and Social Studies texts. You and some of your friends want to study modern literature like Camus, Mailer, Malcolm X, Phillip Roth and John Hersey instead, and have a course on the origin and development of the Vietnamese War. If a teacher can't work on it, you want to run it yourselves.

SCENE II

GENERAL SITUATION

The students from Scene I, in addition to the following role occupants, are now gathered together in the principal's office for a meeting.

ROLES

Principal: You are now at the center of a rather difficult situation. You have been principal here for 9 years. When you came nobody ever protested anything out loud, and nothing here has changed, so its hard to understand why there's so much noise now. Over 75% of these kids do go on to college, so they must be getting a good education.

Superintendent: (acting as an alter-ego to the principal) You want to impress upon the principal that he should not make any rash moves that would upset the community. Certainly he must be aware of the need for stability in the schools.

Assistant minister of large church: (acting as an alter-ego to the principal) You are anxious for the principal to take students seriously. Most of their demands sound rather reasonable, especially when compared to the strict rules the school system has now established. The principal is in your congregation.

Newspaperman: You will knock on the door shortly after the meeting starts, introduce yourself and ask if you can attend. This sounds like hot stuff and you'd like to get in on it.

Several students: (As in Scene I)

Interracial Focus

SCENE I

GENERAL SITUATION

Civil disturbances have occurred in your city during the summer. Partly as a result the principals' advisory council has set a number of new rules on a city-wide basis. In your school there have been no serious incidents or disturbances yet. This is a large high school, drawing its students from several areas of the city. About 60% of the students are white and about 40% are black.

The new rules consist of the following:

1. No large groups shall congregate in the halls.

2. There will be appropriate dress worn—no shorts, blue jeans, excessive jewelry, exotic hairdos or dark glasses.

3. No groups that are not officially sponsored by the school will be allowed to meet or gather in or near the school building.

4. There will be no public display of affections between students.

5. Radios will not be played in school.

6. When moving in the halls, students will walk and keep to the right at all times.

There are several policemen stationed in the halls of the school during the first week; they are there to prevent trouble that there has been rumors about.

ROLES

Student #1:   Yesterday you were sent home by the assistant principal for wearing African jewelry to school.

Student #2:   You heard from a friend of yours that last week a policeman had told him, "slow down, nigger, don't run in the halls."

Student #3:   Last week, on the first day of class, 3 students asked the history teacher about some black history. The teacher replied that she couldn't do that until it was instituted as part of the school curriculum. Besides, she said, the whole idea of black history is very controversial now; she wasn't sure anything like that existed.

Student #4: You are taking the leadership in establishing an Afro-American fraternity in school, and have organized a group of students who have asked for official approval. Other fraternities sometimes function as clubs, and meet in the school. The principal has not met with you to answer this request yet.

Student #5: You have heard a number of stories and incidents similar to the ones being shared by your colleagues, but you're not sure any of them are important enough to make a fuss about. Probably the teachers and the principal will take care of them without much fuss.

SCENE II

GENERAL SITUATION

The students from Scene I, as well as the following role occupants, are now gathered together in the principal's office for a meeting.

ROLES

Principal: You are now at the center of a rather difficult situation. You are white, and you have been principal here for 9 years. When you came the school was 95% white and nobody ever protested anything out loud.

Superintendent: (acting as an alter-ego to the principal) You want to impress upon the principal that he should not make any rash moves that would upset either the white or black communities. Certainly he must be aware of the need for stability in the schools.

Assistant minister of a large white church: (acting as an alter-ego to the principal) You are anxious for the principal to take the students seriously. Most of their demands sound rather reasonable, especially when compared to the strict rules the school system has now established. The principal is in your congregation.

Newspaperman: You will knock on the door shortly after the meeting starts, introduce yourself, and ask if you can attend. This sounds like hot stuff and you'd like to get in on it.

Several students: (As in Scene I)

STUDENT INVOLVEMENT
A BRIDGE TO TOTAL EDUCATION

TASK FORCE ON STUDENT INVOLVEMENT

RECOMMENDATIONS FOR POSITIVE STUDENT INVOLVEMENT

I. GENERAL ADMINISTRATIVE POLICIES

A. Maintain a constant dialogue with students. Don't just say the line of communication is open—use it!

B. Assure students that any legitimate request will be dealt with in a fair manner, promptly and with genuine concern. If no action can be taken immediately on a request, the reasons for delay should be adequately explained.

C. Sanction legitimate, responsible dissent if it does not disrupt the educational activities of the school.

D. Provide for dialogue or seminar sessions for *all* students held on regularly scheduled dates for discussion of current school problems, communication among students of different backgrounds and interest, and general surveillance of current events.

1. Faculty members and administrators may or may not be included at these sessions according to the topics or needs of the group. However, some system of student-to-adult feedback should be arranged in advance.

2. One regularly scheduled class period per two-week or monthly period could be utilized for these sessions, with the time being rotated between periods so as to relieve any one period of an excessive loss of time.

3. Study halls might also be used at regular intervals for such seminars.

E. Allow students to formulate and organize emergency committees with the powers to investigate and derive solutions to problems of unrest. By placing a larger burden of responsibility on the students, greater awareness of student capability and responsibility is engendered within the student body.

F. Urge students of all types of backgrounds to respect the school as *their* institution of learning rather than the institution of a small body of select students.

G. Give the local high school administrative staff responsibility for all rules and regulations at the school and allow them to be as flexible as

From *Student Involvement* (Raleigh: State Department of Public Instruction; revised, 1971). Reprinted with the permission of the publisher.

possible. Rules set by higher administrative levels (i.e., the Board of Education and the Superintendent) are often points of contention between a responsible but "hands-tied" principal and a conscientious but inhibited student body.

H. Maintain constant communication between administration, faculty, and students so that all three strata of the high school will be aware of the problems, interests, and new ideas of the others. A formal committee or informal "dialogues" could facilitate this communication.

I. Encourage complete participation by students at the junior high school level and allow the junior high school student government as much responsibility as possible.

J. Distribute students alphabetically in homeroom assignments rather than by the trackings of students in order to give each student a wider perspective on the entire student population and to foster better understanding between different student backgrounds.

K. The principal's or faculty advisor's relationship to the school newspaper should be worked out early in the year to save embarrassment and misunderstanding. The principal should advise the paper, but neither he nor any other faculty member should ever censor or alter the newspaper. Rather, also early in the year, the student staff should establish guidelines under which they will print articles (these should probably deal with the areas of obscenity and libelous statements). It is recommended that a "Principal's Column" be included in the paper to allow him to communicate his feelings on any and all areas of school concern. By this column a principal may communicate to the students on specific situations which warrant concern (congratulations to successful school groups, clarification of misunderstandings, and comments on future activities). This column should in no way limit the principal's concern with and practice of other forms of communication but should be yet another avenue towards complete communication.

II. ATTITUDES AND ACTIONS OF ADMINISTRATORS

A. Be honest, straightforward, and frank with students. Do not treat them as less than adults until some action gives you cause to do so.

B. In all cases where propriety permits, give a full explanation for all actions taken, both positive and negative in nature.

C. Despite all justifications raised otherwise, tell the entire truth about all incidents, for rumors are found to be a major stumbling block to unity and communication within the high school. The responsibility for removing rumor and rumor potential lies with the administrator as well as with the students.

D. Support students when they are right.

E. Limit arbitrary rules to a minimum. Never implement a policy without fully explaining the rationale behind it to the student body.

F. Levy equal rewards and punishments for equivalent acts and in proportion to their importance.

G. Do not threaten or intimidate students with real and/or imagined punishments.

H. Refrain from forcing students into positions where they are required to reveal fellow student offenders or face stricter punishments.

I. Use suspensions and expulsions as punishments only as a last resort. It is strongly recommended that offenders committing even major infractions be assigned punishment commensurate with their offense rather than be forced to lose valuable and often crucial academic time.

J. The principal should establish and disseminate to all students and parents the grounds on which a student will be disciplined, suspended, or expelled. These guidelines should list specifically those areas considered minor infractions, major infractions, and grounds for suspension or expulsion. Also, the principal should make known to all students and parents the procedures he will follow if any major disciplinary action, suspension, or expulsion should be necessary. This is to insure awareness and responsibility within the student body, to inform parents, and to prevent misunderstanding and confusion in the event of disciplinary action.

K. Use police minimally and then only to protect, not discipline, students.

L. Establish a student advisory committee (perhaps a sub-committee of the Student Council) to help decide disciplinary policies, not to judge individual cases.

.   .   .   .

IV. EXTRACURRICULAR ACTIVITIES

A. Use cheers which reflect all segments of the student body to increase the unity created by athletic events.

B. Develop a system of student-oriented clubs which will offer the opportunity to every student to participate in areas of his choice. Adult guidance (but not domination) should be provided when needed.
   1. Support the creation of more service-oriented clubs and interest clubs (i.e., photography, ecology) to meet expanding student interest and willingness to participate.
   2. Encourage all clubs in the school to be open to students of all types of backgrounds—economic, social, religious, racial, and academic.

3. Provide transportation as often as possible to as many events as possible.
   a. Perhaps special rate arrangements can be made with local mass transit systems for special events.
   b. In consolidated schools where students are bussed long distances, activity busses could be made available in the later afternoon so that students without private transportation can remain for activities after school.
   c. In clubs which operate under a point system or other systems placing value marks on service, providing transportation for other members should receive points because of the service rendered.
4. Encourage minimum monetary expenditures to be required for student participation, thus encouraging those of low economic status to be involved as well as those of stronger economic background.
5. Keep club membership open at all times or have several times during the year when new members may be added so that a student may join anytime he becomes aware of or interested in any specific organization.
6. Eliminate all grade requirements for membership and office-holding in clubs except those of an honorary academic nature. Too often extracurricular activities exclude all but those students of high academic standing when participation might be a good learning experience for students with lower grades and encourage them to become more involved in the school at all levels.
7. Define the role of the adult advisor according to the nature of the club. Guidance, but not dominance, should be stressed.

C. Include time during the school day when students may participate in extracurricular activities. Thus students who have jobs or home responsibilities after school may participate.
   1. One day per month or per two-week period could be set aside as a "free day" in which both students and faculty could engage in non-classroom activities such as club meetings, tutoring, independent study, special projects, field trips, visits to other schools, etc.
   2. One day a week each period might be shortened by ten minutes to leave a free hour at the end of the day for non-classroom activities.
   3. One regularly scheduled class period per week could be designated as an activity period with the time being rotated to prevent excessive time loss for any particular period.
   4. The number of school-wide assemblies could be reduced and the extra time used for more individualized activities.

D. Encourage students to accept a greater degree of responsibility in areas where they may play a primary role. "Involvement breeds involvement" is quite true, and with greater student involvement the educational process will surely improve. Though not a business, a school functions much like any enterprise: it is only as productive as each of its members turns out to be. Some suggested areas for greater student involvement and responsibility are:

1. Advisory committees to academic departments on such topics as textbooks, class format, course content, or possible new programs.
2. Student-administered tutorial programs under teacher guidance.
3. Student-administered study halls during lunch periods and before school.
4. Advisory committee to the principal on rules and disciplinary policy. (See Section II-L.)
5. Student-administered monitor systems when needed.
6. Guides for field trips and groups visiting the school.
7. Advisory committees to the guidance departments. Students could:
   a. Research and develop college and scholarship files and disseminate information to all students.
   b. Assist the counselor in helping potential drop-outs and students with grade problems.
   c. Counsel other students about course offerings, career opportunities, and clubs and extracurricular activities which may be open to them.
8. Student-faculty-administration committee to deal with problems and concerns related to the total school community.
9. Student-teacher administered discussion groups between various segments of the student population—those of different races, religions, geographical areas, etc.
10. Student committee for curriculum evaluation and innovation. Faculty input but not control should be encouraged.
11. A community-relations committee to extend student ideas and concerns to the community through the news media and organizations such as the PTA, school board, city or county Board of Commissioners, the Chamber of Commerce and other civic organizations.

.   .   .   .

VI. HUMAN RELATIONS

A minority group will be defined for the purposes of this section as any group of students whose socio-economic background, race, religion, interests, academic concerns, geographical location, or vocational aspirations tend to set them apart from the majority or controlling segment of the student body. Good human relations consists of recognizing and adapting the school's operation to meet the needs of all such groups and to allow them equal opportunities to participate in school functions.

A. Treat all students as individuals. Avoid stereotyping and group identification.
B. Strive for fair representation of all minority groups in school activities—student government, athletics, cheerleading squads, beauty contests, clubs and

organizations. One of the suggested election procedures in Section V or VII might help achieve this goal.

1. Minority students should not be reluctant to join in school activities. Offer services to the school and participate in all its functions. Don't wait to be invited—volunteer!

2. Members of the majority or controlling segment of the student body should actively recruit and extend sincere invitations to members of minority groups to take part in school activities.

C. Encourage faculty to participate in ethnic sensitivity training during their re-certification periods and in-service training. Encourage faculty assistance in ethnic sensitivity, and capitalize on minority faculty members' experience.

D. Provide channels of communication to air grievances. Let the student body know of these channels in advance and help in determining methods of handling problems.

E. Establish a human relations council to deal with special problems and suggest policies and activities. Such a group is most helpful in areas where integration or consolidation of schools has recently occurred. The student human relations council should be dedicated to promoting and safeguarding within the school community an environment in which dignity, respect, and equal opportunity are of primary importance.

1. Membership
   a. Formulating the council
      1) Have an equal representation of black and white or any other minority groups that may be prominent, especially when racial problems are a major topic, or

      Have a cross section of the entire student body with racial makeup equal to the percent of representation of each race found in the school, or

      Have an equal number of representatives from each school involved in a consolidation move.

      2) Members should have varied interests and be able to voice the opinions of various segments of the student body.

      3) Since people and trends are constantly changing, members should try to keep abreast of new developments ranging from dress fads to political opinions.

      4) The council should be large enough to sufficiently represent the opinions of all students—yet not so large that there cannot be meaningful dialogue in working to attain its ends.

      5) The members of the council should be introduced to the whole student body so that they will know whom to contact with ideas or problems.
   b. Selection—There are several ways in which members might be selected. It is important to note that each school should try to select its com-

mittee members to adapt best to situations which exist within the school.

1) All members may be elected by students.
2) Part of the members may be chosen by the administrators with the remainder elected by the students.
3) Members may be elected by their race or respective groups in caucus.

c. Faculty Advisors—Persons serving in this capacity must have a keen insight into social conditions which are rapidly changing in today's schools. They should serve as consultants rather than as directors. Above all, faculty advisors should have an understanding and sympathetic attitude toward the many complexities which create friction within the school community. In making this selection, students will undoubtedly choose persons to whom they feel they can relate easily and who will be good listeners.

1) Have the council select the advisors themselves.
2) Have two advisors, one black, one white.

d. Chairmanship—This also is something that needs to be determined by the committee itself.

1) Have one chairman, but frequently rotate the position between black and white council members, or
   Have co-chairmen, one black, one white, and let them divide the responsibilities according to the best method, or
   Have a chairmanship rotating among representatives from each school involved in consolidation, or
   Have a chairman elected by the group.
2) Whoever is serving in this capacity must be perceptive and tactful. He must ensure that each member of the committee can fully express his opinions and attitudes without hurting the dignity of the individual or hindering the progress of the committee. He must also allow any member or guest to retreat from a hasty or ill-considered position without loss of face.
3) He should serve as spokesman for the committee to the student council and various school and community organizations.

2. Meetings

a. Meetings should be held at a regularly scheduled time and place which is known by the entire student body, faculty, and administration.
b. In order for the council to be accessible to the maximum number of people, meetings should be held during school time if it is at all possible.
c. Some meetings should be open to the public, while others may have segments that need to be confidential.
d. Emergency meetings should be called when necessary.
e. There should always be some positive activity to avoid complacency

and discourage the development of negative attitudes among the student body.

3. Guests
   a. At periodic meetings each council member and the advisors should bring other students and faculty members.
   b. Persons who deal with Public Relations in the community should be invited in as well as parents. This would include members of the news media.
   c. Opportunities should be made for all students to express opinions and suggestions to the council through open forum sessions, suggestion boxes, or attendance at regular meetings.
   Accurate records of each meeting should be kept.
4. Records
   a. Accurate records of each meeting should be kept.
   b. Records should be made available to all students, faculty, and administrators for review except in cases where confidential sources play a roll in decisions.
5. Responsibilities
   a. A first task of the council is self-education. Members should make use of acquaintances, experiences, and services of consultants in the field of human relations. Each member should have a working knowledge of existing problems within the school.
   b. The council should listen to any complaint, problem, or question which might be posed by any student, faculty member, or administrator.
   c. There should always be room for honest disagreement between members of the council since it is composed of people coming from different backgrounds.
   d. Since the council is oriented toward obtaining harmony within the school, its members should suggest or recommend positive action to increase cooperation and promote the understanding that differences do exist in people, yet this need not prevent successful interaction.
   e. The council should have the right to work on problems which it foresees before these problems are brought before it. This means that some positive show of concern or action may prevent negative reaction to a situation.
   f. The sessions, while not highly structured, should center around:
      1) What is the cause of concern?
      2) What are the sources of the problem?
      3) What are possible solutions?
         a) How realistic is each?
         b. How are they to be implemented?
      4) What resources for help are available?
      5) What steps are to be taken?
   g. Recommendations

1) All recommendations should be sent to the principal, student council, and faculty council, if one exists. These recommendations should be made known to the entire student body through assembly programs, bulletin boards, and distribution of printed copies.

2) For the best communication and understanding, the following steps are recommended to the principal as responses to the council's recommendations:

   a) The principal should agree to the recommendations and work to enact it if possible. If he disagrees with the recommendation, he should meet with the council to discuss his position and seek alternative solutions.

   b) The principal should refer recommendations to an appropriate committee or board if it is not within his power or jurisdiction to take action. In doing so, he should specify where it is and what action may be expected.

F. Remember that the basic concepts of good human relations—honesty, mutual respect, tolerance of others' opinions, and equal opportunities for everyone —apply to all relationships within the school: student-student, student-faculty, faculty-administration, and administration-student. Each member of the school, community, and especially the human relations council, should promote better relations in all these areas.

PORTLAND'S UNCONVENTIONAL ADAMS HIGH

JOHN GUERNSEY

When school lets out for the summer in a month or so, the John Adams High School in Portland, Ore., will be one school year old. Its brief life has been a volcano of controversy because of its almost complete departure from the conventional approach to high school education.

"Adams High does not teach respect for authority, discipline, basic scholarship, or orderly use of time. The school teaches gross egotism, extreme self-centeredness, myopic self-delusion, and general anarchy," says one Portland resident.

"We're learning to live with other races and other people here at Adams," says a student. "And all the math, English, Chaucer, and history teaching in the past didn't teach our parents how to do that."

"My daughter's education is being neglected at Adams, and I am having her transferred to another high school," says a parent who meant it. His daughter now attends a different high school.

From *American Education*, 6 (May, 1970), 3-7. Reprinted with the permission of the author and the publisher.

John Guernsey is Education Editor of The Oregonian, *Portland, Oregon.*

"I'm all for Adams," says another parent. "My daughter went to another high school for two years, but this is the first time she has taken the initiative to do studies and projects on her own."

Robert Schwartz, the 32-year-old, mercury-minded principal, describes Adams as "a school where students want to go, and want to learn because they are curious and interested—not because an attempt is made to force them to learn." He has stayed in the saddle during the bucking first months of the operation, and is now convinced that "the school will gain momentum and support as it goes."

What's so different about Adams that has inspired such diametrically opposed opinion?

For one thing, it's the school's curriculum itself, which is split into general education problem-solving courses and an electives program. The general education part works like this:

All students spend about half of each school day, either the morning or the afternoon, on different teams that study ways to cope with such problems as air and water pollution, unemployment and welfare, reducing student unrest, improving student-adult understanding, keeping the automobile from destroying the metropolitan area, reducing the crime rate, and lessening race-related friction in the school and community.

There is no breakdown by grades or ability in these problem-solving sessions: All study teams are mixtures of juniors, sophomores, and freshmen (the school will not have a senior class until 1970-71).

Teachers attempt to encourage older students to help the younger ones, the faster ones to help the slower ones, and each student works on the part of a problem that is compatible with his ability. The problem-solving tactic also avoids the compartmentalization of subjects: The students do not study English for 40 minutes, or social studies, math, science, or history as specific courses; they deal with all these basic subjects as parts of a study of a given real problem during the general education program.

As an example of the value of the general education approach, Schwartz refers to an incident that occurred just as Adams opened last fall. Several Portland high schools began the year with serious race-related student problems, resulting in numerous assaults and police action. The most severe disturbances were at Adams, where the philosophy is to bring together students from all backgrounds, representing many ranges of abilities, and where the student body is 22 percent black.

General education study teams jumped right into the action and undertook to develop solutions to Adams' racial problems. In fact, race relations occupied the whole general education program for the first couple of weeks of school. A race relations committee held assemblies where students could talk matters out, and black and white student leaders began to take command of the situation. Since then, although assaults and confrontations haven't ceased altogether, there has not been another major racial flare-up at the school.

Schwartz explains the problem-solving education approach: "Students need to learn what will help them function effectively in society, regardless of what type of work or what further education they plan to go into after high school."

The courses at Adams were put together almost entirely by the teachers, with help from about 100 students, during the summer of 1969. Schwartz would have liked to have had even more of the school's 1,300 students take part in curriculum planning.

The teachers kept several questions in mind while putting together the courses. What should students know and be able to do after leaving high school? What parts of the individual disciplines can contribute the most to the overall general studies courses?

"The program is tied to something inside the kid that interests him," says Schwartz. "Then it must be tied to something on the outside that is real." By real, Schwartz and his teachers mean the problems of today—race, pollution, crime, and so forth—not material that deals with national problems of 100 or 200 years ago, although they insist they do not ignore historical perspective.

"The important thing is that students should learn the techniques of problem solving and how to adjust to change. These abilities should prove useful throughout the rest of their lives," Schwartz adds.

It is noon now, and half the students have completed their problem-solving sessions. During the afternoon they will attend specific classes—but they take what electives they please—or they can do independent study, meet with student-faculty committees, or even goof off a part of the time. Each student is scheduled for some electives at which attendance is expected.

Of the elective courses, some require a full school year and others are mini-courses that last about six weeks. The mini-courses meet just about every imaginable interest: computer application and technology, astrology, coed badminton, and even such special studies as "From Bach to Bartok." Schwartz explains the large number of elective courses and the free time in which students can study what they wish: "Give kids a chance to try some of the things they're interested in. They must have the chance to be curious, to explore adult roles and have meaningful choices."

Schwartz also points out that the academic and college bound students can use the elective periods for taking in-depth and continuous studies in math, English, physical and social sciences, history, and other college requirement courses.

Adams is well tuned to the fact that of each 10 students who begin as freshmen in high school, only about two will go on to complete college. Consequently, the $5.8 million high school has strong and wide ranging job-related programs in which a good percentage of Adams students are enrolled.

Schwartz and his staff hope eventually to encourage business, industry, and the professions to participate in the school's training program and to sponsor students in half-day on-the-job training apprenticeships. They also hope to invite business and industrial representatives as guest lecturers and assistant teachers, and they plan to arrange for some vocational-technical classes at outside plants during the evenings.

For 60 students who don't really seem to be turned on by the academic or vocational program at Adams, there is a mobile school where they spend most of their general education time. A big bus, accommodating about 30 youths each morning and afternoon, roams the metropolitan area on scheduled visits to industrial plants, art museums, city and county operations, conservation projects, airports, and the like. In an attempt to add relevancy, Adams uses the community itself as a basis for these youngsters' education. On returning to Adams, the students write, tell stories, or make movies concerning their outings, and teachers try to motivate them toward more concrete learning experiences.

Some parents, especially those whose youngsters are headed for college, are uneasy about the school's relatively lax requirements that specific courses be completed in order to qualify for graduation. However, college officials have assured them that their children will not be denied college admission because of that. Grades are optional at Adams. At the beginning of each course students can, with their parents' approval, choose to receive either a regular letter grade or a pass-fail notice.

Another of Adams' major educational tenets is that students learn better and teachers teach better when the students and teachers have a close understanding of one another via more personal contact and less formal relationships.

To combat the impersonality of largeness, Adams operates as four smaller high schools in one—at least for the general education program and for administrative purposes such as counseling and disciplining. Each smaller school—known as a house—has about 300 students, mixed as to class (freshmen, sophomores, juniors), race, and social and economic background. Two teams of teachers work with the students in each house, and the same teachers stay with the same students as much as possible for more than one academic year.

Counselors are part of each house team and work with the students and other teachers all day long. In this manner the counselors get to know the students better and can do more to help them with their problems. They also help teachers improve their counseling abilities.

One of the most innovative changes at Adams is in the area of school policy-making. While the ultimate responsibility for the operation of the school rests with the principal, Adams is experimenting with a mechanism to permit majority rule voting by students and faculty members on some issues. With the aim of teaching students how democracy works so they will be better qualified citizens when they reach voting age, the Adams operation duplicates, in some respects, the functioning of the U.S. Government.

"The whole issue of decision-making in conventional high schools is wrong," says Schwartz. "The students and faculty members want more voice, so we're experimenting with the delegation of authority."

At Adams there is a school legislature made up of a student-elected student senate and a faculty-elected faculty senate. Joint committees representing these bodies meet jointly on such issues as curriculum and grading, or on policies that most directly affect students and teachers.

In other cases the senates function separately. If the issues involve student conduct, dress codes, and so forth, the policies are made and enforced by the student senate. If they involve working conditions and other areas of primary interest to teachers, they are dealt with by the faculty senate.

Schwartz and other administrators make up the executive branch of the school government. Changes or new policies developed and approved by the senates, jointly or separately, require the principal's signature before they can become school policies. Although the principal has veto power over bills sent to him, the legislative bodies have been empowered to override the principal's veto by a two-thirds vote. The override policy, however, is currently under reconsideration.

Adams also plans to set up a judicial branch which will probably be some sort of appeals body made up of students, faculty members, and administrators. However, Schwartz and his staff have found that there are many legal implications involved that require careful study. "A school is not a court," said Jerry Fletcher, coordinator of research and evaluation at Adams. "We have to be very careful in setting up quasi-judicial procedures."

In addition to introducing changes that could make education more interesting and relevant to students and teachers, Adams includes numerous clinical programs to influence teacher preparation, teacher enthusiasm for teaching, and community involvement. Schwartz and his staff feel that the clinical approach is one of the most important aspects of the experimental school. They challenge the long-standing education concept that college and university campuses are the best places for training teachers and performing educational research.

"The truth is that a university is just not a very relevant setting for training teachers and doing much educational research," says Schwartz. "As it is now, a college student training to be a teacher does not get into a regular school classroom until very late in his training—the last part of the senior year. He gets far too much of his material from theory and hearsay from a professor." So Adams has worked out an arrangement with officials of Reed College, Lewis and Clark College, and Oregon State University that permits junior year teacher trainees to receive college credit for working in Adams classrooms. Nearly all of Adams' 80-member faculty is made up of experienced teachers, but the school also has a great many trainees—nearly 100 of them this year. They are teamed off with regular teachers so that the inexperienced learn from the experienced in actual classroom situations.

Some of the teachers at Adams also hold assistant professorships at the colleges with which the high school cooperates. Schwartz views this as a very necessary advancement in education. "There must be closer educational ties between the four-year campuses and the grade schools and high schools," he stresses.

In one training program that Adams carries out in cooperation with Oregon

State University, eight interns, most of them black, are being trained for teaching in inner-city schools. The interns either have no college degrees or majored in something other than education. They are learning on the job at Adams, getting a full year of actual classroom experience and taking training for college credit from the Adams teachers who double as professors. Schwartz hopes that the experiment, sponsored under the Education Professions Development Act, will result in more blacks with teaching potential being able to enter the teaching field.

Schwartz believes the on-the-job training for both blacks and whites without college training in the field of education can have two major impacts:

1. Elementary schools and high schools throughout the Nation want more black teachers than they can find, because not enough blacks have college backgrounds—especially in the field of education. On-the-job training like that provided in the Adams-OSU program could qualify many more in a hurry.

2. Preparing teachers without an overload of educational theory courses could modify long-standing teacher credential requirements which deny schools the use of many persons who are experts in their fields and who would like to teach but will not take the methods courses necessary to qualify.

Adams also hopes to add to the significance of educational research, since the school has its own researchers and evaluators right there on the job as part of the teaching teams. "Research is much more meaningful and reliable when conducted in and around actual classrooms," Schwartz emphasizes.

This 21st century high school is the creature of Schwartz and six other secondary school teachers who, in 1967, were in their final year of study at the Harvard Graduate School of Education. They set out to develop a model for a school program that would make possible the achievement of many of the educational objectives that were commonly voiced by educational and social analysis but had not been established in practice or adequately tested.

The Harvard graduate students envisioned, in short, a clinical high school—one where instruction of students, curriculum development, preservice and inservice training, and research could all go on simultaneously. A high school, they believed, might be made to function somewhat like a teaching-hospital does in medicine.

"We realized that our individual voices would be drowned out, but if we had our own high school and worked as a team, we could make the changes we believe are necessary," says Schwartz.

The seven graduate students developed a detailed plan of how they believed a high school should operate. Then they sent a proposal to half a dozen metropolitan school districts and kept their fingers crossed that they would get a taker. They got several but were most impressed by the enthusiastic reply from Portland school officials and school board members.

Now, after eight months, is the school living up to the expectations of Schwartz and his codesigners?

"It's hard to say," the innovative principal is frank to admit. "The battle was simply for survival when the school first opened. Then the problems with questioning parents occupied much of our time. It has moved so fast, so far, that we haven't had much time for measuring and analysis. I believe we are through the roughest part now, and can get on with better teaching, learning, and measuring."

There's no question that parent opposition to the school has simmered down. Adams now has four parent advisory groups, one for each student house, totaling more than 160 persons. These groups usually meet at least once every two weeks, and some of the members are parents who continue to look askance at the school.

"And that's the way we want it," Schwartz says. "We don't want the parent groups made up totally of parents who are there to tell us what a great job we are doing. We have learned a lot—and continue to learn—from what the critical parents have to say. What we want most is to have them all involved with the school."

Adams won't claim that it has solved all attendance problems or convinced 1,300 students there to love school. But many of the students obviously do like Adams, and their enthusiasm has been instrumental in quieting down a large number of questioning parents. As one parent put it: "I still don't understand the damned place, but it's the first time my kid has actually been excited about going to school. So how can I knock it?"

Some students feel they are learning more at Adams. Others like the school because they have more voice in what they will study or a chance to be on their own. Then there are some who really don't know why they like it more than other high schools. "We just feel better here," they'll say. But most will tell you, "We're getting more out of school here because our teachers are more than teachers—they help you with all kinds of problems."

Since Adams teachers have less time scheduled in classes than teachers at other Portland schools, they have more time for other contacts with students. "A very positive point," says Patricia Wertheimer, coordinator of social services at the school, "is that the teachers have a genuine interest in their kids. How many other schools do you know where teachers visit a student's home or phone if the student is absent too many times?"

A visit to the school at 3 p.m. verifies this. People aren't stampeding one another to check out and leave for the day. Many students and teachers stay until five, six, or seven because they're working on something—or with somebody—they're interested in.

HIGH SCHOOL WITH NO WALLS—
IT'S A HAPPENING IN PHILADELPHIA

HENRY S. RESNIK

In the great jungle of public education, the high schools are open game these days, and the onslaughts of the critics, from respected academics to long-haired student activists, are having a devastating effect. The severest criticisms define the typical American high school as a prison-and-factory, but even establishment insiders have admitted that most high schools are several generations behind the times. Everybody, it seems, is looking for alternatives, and the school system of Philadelphia has found what many educational reformers consider a truly exciting possibility: an experimental high school called the Parkway Program.

A year-round happening, the program is a school without grades, marks, arbitrary rules, authority figures, a building—or, its advocates claim, boredom.

The locale is in and around central Philadelphia: in offices, museums, science centers, hospitals, theaters, department stores; in luncheonettes, in the Automat, on street corners and stairways. Students can opt for such courses as: law enforcement at the administration building of the Police Department, library science at the public library, and biology at the Academy of Natural Sciences. In fact, with all of Philadelphia as a resource, Parkway students are free to study just about anything that may interest them.

When most administrators want to boast about a new high school, they produce drawings of a $14-million edifice that took three years to build; the best picture of the Parkway Program is an aerial view of Philadelphia's Center City. The program is named after the Benjamin Franklin Parkway, a mile-long boulevard lined with cultural institutions that begins at City Hall and culminates in the Greek-revival Museum of Art on a hill overlooking the Schuylkill River. The Parkway Program brushes aside the traditional notion that learning must be acquired within four-walled boxes called classrooms and acknowledges that life and learning are all part of the same ongoing process. The city itself is the classroom, and the life of the city is the curriculum.

NO LID TO BLOW

There are no dropouts here. Parkway students linger long after scheduled classes are over and often volunteer to come in for various weekend activities. As far as the program is concerned, no administrators are worried that "the lid will blow." There *is* no lid.

Perhaps most important the program is structured to acknowledge the value

Reprinted by permission of the author and of THINK Magazine, 35 (November-December, 1969), 33-36, published by IBM, Copyright 1969 by International Business Machines Corporation.

and uniqueness of every individual. For most of the people the program serves—teachers and students as well—school has become a portal to self-fulfillment.

Philadelphia's "school without walls" began as a brilliant gimmick for decreasing overcrowding—at virtually no cost to the school system—and publicizing the climate of innovation that a new Board of Education had been trying to establish since the beginning of 1966.

According to local legend, a board official looked out his office window in the board's Parkway headquarters one day, saw the huge palaces of culture—the Free Library, the Franklin Institute, the Art Museum and dozens of others—that line the Parkway for most of its length, and said, "Why not use all this as the campus of a high school?" When the proposal was announced in February 1968, it was the talk of Philadelphia—the combination of economy and novelty lent the idea an almost irresistible magic. Several leaders of Parkway institutions complained that they had not been consulted and that their participation was far from guaranteed, but these objections were lost amid the general din of rosy publicity.

Old guard administrators at the Philadelphia Board of Education still maintain, as they did at the beginning, that the program is no more than a good job of public relations on the part of the reformist board and the liberal administration of Superintendent of Schools Mark Shedd. It is indeed good copy, but, more than any other single experiment in Philadelphia's huge reform movement, the Parkway Program delivers the basic educational changes that Shedd promised when the board hired him early in 1966. Although the program has a good deal of surface glitter and seems so much a merely slick idea, it questions basic assumptions about the structure of schools. Its supporters believe that its potential for effecting change is virtually unlimited.

"THE RIGHT MAN"

In retrospect, it is clear that the possibilities of the proposal might never have been realized if it had fallen into the wrong hands. For months after the board's announcement, traditionalists within the school system limited their reaction to questions about how administrators could ever coordinate the activities of so vast and sprawling a campus. For them, the proposed "Parkway High School" was merely a difficult exercise in scheduling, a nightmare vision of shuttle buses jamming the parkway and harried vice principals imploring systems analysts to help them out of the mess. If this attitude had prevailed, the program could easily have amounted to a bizarre variation on the usual humdrum theme.

But then, in June 1968, the board announced the appointment of 42-year-old John Bremer as the program's director. An Englishman and a born rebel, Bremer had roughly twenty years of educational experimentation to his credit. Nine of these he had spent in England, principally in connection with the Leicestershire Schools, which are now being widely hailed as models for reform in elementary education throughout the United States. Most recently, after emigrating to America and teaching education at the university level, Bremer had been unit administrator of New York's Two Bridges district, a tempest-torn effort at decentralization and community control. Bremer was so soft-spoken and mild-mannered that some observers within the central administration wondered in the beginning whether he could handle the politics of the job. Soon, however, their fears were set firmly to rest, for it became clear as time went on that, in the words of an educational consultant close to the program, Bremer has been "the right man in the right place at the right time."

Typical of Bremer's approach was his insistence, from the earliest days of his appointment, that, contrary to popular belief, there would be no shuttle buses connecting the various parkway institutions—students would have to find their own way of getting from one place to another, no matter what the distance. The decision reflects a philosophy that has come to dominate the program and to determine its basic shape and style: Bremer is committed to individual growth, creativity and autonomy; he is an enemy of bureaucracies that tell people exactly what to do and think (or how to get to a destination); he delights in public criticism of the educational establishment. At the opening of the summer session in July 1969, he told a group of students entering the program for the first time, "In terms of behavior and attitudes, you're going to have to unlearn everything you've learned in your public school education so far, as quickly as possible."

The pilot "unit" of the Parkway Program opened in February 1968, with approximately 140 students, among whom half were black and 20 were from Philadelphia suburbs; nine full-time teachers; another ten or so student-teachers or undergraduate interns; and a huge second-story loft headquarters two blocks from City Hall. A second unit was opened, in rented office space five blocks from the first, at the beginning of the summer session, enrolling another 130 students. In September 1969, a third unit, about ten blocks from the first, was opened in an old school building. This consists of an elementary school for 130 children in kindergarten through fourth grade, modeled on the libertarian British infant schools that Bremer helped to pioneer, and a high school for 130 students who participate in and study, among other things, the entire operation of the elementary school. A fourth unit, again with 130 high school students, has just opened. The original plan called for a high school of 2,400 students, and although Bremer has considered such modifications of the plan as a "nongeographical school district" encompassing much larger numbers of students throughout the city, each unit in the growing program has been modeled on the same basic pattern.

One of the greatest attractions of the Parkway Program for students is the tremendous freedom it allows—some observers believe that the program is merely chaotic. Bremer insists, however, that he has provided a tight "internal" structure. While each unit has taken on a distinct character of its own, at any rate, certain structural elements are common to the entire program:

LIKE A FAMILY

Tutorial groups: These groups of about fifteen students and two teachers are the principal base, rather like a family, of each student's Parkway career. In the tutorial group, which meets for two hours four days a week, the student plans his schedule, receives personal counseling, and makes up deficiencies in such basic skills as reading and math. Some tutorial groups plan parties and outings; others organize informal athletic events; others agree to study a subject of mutual interest. The tutorials are also responsible for the extensive written evaluations of both students' and teachers' work that take the place of grades.

Selection by lottery: One of Bremer's educational axioms is, "Anything that can be measured is educationally worthless." Consequently, the Parkway Program bypasses standardized tests as a basis for admission and favors the totally random method of drawing names from a hat. There were 10,000 applications for the 130 places in the second unit; some teenagers burst into tears when they missed their chance at the public drawing.

HOW TEACHERS ARE CHOSEN

Faculty selection by committee: Most teachers in the Parkway Program are selected by committees consisting of university students, parents from the community, visiting teachers, and students and teachers from other units. After the initial interviews, a few dozen of the most promising applicants are assigned the task of deciding what process of elimination they should use in filling the limited number of openings, and are then observed by Bremer and key advisers as they thrash out the problem.

Institutional offerings: Each unit is responsible for enlisting the aid of the various downtown institutions, both public and private, in the form of courses and other projects, which range from discussion and planning groups to paid employment. So far, each unit has managed to line up more than thirty offerings. The Parkway catalog lists 90 "cooperating institutions."

Faculty offerings: Since the program operates only within general requirements for the high school diploma in the State of Pennsylvania, the permanent faculty members have been able to explore many subjects and courses of study that the traditional high school would never allow. During the first session, for example, students could choose from such unusual fare as: "Psychology and Personal Problems," "Multi-media Journalism," "Film-making," "Vagabond Sketching," "Kite-flying," numerous workshops in creative writing, and courses in 10 languages.

Town meetings: Sometimes shouting sessions, sometimes orderly public debates, the program's weekly town meetings have emerged as the principal form of government in each unit. Discussions range from such basic questions as what kinds of rules and philosophies the unit should adopt to such mundane matters as the filling out of forms, but the emphasis throughout is on total participatory democracy.

"EVERYBODY'S YOUR FRIEND"

What may be the most important factor in the program's success, however, is the emphasis on community that has come to motivate the behavior of most participants as if it were a religious force. The various structural elements have certainly encouraged this sense of community, but it seems to derive as much from Bremer's inspiring, almost charismatic vision as any other single factor. According to Mario Fantini, the program's liaison with its initial sponsor, the Ford Foundation, "John Bremer made the program *human*." Most teachers are known, at any rate, by their first names only, and students usually describe the warmth and intimacy of the program as if they can scarcely believe they have found such things in a place called school. "Here you get the feeling that everybody's your friend" is a typical reaction.

Bremer insists that the almost random selection of students and faculty has neutralized his power to create a private fiefdom; nevertheless, it is clear to any visitor that he has set the tone for the entire operation and that this tone is almost always informal and spontaneous. Members of the first unit were so friendly and drew so close, in fact, that they may have inadvertently perpetuated a certain anti-establishment cliquishness.

"The first day of the program," reports one teacher who had had more than a decade in the traditional system, "one of the students said 'What do you want to be called? Some of the teachers are called "Mr." or "Mrs." Some are called by their first names.' I said "You call me 'Mrs.' After 10 days time I didn't want anybody calling me 'Mrs.' again."

Another teacher defines what seems to be the most important factor in the self-education of everyone in the Parkway community: "One of the things I've gotten," he observes, "is a sense of power. In the regular school situation you have it within the confines of the classroom, but here I'm really in control of myself and the program as it affects me and the people I'm working with. There's always the sense that the kids are teaching you and you're teaching the kids."

"My kid had already dropped out, even though he was still going to school," says the father of a Parkway student. "They discouraged him at his old school; they discouraged his musical talent, one of his main interests. He's a much different person now—he's interacting with the other kids and the faculty to a far greater extent. . . ."

Constantly attracting such testimonials from throughout the city, the Parkway Program flaunts its own inability to be evaluated in traditional terms.

"It's founded on a new principle of what education is," says Mario Fantini, who is also one of Ford's leading educational theorists. "The existing system isn't working. If you look at the student unrest as a symptom of the inability of the educational system, forged in another century, to be responsive to the concerns of this generation, it seems that many of those concerns would be addressed in a Parkway-like school."

MORE PARKWAY PROGRAMS

Some educators across the country seem to agree. By the fall of 1969, similar programs were under way in at least four major cities; several community groups in Philadelphia were eager to align themselves with Bremer and his philosophy; the Board of Education had voted to increase the size of the student body in 1969 to 700; and Bremer had a pledge of $500,000 from the school system's operating budget. For once, it seemed, a school had managed to please just about everybody.

There have been critics, of course. The program has been attacked as just another of the board's fancy experiments and there have been threats to block city funding. Yet the Parkway Program costs no more than what the board would need to educate the Parkway students in regular high schools.

Some observers argue that despite his emphasis on individual initiative, Bremer has often been hypocritically, arbitrarily authoritarian. A few teachers contend, moreover, that the most important advantage of the program is not its structure but the intimacy provided by a smaller teacher-student ratio—an intimacy that Bremer may have trouble maintaining as the program grows.

Though riding the crest of a wave, Bremer appreciates what he often refers to as the "messiness" of learning. He is almost proud to admit that the first sessions were not without their problems. Principally, too many students have not received the training in basic skills which is supposed to be a primary function of the tutorials. He is confident, however, that the problems will be solved—solving educational problems, is, after all, what the program is about.

PUPIL ACTIVISM CAN BE A POSITIVE FORCE

LaMAR P. MILLER

School systems, once again, are attempting to respond to the pressures of a rapidly changing society. From secondary to elementary schools the educational boat is being rocked by a variety of protests. These include demands for a more relevant curriculum by blacks and Puerto Ricans, increased pay for paraprofes-

From *Instructor*, 80 (August-September, 1970), 65-66. Reprinted with the permission of the author and the publisher.

LaMar P. Miller is Education Director of the Institute of Afro-American Affairs, and Professor of Education at New York University.

sionals and teachers, demonstrations by parents from the right and left, protests against the war in Southeast Asia.

As a new school year begins, we wonder when and over what issues will the emphasis on dissent and protest affect the elementary schools. The multiplicity of protests and the urgency of the resulting crises require we consider the challenge of change that most certainly will occur.

If we have learned anything from the events of the past two years, it is that no school is immune to the increased emphasis on student participation in educational activities. The unrest is confined neither to one particular area of the country nor to one particular group of people. The involvement of individuals and of groups covers the entire range of social, political, economic, and educational problems. Moreover, much of the activity has centered around the neighborhood elementary school.

The most casual visitor to an elementary school during a normal day can observe the increased participation by parents and by individuals representing many sections of the community. Obviously, our children watch and learn from the activities of these adults, many engaged in various forms of dissent.

One of the greatest challenges elementary teachers will be faced with in the coming years is the pupil demand to be involved in planning and decision making that is more than just lip service. Teachers will have to find ways to let students express their opinions with the knowledge that they will be heard and that their ideas will be considered.

One element of change that must be considered is the role of the teacher. Typically, elementary schools have operated on the theory that a child should first learn about his immediate surroundings and then in ever increasing circles explore the rest of the world. This theory assumes that the child has never asked questions, never watched television, and never had a life outside of school. Television alone has changed the role of the teacher. Students come to school conditioned with an awareness of life, experienced vicariously through a TV channel. No longer can a teacher be simply a dispenser of information; there is too much of it. And students will not wait for the teacher to tell them everything, for there are too many other efficient ways to acquire knowledge. If we can accept the premise that the role of the teacher and the school has changed dramatically, then it is reasonable to consider guidelines for making student involvement an exciting challenge.

Elementary school students should learn the Bill of Rights through practice and policies in the school and in the classroom.

Ira Glasser, Associate Director, New York Civil Liberties Union, believes that our public schools steadfastly deny that the Bill of Rights applies to them. He states,

Everyone goes through our schools. What they learn—not from what they are formally taught but from the way the institution is organized to treat

them—is that authority is more important than freedom, order more precious than liberty, and discipline a higher value than individual expression. That is a lesson which is inappropriate to a free society—and certainly inappropriate to its schools.[1]

The question of whether or not Glasser is correct in his assertion is not the issue here. He does, however, cause us to raise questions about how we provide experiences for pupils to learn about government. We know that government is becoming more and more complicated. Nevertheless, children must have a chance to learn what it is and how to react to it. The problem is that we have not given our pupils meaningful exposures to representative government. Children do not have a real opportunity to learn what the Bill of Rights is, or the meaning of "due process." I doubt if there is an elementary school in the country without at least one teacher who would say, "No one is going to leave this room until I find out who threw that eraser"—a direct violation of due process.

The question is how can we encourage reasonable dissent consistent with the Constitution. We need to establish clear-cut ways for students to know and learn through practice what their rights are. We should also be concerned with the effect of the elementary curriculum on the maturing adolescent. Today's student protests may well be a reflection of the ineffectiveness of our social studies curriculum. Some researchers suggest, for example, that in the elementary school teachers give an unrealistic view of the political world. Though they supply the child with necessary information about government, they teach the child nothing about the role of pressure groups of special interests in politics. Nor are they likely to examine the controversies which dominate the political scene. In short, the school seems to avoid discussion of political issues. By seventh or eighth grade the child has acquired many facts about government. What he needs to learn is how to *apply* them.

In view of the need for more meaningful experiences, we might consider some specific activities.

A bill of rights for elementary school students should be placed in every classroom and discussed so that it is clear to students what their rights are. Teachers should take seriously the matter of individual rights of students. At the same time, the rights of teachers should be spelled out.

Another practical suggestion is the creation of a school council, including students, teachers, parents, and administrators. The responsibilities and the authority of the council should be clear to all. The student representatives must be given an equal voice. Students should be encouraged to elect their own representatives through a process not influenced by a teacher. All ethnic groups attending the school should be represented on this council. The council should be of a size to be efficient, perhaps ten to twelve. Members for a twelve-man council would be

[1] Ira Glasser: "Schools for Scandal—The Bill of Rights and Public Education," *Phi Delta Kappan,* December 1969.

two administrators, two teachers, two parents, six students, each with an equal vote.

Children need to have exercise in executive, legislative, and judicial decision making. For the most part, student government in our schools has merely been the right of the students to agree with the principal. In elementary school we ought to be giving students the opportunity to experiment wih a represeative government that is real. They need opportunities to make mistakes and learn from those mistakes. They need opportunities to generate rules which govern people's behavior and find out why they don't work, and to look at judicial practices and see why they do.

Elementary school pupils should be given meaningful responsibilities in the school and the classroom as a means of capitalizing on dissent.

Enlightened educators know that responsibility is not something we teach, it is something we give. They know also that too often we have relegated pupils to certain positions in life by the kinds of things we ask them to be responsible for in the classroom. We teach them that it is more important to be responsible for cleaning erasers than it is to be responsible for what one says and does or for the effect one's behavior has on others.

Teachers should be encouraged to develop classroom activities that provide an opportunity for students to take part in and disagree with matters that are realistic to them. I do not propose make-believe activities. Whatever happens to be the concern of students should be negotiable, including such things as homework. In other words, wherever students have concerns about their treatment in school and in class, teachers ought to encourage their right to discuss the issue.

A way to implement this guideline would be the use of discovery and inquiry techniques as a means of utilizing concepts and skills that are taught, drawing upon the personal experiences of children, and dealing with important natural and social problems. Teachers who use such techniques find themselves and their students in new roles. The teacher in this role must have the general attitude of an inquirer who has no final answers. He makes clear that all statements are to be examined and accepted or rejected in the open forum of ideas. The teacher may play the role of the devil's advocate, constantly making students prove the defensibility of their positions. For the students, an important result of the inquiry technique is that they must take responsibility for what they say. They will begin to view knowledge as tentative rather than absolute. Moreover, ideas are continuously challenged by peers. Finally, they learn to handle dissent in a meaningful way.

Students should also be allowed to perform classroom tasks that are commensurate with their abilities. There are many lessons that can be taught by students to an entire class or to small groups. These should be realistic and not contrived. In most instances students can also handle equipment. They can develop slide sequences and films.

Children should be responsible for their own behavior when doing such things as going to the restroom, checking out library materials, and arriving at class on time. It should be clear through teacher practice that behavior is an individual responsibility.

The importance of group activities should not be overlooked, but the responsibility for these activities should be with the group and not with the teacher. Children can conduct their own affairs, arrive at their own solutions, and create new and innovative approaches to classroom activities if encouraged to do so.

The school should look for and develop levels of leadership in pupils. The scope of activities for enhancing leadership qualities should be extended to such facets of the school program as student service clubs, seating arrangements at lunch, plays and skits for assembly programs, and so on. Students can even assume leadership in curriculum matters. While they may not be able to determine whether or not the knowledge imparted is correct, they can certainly determine whether or not the teacher or other students are getting it across to them. They can determine some of the problems they are having in understanding what the teacher is talking about and can raise questions about whether or not the subject is relevant.

Since we live in a world of continued growth and rapid change, the great majority of problems relating to the school and to our ability to capitalize on dissent are of the continuing variety. Thus, the question of how we handle dissent in the elementary school is one that demands a continuing solution. Efforts to answer this question should be a *constant* in the school's program. If we are to eliminate negative dissent and cope with the negative aspects that arise, we must recognize that even a six-year-old knows a great many things. We must involve him in realistic activities and stop insulting his intelligence.

INDEX